Tax Law, Religion, and Justice

This book asks why tax policy is both attracted to and repelled by the idea of justice.

Accepting the invitation of economist Henry Simons to acknowledge that tax justice is a theological concept, the work explores theological doctrines of taxation to answer the presenting question. The overall message of the book is that taxation is an instrument of justice, but only when taxes take into account multiple goods in society: the requirements of the government, the property rights of society's members, and the material needs of the poor. It is argued that this answer to the presenting question is a theological and ethical answer in that it derives from the insistence of Christian thinkers that tax policy take into account material human need (*necessitas*). Without the *necessitas* component of the tax balance, tax systems end up honoring only one of the three components of the tax equation and cease to reflect a coherent idea of justice.

The book will be of interest to academics and researchers working in the areas of tax law, economics, theology, and history.

Allen Calhoun is a McDonald Distinguished Fellow at the Center for the Study of Law and Religion at Emory University. He has been a tax lawyer and a tax law editor, obtaining a JD from Notre Dame Law School and an LLM from Washington University. He received an MTh and then a PhD in theological ethics from the University of Aberdeen, Scotland.

Law and Religion

The practice of religion by individuals and groups, the rise of religious diversity, and the fear of religious extremism, raise profound questions for the interaction between law and religion in society. The regulatory systems involved, the religion laws of secular government (national and international) and the religious laws of faith communities, are valuable tools for our understanding of the dynamics of mutual accommodation and the analysis and resolution of issues in such areas as religious freedom; discrimination; the autonomy of religious organisations; doctrine, worship and religious symbols; the property and finances of religion; religion, education and public institutions; and religion, marriage and children. In this series, scholars at the forefront of law and religion contribute to the debates in this area. The books in the series are analytical with a key target audience of scholars and practitioners, including lawyers, religious leaders, and others with an interest in this rapidly developing discipline.

Titles in this series include

Law and Christianity in Latin America
The Work of Great Jurists
Edited by M.C. Mirow and Rafael Domingo

Tax Law, Religion, and Justice
An Exploration of Theological Reflections on Taxation
Allen Calhoun

For more information about this series, please visit: www.routledge.com/Law-and-Religion/book-series/LAWRELIG

Tax Law, Religion, and Justice

An Exploration of Theological Reflections on Taxation

Allen Calhoun

Routledge
Taylor & Francis Group
LONDON AND NEW YORK

First published 2021
by Routledge
2 Park Square, Milton Park, Abingdon, Oxon OX14 4RN

and by Routledge
52 Vanderbilt Avenue, New York, NY 10017

Routledge is an imprint of the Taylor & Francis Group, an informa business

British Library Cataloguing-in-Publication Data
A catalogue record for this book is available from the British Library

Library of Congress Cataloging-in-Publication Data
Names: Calhoun, Allen, author.
Title: Tax law, religion, and justice : an exploration of theological reflections on taxation / Allen Calhoun.
Description: Milton Park, Abingdon, Oxon ; New York, NY : Routledge, 2021.
| Series: Law and religion | Includes bibliographical references and index.
Identifiers: LCCN 2020043544 (print) | LCCN 2020043545 (ebook) | ISBN
9780367483722 (hardback) | ISBN 9781003039556 (ebook)
Subjects: LCSH: Taxation--Law and legislation. | Taxation--Religious aspects. | Taxation--Economic aspects. | Equality.
Classification: LCC K4460 .C35 2021 (print) | LCC K4460 (ebook) | DDC
343.04--dc23
LC record available at https://lccn.loc.gov/2020043544
LC ebook record available at https://lccn.loc.gov/2020043545

ISBN: 978-0-367-48372-2 (hbk)

ISBN: 978-0-367-71347-8 (pbk)

ISBN: 978-1-003-03955-6 (ebk)

Typeset in Galliard
by Deanta Global Publishing Services, Chennai, India

For Mary Ann

Contents

Acknowledgments

There are many debts of gratitude that I would like to acknowledge in bringing this book to print. The wisdom and depth of knowledge of the supervisors of my doctoral work, from which this book springs, at the University of Aberdeen, Brian Brock and Andrew Simpson, impress and humble me to this day. The same can be said for John Witte, Jr., and Justin Latterell of Emory University's Center for the Study of Law and Religion.

I am grateful as well to the editors and publishers at Routledge for their professional guidance and wisdom in bringing about this completed product.

The encouragement and feedback of numerous colleagues, mentors, and friends at the University of Aberdeen made my doctoral dissertation possible. Among those, I would like especially to acknowledge Amy Erickson, Andrew Errington, Kevin Hargaden, Emily Hill, Michael Morelli, and Carlos Thompson. My time as a McDonald Distinguished Fellow at Emory University has also brought me into contact with some exceptionally gifted scholars, and I wish particularly to thank Andrew Hayashi, Samuel Bray, and Nathan Chapman.

Gratitude is due as well to my parents, Anne and David Calhoun, who instilled in me the desire for knowledge, and to my sister and brother-in-law, Isabel and Jon Farrar, for their kind support and encouragement.

My deepest gratitude goes to my wife, Mary Ann, without whose adventuresome spirit, belief in my abilities, and remarkable patience I would never have undertaken this project—let alone finished it. This book is dedicated to her.

Introduction

Purpose and approach of the book

Why does the institution of taxation occupy a precarious place in our societies, seemingly suspended between its potential to redistribute resources and its status as a necessary evil? In other words, why is taxation held out as the means for achieving greater social equity while it is, at the same time, under constant pressure to limit itself for the sake of economic productivity? Why, to put the question succinctly, is tax policy driven by the competing principles of equity and efficiency? That is the question this book is designed to answer—but to answer in a particular way. The approach of this project is both historical and conceptual. It is an excavation of theological commitments throughout the history of Christianity in the West that have formed and shaped taxation as we know it and, thus, that help to explain the ambiguous nature of our conceptions of taxation.

Thus, beneath the central question—why tax law is suspended between different guiding principles—lies a more specific question: why does taxation serve an adjunct role in legal systems, functioning as the means of achieving redistributive justice while other areas of law protect private property and foster the production of wealth? Christian theology has had much to say about property rights and wealth as moral categories. This work offers a contribution to what historian Jennifer Hole calls "economic ethics," i.e., studies of the "moral evaluation" of contemporary economic practices.[1] The subject matter of economic ethics, according to Hole, centers on the struggle in Christian thought over the category of wealth, and more specifically, the tension between acquiring wealth and the ideals of poverty exemplified by Jesus' life.[2]

This book, therefore, treats the categories of contemporary tax theory as inherited from earlier political, legal, and economic commitments that were infused with theological concepts. The categories remain even though evacuated of their original theological content.[3] In this respect, the present project follows the example of the theologian E. Clinton Gardner, who, quoting Harold J. Berman, writes:

> The secular and increasingly global context of present-day law precludes the possibility of return to the legal systems of the past. Nevertheless, a study of

> the tradition is an essential preparation for the constructive task which lies ahead. . . . Such a study reveals the distinctive character of modern Western law. . . . Today, however, secular law, bereft of its original foundation, is left "suspended, so to speak, in mid-air."[4]

Taxation, by its very nature, calls for "theological" input, as the economist Henry Simons noted.[5] Although Simons may have meant "theological" metaphorically, the term is suggestive; and this project accepts the invitation to excavate the theology or theologies that direct taxation toward a redistributive goal not readily explicable by most prevailing theories of tax equity.

The material that follows is necessarily presented historically, but its objective is not merely to increase the historical understanding of theological reflections on taxation. The following chapters draw on political, social, and economic developments, but the overall approach of the book is based in theological ethics.[6] The material refers at times to the influence that ideas had on economic legislation and the impact that law and politics had on theology, but it is chiefly concerned with examining the ideas of theologians.[7] Its primary method is to examine texts in selected theological traditions.[8] It is, in other words, a theoretical study with sociocultural features. The impact of theological and philosophical ideas on legislation and on attitudes of the people is hard to gauge. The chapters that follow, however, are informed by the belief that ideas are often criticisms of, and reactions to, social, economic, and political circumstances.[9] Moreover, these criticisms and reactions can, and sometimes do, influence actions and decisions.[10] At the very least, theologians throughout the history of the Christian church have liberated categories and vocabularies that made sense of, and allowed people to articulate, changing social and economic circumstances.[11]

Though it aspires to none of the magnificence of Peter Brown's *Through the Eye of a Needle*, this book is influenced by the ease with which Brown interweaves political, economic, and social currents with the ideas of "elite" thinkers—Ambrose and Augustine foremost among them. Anticipating the challenge that his chosen authors are not wholly representative of the thinking of average people in the later centuries of the Roman Empire, Brown writes that "[i]n matters of religion—and especially in the study of major religious movements such as the formation of the Christian churches—the word 'elite' can be misleading." He continues:

> It invites us to assume an absence of contact between leading minds and the wider body of opinion and practice that surrounds them. This is a false assumption. I prefer the judgment of Louis Gernet, writing on Greek religion in the classical period: "An elite does not invent. It renders explicit what many others think."[12]

This work also proceeds in accord with that judgment.

This is a work of political theology and philosophy and, as such, bridges the gap between past and present. It follows the methodological perspective that

Richard Tuck sets out in the preface to his *Philosophy and Government 1572–1651*, according to which one must be a historian to understand political philosophers (and theologians) of any period, depicting "the character of the actual life which these theorists were leading, and the specific political questions which engaged their attention." At the same time, however, a work of political philosophy must make "a contribution to our understanding of how people might cope with broadly similar issues in our own time."[13] Tuck suggests, correctly, that the differences between past and present are not as great as we often think. "[T]he better our historical sense of what those [past political] conflicts were," he writes, "the more often they seem to resemble modern ones."[14]

American work on political economy has tended to proceed ahistorically. This is a mistake, according to Susan Strange, and the present work follows Strange's advice in inquiring into the *causes* of today's consequences.[15] Strange argues that any economic arrangement that affects "systems of production, exchange and distribution, and the mix of values reflected therein" necessarily results from "human decisions." We must, therefore, "peer behind the curtain of passing time into what went before."[16]

Limits of the book

This work, nevertheless, does not offer detailed policy recommendations or insight into how the mechanics of the American tax system might be improved. The purpose of these chapters is certainly not to suggest that American or British tax policy be guided by any particular theological doctrine, nor is it to argue that medieval and Reformation-era doctrines of taxation supply the technical precision needed to formulate contemporary tax policies. Regarding the connection between theory and policy, Susan Strange argues that any theorist must eventually choose whether "to proceed from explanatory theory" or to engage in "policy prescription." It is not essential for the theorist to apply theory to policymaking, she writes, because "policy-making necessarily involves value judgments and risk assessments that are exogenous to theory and that are better made by practical policy-makers than by irresponsible academic theorists."[17] While offering general thoughts about how tax policy might better proceed, this book is content to remain primarily in the realm of irresponsible academic theorizing.

Rather than telling policymakers exactly what they should do in Washington or London, this work offers three broad messages, each to a different audience.

To the historian, it offers an explanation of the ambivalent position in which tax theory currently finds itself.

To the church, this project extends an invitation. The church has often shown suspicion of government-administered poor relief, of various forms of social justice, and of certain types of equality. These chapters ask the Christian believer to consider re-imagining redistributive taxation as a means of taking on the burdens and needs of her neighbor. In the United States, conversations about economics and public finance were briefly open to ideas about equity after the financial crisis beginning in 2008 and briefly again in the early days of the 2020 presidential campaign. Equity may have surfaced in those conversations only as an instrumental kind of equity, the consequence of a realization that inequality can destabilize the economy, but the opportunity to bring a more theological account of equity into public discourse was there. It was a missed opportunity; it should not be missed in the next crisis.

To policymakers, this project issues a warning. Tax theory and tax policy will necessarily remain incoherent if they are beholden to one and only one social goal, such as economic growth. Taxation must, by definition, take into account plural goods, and those goods must be commensurable. The meaning of this undoubtedly cryptic paragraph will, I hope, unfold throughout the course of this book.

The book is limited in its scope. Discussions of just taxation have largely presupposed a domestic rather than a global setting, because the former is the context in which most political philosophy (and theology) has traditionally been worked out. This work is no exception. It takes American and British tax theory and policy as its contemporary point of departure to make the scope of the analysis more manageable. For the same reason, it limits its historical excavation to theologians of the Western church. Contemporary treatments herein focus on progressive income tax systems because those systems have been identified in much of the nineteenth-, twentieth-, and twenty-first-century literature as the primary bearers of tax justice.[18]

Because this book bridges the gap between past and present, it runs the risk of anachronism. A few words are in order concerning that risk. No doubt the great economic historian M. I. Finley is right to caution that the *economy* was not a conceptually differentiated segment of thought or practice in ancient society.[19] Concepts like laissez-faire are meaningless when applied to antiquity; they cannot be imposed on a world that had no prior conception of economy.[20] Regarding taxes specifically, Finley maintains that no evidence whatsoever leads us to conclude that the ancient Greeks ever thought of tax as having an effect on the economy. For instance, he concludes that they understood no connection at all between taxation and competition, the balance of trade, and productivity. Athens did not even use taxes to control its own food supply. Nor did Rome contribute any greater understanding; its sole objective in levying taxes was to raise revenue.[21] The term "economy" itself initially meant regulation, administration, and organization. The meaning of the term was only gradually extended to the ideas of management and then *revenue management*.[22]

To impose the categories and vocabulary available to us in our understanding of the economy and its interaction with taxation on the ancient world would indeed be an anachronism. But to build on ethical insights of ancient thinkers—be they "elite" or not—to gain an understanding of the moral richness and poverty of our contemporary ideas about the political economy is surely permissible. R. J. Hernández-Díaz writes concerning the methodology in his essay on Augustine and political economy: "The chief concern of this essay is not to understand Augustine himself but to reflect on an insight of Augustinian moral theory and its consequences for contemporary ethical debates on the political economy."[23]

The same could be said of this book—not just with respect to Augustine, though that is definitely the case, but also with respect to Thomas Aquinas, William of Ockham, Luther, Calvin, and those who play supporting roles in the narrative that unfolds on the following pages.

The error of the ahistorical, typically American analysis of the ethical implications of public finance, particularly the *theological*-ethical implications, stems from the tendency to define terms narrowly and the proclivity for compartmentalization for which our time is well known. This book rejects those tendencies. Embracing the methodological critique of those who—like Susan Strange and R. J. Hernández-Díaz—resist compartmentalization, this work relies entirely on the conviction that political and economic views "flow seamlessly" from theological commitments.[24] Indeed, this book accepts the thesis of political theologians and philosophers like Carl Schmitt and Erik Peterson that, as philosopher Giorgio Agamben puts it, "[s]ignatures move and displace concepts and signs from one field to another," with the result that "secularization operates in the conceptual system of modernity as a signature that refers it back to theology."[25]

Donald Shriver and Richard Knox write that tax "received only episodic attention in the writings of the early Protestant Reformers and has received, if anything, less attention in the writings of their intellectual descendants," even though taxation is, they claim, "the most important *economic* dimension of relations between Christians and the state."[26] The invitation of the present work is for readers not to be deterred by the relative paucity of explicit "tax theology," in the Reformation and its aftermath as well as throughout church history, and to look at considerations that hide behind other issues in the thinking of theologians through the ages. It is an invitation to find elusive yet important connections between ancient philosophical and theological ethics and today's concrete implications.[27]

One additional caveat is in order. This book is a work in law and ethics, but not in the sense in which the phrase "law and ethics" is usually understood. In the United States, the subdiscipline of legal ethics goes by the name "professional responsibility." The bar association of each state adopts rules designed to guide the conduct of lawyers in that jurisdiction.[28] Texts that seek to encapsulate rules of professional responsibility and place them in context ultimately try to answer one question: can a person "be both a good lawyer and a good person?"[29] These texts navigate the fraught relationship between law and morality, often working toward a definition of justice along the way.[30]

This book does not seek to navigate the complicated connection between law and morality so much as to look behind that relationship in a specific area of law—taxation—with the goal of understanding how tax justice, or tax equity, became mired in ambiguity in the first place. The project might better be described as a work of jurisprudence than of law and ethics, but jurisprudence—"the nature of law and its working"—has assumed strongly positivist connotations.[31] Without denying the value of positivist accounts of taxation, this project focuses instead on the use that theologians have seen fit to make of the institution of taxation. It inquires into the sources of tax legitimacy, but it considers those sources as lying outside the science of public finance itself. The story told here, to be sure, assumes that the institution of taxation existed long before Christian theologians sought to explain how tax could be legitimate, but the story centers on the ways in which Christian thinkers infused tax with meaning and theological legitimacy and how those infusions shaped contemporary tax philosophy so significantly that positivist jurisprudence is incapable by itself of untangling the confusions facing tax philosophers and policymakers today.

Outline of the book

At one level, this book addresses the tension between the realism demanded of policymakers and the relative ideological purity of calls for redistributive taxation. The theologians discussed herein never questioned a ruler's prerogative to raise revenue for the common good, as long as the revenue raised was indeed used for the common good. What the theologians required was that the ruler's objectives be infused with concern for the needs of society's disadvantaged members. In other words, the needs of the poor should balance the needs of state and the interests of property owners and wage earners.

In form, the theologians' call resembles the recessive voice of tax justice in the contemporary American discussion. The goal of liberal-egalitarian tax theories in particular is to inject explicitly redistributive considerations into tax policy.[32]

In substance, however, the contemporary and historical calls for redistributive justice differ. Taxation as a tool for reducing economic inequality has recently received significant attention in the United States.[33] Many view inequality as a strike against American democracy. Reasons for decrying the wealth gap range from a desire to see all of society's members share in economic growth and prosperity (limited always by the overriding commitment not to hinder growth) to the pragmatic concern that too much inequality jeopardizes the rule of law and, thus, the conditions for growth.

As the following chapters will show, the reduction of inequality itself was not a particularly high priority for Augustine, Aquinas, Ockham, Luther, and Calvin. Instead, what is common to these theologians' accounts of property (and tax) is simply this: the inescapable imperative that property (and tax revenue) be used to meet the needs of the poor.

As the Christian church grew during the history of the Roman Empire, it increasingly faced questions about the morality of wealth and poverty. Its representatives—not least Ambrose and Augustine—worked to delineate an appropriately Christian response to extreme wealth, poverty, and economic inequality in their society. Other Christians approached the problem differently. The "theology of redistributive taxation" herein begins there, with the early theological efforts to heal the wound between rich and poor.[34]

Thomas Aquinas was the thinker who gave the concept of *need* its redistributive force. He offered a robust account of individual property rights as an affirmative good, but one that is nonetheless limited by the natural law of communal property.[35] *Necessitas* is a kind of triggering mechanism in Thomas' political theology, in that the need of the poor person reactivates the natural law of common possession, suspends human laws on private property, and places the one with superabundance in the debt of the one lacking *necessitas*.

William of Ockham, who wrote about taxes quite directly, anticipated various modern tax theories. He also reinvigorated the recessive voice, represented in Chapter 2 by the likes of Jerome and Pelagius, regarding wealth and the Christian life. Tax was ultimately for Ockham a way of renouncing what was Caesar's and thus living more consistently in the spiritual *dominium*.[36]

For Martin Luther, inequality was an unimportant concept. According to Luther, the assurance that the believer has received an abundance of all good things—spiritual and material—by virtue of having changed places with Christ frees her to focus exclusively on the needs of others without reservation or anxiety.[37]

Inequality does enter the theological narrative in the thinking of John Calvin,[38] but more as a catalyst for relieving others' needs and binding people together in an arrangement of mutual dependence than as a central problem of its own.

In the end, Calvin's vision was inverted by Enlightenment thinkers. His eschatological reserve was replaced by the confidence—if not hubris—of using taxation to reach an ideal state of affairs in society. The assumption that an optimal social condition is reachable answers the presenting question: why does taxation occupy ambiguous ground between moral and amoral considerations?[39]

Notes

1 Jennifer Hole, *Economic Ethics in Late Medieval England, 1300-1550*, Archival Insights into the Evolution of Economics, ed. Robert Leeson (Basingstoke: Palgrave Macmillan, 2016), 19.

2 Hole, *Economic Ethics*, 22.

3 Legal historian Chris Thornhill calls this phenomenon "theoretical secularization." Any researcher exploring theoretical secularization, he writes,

> argues that the problems and concepts of political theory are often distilled from, or express responses to, points of theological or legal-theological debate, that legal and political principles evolve through a reshaping or a transformation of paradigms first pertaining to religion or religious conceptions of law, and that theological or legal-theological ideas retain impact in political debate even when the specifically religious content of these problems has begun to diminish in relevance.

Chris Thornhill, *German Political Philosophy: The Metaphysics of Law*, Routledge Studies in Social and Political Thought (London: Routledge, 2007), 1.

4 E. Clinton Gardner, *Justice and Christian Ethics*, New Studies in Christian Ethics 7 (Cambridge: Cambridge University Press, 1996), 1–2.

5 Henry C. Simons, *Personal Income Taxation: The Definition of Income as a Problem of Fiscal Policy* (Chicago: The University of Chicago Press, 1938), 13.

6 Chapter One is an outlier, presenting the contemporary debate over theory on its own terms.

7 The project follows in some respects the model provided by Carter Lindberg's *Beyond Charity: Reformation Initiatives for the Poor* (Minneapolis: Fortress Press, 1993). Lindberg states early on in his book that he considers "the interpretations of some social historians to be unnecessarily reductionistic." Lindberg, *Beyond*

Charity, 13. He readily acknowledges that ideas and events influence each other, and that his "presentation of theories" must be "supplemented by accounts of . . . legislative and administrative praxis"; but he emphasizes that his approach is not that of a social historian. Lindberg, *Beyond Charity*, 4–6. In the final analysis, Lindberg insists, judgments about the relationship of values and ideologies to political and economic policies must rest "not only upon empirical observations but also upon nontestable assumptions" held by, among others, historians and theologians. Lindberg, *Beyond Charity*, 2.

8 For a similar statement of purpose, see Gardner, *Justice and Christian Ethics*, 6–9.

9 See Hole, *Economic Ethics*, for statements of a similar methodological position.

10 Historian Elizabeth A. R. Brown writes that "there is evidence that in some parts of western Europe," the social, political, and economic teachings of medieval theologians "resulted in the performance of acts which, rather than promoting the immediate practical interests of the ruler and his realm, actually mitigated against them. In these instances the precepts of the theologians would appear to have fallen on fertile ground and to have prompted actions which would not otherwise have been performed." Elizabeth A. R. Brown, "Taxation and Morality in the Thirteenth and Fourteenth Centuries: Conscience and Political Power and the Kings of France," *French Historical Studies* 8, no. 1 (Spring 1973): 9, accessed August 15, 2020, http://www.jstor.org/stable/285956.

11 This is the claim that Carter Lindberg stakes in response to the debate over the influence of Luther's ideas on changing economic and social conditions in the sixteenth century. Lindberg, *Beyond Charity*, 68–69.

12 Peter Brown, *Through the Eye of a Needle: Wealth, the Fall of Rome, and the Making of Christianity in the West, AD 350–AD 550* (Princeton: Princeton University Press, 2012), xxiii–xxiv, quoting Louis Gernet, *Le genie grec dans la religion* (Paris: Renaissance du Livre, 1932), 370.

13 Richard Tuck, *Philosophy and Government 1572–1651*, Ideas in Context, ed. Quentin Skinner, Lorraine Daston, Wolf Lepenies, Richard Rorty, and J. B. Schneewind (Cambridge: Cambridge University Press, 1993), xi.

14 Tuck, *Philosophy and Government*, xi–xii.

15 Susan Strange, *States and Markets*, 2nd ed. (London: Continuum, 1994), 21.

16 Strange, *States and Markets*, 18.

17 Strange, *States and Markets*, 11–12.

18 Dennis J. Ventry, "Equity versus Efficiency and the U.S. Tax System in Historical Perspective," in *Tax Justice: The Ongoing Debate*, ed. Joseph J. Thorndike and Dennis J. Ventry, Jr. (Washington, DC: The Urban Institute Press, 2002), 43.

19 M. I. Finley, *The Ancient Economy* (Berkeley: University of California Press, 1999), 21.

20 Finley, *The Ancient Economy*, 155.

21 Finley, *The Ancient Economy*, 164, 165, 200.

22 Finley, *The Ancient Economy*, 17, 20.

23 R. J. Hernández-Díaz, "Augustine and Political Economy," in *Augustine and Social Justice*, ed. Teresa Delgado, John Doody, and Kim Paffenroth (Lanham, MD: Lexington Books, 2015), 114.

24 See Hernández-Díaz, "Augustine and Political Economy," 115. Hernández-Díaz decries both the failure of contemporary theorists to recognize that economics and the study of political economy are inseparable, and the tendency of interpreters of Augustine to treat his political economic thought in isolation from his theology and to "study his theology without reference to his political-economics." While this "truncation" may be appropriate in modern scholarship, it "is ill suited to Augustine's own thinking." Hernández-Díaz, "Augustine and Political Economy," 114–15.

25 Giorgio Agamben, *The Kingdom and the Glory: For a Theological Genealogy of Economy and Government* (Homo Sacer *II, 2*), trans. Lorenzo Chiesa and Matteo Madarini (Stanford: Stanford University Press, 2011), 4.
26 Donald W. Shriver, Jr., and E. Richard Knox, "Taxation in the History of Protestant Ethics," *The Journal of Religious Ethics* 13, no. 1 (Spring 1985): 135.
27 See Shriver and Knox, "Taxation in the History of Protestant Ethics," 151–52.
28 See, e.g., "Legal Ethics," Duke University School of Law Research Guides, accessed August 16, 2020, https://law.duke.edu/sites/default/files/lib/legal ethics.pdf.
29 Monroe H. Freedman and Abbe Smith, *Understanding Lawyers' Ethics*, 4th ed. (New York: LexisNexis, 2010), 1.06.
30 See, e.g., Grace M. Giesel, *Mastering Professional Responsibility*, 2nd ed. (Durham, NC: Carolina Academic Press, 2015); Geoffrey C. Hazard, W. William Hodes, and Peter R. Jarvis, *The Law of Lawyering*, 4th ed. (New York: Wolters Kluwer, 2018); Ronald D. Rotunda, *Legal Ethics in a Nutshell*, 4th ed. (St. Paul: West Thomson Reuters, 2013); Thomas Shaffer, *American Legal Ethics* (New York: Matthew Bender & Co., 1985).
31 Hilaire McCoubrey and Nigel D. White, *Textbook on Jurisprudence*, 2nd ed. (London: Blackstone Press Ltd., 1993), 1.
32 See Chapter One.
33 See, e.g., Zachary Karabell, "Why Taxing the Rich May Not Save Democracy," *Wired* (January 29, 2019), accessed August 16, 2020, https://www.wired.com/story/why-taxing-the-rich-may-not-save-democracy/ (reviewing Representative Alexandria Ocasio-Cortez' proposal to raise the marginal tax rate to seventy percent on income above $10 million and Senator Elizabeth Warren's proposed "wealth tax" on assets over $50 million).
34 See Chapter Two.
35 See Chapter Three.
36 See Chapter Four.
37 See Chapter Five.
38 See Chapter Six.
39 See Chapter Seven.

References

Agamben, Giorgio. 2011. *The Kingdom and the Glory: For a Theological Genealogy of Economy and Government* (Homo Sacer *II, 2*). Translated by Lorenzo Chiesa and Matteo Madarini. Stanford: Stanford University Press.

Brown, Elizabeth A. R. 1973. "Taxation and Morality in the Thirteenth and Fourteenth Centuries: Conscience and Political Power and the Kings of France." *French Historical Studies* 8, no. 1 (Spring): 1–28. Accessed August 15, 2020. http://www.jstor.org/stable/285956.

Brown, Peter. 2012. *Through the Eye of a Needle: Wealth, the Fall of Rome, and the Making of Christianity in the West, 350 AD – 550 AD*. Princeton: Princeton University Press.

Duke University. 2017. "Legal Ethics." Duke University School of Law Research Guides. Accessed August 16, 2020. https://law.duke.edu/sites/default/files/lib/legalethics.pdf.

Finley, M. I. 1999. *The Ancient Economy*. Berkeley: University of California Press.

Freedman, Monroe H., and Abbe Smith. 2010. *Understanding Lawyers' Ethics*. 4th ed. New York: LexisNexis.

Gardner, E. Clinton. 1995. *Justice and Christian Ethics. New Studies in Christian Ethics 7*. Cambridge: Cambridge University Press.

Hernández-Díaz, R. J. 2015. "Augustine and Political Economy." In *Augustine and Social Justice*, edited by Teresa Delgado, John Doody, and Kim Paffenroth, 113–27. Lanham, MD: Lexington Books.

Hole, Jennifer. 2016. "Economic Ethics in Late Medieval England, 1300–1550". In *Archival Insights into the Evolution of Economics*, edited by Robert Leeson. Basingstoke: Palgrave Macmillan.

Karabell, Zachary. January 29, 2019. "Why Taxing the Rich May Not Save Democracy." Wired. Accessed August 16, 2020. https://www.wired.com/story/why-taxing-the-rich-may-not-save-democracy/.

Lindberg, Carter. 1993. *Beyond Charity: Reformation Initiatives for the Poor*. Minneapolis: Fortress Press.

McCoubrey, Hilaire, and Nigel D. White. 1993. *Textbook on Jurisprudence*. 2nd ed. London: Blackstone Press Ltd.

Shriver, Donald W., Jr., and E. Richard Knox. 1985. "Taxation in the History of Protestant Ethics." *The Journal of Religious Ethics* 13, no. 1 (Spring): 134–60.

Simons, Henry C. 1938. *Personal Income Taxation: The Definition of Income as a Problem of Fiscal Policy*. Chicago: The University of Chicago Press.

Strange, Susan. 1994. *States and Markets*. 2nd ed. London: Continuum.

Thornhill, Chris. 2007. *German Political Philosophy: The Metaphysics of Law*. Routledge Studies in Social and Political Thought. London: Routledge.

Tuck, Richard. 1993. "Philosophy and Government 1572–1651." In *Ideas in Context*, edited by Quentin Skinner, Lorraine Daston, Wolf Lepenies, Richard Rorty, and J. B. Schneewind. Cambridge: Cambridge University Press.

Ventry, Dennis J. 2002. "Equity versus Efficiency and the U.S. Tax System in Historical Perspective." In *Tax Justice: The Ongoing Debate*, edited by Joseph J. Thorndike and Dennis J. Ventry, Jr., 25–70. Washington, DC: The Urban Institute Press.

1 Equity and efficiency

Introduction

In June 2019, a call for a US federal wealth tax was published under the title "An Open Letter to the 2020 Presidential Candidates: It's Time to Tax Us More." It was written by 20 very wealthy Americans. "A wealth tax," the letter argued, "would help close the large gap in effective tax rates between very rich families and everyone else." The current economic imbalance that the billionaire authors sought to redress "creates resentment and makes it harder for working-class Americans to achieve social mobility. ... The most fortunate should contribute more." The signatories concluded: "It is not in our interest to advocate for this tax, if our interests are quite narrowly understood. But the wealth tax is in our interest as Americans."[1]

The letter is mentioned here not for the merits of its proposal, but to draw attention to the fact that its authors felt the need to write it in the first place. The idea that taxes on the wealthy are, at best, a necessary evil is so ingrained in American tax policy and in the popular imagination that these wealthy Americans felt obliged to implore presidential candidates to consider taxing them in new ways for the benefit of society. Twenty billionaires speaking against their own immediate economic interests was seemingly required to break through the single guiding principle of American tax policy, i.e., that taxes must not impede the preservation and maximization of wealth any more than is necessary.

Tax policy in the United States is a puzzle: its domain is "thoroughly moralized territory" but it lacks an abstract moral principle to structure it. Tax justice, consequently, is approached in a piecemeal manner, both in theory and in policy. On the one hand, tax theorists and policymakers refer frequently to concepts such as inequality but have no consistent conception of justice to guide them.[2]

This puzzle manifests itself in the way taxation works in society. On the one hand, the full weight of distributive justice falls on the tax system, thus freeing other areas of law to focus on maximizing economic growth. The tax scholar Linda Sugin writes:

> For better or for worse, the tax law is the major tool of redistribution we have. Tax policy debate is one of very few areas of the law in which discussions of

> distributive justice are considered appropriate. The political reality is that most other economic regulation is oriented towards maximization of wealth, rather than its distribution. The tax law comes in after productivity is maximized, and it should—to some extent at least—rearrange the results produced by markets that operate to concentrate wealth and opportunity.[3]

On the other hand, tax theorists often push equity considerations aside. Taxation tends to be regarded as a "black box" that is called on "to put into effect whatever distribution of economic benefits and burdens ... is required by the normative theory under discussion."[4] The degree of concern over inequality in society is a "normative" question "that cannot be answered with data" and must, therefore, be segregated from economic considerations.[5] A barrier is required, it seems, between "uncontroversial" considerations such as "productivity, efficiency, and real income" and "controversial," distributional concerns.[6]

This barrier leaves taxation in an untenable position; it is the best—perhaps only—instrument of distributive and redistributive justice available, but distributive concerns are not regarded as appropriate subject matter for tax theory. Why, Sugin asks, would we want to "discount the one real-world tool that is regularly employed toward achieving" distributive justice?[7]

(Re)distributive taxation

A tax is an enforceable "financial charge" that the state makes on an individual, corporation, or other entity "for the support of state operations and programs." The revenue from taxation is generally considered "just" if it is used for one or more of three purposes: (1) paying for government and public services; (2) shaping the behavior of citizens; and (3) redistributing resources.[8] The first purpose—paying for public, "non-rival" goods—is the least morally controversial, although even that use of taxation lacks a moral account of "which public goods warrant coercive supply."[9] The second use—taxation for the purpose of altering the way people use resources—is more controversial. It is not the focus of this book, although it appears when necessary.

The focus of this book is on the third purpose of taxation, its redistributive function. Taxation is, as we have already seen, "the most important instrument by which the political system puts into practice a conception of economic or distributive justice."[10] Justice is the subject matter of economics to the extent that economics "is concerned with the proper distribution of scarce resources in society,"[11] and no aspect of economics or politics affects that distribution more than redistributive taxation.[12]

The two criteria by which the majority of economists today measure the outcomes of tax policy are efficiency and equity.[13] Efficiency is understood here to mean "non-distortional," i.e., as causing minimal interference in the decisions that taxpayers make.[14] In tax scholar James Repetti's words, "[t]he 'efficiency' of a tax system frequently refers to its 'excess burden,' which reflects the decrease in utility attributable to behavioral changes that would not occur in a tax-less world."[15]

Equity is regarded as the element of justice in the sphere of taxation, but it is difficult to define. On one level, tax equity refers to "how taxes should be distributed among the public."[16] Tax equity is typically thought of in terms of "horizontal equity" and "vertical equity," but these two concepts do not offer the same definition of equity. Horizontal equity refers to the idea that equal incomes should bear the same tax burden, vertical equity to the idea that the burden of taxation should increase as income increases.[17] These two conceptions of equity sometimes conflict.[18]

Even when standing alone, moreover, neither conception of equity carries a stable and uncontestable meaning. The exact shape of an equitable curve in a progressive tax system (i.e., one in which rates increase as income increases) has proved elusive. Vertical equity is a principle that simply cannot be reduced to an actual rate structure.[19] Horizontal equity fares a little better. The 2017 federal Tax Act, for instance, adopted a "schedular" system "that applies different tax rates, or schedules, to different types of income" in an effort to "avoid the distortions and economic inefficiencies given the practical inability to include all income in the tax base."[20] These moves "effectively upended the key principle of the Tax Reform Act of 1986, namely that an ideal revenue system should tax a broad base of income at low rates."[21] These two tax reform acts present two different conceptions of horizontal equity. The 1986 Act operated with the assumption that taxpayers with similar amounts of income should be taxed at approximately the same rate; the 2017 Act took into account the varying effects of different types of income in attempting to achieve approximate equality of treatment across the tax base.

At another level, tax equity refers to *redistributive* justice, i.e., the change of resources across society rather than merely the allocation of the tax burden.[22] The line between distributive justice and redistributive justice is blurred, however. The two terms—distributive and redistributive—are not used consistently. "Distributive justice" sometimes means something broader, and vaguer, than the fair allocation of tax burdens.[23] Even assuming consistent definitions, the distinction between the two types of justice is not always clear. Vertical equity is a case in point. It is a kind of distributive justice, because it seeks to allocate more of the overall tax burden to the relatively wealthy than to the less wealthy. However, under utilitarian assumptions, a progressive rate structure is only distributive—and not redistributive—if that structure reflects the exact rate at which the marginal utility of income declines. A taxpayer with greater pre-tax income pays a higher dollar tax than a person with less pre-tax income, but tax burdens measured in utility are the same. No redistribution of income occurs.[24] That, however, is an unlikely scenario. Distributive justice often evolves into redistributive justice without any intention or even awareness on the part of policymakers: "When governments try to rectify some real or perceived vertical inequity, some amount of redistribution is almost inevitable."[25]

The ambiguous meaning of tax equity has undoubtedly hampered efforts to balance efficiency and equity.[26] Nevertheless, a balance of some kind is what tax theorists seek. The right trade-off between equalizing welfare and preserving incentives is a driving force in tax theory, if not in tax policy.[27] Indeed, this balance is an animating force in political economy more generally, beyond the confines of taxation. Susan Strange, for instance, notes that the three political-economic models—which she calls nationalism, socialism, and liberalism—all balance the values of wealth, security, freedom of choice, and justice. What distinguishes these models is the order in which they rank the four commitments and the relative weight they give them.[28]

The rest of this chapter questions whether American and British tax policy in fact reflects the kind of balance that tax theorists seek as their holy grail. While not providing a historically developed answer to the presenting question (i.e., why taxation is and yet is not tied to justice)—that is the task of the rest of the book—the following sections of this chapter at least work toward clarifying the question.

The role of "side constraints"

The trade-off between efficiency and equity (or, more strongly, equality) is a peculiar kind of balance. The two values do not confront each other head on, as equal combatants. Libertarian conceptions of justice demonstrate more clearly than other ideas of justice that a society's pre-established commitments operate more as "absolute 'side-constraints' on action" than as commensurable principles susceptible to actual balancing. Agents may do what they wish "within the constraints imposed."[29]

Libertarian rights

The philosopher Robert Nozick (1938–2002) understood redistributive tax-and-transfer systems as "rights-infringing transfers" because these systems transfer holdings away from those entitled to them. "Historical" distributions, in Nozick's view, are preferable to "end-result" principles of justice because the former do not necessitate redistribution, which is just another word for "interference." Maintaining what Nozick called "patterned justice" of some kind—e.g., a distribution according to "moral merit, or needs, or marginal product, or how hard [one] tries," to name just a few candidates—requires someone to "either continually interfere to stop people from transferring resources as they wish to, or continually (or periodically) interfere to take from some persons resources that others for some reason chose to transfer to them." Nozick questioned why justice must be expressed in terms of a "resulting pattern" instead of "underlying generating principles." [30]

Nozick's analytical baseline (i.e., property rights) is also a morally privileged baseline (i.e., "entitlement"). Judged against the sole criterion of inviolable, "negative" property rights, taxation is for Nozick a necessary evil and redistributive taxation an *unnecessary* evil. Taxation may be necessary, Nozick conceded, to fund a minimal state capable of defending the very property rights that he held to be primal and primary. If its function extends beyond that role, taxation must be denounced. Despite Nozick's contention that taxation should not accommodate disparate social goods, a basic balancing approach is necessary even in libertarianism.[31] The libertarian goal is to find the minimal quantum of taxation that maximizes property rights. It is a one-sided balancing test, however, in that it sets the right to property in a logically prior and morally privileged place; the burden is on the limited needs of the state to demonstrate how, why, and to what extent that prior and privileged right must be attenuated.

Consequentialists and non-consequentialists alike all adopt some version of the side-constraint model that is most clearly visible in libertarian philosophy.

Classical utility theories of sacrifice

Classical utilitarian tax theories assumed that happiness or well-being, referred to more technically as "utility," was the fundamental value that social policy choices should take into account. The notion of *sacrifice* as a measure of taxation arose because taxes were assumed to reduce a subjective sense of well-being, or happiness.[32] Sacrifice is the inverse of utility; as one increases, the other decreases. Sacrifice thus became the measure of utility in a negative sense.

John Stuart Mill (1806–73), the political economist F. Y. Edgeworth (1845–1926), the mathematical economist Arnold Jacob Cohen-Stuart (1855–1921), and the economist A. C. Pigou (1877–1959) all sought a principle of taxation that would equate the sacrifices of a society's members. In the end, "equal marginal sacrifice" was enshrined as the standard principle of tax fairness.[33] The principle of equal marginal sacrifice seeks the least total sacrifice from society. It asks each taxpayer to give up the portion of her income that produces the least aggregate sacrifice, thus requiring the government to assess tax to meet the desired revenue in a way that maximizes the sum of the post-tax utility of all taxpayers.[34] Equal marginal sacrifice yields maximum progression, "lopping off income from the top down until the tax system cumulates the required revenue."[35] The economist Richard Musgrave has suggested that the success, albeit temporary, of equal marginal sacrifice stemmed from the fact that the principle's formulation of tax fairness coincided with "the economist's goal of maximizing society's aggregate welfare."[36]

The principle of equal marginal sacrifice, however, was never without its detractors. If fully implemented, the principle would have led to "[e]xclusive taxation of the rich, at probably close to confiscatory rates," violating "even minimal considerations of fairness based on merit or just dessert."[37] In fact, the utilitarian approach to taxation in general was widely criticized on the grounds that well-being, or utility, simply cannot be translated into definite units in the way that money can be. The economist Harold Groves, for instance, wrote: "The whole utilitarian view assumes the measurability of the immeasurable and a comparison of the incomparable. It is not possible to define an objectively correct distribution of happiness."[38]

Utilitarian tax philosophy seemed to have run its course by the middle of the twentieth century, when economist T. N. Carver (1865–1961) observed that taxation consists of twin "evils," i.e., the sacrifice required of the taxpayer and the repressive effect that taxes have on productivity, that utility theories failed to provide a measure of the trade-off between these two evils, and that these theories therefore could offer no guidance on the shape of rate schedules.[39]

At the heart of the demise of classical utility theories lay the difficulty of interpersonal comparisons. Gauging how much of a subjective sacrifice individuals X and Y make, i.e., how much happiness they lose, when they pay taxes is simply impossible. It was well and fine for thinkers of the utilitarian persuasion, wedded to the principle of diminishing marginal utility,[40] to argue around the turn of the twentieth century "that overall welfare is in fact maximized by equalizing incomes as much as is consistent with retaining incentives to produce."[41] What they could not do is show why 100 dollars contributed as much to the well-being of individual X as 100 dollars contributed to the well-being of individual Y, assuming X and Y had the same income—let alone show why 100 dollars contributed *more* to B's well-being (and by how much) than to C's well-being when B had less income than C and thus subjectively valued 100 dollars more.

In the 1930s, economists like Lionel Robbins (1898–1984) and Henry Simons (1899–1946) dismissed subjective interpersonal comparisons from the sphere of tax philosophy—Robbins because he thought they were unscientific, and Simons because he regarded them as useless at best, at worst dishonest.

Simons conceded that a minimum sacrifice principle, if true, implies that taxes should be progressive, but he believed that the concept of sacrifice was lacking in content: "One derives practical implications from the criterion of equality, or proportionality, of sacrifice precisely in proportion to one's knowledge of something which no one has ever known, or ever will know, anything about."[42]

Furthermore, Simons asked, why should utility theory be based on suffering in the first place? Simons considered utility theory's fundamental hedonism only thinly veiled behind its "pseudo-scientific statement of the case against inequality"; what really drove the theory was the conviction "that all individuals are, or must be treated as, equally efficient as pleasure machines."[43]

Simons was convinced that the rejection of inequality is a value judgment that necessarily comes from outside the science of public finance. He famously wrote:

> The case for drastic progression in taxation must be rested on the case against inequality—on the ethical or aesthetic judgment that the prevailing distribution of wealth and income reveals a degree (and/or kind) of inequality which is distinctly evil or unlovely.[44]

Attempts to argue for progression on utilitarian grounds, Simons thought, can only be subterfuge that disguises a person's, a political party's, or a nation's hedonistic impulses and yet suppresses a visceral but unconfessed discomfort with inequality.[45]

The rise of welfarism

By exposing the scientific sham of sacrifice theories, Simons contributed to the sequestration of "ethical and aesthetic judgments." Rather than admitting them "through the back door," to use Simons' terms, British and American economists refused them admittance altogether. Substantive conceptions of well-being, such as happiness, were put aside in the 1930s and economists replaced them with *satisfaction of preferences.* These interpersonal utility comparisons, i.e., comparisons of how well preferences are satisfied instead of how much satisfaction people feel, "are not comparisons of mental or physical states but rather of the extent to which the world is as" individuals X and Y "prefer" in some sense. X and Y may not even know if their preferences are satisfied. The serious difficulty with this definition of welfare lies, of course, in determining who decides which preferences X and Y have.[46]

Economists have tried to solve the problem of who gets to decide by setting in place two constructs: rational choice theory and the Pareto principle. Rational choice theory assumes that economic agents "have well-ordered preferences" and that they "make optimal choices given those preferences and the various constraints they face."[47] The theory breaks down into two separate theories. First, preferences, (i.e., goals or ends) are assumed to be rational, which means that they satisfy conditions such as completeness (i.e., for all objects of preference x and y, a person either prefers x to y or y to x or is indifferent) and transitivity (e.g., a person prefers x to z if she prefers x to y and y to z). According to the second sub-theory, the economic agent is presumed to act in the most efficient way (i.e., the "instrumentally rational way") to achieve the ends in question.[48]

The Pareto principle is said to have replaced the substantive utilitarian notion of the good as the evaluative standard in welfare economics.[49] The principle depends on the concept of "Pareto improvement." State of affairs X is a Pareto improvement over state of affairs Y if no one prefers Y to X and at least one person prefers X to Y. The Pareto principle holds that if X is a Pareto improvement over Y, then X is morally better than Y.[50]

A "social welfare function" is any ranking of social states. In "welfarist" thought, social welfare functions depend on social preferences as ranked by the Pareto principle. A social welfare function, for instance, will rank state of affairs R over state of affairs S if someone prefers R to S and no one prefers S to R.[51] Welfarists want nothing to do with substantive inputs. Only preference-ranking is admissible. Welfarism perhaps reaches its most consistent expression in the Hicks-Kaldor criterion analysis, which posits that welfare economists need not and should not "pass moral judgments on economic distribution"; all that they need to worry about is efficiency—enlarging the pie—leaving division of the pie to politicians. And to determine if state of affairs X is more efficient than state of affairs Y (i.e., whether X has greater capacity to satisfy preferences than Y), they only need to determine if X is a potential Pareto improvement over Y.[52]

Economists tend to think of rational choice theory as a positive theory, while philosophers view the same theory, which they tend to call "practical rationality," as normative because it tells agents what they "ought" to do "to act rationally."[53] It would be an understatement to say that the relationship between philosophy and economics changed in the first third of the twentieth century. Philosophy was largely banished from welfarist approaches, abandoned in favor of "scientific economics."[54] Welfarism is "relentlessly consequentialist": procedural matters like fairness and due process are only interesting insofar as they affect outcomes.[55] As consequentialists, welfarists take an action, policy, or institution to be morally permissible if its results are no worse than those of any alternative, and to be morally obligatory if the results are better than those of any alternative. As Daniel Hausman and Michael McPherson put it, "The fundamental thesis of utilitarianism is that one should do whatever maximizes the overall welfare."[56] Economists hoped in the middle of the twentieth century to separate "uncontroversial" improvements in productivity, efficiency, and real income from "controversial" concerns, primarily distributional considerations.

The latter were left to politics. As philosopher T. M. Scanlon argued, "the value of resources, capabilities, or primary goods should be determined by public moral deliberation concerning their importance in facilitating a range of good lives."[57] Not just at the policy level, but also at the level of fundamental assumptions about how citizens should act, egalitarian, utilitarian, and the welfarist traditions all assume that individuals are supposed to have the principles of justice in mind in the conduct of their *political* actions but not in the conduct of their market relations.[58]

Tax, however, is more than a purely economic matter. "It is now widely recognized in the literature," political economists Walter Hettich, Lawrence Kenny, and Stanley Winer write, "that observed tax systems reflect the interplay among political forces together with the influence of current and past economic factors."[59] Actual tax systems can be modeled in both democratic and non-democratic regimes "as direct outcomes of political competition, tempered by economic factors."[60] Thus, U.S. taxation follows, at least in theory, a "side-constraint" pattern in which certain parameters are set through operation of the political process and then the contours of the taxes in question are developed through exclusively economic welfare rankings and assumptions about how economic agents think and act.

Optimal tax theory

Nowhere is the "side-constraint" pattern more evident than in the optimal tax theory that emerged in 1971 with the publication of J. A. Mirrlees' groundbreaking work.[61] Optimal tax theory posits a tax system "chosen to maximize a social welfare function subject to a set of constraints."[62] This means that the tax system will reflect the highest ranking of social states subject to some overriding commitment or commitments of the society that limits, in an *a priori* way, the options to be ranked.

The "social planner" or policymaker contemplated by optimal tax theory is typically utilitarian. The social welfare function is based on the "utilities"—indicators of preference orderings—of individuals in the society. Because the theory assumes that society is homogenous, the "social planner's goal is to choose the tax system that maximizes the representative consumer's welfare," i.e., satisfaction of preferences, in light of the reality that incentives supplied by the tax system will influence the taxpayer's choices and behavior.[63]

If the social planner were unconstrained, the optimal tax would simply be a lump-sum tax, which would not "distort the choices" of taxpayers at all and would thus be perfectly efficient.[64] But a lump-sum tax is politically unacceptable. Gregory Mankiw, Matthew Weinzerl, and Danny Yagan write:

> In the world, there are good reasons why lump-sum taxes are rarely used. Most important, this tax falls equally on the rich and the poor, placing a greater relative burden on the latter. When Margaret Thatcher, during her time as the Prime Minister of the United Kingdom, successfully pushed through a lump-sum tax levied at the local level (a "community charge") beginning in 1989, the tax was deeply unpopular. As the *New York Times* reported in 1990, "[W]idespread anger over the tax threatens Mrs. Thatcher's political life, if not her physical safety. And it may prove to be the last hurrah for her philosophy of public finance, in which the goals of efficiency and accountability take precedence over the values of the welfare state." The tax was quickly revoked, and not coincidentally, Thatcher's term of office ended not long after.[65]

Failing the lump-sum-tax solution, the social planner, according to optimal theory, would resort to the ability-to-pay principle. That principle emerged in the English-speaking world as an alternative to benefit theory, coming into its own when John Stuart Mill sharply criticized benefit theory and sought to replace it with his reformulated version of the ability-to-pay principle, i.e., equal sacrifice.[66] The intuitive appeal of the ability-to-pay principle lay in its fairness: since each person incurs a loss when paying tax, the losses should be spread equitably, and if they are spread according to individuals' ability to sustain them, the spread can be considered equitable.[67] However, because ability to pay is not directly observable, the principle "fails to deliver useful and realistic prescriptions," at least without refinement.[68]

Mirrlees' model provided that refinement by "recognizing unobserved heterogeneity, diminishing marginal utility of consumption, and incentive effects," thus formalizing "the classic tradeoff between equality and efficiency that real governments face."[69] By assigning leisure a utility value, Mirrlees' 1971 income tax model attempted to take into consideration the fact that taxation can lead taxpayers to choose leisure over work. In classical utility theory, utility had been, for each level of ability in society, earnings minus taxes paid.[70] That is, society's total welfare was the sum of (1) the earnings of each member of society with a particular ability type less taxes paid by each member of society with that ability type, (2) multiplied by the total number of members of society with that ability type, and then (3) added to the same calculations for all other ability types in society.[71]

Mirrlees' model changed the formula by assigning leisure itself a utility value. Society's total welfare became the sum of (1) a utility function for each ability type's before-tax income less taxes paid on the before-tax income and time spent at work by that ability type, (2) added to the same calculations for all other ability types in society.[72]

Among numerous additions and refinements to Mirrlees' 1971 model over the years, of note is A. B. Atkinson's observation that social welfare is highly sensitive to society's egalitarian preferences.[73] Atkinson concluded that as that egalitarian preference decreases, the marginal utility of income diminishes more rapidly and the loss of aggregate utility resulting from inequality increases. Using income instead of utility, Atkinson placed "a social value on different incomes dependent 'on the degree of aversion to inequality in society.'"[74] The introduction of a "weighting parameter" transformed the welfare function "from a mere counting operation, wherein each individual's utility counted equally, to a political or social calculation for arriving at that parameter." As a result, "decision makers could select the value of equality desired, and the models would then crank out the appropriate tax rates."[75]

The reality that the optimal tax models cannot generate a social welfare function, which remains "a normative question that cannot be answered with data,"[76] is not necessarily a weakness. Their reticence as to how much we should care about inequality makes the models flexible:

> Users of the model can input various patterns of income distribution and efficiency costs of taxation to evaluate alternative tax regimes. The model is amenable to different definitions of distributional fairness and can adjust to accommodate specific limitations in tax design that may arise from political or administrative constraints.[77]

The models work backwards from a goal "defined in terms of a final distribution of utilities" to a tax system that is best suited to induce that distribution *after* agents react to the formula.[78] The models first specify a social welfare function that is regarded as representing society's objective, and then generate the formula that generates the optimal tax given that constraint.[79] There is, properly speaking, no optimal *theory* of taxation. The models only supply a formula that demonstrates "how social welfare and tax burdens might interact in ways unimagined by previous public finance experts" but provide no guidance in determining what social welfare is or what tax burdens should be.[80] Choosing the social welfare function is always *the* ethical issue in the process.[81] As an ethical issue, the social welfare function is a "political" side-constraint.

Philosophers as well as economists have been responsible for the transformation of balance into a schizophrenic system of side constraints, as the next section explains. The peculiar position that political philosophy (in addition to economics) has placed taxation goes a long way toward revealing why tax is "moralized" but lacks an ethical guiding principle.

Politics and economics

Such a solution fits well with the division of labor in Western democracies between political policymaking and the machinations of economic implementation of the policies generated. The barrier between the "uncontroversial" balance reached between equity and efficiency on the one hand and the "controversial" decisions about how much equity society desires on the other is not solely the work of economists. Philosophers are also responsible, because they have not been able to come to a consensus on the moral basis for equality or weaker forms of equity in society. Regarding the American scene, Hausman and McPherson write: "A commitment to moral and political equality is deeply embedded in American political traditions and in Kantian moral philosophy, but the basis for this commitment and its implications for economic equality are controversial."[82]

Since John Rawls first published *A Theory of Justice*, also in 1971, American philosophers have distinguished between the parameters of justice and the "outcomes" of justice within those parameters. Rawls did not offer an alternative theory of well-being. He was content to interpret well-being as preference-satisfaction, as long as well-being is based in part on one's own efforts. That was not his primary concern. Social policy should focus on "primary goods," which represent the aspect of welfare for which society, not the individual, is responsible.[83] "Outcomes," therefore, are to be judged entirely by the validity of the procedures that gave rise to them. As Hausman and McPherson describe the workings of Rawls' system of justice, "If the rights and institutions satisfy Rawls's principles, then the results are just, regardless of their details."[84] Outcomes are like lottery winnings; if procedures were followed, then "the results are automatically just because there is no other criterion by which to judge those outcomes."[85]

Rawls is by no means alone in strictly separating institutions from outcomes; Amartya Sen's "capabilities" approach and Ronald Dworkin's "equality of resources" theory, to name just two, follow the same pattern in form. The "Leviathan model" of politics advanced by Geoffrey Brennan and James M. Buchanan assumes that revenue-maximization is the sole characteristic of governments and their tax systems, limited only by the restraints that a people manage to put in place at the "constitutional stage of decision" in a state's formation. The Brennan-Buchanan paradigm is structured around the distinction between the constitutional stage of decision and the far more limited "in-period" electoral outcomes.[86] Brennan regards Rawlsian thought and the Leviathan model as similar in that they both have a "constitutional" character, by which he means that they both insist on a distinction between the "rules of the game" (basic institutions) and "plays of that game" (outcomes). Once again, "normative evaluation works backwards" from the justice evident (or not) in "the pattern of social outcomes" to the basic institutions that gave rise to that pattern.[87]

Rawls' "first principle of justice" is that "each person is to have an equal right to the most extensive scheme of equal basic liberties compatible with a similar scheme of liberties for others."[88] The philosopher and political scientist Colin Farrelly points out that Rawls assumed these basic liberties to be "negative" rights in the sense that the government guarantees them by "simply refraining from interference," but that this cannot possibly be the case. The liberties that both libertarians and "egalitarian liberals" like Rawls consider basic—liberties such as property rights—have "budgetary costs," Farrelly argues.[89] Taxation provides the revenue to cover those costs. It is "a necessary instrument of rights protection."[90] The efforts of American philosophers like Rawls to sequester basic goods or "political" rights behind a veil of ignorance so as to preserve them untainted from the vicissitudes of fortune, individual temperament, the workings of the market, and the like, begin to unravel when they encounter the institution of taxation. Taxation reflects "the interplay among political forces together with the influence of current and past economic factors," as Hettich, Kenny, and Winter put it.[91]

The tax scholar Alex Raskolnikov, referring specifically to the utilitarian principle of ability-to-pay, faults philosophers for failing to provide economists with the necessary guidance:

> Economists must choose the basis of redistribution because without this choice, the analysis stops in its tracks. Yet for whatever reason, Kant and Hegel, Nietzsche and Kierkegaard, Rawls, Raz, and Dworkin have not been particularly interested in addressing the question. So economists did the best they could, settled on ability to pay as the answer, and proceeded with the analysis.[92]

But it is not too hard to see why these philosophers avoided the question of taxation. Not only because it is boring—although they may well have regarded it as such—but because it is not susceptible to categorization as an institution or outcome, these negligent philosophers simply did not know what to do with it. Taxation has fallen through the cracks precisely because it is neither entirely what we may call "political" nor entirely what we can term "economic."

Brennan argues that taxation occupies a "middle ground" between basic institutions and in-period operations, i.e., between institutions and outcomes or between the basic rules of democracy like majority rule and day-to-day public policy decisions.[93] The "rules of tax justice" are quasi-constitutional, in Brennan's view, because they embody relatively stable cost-sharing arrangements, base definitions, and rate structures that persist over multiple electoral cycles.[94] At the same time, "the tax system is not simply an articulation of individuals' conceptions of justice." Much else goes into such a system, including "a good dose of thinly disguised self-interest."[95] Taxation simultaneously reflects both the "democratic processes" that "give greater voice to the egalitarian values of the citizenry" and "those same individuals' market choices."[96]

I want to suggest that taxation is the bridge between the political value of equity and the economic value of efficiency. I mean "economy" primarily in that word's original sense. The Greek word *oikonomia* carried the sense of regulating, administering, or organizing. Xenophon's *Oikonomikos*, which represents more than any other the original use of the term *oikonomia*, "is a guide for the gentleman landowner ... with a long introduction on the good life and the proper use of wealth."[97] To the ancients, the *oikonomia* treated the rights and obligations of the "family." The Latin *familia* ("household") referred to "all the persons, free or unfree, under the authority of the *paterfamilias.*" Both *oikonomia* and *familia* bore "a heavy accent on the property side."[98] From that starting point, the meaning of the word *oikonomia* began "its extension to any sort of organization or management," even, in Quintilian's usage, to the plan of a poem or piece of rhetoric.[99] Occasionally "it was used to mean the management of public revenues," which necessarily loomed large in the management of affairs of state—although the term "economics" was not used in its current, specialized sense until the late nineteenth century (that is, the social science of the use of scarce resources to obtain the maximum satisfaction of society's virtually unlimited wants[100]). The elements of what we call "the economy" were present to some degree in antiquity, but they were not gathered into a conceptually discrete unit until centuries later.[101] A description proposed by the philosopher Giorgio Agamben seems broad enough to capture the senses of both the ancient Greek *oikonomia* and the current usage of the word "economy": "This activity rather implies decisions and order that cope with problems that are each time specific and concern the functional order (*taxis*) of the different parts of the *oikos*"—whatever the *oikos* may be.[102] It is, in other words, a dynamic interplay of competition and decision-making, and of exchange and trade-offs. Its restless activity often centers on property rights, seeking to negotiate how absolute or how attenuated they are and should be and how they can be balanced against other rights, duties, and values. Economy so understood is close in concept to the in-period operations of the Brennan-Buchanan model. For this reason Brennan can regard "democratically made collective decisions" and "maximally just private property rights" as existing in tension, both with "independent normative force." The "appropriate terms" on which "these two normatively grounded elements should interact" is for Brennan "*the* issue of taxation."[103]

It seems that Raskolnikov's negligent philosophers were not interested in a middle ground between constitutional and in-period stages, or in an institution that partakes of the qualities of both of those stages and effects a compromise between them. Like the "image of divine monarchy in the formula 'Le roi règne, mais il ne gouverne pas'" ["the king reigns, but he does not govern"], so important to political theologians Carl Schmitt and Erik Peterson in the mid-twentieth century,[104] equity remains in the background, silently setting the rules by which the value-neutral forces of efficiency will play.

The demise of equity

A predictable consequence of the "backgrounding" of equity has been the near eclipse of equity by efficiency in tax policy, if not in theory. Inequality-aversion has remained low in the United States, as have top marginal individual income tax rates.[105] Especially since the popularization of the "Laffer curve" in the 1980s, many Americans have assumed that lowering taxes can increase revenue. The assumption, more specifically, has been that income taxes begin to take a toll on economic productivity at relatively low rates, so that less wealth is produced from which revenue can be raised.[106] Regardless of the validity of these assumptions, they reflect an important social belief in the United States and many other liberal democracies: society as a whole is better off materially when the tax system preserves the maximum amount of private wealth, and creates conditions for the maximum amount of private wealth-creation, that it possibly can.

This strong commitment to efficiency is also evident in the 2017 Tax Act, which opted for efficiency over horizontal equity in its attempt "to limit the benefits of behavioral responses based on differences in tax rates among similar kinds of activities." Whether or not the effect of the tax act is an increase in efficiency, that was certainly the intent of its drafters. For instance, the act made a large reduction in the corporate tax rate, changed the treatment of foreign-source income, and added a preferential tax regime for some "pass-through" income from partnerships, limited liability companies, and S corporations.[107] Harvey Galper considers the act an equity failure, as it violates vertical equity by significantly reducing the taxation of capital income compared to earned income, thus giving "high-income households, who own most capital, larger tax cuts as a share of after-tax income than lower-income households, in some cases, by very large margins." Disparate treatment of different kinds of income, i.e., capital versus earned income, introduced by the act "can result in quite different tax treatment for those earning the same amount of income" and, thus, also undermines horizontal equity.[108] The 2017 Act marks the latest step in the several-decades-old "trend toward treating efficiency as the prime normative goal of tax policy."[109]

It is perhaps more accurate to say that efficiency has *absorbed* equity than to say that it has eclipsed it. A sense of equity endures, but it is built into the rate structure of the federal income tax itself in the United States. Equity, in Galper's analysis of the 2017 Tax Act, means horizontal or vertical equity—a "thin" kind of equity that has more to do with whether the allocation of the tax burden is fair. To be sure, a progressive income tax inevitably redistributes income,[110] but the relatively small spread between the highest and lowest rates in the US federal income tax and the UK income tax limits the potential for redistribution. In the United States, even with its limited redistributive goals, three-quarters of redistribution at the federal level in 2018 was attributable to spending and only one-quarter to tax itself.[111] Distributive justice, and equity with it, has come to mean little more than spreading the pain of taxpaying so that each taxpayer feels as little of it as possible. This was the conclusion of the influential essay "The Uneasy Case for Progressive Taxation," published in 1953, by Walter Blum and Harry Kalven.[112] Blum and Kalven described taxes as "a necessary evil falling upon a distribution of money, and therefore upon a distribution of satisfactions, which is otherwise acceptable." "With this assumption," they continued, "the problem is not to use the tax system to adjust existing inequalities in that distribution but simply to leave all taxpayers equally 'worse off' after taxes."[113]

Once equity is taken to merge with efficiency, equity is no longer a separate variable in the tax balance. It is seen as a fortuitous byproduct of the alliance between government on the one hand and job-producing, wealth-creating large corporations and top income-earners on the other. If efficiency in the sense of freedom from market distortions is needed for economic growth, then the state has a vested interest in efficiency. The state's interests become aligned with the efficiency factor in tax equations. Even the leftist British political philosopher Dudley Knowles acknowledged, if somewhat ruefully:

> The social democratic societies of Western Europe have all given lip-service to this idea of equality in respect of meeting needs, but the attainment of it is beginning to have the air of an intractable problem. When sociologists (or, more likely social workers) point out the level of unmet needs in a variety of different policy contexts, e.g., health, education, housing, provision for the elderly, and urge a greater measure of redistribution of resources, politicians, increasingly of *all* mainstream parties, respond that meeting these needs first requires further economic growth, that the strategic political priority must be the effectively painless process of raising more resources, achieving a greater social fund of income and profit which can be taxed without creating disincentive effects.[114]

Yet efficiency is a strange choice for a goal of *any* tax policy. Tax is, simply put, inefficient. Underlying the efficiency baseline is a commitment to growth, and growth, Linda Sugin writes, "is an incoherent standard for a tax system." "Taxation," she continues, "always reduces the net individual rewards from economic activity." As a result, "[e]very tax system actually in use impedes growth in some way, so a growth norm favors repeal of every existing tax."[115]

The tax system's paradoxical commitment to efficiency seems to result from the unrealistic desire to remove "controversial" elements (justice, equity, equality, freedom) from the field on which the "uncontroversial" elements (market dynamics, property rights, Pareto improvements) can play out. The tension between economic efficiency and freedom—another possible ingredient of equity, depending on the political philosophy at work—illustrates the blurry lines between controversial and uncontroversial elements. Hausman and McPherson write:

> The efficiency case has been considered a part of "scientific" welfare economics because it has appeared to rely only on uncontroversial moral premises, while the argument in terms of freedom has been reserved for "unscientific" essays because its moral premises have appeared to be of a more philosophical nature.

But at the same time, economists seem content with the efficiency standard for the reason that they think on some level "that the Pareto standard itself promotes liberty because it values outcomes that best accommodate the voluntary choices of individuals."[116] This perhaps unconscious belief is a false one in Hausman and McPherson's estimation, but it undoubtedly plays a role in the counterintuitive choice of economic efficiency as the guiding principle of tax systems.

I wish to suggest that no amount of segregation between controversial and uncontroversial—political and economic—elements satisfies the human impulse toward justice in the economic sphere. The more controversial moral questions will be pulled down, as it were, from the political background—with its semi-divine aura, its sacred principles of consent, political competition, and inalienable rights—into the more "ministerial" realm of exchanges, trade-offs, and in-period decisions that respond to events and changing circumstances. Even when redistributive concerns are most hidden from view, they lie beneath the surface—not only in result (as when the rate structure effects redistribution), but even as a goal. The goal may not be articulated, but, as Daniel Shaviro contends, the fact that we choose to tax consumption, income, and wealth reveals that we simply dislike inequality. In Shaviro's argument, consumption taxes burden decisions to work, while income and wealth taxes burden work and saving. Saving, work, and decisions about work cannot possibly be what we want to tax, Shaviro writes; "[t]he defense of any of these tax bases therefore lies in its capacity to provide a crude proxy for some set of attributes that are relevant to distributive justice but cannot be observed directly." [117]

There is something of the divine-monarchy model in the hiddenness of the equity-impulse and, with it, the social drive for redistribution. "[I]n Aristotle," Agamben writes, "God is the transcendent principle of any movement, who leads the world as a strategist leads his army." But in the pseudo-Aristotelian treatise *De mundo*, analyzed in political-theological terms by Peterson and Agamben, "the monarch, hidden in the rooms of his palace, moves the world as the puppeteer leads his puppets on strings." This again is the "image of divine monarchy in the formula 'Le roi règne, mais il ne gouverne pas.'"[118] Decisions about redistribution remain behind a political veil. As Hettich, Kenny, and Winer observe, the type of democratic apparatus in place determines the redistributive operations of the economy. Studies have shown that proportional representation tends to lead to more redistribution, but "an increase in the number of veto points reduces the extent of it." "Veto players" are actors, whether individual or collective, "whose agreement is required for a change of the status quo"[119] and thus apparently operate at the constitution or basic-institutions stage of decision-making. But we have seen that tax can change the distribution of goods—in fact, that it inevitably will do so—because it occupies a middle position between constitutional and in-period operations, partaking of the qualities of both.

Property rights

A word about property rights is in order, because they, like taxation, occupy an ambiguous and contested position between the constitutional and in-period stages of decision-making in democratic societies, and because they are intertwined with taxation. Presumptions, from whatever source, about pre-tax distributions are more specifically presumptions about "ownership claims,"[120] and those claims are claims about property rights, which even social-constructivists like philosophers Liam Murphy and Thomas Nagel reluctantly admit constitute "the moral category most directly relevant to tax policy."[121] Framing debates about taxation around the question of the extent to which the state can legitimately interfere with its citizens' property rights has, in philosopher Laura Biron's words, "a remarkable effect on the perceived legitimacy of the tax system."[122]

At one end of the spectrum, libertarians place property rights in the basic-institution category, regarding "pre-existing civil and property rights" as the only permissible "limitations on freedom that are of social concern."[123] Even Brennan and Buchanan follow libertarianism to this extent, elevating property rights to a higher priority than tax structures. Brennan argues that a "change in the property rights structure is *a change in the basic institutions of society*, whereas a change in tax arrangements ... is an operation under the rules of in-period politics."[124]

At the other end of at least the American spectrum is the "conventionalist" approach advanced by Murphy and Nagel in their much-discussed book *The Myth of Ownership: Taxes and Justice*. There they reject "everyday libertarianism" in favor of the following view:

> Private property is a legal convention, defined in part by the tax system; therefore, the tax system cannot be evaluated by looking at its impact on private property, conceived as something that has independent existence and validity. Taxes must be evaluated as part of the overall system of property rights that they help to create. Justice or injustice in taxation can only mean justice or injustice in the system of property rights and entitlements that result from a particular tax regime.[125]

Pre-tax property rights remain, at least morally, in the mix of the *oikonomia* for Murphy and Nagel, except perhaps to the extent those rights are needed for purely analytical purposes.[126]

Brennan thinks that Murphy and Nagel have committed a fundamental violation of the Rawlsian premise of justice, that there is a distinction between "institutions" and "outcomes," and that "the institutions endorsed under the principles of justice must have some independent status."[127] Theorists like Ruby Shao seem to agree, arguing that all forms of "primary goods" liberalism—whether of the Rawlsian variety or more influenced by Sen or Dworkin—require natural property rights to secure the basic goods in question.[128]

Colin Farrelly, on the other hand, points out that *taxation* is a more logically privileged institution than Brennan is likely to admit, because tax revenue is needed to support the very expensive basic institutions, like property rights, that libertarians like Nozick, liberal egalitarians in the Rawlsian tradition, and constitutionalists like Brennan all want to hide away in some kind of primordial political space.[129]

Peter Vallentyne offers a compromise, in which property ownership is conceived as a bundle of rights over a thing. A "maximally strong bundle," which would be called full ownership, would in fact preclude the "legal permissibility of taxation."[130] Once property rights are morally privileged, two questions remain: (1) can property rights be weakened just enough to permit taxation; and (2) is the tax in question used for a morally suitable purpose? In other words, "just taxation is compatible with 'almost' full ownership of a thing." Vallentyne writes: "One could have all the rights of full ownership except that one was liable to certain kinds of taxation."[131] Vallentyne's view seems to be the correct reading of the actual arrangement reached by societies like the American and British ones, with their high view of property rights but their need to levy taxes. His view implies that it is not property rights themselves, but the decisions about how to define those rights, which are established inviolate and sacrosanct at the political or constitutional stage of decision-making.

To return to the original question posed in this chapter—why taxation is moralized territory even though it lacks a guiding principle of justice—the provisional answer is that taxation occupies a middle position between the basic moral decisions that a society makes about that society's structures of justice and the purportedly value-neutral space of efficiency calculations. The moral component is removed from view but not altogether successfully. More than a hint of the ethos of justice lingers around the mechanics of tax systems. The next chapter begins an excavation of how, theologically, taxation (with property rights as well) comes to occupy this hybrid position in political economics.

Notes

1 Louise J. Bowditch, et al., "An Open Letter to the 2020 Presidential Candidates: It's Time to Tax Us More," *Medium*, June 24, 2019, accessed June 6, 2020, https://medium.com/@letterforawealthtax/an-open-letter-to-the-2020-presidential-candidates-its-time-to-tax-us-more-6eb3a548b2fe.

2 Daniel Halliday, "Justice and Taxation," *Philosophy Compass* (2013): 1, 10.

3 Linda Sugin, "Theories of Distributive Justice and Limitations on Taxation: What Rawls Demands from Tax Systems," *Fordham Law Review* 72, no. 5 (1994): 2013–14. Redistribution can be thought of as a modification "of the holdings of particular persons, collective agents, or groups." To quantify how a system redistributes resources, therefore, one needs to measure redistribution against these "holdings," that is, against a benchmark or baseline, i.e., against an "initial distribution of goods to which some other distribution is seen as a redistributive modification." Barry Christian, "Redistribution," *The Stanford Encyclopedia of Philosophy*, ed. Edward N. Zalta, last modified Spring 2018, accessed June 6, 2020, https://plato.stanford.edu/entries/redistribution/.

4 Alan Hamlin, "What Political Philosophy Should Learn from Economics About Taxation," in *Taxation: Philosophical Perspectives*, ed. Martin O'Neill and Shepley Orr (Oxford: Oxford University Press, 2018), 17.

5 N. Gregory Mankiw, Matthew Charles Weinzierl, and Danny Ferris Yagan, "Optimal Taxation in Theory and Practice," *Journal of Economic Perspectives* 23(4) (2009): 154.

6 See Daniel M. Hausman and Michael S. McPherson, *Economic Analysis, Moral Philosophy, and Public Policy*, 2nd ed. (Cambridge: Cambridge University Press, 2006), 147.

7 Sugin, "Theories of Distributive Justice," 2014.

8 Peter Vallentyne, "Taxation, Redistribution and Property Rights," in *Routledge Companion to Philosophy of Law*, ed. Andrei Marmor (New York: Routledge,

2015), 291. See also Martin O'Neill and Shepley Orr, introduction to O'Neill and Orr, *Taxation: Philosophical Perspectives*, 1; Richard A. Posner, *Economic Analysis of Law* (Boston: Little, Brown and Co., 1973), 223.

9 Halliday, "Justice and Taxation," 2.

10 Liam Murphy and Thomas Nagel, *The Myth of Ownership: Taxes and Justice* (Oxford: Oxford University Press, 2002), 3.

11 Hausman and McPherson, *Economic Analysis*, 198.

12 For a discussion of models demonstrating that income tax is uniquely suited to redistributing income, see Louis Kaplow and Steven Shavell, "Why the Legal System is Less Efficient than the Income Tax in Redistributing Income," *The Journal of Legal Studies* 23, no. 2 (June 1994): 667–81.

13 "Basic Welfare Economics and Optimal Tax Theory," EML Econometrics Library, University of California Berkeley, accessed June 6, 2020, https://eml.berkeley.edu/~burch/conf04/d1.pdf.

14 See Alex Raskolnikov, "Accepting the Limits of Tax Law and Economics," *Cornell Law Review* 98 (2013): 527–28.

15 James R. Repetti, "The Appropriate Roles for Equity and Efficiency in a Progressive Income Tax," 24 *Florida Tax Review* (forthcoming 2020). It should be noted that the focus in this chapter is on income tax rather than on other kinds of taxes, such as consumption, property, or wealth taxes. Most Anglo-American tax philosophers of the past two centuries have chosen to incarnate their conceptions of tax justice in a progressive income tax. This choice was motivated by the replacement of the benefit theory of tax with the ability-to-pay theory after Adam Smith put forward his maxims of taxation. See Richard A. Musgrave and Alan T. Peacock, introduction to *Classics in the Theory of Public Finance*, ed. Richard A. Musgrave and Alan T. Peacock (London: Macmillan, 1958), ix (during the course of the nineteenth century, "income came to be accepted widely as the index by which to measure ability to pay"); Richard A. Musgrave, "Fairness in Taxation," in *The Encyclopedia of Taxation & Tax Policy*, 2nd ed., ed. Joseph J. Cordes, Robert D. Ebel, and Jane G. Gravelle (Washington: The Urban Institute Press, 2005), 136 (once ability-to-pay emerged as the dominant principle of tax justice, "an index was needed by which to measure 'ability'"; "[t]hat index has traditionally been thought of in terms of income, with income seen to provide the best measure of economic capacity"). Richard Musgrave writes: "Adam Smith had already formulated his first maxim in terms of income only, and through the [nineteenth] century income came to be accepted more or less generally as the proper index of ability to pay. The personal income tax accordingly came to be considered the most equitable tax." Richard A. Musgrave, *The Theory of Public Finance: A Study in Public Economy* (New York: McGraw-Hill Book Co., Inc., 1959), 94.

16 Richard A. Musgrave, "Equity and the Case for Progressive Taxation," in *Tax Justice: The Ongoing Debate*, ed. Joseph J. Thorndike and Dennis J. Ventry, Jr. (Washington: The Urban Institute Press, 2002), 9.

17 See, e.g., Musgrave, "Fairness in Taxation," 136.

18 For an example of this conflict, see Anne L. Allstott, "Updating the Welfare State: Marriage, the Income Tax, and Social Security in the Age of Individualism," *Tax Law Review* 66 (2013): 705, accessed June 6, 2020, http://digitalcommons.law.yale.edu/cgi/viewcontent.cgi?article=5876&context=fss_papers. Allstott provides a history of the "marriage penalty" and the "marriage bonus" in U.S. federal tax law and concludes:

> Husbands and wives with divergent earnings still claim a marriage bonus, but two-earner couples with similar earnings pay a marriage penalty. The marriage penalty/bonus problem is, of course, insoluble. The well-known "trilemma"

> holds that an income tax cannot simultaneously impose progressive marginal tax rates, assess equal taxes on married couples with equal earnings, and maintain marriage neutrality (so that the total income taxes paid by two unmarried individuals neither increase nor decrease when the couple marries).

See also Geoffrey Brennan, "Striving for the Middle Ground: Taxation, Justice, and the Status of Private Rights," in O'Neill and Orr, 65–66.

19 See, e.g., Marc Fleurbaey, "Welfarism, Libertarianism, and Fairness in the Economic Approach," in O'Neill and Orr, 37.

20 Harvey Galper, "The TCJA Has Replaced the 1986 Tax Act, But Is It Tax Reform?," *TaxVox Blog*, March 30, 2018, accessed June 6, 2020, https://www.taxpolicycenter.org/taxvox/tcja-has-replaced-1986-tax-act-it-tax-reform. More specifically,

> The [2017] Tax Cuts and Jobs Act maintained the preferential income tax rates for long-term capital gains and for dividends. But it added new tax regimes for income from pass-through entities (many of which are smaller businesses, but some of which are very large entities) that provide lower tax rates than for comparable wage earners, for income from exports by US multinational firms, and added a Base Erosion Anti Abuse Tax on certain intra-company transactions with foreign affiliates.

Mark J. Mazur, "Reflections on the Tax Cuts and Jobs Act" (testimony, hearing on "Unleashing America's Economic Potential," Joint Economic Committee, April 11, 2018), accessed June 6, 2020, https://www.jec.senate.gov/public/_cache/files/119bdfe4-c47c-4069-8be3-1d939c491ab4/mark-mazur-testimony-4-11-18.pdf.

21 Galper, "TCJA Has Replaced the 1986 Tax Act."

22 Richard A. Musgrave and Peggy B. Musgrave, *Public Finance in Theory and Practice*, 5th ed. (New York: McGraw-Hill Book Co., 1989), 82.

23 See, e.g., the use of the term "distributive" in Samuel Fleischacker's *A Short History of Distributive Justice* (Cambridge, MA: Harvard University Press, 2004), where taxation that "gives one citizen goods belonging to another" falls under the rubric of distributive justice. See also Linda Sugin, "Tax Expenditures, Reform, and Distributive Justice," *Columbia Journal of Tax Law* 3 (2011) (using the term "distributive justice" in the broader sense).

24 Stephen Utz, "Ability to Pay," *Whittier Law Review* 23 (2002): 895.

25 C. Eugene Steuerle, "And Equal (Tax) Justice for All?," in Thorndike and Ventry, 260.

26 See Repetti, "The Appropriate Roles for Equity and Efficiency."

27 See, e.g., Hausmann and McPherson, 184, 188.

28 Susan Strange, *States and Markets*, 2nd ed. (London: Continuum, 1994), 3, 5, 17.

29 Hausman and McPherson, *Economic Analysis*, 167, quoting Robert Nozick, *Anarchy, State and Utopia* (New York: Basic Books, 1974), 28–35.

30 Nozick, *Anarchy, State, and Utopia*, 150–63.

31 Nozick rejected "balancing" social theories as expressions of "current time-slice" principles of justice. Nozick, *Anarchy, State, and Utopia*, 154.

32 John F. Witte, *The Politics and Development of the Federal Income Tax* (Madison, WI: The University of Wisconsin Press, 1985), 33.

33 Musgrave, "Fairness in Taxation," 136.

34 Utz, "Ability to Pay," 891–92. The other versions of equal sacrifice are *equal absolute sacrifice*, which treats sacrifices as equal when the value of what each taxpayer gives up is equal "in whatever terms are considered most relevant" to the value that every other taxpayer gives up (e.g., if taxpayer X gives up ten units of utility, then taxpayer Y must also give up ten units of utility, regardless of how

many units of utility X and Y have before and after their tax payments), and *equal proportional sacrifice*, which requires that all taxpayers give up equal fractions of the utility that they otherwise would have enjoyed (e.g., if X received one thousand units of utility before tax and is required to give up 100 units, then, if Y started with one hundred units, Y must give up ten). Utz, "Ability to Pay," 891–93. Thus, equal absolute sacrifice "calls for equal disutility cost among taxpayers," equal proportional sacrifice for "contributions that will leave taxpayers with the same relative proportion of total utilities as they had before tax," and equal marginal sacrifice for the leveling of incomes "to the point where taxes run out." Harold M. Groves, *Tax Philosophers: Two Hundred Years of Thought in Great Britain and the United States*, ed. Donald J. Curran (Madison, WI: The University of Wisconsin Press, 1971), 55.

Mathematical economist Arnold Jacob Cohen-Stuart (1855–1921) argued that equal absolute and equal proportional sacrifice can lead to different tax rate schedules. Assuming, as did his contemporaries, that marginal utility decreases as income rises (e.g., that $10 is worth less to someone who has $100,000 than to someone who has $100), Cohen-Stuart concluded that equal absolute sacrifice implies a constant tax percentage rate, while equal proportional sacrifice (which idea he introduced) requires a progressive rate structure. Witte, *Politics and Development*, 33; Groves, *Tax Philosophers*, 52. For example, assume that taxpayers X and Y have incomes of $2,000 and $4,000, respectively, that marginal utility falls as fast as income advances, and that a proportional 1% tax is imposed on all income. X's tax, in this case, is $20 and Y's is $40. Meanwhile, the utility of a marginal dollar to X must be twice that of Y. If utility starts with some marginal amount, the utility of X's marginal utility could be 100 while the utility of Y's marginal utility is 50. The utility taken by tax is $2,000 ($20 × 100) for X and the same amount for Y ($40 × 50). However, X's *total* utility (as opposed to marginal utility) must be substantially more than half of Y's total utility. Assume, for instance, that X's average utility is 200 rather than 100, and that Y's is 150 rather than 50. Now, X's total utility is 400,000 (200 × 2,000) and Y's is 600,000 (150 × 4,000). To take an equal amount of utility from each would now leave X relatively less well-off than before. Therefore, to achieve "leave them as you found them" sacrifice, the tax structure needs to be progressive. Groves, *Tax Philosophers*, 52.

Edgeworth quickly dismantled Cohen-Stuart's formulation, even though he too assumed decreasing marginal utility of income, by showing that other utility functions nevertheless yield inconsistent tax rates for equal sacrifice and for proportional sacrifice. Edgeworth demonstrated, for instance, that if utility equals the square root of income, then equal sacrifice requires a regressive rate structure and proportional sacrifice a constant percentage rate. Edgeworth proposed the theory of equal marginal sacrifice in place of equal and proportional sacrifice theories. He argued that, because each income increment has less utility than the one preceding it, taxing the highest incomes will produce the least amount of utility loss. Witte, *Politics and Development*, 33–34.

35 Musgrave, "Equity and the Case for Progressive Taxation," 9.
36 Musgrave, "Equity and the Case for Progressive Taxation," 9.
37 Witte, *Politics and Development*, 35–36.
38 Groves, *Tax Philosophers*, 57.
39 Witte, *Politics and Development*, 36.
40 That is, the idea that $10, for example, is worth more to someone who has $100 than to someone who has $100,000.
41 Hausman and McPherson, 104–105.
42 Henry C. Simons, *Personal Income Taxation: The Definition of Income as a Problem of Fiscal Policy* (Chicago: The University of Chicago Press, 1938), 8.
43 Simons, *Personal Income Taxation*, 11.

44 Simons, *Personal Income Taxation*, 18–19.
45 "Such curious methods of defending progression are commonplace. The practice typically is that of admitting progression through the back door, under the cloak of Adam Smith's first maxim [i.e., that taxes should be proportional to how much the taxpayer benefits from the state]." Simons, *Personal Income Taxation*, 17.
46 Hausman and McPherson, *Economic Analysis*, 105.
47 D. Wade Hands, "Philosophy and Economics," in *The New Palgrave Dictionary of Economics*, 12, Living Edition, ed. Matias Varnengo, Esteban Perez Caldentey, and Barkley J. Rosser, Jr., first online March 14, 2017, accessed June 2, 2020, https://doi.org/10.1057/978-1-349-95121-5_1622-2.
48 Hands, "Philosophy and Economics," 12; Hausman and McPherson, *Economic Analysis*, 309, 312.
49 Hands, "Philosophy and Economics," 3.
50 Hausman and McPherson, *Economic Analysis*, 136. In addition, "Pareto efficiency" has been reached when no further Pareto improvements can be made. A "potential Pareto improvement" is state of affairs P that could *become* a Pareto improvement through some redistribution of goods or compensation of those who do not prefer P. Hausman and McPherson, *Economic Analysis*, 136, 145.
51 Hausman and McPherson, *Economic Analysis*, 217–18.
52 Hausman and McPherson, *Economic Analysis*, 145.
53 Hands, "Philosophy and Economics," 13.
54 Hands, "Philosophy and Economics," 1.
55 Hausman and McPherson, *Economic Analysis*, 218.
56 Hausman and McPherson, *Economic Analysis*, 99.
57 Hausman and McPherson, *Economic Analysis*, 192, citing Thomas Scanlon, "Preference and Urgency," *Journal of Philosophy* 72 (1975): 655–70, and Thomas Scanlon, "Equality of Resources and Equality of Welfare: A Forced Marriage?" *Ethics* 97 (1986): 111–18.
58 Brennan, "Striving for the Middle Ground," 71.
59 Walter Hettich, Lawrence W. Kenny, and Stanley L. Winer, "Political Regimes, Institutions and the Nature of Tax Systems," 2, Academia.edu, July 22, 2009, accessed June 8, 2020, https://www.academia.edu/3153509/Political_Regimes_Institutions_and_the_Nature_of_Tax_Systems.
60 Hettich, et al., "Political Regimes," 2.
61 J. A. Mirrlees, "An Exploration in the Theory of Optimum Income Taxation," *The Review of Economic Studies* 38, no. 2 (April 1971).
62 Mankiw, Weinzierl, and Yagan, "Optimal Taxation in Theory and Practice," 3.
63 Mankiw, Weinzierl, and Yagan, "Optimal Taxation in Theory and Practice," 3.
64 Mankiw, Weinzierl, and Yagan, "Optimal Taxation in Theory and Practice," 4.
65 Mankiw, Weinzierl, and Yagan, "Optimal Taxation in Theory and Practice," 4, quoting Peter Passell, "Furor over British Poll Tax Imperils Thatcher Ideology," *New York Times*, April 23, 1990.
66 The traditional benefit principle, associated with eighteenth-century Enlightenment political theory, used the principle to justify republican and nondespotic government in contractarian terms. As employed by Locke, Montesquieu, and Kant, the benefit principle had little to say about the details of tax systems. Joseph M. Dodge, "Theories of Tax Justice: Ruminations on the Benefit, Partnership, and Ability-to-Pay Principles," *Tax Law Review* 58 (Summer 2005): 402. Locke wrote: "'Tis true, Governments cannot be supported without great Charge, and 'tis fit every one who enjoys his share of the Protection, should pay out of his Estate his proportion for the maintenance of it." John Locke, *Two Treatises of Government*, ed. Peter Laslett, Cambridge Texts in the History of Political Thought (Cambridge: Cambridge University Press, 1988) 2.11.140. According to Montesquieu, "The revenues of the state are a portion each citizen

gives of his goods in order to have the security or the comfortable enjoyment of the rest." Montesquieu, *The Spirit of the Laws* 13.1, ed. and trans. Anne M. Cohler, Basia C. Miller, and Harold S. Stone, Cambridge Texts in the History of Political Thought (Cambridge: Cambridge University Press, 1989), 213. And Kant stated: "[I]n so far as he takes the duty of the people upon himself, the supreme commander has the right to impose taxes upon the people for their own preservation ...." Immanuel Kant, "The Metaphysics of Morals," in *Kant: Political Writings*, ed. Hans Reiss, trans. H. B. Nisbet, Cambridge Texts in the History of Philosophy, ed. Raymond Guess, Quentin Skinner, and Richard Tuck (Cambridge: Cambridge University Press, 1991), 149.

Mill also described the benefit principle, but only so that he could expose the principle as leading to regressive tax rates. Assuming a version of the principle in which individuals pay taxes in exchange for specific goods and services in situations where market exchanges are impractical, Mill concluded that the problem with the benefit principle is that the poor benefit more than the rich and, thus, should have to pay a higher share of the overall tax burden than the rich. John Stuart Mill, *Principles of Political Economy, with Some of Their Applications to Social Philosophy* (London: Longman, Green, Longman, Roberts, and Green, 1865) 5.2.2. See also Dodge, "Theories of Tax Justice," 404–405; Musgrave, *The Theory of Public Finance*, 92.

67 Musgrave, "Fairness in Taxation," 136. Not everyone has been equally impressed with the choice of ability as the principle of fairness. Tax scholar Alex Raskolnikov finds the choice arbitrary: "Maybe we should redistribute based on ability, maybe based on benefits, sacrifice, opportunities, luck, sunny disposition, good looks, or something else." Raskolnikov, "Accepting the Limits of Tax Law and Economics," 562.

68 Mankiw, Weinzierl, and Yagan, "Optimal Taxation in Theory and Practice," 5.

69 Mankiw, Weinzierl, and Yagan, "Optimal Taxation in Theory and Practice," 5.

70 That is, $U_n = Z(n) - T(n)$, where n represents an ability type with income Z, T represents taxes, and U represents utility.

71 Witte, *Politics and Development*, 37. Expressed mathematically, utility for ability type n was multiplied by the frequency of ability type n, or $f(n)$, and then this multiplication was repeated for all ability types in society and summed to obtain W, which is total welfare:

$$W = \sum_{n=1}^{N} [Z(n) - T(n)] f(n)$$

72 Witte, *Politics and Development*, 37. Once $x(n)$ was added to represent after-tax income for ability type n and $y(n)$ was added to represent the proportion of each day spent at work for ability type n, the general utility function became:

$$W = \sum_{n=1}^{N} U_n[x(n), y(n)] f(n)$$

Because $x(n) = z(n) - T[z(n)]$, i.e., the obvious fact that after-tax income equals before-tax income less taxes paid on the before-tax income, the optimal utility function could be expressed as follows:

$$W = \sum_{n=1}^{N} U_n\{[z(n) - T(z(n))], y(n)\} f(n)$$

73 Atkinson generalized the social welfare function as follows:

$$W = (\Sigma\ U_i p)\tfrac{1}{p}$$

where "W is social welfare and p is a parameter that represents the egalitarian preference of society" and i is income. Witte, *Politics and Development*, 39.

74 Witte, *Politics and Development*, 39–40, quoting A. B. Atkinson, "How Progressive Should Income Tax Be?" in *Essays in Modern Economics*, ed. Michael Parkin and A. R. Nobay (London: Longman, 1973), 90–109.
75 Witte, *Politics and Development*, 40.
76 Mankiw, Weinzierl, and Yagan, "Optimal Taxation in Theory and Practice," 8.
77 Linda Sugin, "A Philosophical Objection to the Optimal Tax Model," *Tax Law Review* 64 (2010–2011): 229.
78 Fleurbaey, "Welfarism, Libertarianism, and Fairness," 38.
79 Hamlin, "What Political Philosophy Should Learn from Economics About Taxation," 22.
80 Utz, "Ability to Pay," 928.
81 Fleurbaey, "Welfarism, Libertarianism, and Fairness," 47.
82 Hausman and McPherson, *Economic Analysis*, 177.
83 Hausman and McPherson, *Economic Analysis*, 130.
84 Hausman and McPherson, *Economic Analysis*, 205.
85 Hausman and McPherson, *Economic Analysis*, 205.
86 Geoffrey Brennan and James M. Buchanan, *The Power to Tax: Analytical Foundations of a Fiscal Constitution*, The Collected Works of James M. Buchanan 9 (Indianapolis: Liberty Fund, 1980), 22–24.
87 Brennan, "Striving for the Middle Ground," 68.
88 John Rawls, *A Theory of Justice*, rev. ed. (Cambridge, MA: The Belknap Press of Harvard University Press, 1999), 53.
89 Colin Farrelly, "Taxation and Distributive Justice," *Political Studies Review* 2 (2004): 188.
90 Farrelly, "Taxation and Distributive Justice," 189.
91 Hettich, Kenny, and Winer, "Political Regimes, Institutions and the Nature of Tax Systems," 2.
92 Raskolnikov, "Accepting the Limits of Tax Law and Economics," 562.
93 Brennan, "Striving for the Middle Ground," 72–73.
94 Brennan, "Striving for the Middle Ground," 72.
95 Brennan, "Striving for the Middle Ground," 73.
96 Brennan, "Striving for the Middle Ground," 73.
97 M. I. Finley, *The Ancient Economy*, updated edition, Sather Classical Lectures 43 (Berkeley: University of California Press, 1999), 17–18.
98 Finley, *The Ancient Economy*, 18.
99 Finley, *The Ancient Economy*, 20.
100 See Campbell R. McConnell and Stanley L. Brue, *Microeconomics: Principles, Problems, and Policies*, 16th ed. (New York: McGraw-Hill Irwin, 2005), G-5.
101 Finley, *The Ancient Economy*, 20–21, 23.
102 Giorgio Agamben, *The Kingdom and the Glory: For a Theological Genealogy of Economy and Government* (Homo Sacer *II*, 2), trans. Lorenzo Chiesa and Matteo Madarini (Stanford: Stanford University Press, 2011), 17–18.
103 Brennan, "Striving for the Middle Ground," 64–65 (italics in the original).
104 Agamben, "The Kingdom and the Glory," 9.
105 The Gini coefficient is a tool for measuring a nation's distribution of income using values ranging from zero to one, in which zero means that income is distributed equally among all income groups and one means that the highest-income group receives all income while the others receive none. The Gini coefficient for market income in the United States rose from 0.47 to 0.60 between 1979 and 2014; for income before taxes and transfers, the Gini coefficient rose from 0.41 to 0.52, and for income after transfers and taxes, it rose from 0.35 to 0.44, during the same period. Repetti, "The Appropriate Roles for Equity and Efficiency," 7. In the United States, the maximum statutory federal income tax rate for individuals has fallen from 91% in 1956 to 37% in 2019. That trend, Repetti states, was simply

"an attempt to increase efficiency." Repetti, "The Appropriate Roles for Equity and Efficiency," 3. The drop in top income tax rates, coinciding with increases is the payroll tax, which falls primarily on the relatively poor, and decreases in dividend and estate taxes, which are paid by the wealthy, has accentuated inequalities in the United State. Hausman and McPherson, *Economic Analysis*, 196. In 2004, the Congressional Research Service compared the disposable household income of the top ten percent (in terms of income) with the bottom ten percent in eighteen countries. The top ten percent in the United Kingdom had income that was 4.4 times greater than the income of the bottom ten percent; in the United States, that figure was 5.5. Denmark, Sweden, Norway, and Slovenia had the lowest values of the countries compared: 2.8, 2.8, 2.9, and 2.9, respectively. Only Mexico (with a value of 8.5) and Colombia (11.3) had higher values than the United States. Repetti, "The Appropriate Roles for Equity and Efficiency," 10.

106 Even apart from the question of where on the curve economic productivity generates enough revenue to offset lower rates, the percentage at which income taxes have any negative effect on the economy at all may be higher than often thought. One recent OECD study suggests that income tax rates up to 60% may actually *promote* economic growth. Santo Milasi and Robert J. Waldmann, "Top Marginal Taxation and Economic Growth," *Applied Economics* 50 (2018): 2156, 2162–65, cited in Repetti, "The Appropriate Roles for Equity and Efficiency," 38. This result presumably reflects, among other things, that the "income effect" (i.e., that higher rates make people work and earn more so that they can pay their taxes and have something left over) outpaces the "substitution effect" (i.e., that higher rates make people substitute leisure for work because they have less incentive to earn).

107 Galper, "TCJA Has Replaced the 1986 Tax Act."

108 Galper, "TCJA Has Replaced the 1986 Tax Act."

109 Sugin, "Tax Expenditures," 35.

110 It is quite simple to reduce after-tax income inequality: simply increase the rates on top earners relative to low earners. The impact on wealth inequality is more complex. Repetti, "The Appropriate Roles for Equity and Efficiency," 27. Hence F. A. Hayek's complaint about progressive income taxation:

> If, before taxation, a surgeon gets as much for an operation as an architect for planning a house, or a salesman gets as much for selling ten cars as a photographer for taking forty portraits, the same relation will still hold if proportional taxes are deducted from their receipts. But with progressive taxation of incomes this relation may be greatly changed. Not only may services which before taxation receive the same remuneration bring very different rewards; but a man who receives a relatively large payment for a service may in the end be left with less than another who receives a smaller payment.

F. A. Hayek, *The Constitution of Liberty* (London: Routledge & Kegan Paul, 1960), 316. Since E. R. A. Seligman published *Progressive Taxation in Theory and Practice* in the 1890s, progressive income taxation has been considered, in the United States, the paradigmatic just tax measured by sacrifice and ability principles. As political economists like Hayek and like R. A. Musgrave have stated, American tax philosophy must work within the confines of this verdict of history, even if the choice of progressive income tax is contestable. Hayek, *The Constitution of Liberty*, 307; R. A. Musgrave, "In Defense of an Income Concept," *Harvard Law Review* 81 (1967): 46.

111 Repetti, "The Appropriate Roles for Equity and Efficiency," 28.

112 Walter J. Blum and Harry Kalven, Jr., "The Uneasy Case for Progressive Taxation," *University of Chicago Law Review* 19, no. 3 (Spring 1952): 417–520.

113 Blum and Kalven, "The Uneasy Case for Progressive Taxation," 460.

114 Dudley Knowles, *Political Philosophy* (London: Routledge, 2001), 211–12. *The Guardian*, in Knowles' obituary, described him as a "liberal-communitarian ... one-nation social democrat ... always an old-Labour northerner." John Skorupski, "Dudley Knowles Obituary," *The Guardian*, November 5, 2014, accessed September 9, 2020, https://www.theguardian.com/education/2014/nov/05/dudley-knowles-obituary. Despite his concession to the spirit of the age, Knowles is beset by the nagging worry, originating in his reading of Rousseau, that equality is a good in itself, even when equality makes everyone *worse* off. For Rousseau, Knowles observed, everyone suffers from inequality (as when masters are dependent on their slaves). Knowles asks us to suppose that there are two classes of people (A and B) and that the following are three possible distributions of primary goods:

	A	B
(1)	50	50
(2)	30	150
(3)	55	65

The difference principle, reflecting *maximin* reasoning, ranks (1) higher than (2) but (3) higher than (1). Outcome (3) is "weakly Pareto superior" to (1). Maximum average utility, however, would rank (2) highest. As a psychological answer, Rawls says we would not—as social contractors—dare pick (2). Rawls also insists that (3) has to be better than (1) because envy is irrational. Knowles is not so sure; inequality itself may breed lack of self-respect. In any event, he thinks, the lesser standing that results from inequality—any inequality—"should be factored into the index of primary goods which defines the condition of the worst off." Knowles, *Political Philosophy*, 227–30.

115 Sugin, "Tax Expenditures," 36.

116 Hausman and McPherson, *Economic Analysis*, 159–60.

117 Daniel Shaviro, "Endowment and Inequality," in Thorndike and Ventry, 124.

118 Agamben, *The Kingdom and the Glory*, 9.

119 Hettich, Kenny, and Winer, "Political Regimes, Institutions and the Nature of Tax Systems," 15.

120 Sugin, "Theories of Distributive Justice," 2014.

121 Murphy and Nagel, *The Myth of Ownership*, 43.

122 Laura Biron, "Taxing or Taking? Property Rhetoric and the Justice of Taxation," in O'Neill and Orr, 82.

123 Hausman and McPherson, *Economic Analysis*, 161.

124 Brennan, "Striving for the Middle Ground," 70, 78.

125 Murphy and Nagel, *The Myth of Ownership*, 8.

126 Murphy and Nagel admit that "taxes are essentially modifications of property rights that entitle the state to control over part of the resources generated by the economic life of its citizens." Murphy and Nagel, *The Myth of Ownership*, 8–9.

127 Brennan, "Striving for the Middle Ground," 63.

128 Ruby Shao, "A Natural Case for Taxation," *Princeton Undergraduate Research Journal* 1, no. 1 (Spring 2017): 31.

129 Farrelly, "Taxation and Distributive Justice," 185–96.

130 Vallentyne, "Taxation, Redistribution and Property Rights," 3, 5.

131 Vallentyne, "Taxation, Redistribution and Property Rights," 8, 10.

References

Agamben, Giorgio. 2011. *The Kingdom and the Glory: For a Theological Genealogy of Economy and Government* (Homo Sacer *II, 2*). Translated by Lorenzo Chiesa and Matteo Madarini. Stanford: Stanford University Press.

Allstott, Anne L. 2013. "Updating the Welfare State: Marriage, the Income Tax, and Social Security in the Age of Individualism." *Tax Law Review* 66: 695–759. Accessed June 6, 2020. http://digitalcommons.law.yale.edu/cgi/viewcontent.cgi?article=5876&context=fss_papers.

Atkinson, A. B. 1973. "How Progressive Should Income Tax Be?" In *Essays in Modern Economics*, edited by Michael Parkin and A. R. Nobay, 90–109. London: Longman.

Biron, Laura. 2018. "Taxing or Taking? Property Rhetoric and the Justice of Taxation." In *Taxation: Philosophical Perspectives*, edited by M. O'Neill and S. Orr, 81–97. Oxford: Oxford University Press.

Blum, Walter J., and Harry Kalven, Jr. 1952. "The Uneasy Case for Progressive Taxation." *University of Chicago Law Review* 19, no. 3 (Spring): 417–520.

Bowditch, Louise J., et al. June 24 2019. "An Open Letter to the 2020 Presidential Candidates: It's Time to Tax Us More." Medium. Accessed June 6, 2020. https://medium.com/@letterforawealthtax/an-open-letter-to-the-2020-presidential-candidates-its-time-to-tax-us-more-6eb3a548b2fe.

Brennan, Geoffrey. 2018. "Striving for the Middle Ground." In *Taxation, Justice, and the Status of Private Rights*, edited by M. O'Neill and S. Orr, 60–80. Oxford: Oxford University Press.

Brennan, Geoffrey, and James M. Buchanan. 1980. *The Power to Tax: Analytical Foundations of a Fiscal Constitution.* The Collected Works of James M. Buchanan 9. Indianapolis: Liberty Fund.

Christian, Barry. 2018. "Redistribution." In *The Stanford Encyclopedia of Philosophy*, edited by Edward N. Zalta. Accessed June 6, 2020. https://plato.stanford.edu/entries/redistribution/.

Dodge, Joseph M. 2005. "Theories of Tax Justice: Ruminations on the Benefit, Partnership, and Ability-to-Pay Principles." *Tax Law Review* 58 (Summer): 399–461.

Farrelly, Colin. 2004. "Taxation and Distributive Justice." *Political Studies Review* 2: 185–97.

Finley, M. I. 1999. *The Ancient Economy.* Sather Classical Lectures 43. Updated ed. Berkeley: University of California Press.

Fleischacker, Samuel. 2004. *A Short History of Distributive Justice.* Cambridge, MA: Harvard University Press.

Fleurbaey, Marc. 2018. "Welfarism, Libertarianism, and Fairness in the Economic Approach to Taxation." In *Taxation: Philosophical Perspectives*, edited by M. O'Neill and S. Orr, 37–59. Oxford: Oxford University Press.

Galper, Harvey. March 30, 2018. "The TCJA Has Replaced the 1986 Tax Act, But Is It Tax Reform?" TaxVox Blog. Accessed June 6, 2020. https://www.taxpolicycenter.org/taxvox/tcja-has-replaced-1986-tax-act-it-tax-reform.

Groves, Harold M. 1974. *Tax Philosophers: Two Hundred Years of Thought in Great Britain and the United States.* Edited by Donald J. Curran. Madison, WI: The University of Wisconsin Press.

Halliday, Daniel. 2013. "Justice and Taxation." *Philosophy Compass* 8: 1–12.

Hamlin, Alan. 2018. "What Political Philosophy Should Learn from Economics About Taxation." In *Taxation Philosophical Perspectives*, edited by M. O'Neill and S. Orr, 17–36. Oxford: Oxford University Press.

Hands, D. Wade. March 14, 2017. "Philosophy and Economics." In *The New Palgrave Dictionary of Economics*, edited by Matias Varnengo, Esteban Perez Caldentey, and Barkley J. Rosser, Jr. Living ed. Accessed June 2, 2020. https://doi.org/10.1057/978-1-349-95121-5_1622-2.

Hausman, Daniel M., and Michael S. McPherson. 2006. *Economic Analysis, Moral Philosophy, and Public Policy.* 2nd ed. Cambridge: Cambridge University Press.

Hayek, F. A. 1960. *The Constitution of Liberty*. London: Routledge & Kegan Paul.
Hettich, Walter, Lawrence W. Kenny, and Stanley L. Winer. July 22, 2009. "Political Regimes, Institutions and the Nature of Tax Systems." Academia.edu. Accessed June 8, 2020. https://www.academia.edu/3153509/Political_Regimes_Institutions_and_the_Nature_of_Tax_Systems.
Kant, Immanuel. 1996. "The Metaphysics of Morals." In *Kant: Political Writings*, edited by Hans Reiss, translated by H. B. Nisbet, 131–75. *Cambridge Texts in the History of Philosophy*, edited by Raymond Guess, Quentin Skinner, and Richard Tuck. Cambridge: Cambridge University Press.
Kaplow, Louis, and Steven Shavell. 1994. "Why the Legal System is Less Efficient than the Income Tax in Redistributing Income." *The Journal of Legal Studies* 23, no. 2 (June): 667–81.
Knowles, Dudley. 2001. *Political Philosophy*. London: Routledge.
Locke, John. 1988. *Two Treatises of Government*. Edited by Peter Laslett. Cambridge Texts in the History of Political Thought. Cambridge: Cambridge University Press.
Mankiw, N. Gregory, Matthew Charles Weinzierl, and Danny Ferris Yagan. 2009. "Optimal Taxation in Theory and Practice." *Journal of Economic Perspectives* 23, no. 4: 147–74.
Mazur, Mark J. April 11, 2018. "Reflections on the Tax Cuts and Jobs Act." Testimony, hearing on "Unleashing America's Economic Potential," Joint Economic Committee. Accessed June 6, 2020. https://www.jec.senate.gov/public/_cache/files/119bdfe4-c47c-4069-8be3-1d939c491ab4/mark-mazur-testimony-4-11-18.pdf.
McConnell, Campbell R., and Stanley L. Brue. 2005. *Microeconomics: Principles, Problems, and Policies*. 16th ed. New York: McGraw-Hill Irwin.
Milasi, Santo, and Robert J. Waldmann. 2018. "Top Marginal Taxation and Economic Growth." *Applied Economics* 50, no. 19: 2156–70.
Mill, John Stuart. 1865. *Principles of Political Economy, with Some of Their Applications to Social Philosophy*. London: Longman, Green, Longman, Roberts, and Green.
Mirrlees, J. A. 1971. "An Exploration in the Theory of Optimum Income Taxation." *The Review of Economic Studies* 38, no. 2 (April): 175–208.
Montesquieu. 1989. *The Spirit of the Laws*. Edited and translated by Anne M. Cohler, Basia C. Miller, and Harold S. Stone. Cambridge Texts in the History of Political Thought. Cambridge: Cambridge University Press.
Murphy, Liam, and Thomas Nagel. 2002. *The Myth of Ownership: Taxes and Justice*. Oxford: Oxford University Press.
Musgrave, Richard A. 1959. *The Theory of Public Finance: A Study in Public Economy*. New York: McGraw-Hill Book Co., Inc.
______. 1967. "In Defense of an Income Concept." *Harvard Law Review* 81: 44–62.
______. 2002. "Equity and the Case for Progressive Taxation." In *Tax Justice: The Ongoing Debate*, edited by Thorndike and Ventry, 9–24. Washington: The Urban Institute Press.
______. 2005. "Fairness in Taxation." In *The Encyclopedia of Taxation & Tax Policy*, edited by Joseph J. Cordes, Robert D. Ebel, and Jane G. Gravelle, 135–37. 2nd ed. Washington: The Urban Institute Press.
Musgrave, Richard A., and Alan T. Peacock, eds. 1962. *Classics in the Theory of Public Finance*. London: Macmillan & Co. Ltd..
Musgrave, Richard A., and Peggy B. Musgrave. 1989. *Public Finance in Theory and Practice*. 5th ed. New York: McGraw-Hill Book Co..

Nozick, Robert. 1974. *Anarchy, State, and Utopia.* Oxford: Basil Blackwell.
O'Neill, Martin, and Shepley Orr, eds. 2018. *Taxation: Philosophical Perspectives.* Oxford: Oxford University Press.
Passell, Peter. 1990. "Furor over British Poll Tax Imperils Thatcher Ideology" *New York Times*, April 23, 1990.
Posner, Richard A. 1973. *Economic Analysis of Law.* Boston: Little, Brown and Co..
Raskolnikov, Alex. 2013. "Accepting the Limits of Tax Law and Economics." *Cornell Law Review* 98: 523–90.
Rawls, John. 1999. *A Theory of Justice.* Rev. ed. Cambridge, MA: The Belknap Press of Harvard University Press.
Repetti, James R. forthcoming 2020. "The Appropriate Roles for Equity and Efficiency in a Progressive Income Tax." *Florida Tax Review* 23: ___.
Scanlon, Thomas. 1975. "Preference and Urgency." *Journal of Philosophy* 72, no. 19 (November): 655–69.
______. 1986. "Equality of Resources and Equality of Welfare: A Forced Marriage?" *Ethics* 97, no. 1 (October): 111–18.
Shao, Ruby. 2017. "A Natural Case for Taxation." *Princeton Undergraduate Research Journal* 1, no. 1 (Spring): 25–36.
Shaviro, Daniel N. 2002. "Endowment and Inequality." In *Tax Justice: The Ongoing Debate*, edited by Thorndike and Ventry, 123–48. Washington: The Urban Institute Press.
Simons, Henry C. 1938. *Personal Income Taxation: The Definition of Income as a Problem of Fiscal Policy.* Chicago: The University of Chicago Press.
Skorupski, John. November 5, 2014. "Dudley Knowles Obituary." *The Guardian.* Accessed June 10, 2020. https://www.theguardian.com/education/2014/nov/05/dudley-knowles-obituary.
Steuerle, C. Eugene. 2002 "And Equal (Tax) Justice for All?" In *Tax Justice: The Ongoing Debate*, edited by Thorndike and Ventry, 253–84. Washington: The Urban Institute Press.
Strange, Susan. 1994. *States and Markets.* 2nd ed. London: Continuum.
Sugin, Linda. 2004. "Theories of Distributive Justice and Limitations on Taxation: What Rawls Demands from Tax Systems." *Fordham Law Review* 72, no. 5: 1991–2014.
______. 2010–2011. "A Philosophical Objection to the Optimal Tax Model." *Tax Law Review* 64: 229–81.
______. 2011. "Tax Expenditures, Reform, and Distributive Justice." *Columbia Journal of Tax Law* 3: 1–42.
Thorndike, Joseph J., and Dennis J. Ventry, Jr., eds. 2002. *Tax Justice: The Ongoing Debate.* Washington, DC: The Urban Institute Press.
University of California Berkeley. n.d. "Basic Welfare Economics and Optimal Tax Theory." EML Economics Library. Accessed June 6, 2020. https://eml.berkeley.edu/~burch/conf04/d1.pdf.
Utz, Stephen. 2002. "Ability to Pay." *Whittier Law Review* 23: 867–950.
Vallentyne, Peter. 2012. "Taxation, Redistribution and Property Rights." In *Routledge Companion to Philosophy of Law*, edited by Andrei Marmor, 291–301. New York: Routledge.
Witte, John F. 1985. *The Politics and Development of the Federal Income Tax.* Madison, WI: The University of Wisconsin Press.

2 A society within a society

Introduction

On the one hand, nothing links ruler and subject more obviously than taxes. On the other hand, nothing could have been more remote from the inhabitants of the Roman Empire than tax policy. This chapter describes the distance between ruler and subject represented by the late Roman tax system and the deep regressivity of that system. It then addresses the few explicit Christian perspectives on taxation that the period produced, before turning to ways in which Christians reimagined and began to model a new kind of relationship between the rich and the poor. The chapter then places these developments in a more theoretical political-theological context.

Taxation in the Roman Empire in the fourth and fifth centuries

The institution of taxation dramatically represented the absolute power of the Roman emperor in the fourth and fifth centuries. Each year, in January, the emperor determined the tax budget. The emperor wrote the budget in his own hand. Since the emperor Diocletian's time, the tax budget had ceased to be fixed. It was determined entirely according to the state's needs.[1] Circumstances such as poor harvests were irrelevant; the emperor's revenue target was unimpeachable. It admitted no exceptions, negotiation was an impossibility, and no tax relief was available.[2]

The background to this centrality of taxation in the fourth and fifth centuries lies in the third century. The Roman tax system that emerged during that century of war and economic crises was more burdensome than earlier imperial systems. Tolls were imposed on goods moving from one part of the empire to another; heavier duties were imposed on goods crossing the imperial frontier itself.[3] Some provinces imposed a form of sales tax.[4] Levies imposed on senatorial estates were easily evaded, but those imposed on craftsmen were not.[5] The taxes, moreover, came to be more ruthlessly extracted. By the time of the emperor Diocletian, fiscal official imposed the general assessment and the *annonae* (the systems of providing Rome, certain other cities, and the armies with grain and other food[6]) "in the spirit of armed conquerors," freely using physical force to elicit disclosure of every detail of the wealth of both Italians and provincials.[7]

Diocletian, that "imperial drill-sergeant," proposed coercion as the only means of equating supply and demand in the interest of a "common good."[8] His exactions were consistent with his new administrative structure, which was a matter "not of right but of grace,"[9] and a "new theory of sovereignty" that "admitted no limit to the powers claimed by the state as against the subject."[10] This new theory, though undoubtedly prompted by the end of Rome's expansion early in the second century, leaving taxes as the sole means of supporting the government,[11] nevertheless received philosophical support from what was sometimes interpreted as the turn to political absolutism, on the part of Ulpian (170–223) and other jurists.[12] Diocletian's reign was characterized by an apotheosis of the person of the emperor (*dominus et deus*) on the one hand and, on the other, an "intolerable financial burden" imposed on the taxpayer.[13]

Constantine's conversion did little to mitigate the firmness with which taxes were extracted or the singularly prominent place that taxation occupied in the imperial government. As the system stood in the fourth century, once the emperor had written out the tax budget for his praetorian prefects, they passed on copies to the provincial governor. The town councils in each province were then summoned to the governor's palace, where a demand for specific levies was read out. Each city in the Empire was presented with a lump sum that it was responsible for collecting in its territory.[14] The town councilors, the *curiales*, were typically of modest backgrounds in the early part of the fourth century. It was an honor for them to be admitted to public service, but the honor came with a great price. They were the ones who were given the "grim task of collecting the imperial taxes" from the urban *plebs* and the *rusticuli*—the "little farmers" in the surrounding countryside that comprised their city's territory.[15] Worse, they were responsible for any shortfall in tax collections and were subject, in the event of such a failure, to both "afflicted poverty" and the lash.[16]

Peter Brown has shown that the Empire of the fourth century was not a "melancholy epilogue to the classical Roman Empire" but rather the "climax of the Roman state."[17] It emerged as a successful state after the crises of the third century largely because the emperors Diocletian (284–305) and Constantine (306–337) bequeathed it "an ambitious tax system" and a culture of constant tax demands from the imperial administration. The terms on which Rome survived the crisis of the third century and emerged from it included a stern "rationalization" of taxation, "exacted with unprecedented determination."[18] The impression that churches were largely exempt from these insistent demands is incorrect. The bishops, the clergy, and the churches were only briefly exempt, in the last years of the reign of Constantius II (337–361) from the land tax, "the most important tax of the Empire." Privileges for the church were cut back again after the emperor Julian's ruinous defeat in Persia in 363. Only with such a system could the state maintain the military and bureaucratic structures needed to promote stability and, in the process, great wealth.

Rome needed the wealth of Africa and obtained it through taxation. The Vandals' conquest of Carthage, in 439, was a turning point in the Roman state's ability to dictate the terms of the political arrangement in the west. The civil wars that erupted as a consequence of the Roman state's use of barbarian militias in Britain, Spain, and Gaul had destabilized those provinces, but the fall of Carthage did much more: it "broke the 'tax spine' of the Western empire.[19] Even before 439, the Empire's tax revenues had probably decreased by 50 percent. After the fall of Carthage, the *respublica*, as it was increasingly known, was left with about a quarter of the resources it had enjoyed during the reign of Valentinian I, in the 360s and the 370s.[20] As revenue dwindled, the state found it more and more difficult to pay for regular troops. Without regular troops, the government had no choice but to turn to "barbarian" armies as allies. These armies, to understate the matter, proved hard to control.[21]

In the eastern Empire, in contrast, taxes continued to be collected efficiently throughout the fifth century. The state's institutions and structure had changed little since the days of Constantine and Theodosius I.[22] Once again, taxation remained untouched by the bishops' rise to prominence. The collection of taxes depended on collaboration between local governments and the "local elites," with the result that bishop's role could only be peripheral at best.[23] The story of that peripheral role in the West and how it came to reshape western Roman society's view of the poor and practice of distributive justice follows.

A model of regressivity

In one sense, the late Roman tax system was strikingly efficient. By delegating tax collection (and all other functions except "high justice" and control of the military) to about 2,500 cities "scattered like fairy dust over the surface of an immense empire," Rome was a "'truly minimal state.'"[24] It is not surprising that the system was rife with abuse. Constantine and his successors had tried to combat collusion by removing the collection of taxes from the hands of the town councilors and entrusting it to the provincial governors and magistrates. The inevitable result was an increase in public servants and expense. After 371, collection of the *capitatio*—the head tax on individuals—from the little farmers who worked as tenants on the large *praedia* reverted to the owners of the *praedia* themselves.[25]

The structure of the land tax and the head tax themselves was deeply regressive. "The wealthiest man in Ephesus," David Potter writes, "paid the same head tax as the poorest laborer."[26] Although no one was exempt from transport taxes, Roman citizens were exempt from the *capitatio*. This feature could only have magnified the sense that the poorer members of society bore the greatest tax burden. After the great landowners descended twice—once as tax collectors and then as rent collectors—the little farmers probably faced the year before them with one-third or less of their harvest.[27] If there was a sense of equity in late Roman taxation, it lay in the idea, which was frequently communicated to the Empire's subjects, that only as much tax as necessary for operations of the state would be collected each year.[28]

Roman tax rates were, in fact, relatively low compared to those of eastern Mediterranean governments that the Empire had absorbed, and certainly compared to modern rates.[29] As the fourth century proceeded, however, taxes increased. Typical of mature empires is an effort toward renewal that pushes in the direction of compulsion and higher taxation. Beyond certain limits, high taxes nurture corruption, evasion, "and often a redistribution of income in favour of powerful bureaucrats and of people close to those in power."[30]

Rome was no exception. The price of a manageable tax collection system was large-scale collusion in the shifting of the burden of taxation. Even during Alaric's blockade of the city of Rome in 408–409, when the Senate had to resort to taxation of its own members, noble families continued to prove "notably selfish."[31] Moreover, already regressive, the system became "a source of profit and a basis for local power."[32] By involving themselves with state power, the wealthy emerged during the fourth century as an aristocracy unparalleled in the history of the Empire.[33] The government's unflinching tax policies and ruthless, though delegated, tax collection procedures were turned to the advantage of those close to the center of power and created "seemingly unchallengeable social hierarchies" stretching to Gaul, Spain, and southern Britain "in the glory days of the fourth-century age of gold."[34]

As the Empire crumbled around its edges in the early fifth century, the "network of villas" that had held the population together and linked them to the cities and its *curiales* scattered into more informal groupings of farms and villages. These groups were not free from the burden of taxation, but, in regions where this change occurred, it became "next to impossible to extract . . . the high level of wealth that had supported the affluent residences" of the fourth century.[35] To the extent wealth was to be had in the "gray areas" of the disintegrating Empire, it came from plunder and the slave trade, not from tax revenue.[36] On the other hand, in most of Italy, southern Gaul, coastal Spain, and North Africa, tax revenue continued to come in with "surprising regularity" and the affluence of the villa owners endured until Carthage fell.[37]

The bishops and taxation

For all their growing influence in the fourth century, the Christian bishops could not touch the state's tax policy. Ambrose, though an "insider" to the workings of the imperial government, was unable to attack the fiscal system that contributed to the inequity he saw and decried. The explicit Christian criticism of taxation and its abuses would have to wait a century and a half.[38] Peter Brown writes: "In the one crucial area of taxation and the treatment of fiscal debtors, the late Roman state remained impervious to Christianity."[39]

If anything, taxes and their collection were even more unassailable in the next generation. Numidia, Augustine's province in North Africa, was a land known for "dangerous shortages."[40] In the late fourth and early fifth centuries, grain production was pushed by tax demands, as well as the hope of profit, to its ecological limits. During the course of the fourth century, moreover, town councils became oligarchies, as the wealthier councilors and holders of imperial privileges forced the poorer and less privileged councilors out of power. The rich and powerful maintained their positions by controlling how taxes were allocated. Brown considers manipulation of local alliances to ensure smooth functioning of the tax system to have been the "ultimate test" of a provincial governor's skill.[41] Augustine could not attack this system. Even at the provincial and local levels it "was identified with the emperor" and "out of bounds to criticism." For the most part, Augustine prudently held back. A denunciation of "the actual mechanics of taxation" was coming, but not for another few decades.[42]

A few small breaches of the fortress of imperial taxation did occur. Augustine's lifelong friend and fellow bishop Alypius returned from Africa to Rome in his seventies and hovered around the emperor's court, then in Ravenna, petitioning the authorities concerning the needs of the African provinces and clergy. Augustine wrote to him, in mid-March 420, complaining that tax debtors "were unceremoniously dragged out of church" and that anyone who helped them resist was sued for "obstructing 'necessities of state.'"[43] Augustine asked Alypius to point out to whomever would listen "that fiscal oppression had sapped the clergy of Africa" and suggested that *defensores*—legal advocates who were authorized to challenge tax abuses—should be appointed in Africa as they had been in other parts of the Empire.[44]

Success was limited. Although the Christian bishops grew bolder in the early fifth century and ventured into the area of taxation, they had to accept, for the most part, that taxes were literally the price that had to be paid for a solid empire that could and did provide protection and, at times, privileges to the churches.[45] Despite the high-flown rhetoric of imperial edicts regarding heresy and other religious matters, the one thing that really mattered to the government "was the gigantic annual spasm connected with bringing in the taxes."[46]

The Christian narrative of late Roman taxation

The church's inability to influence tax policy in the late Roman Empire makes the story of how tax became a bearer—at times *the* bearer—of political theology, or more precisely, economic theology, all the more interesting. It begins with a Christian narrative of the emperors' understandable preoccupation with the collection of taxes and then moves to the Christian reaction against the abuses that characterized the final years of the *respublica*'s tax system. These responses did not influence tax policy. The first response is a story told by a Christian apologist at the beginning of the empire's Christian era; the second is the cry of an outraged cleric a century and a half later.

A representation of oppression and inequity

Christianity in the late empire was primarily a lower- and middle-class phenomenon, especially at the dawn of the fourth century.[47] Christians, therefore felt the shift in imperial tax policies acutely.[48] No sooner had the burden of the pagan

Diocletian's exactions fallen most heavily on them, however, than Constantine's conversion offered hope that the burden would be lifted again. The dramatic reversal of the status of Christians early in the fourth century—from the Great Persecution to the Edict of Milan in a matter of one decade—led them to construct a narrative that, with a significant stress on taxation, contrasted the reigns of these emperors.

Lactantius

In the writings of the Christian apologist Lactantius (c. 250 – c. 325), who served both Diocletian and Constantine, the heavy taxation of Diocletian and his colleagues elicited nostalgia for the classical simplicity of Lactantius' political inspiration, Cicero. Lactantius embraced Cicero's high regard for individual property in contrast to the "insatiable greed" of Diocletian, who was "always amassing surplus wealth and funds,"[49] and against the tax-raising efforts of the emperor Maximian Galerius, a member of Diocletian's Tetrarchy.[50]

Lactantius' depiction of Diocletian is of a person consumed with anxiety and insecurity. His restless activity made him "an author of crimes and a deviser of evils; he ruined everything and could not even keep his hands from God."[51] This ruination, in Lactantius' account, came not from tearing down but from authoring and engineering. He had "a limitless passion for building."[52] He would destroy most of a city, forcing its inhabitants to leave "as if the city had been captured by an enemy."[53] Once a building project was completed "and the provinces ruined in the process," Lactantius' Diocletian would say of the buildings, "'They have not been built rightly; they must be done in another way.'"[54]

In keeping with this picture of restless accumulation, Diocletian's tax reforms appear in Lactantius' account as an endless striving for "having," for gratuitous accumulation. Diocletian "was never willing that his treasuries should be depleted; he was always amassing surplus wealth and funds for largesse so that he could keep what he was storing complete and inviolate."[55]

Patience, in contrast to Diocletian's restlessness, was the "supreme virtue" for Lactantius.[56] It was "opposed to all vices and emotions" because "[i]t recalls a troubled and wobbling soul to its calm, it soothes it, and restores man to himself."[57] While not rising to the heights of enthusiasm of his contemporary Eusebius of Caesarea (c. 260–c. 340),[58] Lactantius began *De mortibus persecutorum* by describing the era of Constantine as one in which the serenity of the primitive golden age was being restored: "Now, after the violent whirlwinds of the dark storm, the air is calm and the light that we have longed for has shone forth again."[59]

The primitive golden age had been one in which rulers did not disturb individual property interests. Lactantius maintained, for instance, that Virgil's encomium of communal sharing "when Saturn was king" should not be taken "to mean that there was no private property at all in those days" but rather as "a poetical image of people being so generous that they did not fence off fruits of the earth as their own."[60] Lactantius' account treated taxation—not the possession of private property—as the epitome of greedy acquisition: "Working land stolen from others by violence, for instance, expanding one's own power and levying heavier taxes: none of those is a virtue; they are the overthrow of virtue."[61]

Lactantius died at an advanced age for his day, perhaps 75, around the year 325, midway through Constantine's reign. Constantine's reduction of the tax burden on the middle class was short-lived, but Lactantius' high praise was not wholly without foundation. Constantine did indeed initiate some kind of tax-exemption for Christian clergy, in the interest of maintaining the happiness and prosperity of the empire.[62] It is also true that Constantine acknowledged a form of taxpayer rights, prohibiting imprisonment, chains, and the lash for tax delinquency, using distraint and sale of the property instead.[63] Moreover, his son Constantius II, who closed the pagan temples in 346, enacted further (though short-lived) tax-exemptions for the clergy.[64] The confiscation of temple properties during the first half of the fourth century permitted Constantine and Constantius to spend freely, enhancing the impression that the golden age had returned.[65]

Even Constantine, however, had no choice but to continue "the dreaded indictions of Diocletian and Maximian."[66] If anything, he extended the overall burden of taxation. It was Constantine who initiated the *collatio lustralis*, a general sales tax on business.[67] He also provided his new capital, Constantinople, "with a system of *annonae* similar to that which, since the days of the Gracchi, had made Old Rome the parasite of the world."[68] Moreover, Constantine's efforts, at the end of his life, to force landowners to cultivate neighboring uncultivated lands backfired. As the adjacent lands were usually submarginal, this legislation had the effect of reducing landowners' income and led to greater tax evasion.[69]

Their hopes for an era of restrained taxation at the hands of Christian emperors shattered, Christian writers such as Salvian turned even more hostile to taxation than Lactantius had been. The reason for this hostility, however, was something other than nostalgia for Cicero's "entitlement theory" of justice.

Salvian

In the writings of Salvian the Presbyter (c. 400–c. 490), which have been mined for details about the late Roman tax system,[70] the institution of taxation had become an expression of human sinfulness, a means of instantiating evil desires in the form of cruelty toward others.

Salvian argued that barbarians exhibited more of the love and charity enjoined by divine law than the Romans did, because the former at least loved one another within each tribe, while the latter had sunk to "a new and immeasurable evil . . .: it is not enough for anyone to be happy himself, unless another is unhappy."[71] This unprecedented level of evil was expressed in the way in which the Romans "proscribe one another with exactions."[72] A shocking example of this cruelty, in Salvian's estimation, was the plight of the Bagaudae (Gallic peasant insurgents[73]) who were forced by the greed of the *curiales*-turned-tyrants "to live as barbarians because they were not permitted to be Romans."[74] The Bagaudae were driven to desperation by two aspects of the tax burden imposed on them: (1) its absolute weight, in that the burden exceeded their resources; and (2) its regressivity, in that the burden fell disproportionately on the poor. Salvian wrote:

> This very tax levying, although hard and inhuman, would nevertheless be less heavy and harsh if all would bear it equally and in common. Taxation is made more shameful and burdensome because all do not bear the burden of all. They extort tribute from the poor man for the taxes of the rich, and the weaker carry the load for the stronger. There is no other reason that they cannot bear all the taxation except that the burden imposed on the wretched is greater than their resources. They suffer from envy and want, which are misfortunes most diverse and unlike.[75]

Envy is bound up with payment of the tax; need, with the ability to pay.

An even greater level of injustice surfaced in the case of the *coloni*, for whom the tax burden had become detached from possession. This detachment was characteristic of the Roman Empire in its death throes. The *coloni* were subtenant farmers on large estates (*latifundi*). Some of them, lacking the means to emigrate to the barbarians, had left their own land and effectively sold themselves into serfdom because they could not pay the taxes that were attached to the land.[76] The landed aristocracy into whose hands the *coloni* committed themselves took title to their lands and still continued to avoid taxation.[77]

The cruelties that Salvian associated with the steeply regressive tax structures of the fifth, sixth, and seventh centuries reflected, in economic terms, the collapse of effective central government. As the imperial government became more impoverished, it raised taxes, which, because they could only target the relatively poor, eventually paralyzed the state.[78] In the 430s and early 440s, Roman taxes had to be collected even more ruthlessly than before because of the costly military campaigns launched to reassert, in one final gasp, the power of the *respublica*.[79] The term "regressive" is, admittedly, anachronistic, but the concept is not. As antiquity evolved into the early Middle Ages, the theologians saw tax levies by an increasingly desperate government, and tax evasion by an increasingly powerful landed aristocracy, as together expressing the very essence of human cruelty.[80] The long-standing practice of the rich, that of shifting the burden of high taxes to lesser taxpayers, had become even more pronounced in the 430s.[81] Even the chancery of the emperor Valentinian III, in 441, condemned this sort of tax evasion in terms that echoed Salvian's. What differed in Salvian's writings was the note of finality: the Roman *respublica* was dead, strangled "with the bonds of taxes."[82]

It is not clear, however, that Salvian was describing anything new, and he was hardly describing the emergence of a "proto-feudal" order, as some have maintained. It may be that he was simply highlighting "the normal ups and downs of farmers forced to sell part or all of their land to richer neighbors so as to cover their tax debts."[83]

What was unprecedented in Salvian's writing was a linking of the mechanics of taxation to the moral failure of society. Salvian was clear: at the heart of the "sinister development" he described—that of Romans fleeing to barbarian-controlled provinces (as Salvian himself had done) to escape oppression, and praying that they would never again become subjects of the empire—lay "the fiscal apparatus of the Roman state."[84] As for the almost unspeakable disaster of the *coloni*, Salvian had no problem with social hierarchy itself. What appalled him so about the *coloni* was that the tax system had reduced the farmers to slaves, and that development violated "the Gallic consensus on theology," which "assumed ... sharp asymmetries" in society "as long as the partners remained free agents."[85]

Salvian insisted that "knowledge of the law of God" was "the only criterion according to which God judged any human society."[86] Those societies with the least knowledge of God's law would be treated most leniently; that society—the empire—with the greatest understanding of the law of God would be judged most harshly. Salvian arranged Gaul according to a moral map. The parts remaining in the *respublica* in the 440s would experience the greatest severity of God's wrath—and that at the hands primarily of the Visigoths and Vandals.[87] He saw the empire as an avatar of the Old Testament kingdom of Israel, but the *respublica*—like Israel—had deserted God and would, in turn, be punished.[88]

Christian negativity toward taxation

In some ways, the Christian hostility to overbearing taxation represents the revival of a more classical view of private wealth and restraint on part of the state. Lactantius, as we have seen, revered Cicero's spare vision of taxation. Indeed, Cicero's "mark of a just society," a commitment to seeing that everyone receives her due,[89] formed the backdrop for many medieval and early-modern discussions of tax justice.[90]

Writing in the year before his murder, Cicero (106–43 BC) had demanded that the state—any state—take every precaution "to avoid the imposition of a property tax."[91] Only as a last resort should the state impose such a burden on its citizens, and even then only if it made clear to them that no other option was available and that "if they wish to survive, they must bow to the inevitable."[92]

Cicero's extreme aversion to the taxation of citizens' property was a subcategory of his emphasis on property rights. Such was his concern for the protection of private property that he claimed "[t]he chief preoccupation of the state-administrator must be to ensure that the individual keeps what is his; there should be no public confiscation of the possessions of private persons."[93] The "chief motivation" behind the formation of human communities in the first place, Cicero wrote, "was to ensure the maintenance of private property."[94]

Cicero's *On Obligations* do not separate the concept of public takings from the concept of redistribution: "[Phillipus'] was a pernicious speech, promoting as it did the equalization of property; what could be more baneful than that?"[95] Redistribution appears to have intensified Cicero's hostility to confiscation, but he did not regard the two evils as separate kinds of injustice. He wrote: "So that after I have bought and built my property, maintaining it and sinking money in it, you can enjoy living there against my will? What else is that but robbing some of their possessions, and awarding to others what is not their own?"[96] Cicero understood what the great economist Henry Simons would argue in the twentieth century:[97] taxation is inherently redistributive, regardless of the government's reasons for imposing it.

Cicero's conception of property, taxation, and justice slowly faded from view as the history of the empire unfolded, revived from time to time primarily by those, like Lactantius, who were nostalgic for a less anxious time. The turn toward greater government control and, with it, more bureaucracy was evident by the second century. Nevertheless, the Antonine economy was classically conservative, focused on stability rather than expansion. Charles Norris Cochrane writes that one of Hadrian's favorite mottoes was "*liberalitas* (relating to the cancellation of unpaid taxes)."[98] Increased government regulation "had not as yet degenerated into regimentation."[99]

That degeneration, however, was on full display by the end of the tumultuous third century. To some extent, Rome was a victim of its own success. Describing not just the later Roman Empire, but mature empires in general, the economic historian Carlo Cipolla notes that an "improvement in standards of living is generally reflected, among other things, by the least attractive jobs tending to be deserted."[100] The Roman response to this stage of the empire's economic life was heavy-handed, freezing, for instance, existing miners in their jobs, recalling miners who had found other work, and finally tying the children of miners to that occupation.[101] Against that backdrop, it is not surprising that Christians articulated responses to taxation around the turn of the fourth century that cast taxes in an almost entirely negative light.

On its face, theological engagement with taxation ended there—with a properly Christian disgust at the regressive shape of the tax system and the corrupt and self-seeking use of that system. But that revulsion is noteworthy. It suggests that Christian thinkers were submitting all of society's institutions, even the most unassailable, to ethical scrutiny guided by Christianized views of justice. The inevitable result of that scrutiny would be a kind of "tax justice" in later centuries. First, an idea of distributive justice itself would need to emerge.

"The template for an experiment"

In the fourth and fifth centuries, there was as yet no Christian "doctrine" of taxation. There was, however, an impulse to make of the church and its institutions a microcosm of society where the ways in which wealth mediated relationships among the people of God could be reimagined. Against the backdrop of Cicero's austere classical vision and the new, Christian outrage at the way the powerful used the tax system for their own financial benefit, the Christian model slowly but surely, and inevitably, set the terms for what society could and should express through the institution of taxation.

Peter Brown argues that the church's "atmosphere of relaxed hierarchy" offered relief to both rich and poor in the late empire's stiflingly stratified society. Bishop Cyprian of Carthage (248–58), in Brown's account, provided an early model for an “imaginative erosion of boundaries”—long before Constantine’s conversion—in the church. To Cyprian, the social boundaries of society “vividly concretized” the “imprisoning bonds of sin.”[102] Reaching out to the poor expressed a breaking of the chains of sin. A Christian church, then, could become “a sort of oblique expression of an ideal social order divorced from the compromising realities of life.”[103]

Cyprian was “fiercely inward looking” in that he sought solidarity among Christians above else. He was not interested in reaching out to non-Christians. It was precisely this feature of his vision that made him successful in mobilizing money. Brown reports that on one occasion Cyprian managed to raise through donations of the faithful the equivalent of a month’s salary of 3,000 workmen, or half of an imperial secretary’s annual salary, to ransom Christians taken in a raid by Berber tribesmen. The microcosm of an economic system emerged in Cyprian’s use of alms. Alms flowing from rich to poor “helped bridge social fissures within the Christian community.” Within Cyprian’s community, there was “‘practical evidence of the church constituting a society within a society.’”[104] The subsections that follow trace the gradual turn from an inward-looking church to one that looked out at all members of society.

“Lovers of the poor”

Though the church was still a society within a society 100 years later, the Roman world had begun to feel the presence of the churches in its midst by then. Some of the vision of the ideal society had begun to seep out into the world. The increasing authority that the bishops claimed—and *could* claim—in the fourth century was not only a consequence of Constantine’s conversion and of the Edict of Milan and edicts in the churches’ favor that followed it. The bishops also began to act as “lovers of the poor” in the society surrounding them.[105]

This is not to say that non-Christian Romans lacked generosity. The empire was held together by gifts, which cemented personal ties necessary for the survival of the society as a whole. Both Christians and non-Christians believed that wealth could be legitimized through acts of generosity.[106] Wealthy non-Christians were lavish givers in the fourth century. But their giving took the form of “civic euergetism,” the tradition of performing good deeds for one’s city.[107]

Euergetism was “one of the most striking and idiosyncratic features of the Greco-Roman world,” but it “contained no element of compassion for the poor.”[108] For that reason the bishops seized upon it to transform the giving of wealthy Christians into something dramatically different. The difference between “generosity to one’s city and Christian forms of giving to the poor and to the church” was “an imaginative difference of momentous proportions.”[109]

Non-Christians often saw the churches’ preoccupation with the poor as a distraction. The reason for Rome’s troubles, they believed, lay with the dishonor shown to the ancient gods.[110] To spend as much time and moral persuasion as a bishop such as Ambrose did on the need of the poor must have seemed strange and perverse to Romans of a more classical outlook. For that very reason, the relentless focus of Ambrose and his fellow bishops on the poor allowed them to place in society itself "a series of unmistakable—even shocking—'markers.'"[111]

Ambrose's redirection of acts of euergetism to acts of compassion was all the more shocking to the surrounding world because he received the poor as "brothers." His vision was inspired by the depiction of the poor in the Old Testament, that is, of people coming before the rich and powerful not as "beggars asking for alms" but as victims of oppression seeking justice.[112] Christian generosity was unlike the most salient example of non-Christian benevolence: the *annona civica*, the annual supply of grain to the people of Rome that expressed the emperor's "overwhelming love" for them and "showed that he was the greatest *amator patriae* of all."[113] The *annona*, Brown argues, had in fact nothing to do with poor relief. It too was an act of civic euergetism, for it was never given to the whole population of the city. Only registered citizens of Rome could receive it. It was considered an enviable privilege, a sign that one enjoyed the *securitas Romani populi*, the status of being guaranteed freedom from hunger.[114]

Indeed, probably the single greatest difficulty that the Christian bishops faced in redirecting giving from cities to poor people was that society was not primarily divided into rich and poor but between citizens and non-citizens. The poor, if they were Roman citizens, received entertainment, access to bathhouses, the *annona* in the city of Rome and other doles of food in cities elsewhere, and a kind of privilege. They were the *populus*, the *plebs*.[115] Christians, by presenting "poverty as the sole requirement of generosity," were seen as devaluing the status of the poor citizens.[116] Ambrose wanted to change the terms of the discourse, "to reverse the imaginative effects of standard Christian rhetoric on the poor." He wanted all of the poor, citizens and non-citizens alike, to be seen as part of the "people," not, as Brown puts it, "charged outsiders, sent by God to haunt the conscience of the rich."[117]

Ambrose knew who his *res publica* was. His first emphasis was the "intense cohesion and militancy of the Catholic Church." But, taking its cue from Cicero, his field of vision encompassed two "concentric circles." For Ambrose, cohesion meant human solidarity at the level of the church, just as it had meant unity among the citizens of the city of Rome for Cicero, but it also hinted at something much larger. For Cicero, solidarity was rooted in human nature; for Ambrose, it was inspired by a sense of "the immensity of God." Ambrose envisioned "a universal benevolence that radiated beyond the tight community of the local congregation" to "the limitless circle of humanity as a whole." He saw the potential for "a universal Catholic Church" to "embrace and reunite a fractured world."[118]

On the one hand, it is important not to think of Ambrose and his fellow bishops as setting out a complete and detailed blueprint for social reform. His "shocking markers" were meant as the first cracks in the armor of stratified Milanese society. The goal of the fourth-century bishops was to open up the imaginative space for "intervention in society." Ambrose's sermons "were no more than the preliminary bombardment that preceded the action of the bishop as intercessor with the great."[119]

On the other hand, Ambrose inhabited a different world than Cyprian of Carthage had. The society within a society was beginning to leave its mark on the outer circle of humanity. Ambrose's *De officiis* "amounted to a statement of the role of the Christian bishop in Roman society." It speaks in terms of justice and public duties. Justice is "for others," and it "aids the community." Just people give "money to others" as a duty and "will assume other people's dangers" as their own.[120] There is no doubt that the bishops had become a force for justice in cities like Milan.[121] Even before Ambrose, Constantine had felt himself at liberty to grant exemptions to bishops and churches precisely because they took care of the poor and in that sense aided the larger community. The exemptions were a "quid pro quo," as an edict that Constantine issued in 329 made clear: "The wealthy must be there to support the obligations of the secular world, while the poor are maintained by the wealth of the churches."[122] In the eyes of the first Christian emperors, poor relief had not yet replaced euergetism, and none of the extravagant wealth of the highest ten percent of society was yet thought of as at the disposal of the poor, but the church's preoccupation with the poor had become a matter of justice, parallel in some respects to the traditional Roman culture of giving.

The church's new focus forced it to reckon with the theological problem of wealth and poverty, and from that reckoning an "economic ethics" would be born.[123] It is worth dwelling at some length—with considerable help from Peter Brown's work—on the two broad alternative responses to wealth and poverty, not least because they shaped later political theologies and "tax theologies" contained therein.

Christians and wealth: renunciation or use?

In his own *De officiis*, Ambrose rewrote Cicero's definition of justice. Going beyond Cicero's spare definition that tied justice to the preservation of private property rights, Ambrose wished to foster a conception of justice in which property existed, not simply to be owned, but to be shared.[124] In raising the meaning of justice to the heroic level of assuming other people's dangers as one's own, Ambrose undoubtedly echoed the "ascetic mimesis" of Christians, found particularly in the eastern part of the empire, who had renounced property altogether.[125]

In the next generation, Jerome (342–420) would come to represent this commitment to renunciation of all wealth. He shared the radical, Syrian view that based a life of poverty "on identification with the imagined absolute poverty of Christ." To be a monk in the Syrian sense "meant a total whiteout of the social person." It meant being an heir to the Cynics.[126]

The difficulty for Jerome and other ascetics was that they had to live and work, and that meant they still had to rely on material goods in some way. They "depended on resources only rich patrons could provide."[127] Suspicion of wealth, paradoxically, was one of the driving forces in the articulation of an alternative to ascetic renunciation. The extreme form of asceticism raised questions in the minds of many Christians, Augustine included, because it depended on the wealth of rich supporters. The arrangement seemed insincere.[128]

Moreover, it seemed disingenuous to Ambrose and Augustine to withdraw entirely from the economy that produced the very wealth that could be given to the poor. It was unworthy of the tradition of the Old Testament prophets to retreat from the place where one could be in a position to give justice to the poor who came, not as beggars, but as plaintiffs seeking justice.[129] And, finally, Ambrose, and Augustine after him, recognized that most people with means were simply not free to follow Christ's counsel to the rich young ruler in its literal fullness; they had dependents and obligations.[130] Especially after the wealth of Rome began to dwindle, the radicalization of Pelagius' followers, for instance, seemed not only impractical, but out of date.[131]

Ambrose, a person of means, resolved the tension between embracing poverty and being engaged in the helping of the poor by giving his wealth to the church while retaining control over it and doling it out for the care of those members in society who were in need.[132] Augustine would do much the same when he established his proto-monastic community in Thagaste in North Africa,[133] an undertaking that Brown considers "the most carefully thought-through experiment in creating a community without private property yet to be imagined in the Christian West."[134] Though it was without private property, Augustine's community should not be imagined as one without property. Todd French considers these pious "gifts" to the church more of an identification with the poor in discourse rather than in reality. The Christians who followed the example of Ambrose and Augustine "were eager to reject the desire for wealth, more than the wealth itself," and it is likely "that many received an annuity from the revenues of their given estates."[135]

Augustine was forced to return to the question of wealth and poverty in the Christian community and refine it by the arrival in North Africa of Roman aristocrats fleeing Alaric's sack of the city of Rome in 410. Many of these Romans were influenced by Pelagius (354–418). They were influenced by him, in part, because he tended to validate their lifestyle. There was a certain parallelism between Pelagius' stress on spiritual autonomy and "that high sense of autonomy that had always distinguished the inner circle of the *nobiles* of Rome." The self-image of many Roman aristocrats resembled the "natural nobility" of the soul in Pelagius' theology.[136]

Not all of Pelagius' disciples were as lenient. For the anonymous author of the Pelagian *De divitiis*, wealth had no place in the life of a Christian. All wealth, the anonymous author argued, had its dark history; it was tainted, having inevitably been acquired with at least some measure of injustice. To make matters worse, the relation between wealth and government power—not least in the realm of taxation—was an unremovable blemish.[137] Renunciation was the only available option for wealthy Christians.

As these worrying ideas reached the shores of North Africa, Augustine began to work out the implications of his own version of Ambrose's position. Resisting "the radical call to renunciation associated with the views of the supporters of Pelagius," Augustine argued that wealth was to be *used* in and by the churches.[138]

Augustine's was not a new approach, but rather an intensified reflection on the idea that had been forming for some time among Christians "that it is not wealth itself that matters, but the use one makes of it."[139] As the Roman Empire had relativized individual property interests by gradually subordinating them to the interests of the government, Christian thinkers relativized them in light of the New Testament's apparent preference for poverty over wealth. The theologians' new gauge of ownership was *use* (*utilitas*), and it replaced Cicero's theory of entitlement to property.

Even Lactantius' opposition to imperial taxation had reflected something of a departure from Cicero's views. Lactantius' primary complaint against the tax policies of Diocletian and Galerius was not that they disregarded individual property rights, but that the emperors used taxes to serve their own greed and avarice. The possession of property itself was not sacred for Lactantius. What was important was the use to which property was put, and this principle applied to both sides of the tax equation—to the emperor and to the taxpayer. "[P]eople are not rich," Lactantius wrote, "by possession of wealth but by using it for acts of justice."[140] In Lactantius' account, worshippers in the primitive golden age had possessed private property but they had held it in such a way that, though laboring for wealth themselves, they "allowed the poor a share of the harvest" so that "the storerooms of the just were open in goodwill to all" and "all were equally well off because abundant and generous giving was done by those with to those without."[141]

Ambrose, in his meditation on the story of Naboth, located the goodness of "goods" entirely in the use that was made of them: "Riches are goods for whoever knows how to use them properly, but evils for whoever does not." The correct use turns out to be giving to the poor. Riches are only goods "if you give them to the poor."[142] Ambrose at times seems to have placed the possession of wealth in opposition to its use. The rich, he said, were those who took for themselves "what is common." What was common was "what is given for everyone's use." Therefore, the rich were simply "the few who make no use of their wealth, as opposed to the many who do."[143]

With Augustine, *utilitas* entered its own as an architectonic principle. He employed *utilitas* as a distinguishing mark between the earthly city, characterized by worship to achieve victory and peace, and the heavenly city, where worship expressed "a loving concern for others" instead of "lust for domination over them."[144] "For the good make use of this world," he famously wrote, "in order to enjoy God, whereas the evil want to make use of God in order to enjoy the world." Augustine made this statement in the course of explaining that Cain's sacrifice in Genesis 4 had been simply an act of giving "himself to himself" rather than worship, which is giving "to God something belonging to him."[145]

In those words, Augustine linked *utilitas* to *iustitia*. Cicero's classic definition of justice—*iustitia suum cuique distribuit*—was very much a part of Augustine's repertoire. In fact, the classical definition of *iustitia* reached the Middle Ages "through the echoes of Cicero in Ambrose and St. Augustine," as well as through the lawyers' reliance on a statement by the jurist Ulpian (d. 228), repurposed by Justinian,[146] and through grammar and rhetoric (e.g., from Cicero's *De inventione*).[147] However, other definitions of justice would surface along the way, coexisting sometimes uneasily with *suum cuique*. One such definition, first appearing in the *Formula honestae vitae* of Martin of Braga (d. 579), a treatise on the four virtues,[148] referred to justice as "an unspoken covenant of nature, devised for the aid of many" (*natura tacita conventio in adiutorium multorum inventa*).[149] The canon law scholar Stephan Kuttner speculates that the inspiration for Braga's definition was none other than Lactantius, for whom justice must be "altogether unselfish, disinterested, not expecting rewards."[150]

Another of Augustine's definitions would also circulate in the Middle Ages: *iustitia est amor soli amato serviens*.[151] Thomas Aquinas would use this phrase of Augustine's in the dialectical process of arriving at a definition of justice. If justice is love serving God alone, one of Thomas' "objections" read, then justice cannot "render to each one his right."[152] To this objection Aquinas responded that the love of God includes love of neighbor and, therefore, "includes rendering to each one his due."[153]

Meanwhile, Peter Lombard would borrow yet another of Augustine's definitions of justice, this one from *De Trinitate*: "coming to the aid of the wretched" (*in subveniendo miseris*).[154] Kuttner suggests that Augustine's *soli amato serviens* definition referred to the "ultimate perfection of justice and the other virtues in the state of *beatitudo*," while the *in subveniendo miseris* version pertained to the "transitory" function of justice "here and now."[155] Kuttner writes:

> It is not Augustine the student of Cicero but the disciple of the Gospel who wrote the passage in *De Trinitate*: its language is that of the Sermon on the Mount where St. Matthew's text designates the acts of almsgiving, prayer, and fasting as justice . . . —a connotation oddly lost in the vernacular translations we use.[156]

If anything, Augustine made the traditional formulation of justice more predominant, but in doing so he also expanded the *suum cuique* definition to include piety.[157] As Kuttner observes, *pietas* and *benevolentia* had been parts of justice as classically understood, but in the writings of Lactantius, Ambrose, and Augustine they "became infused with a new Christian fervor."[158]

This move had the effect of blurring the distinction between justice and benevolence; giving to those in need became a sort of payment of debt to them. By giving to the poor, Ambrose told the property holder, you are merely "paying what you owe," and, thus, there is no such thing as a "gratuitous donation."[159] Augustine extended Ambrose's logic by maintaining that the mere fact that something was "taken from an unwilling donor" did not make it "wrongfully taken." Those who "receive their due from unwilling debtors . . . do not acquire anything unlawfully."[160] Six hundred years later, Peter Damien (1007–1072) would echo this teaching, writing that "he who gives to the poor returns what he does not himself own, and does not dispose of his own goods."[161] But that it is to get ahead of Augustine, who wrote to Macedonius: "He who uses his wealth badly possesses it wrongfully, and wrongful possession means that it is another's property."[162]

Augustine was by no means intent on eliminating economic inequality or the private right of possession—even less intent than Ambrose had been. Augustine asked:

> By what right does every man possess what he possesses? Is it not by human right? For by divine right, "The earth is the Lord's, and the fullness thereof." The poor and the rich God made of one clay; the same earth supports alike the poor and the rich. By human right, however, one says, This estate is mine, this house is mine, this servant is mine. By human right, therefore, is by right of the emperors. Why so? Because God has distributed to mankind these very human rights through the emperors and kings of this world.[163]

He believed private property was necessary in civil society, fending off the worst effects of human nature.[164] In fact, for Augustine, the most basic division in society was not between rich and poor, but between the proud "and those who were enabled by God's grace to be humble before God and before their fellows." Some degree of inequality was acceptable, as long as the stratification of society was "softened," in the church, by "abandonment of the toxic byproducts of wealth—arrogance, violence, and the abuse of power."[165]

Augustine's was a more eschatological vision than Ambrose's. Ambrose, imaginatively inhabiting the world of the Old Testament prophets, saw almsgiving not only as a function of the largesse of the wealthy, but also as the correction of past injustices.[166] Augustine, however, was more concerned that Christians hold wealth lightly, using possessions "as though not using them . . . thus proving to unbelievers that they possessed these goods and were not possessed by them."[167] This theme of bitter enslavement to riches carries through to Augustine's *City of God*, where the rich man is described as "tortured by fears, worn out with sadness, burnt up with ambition, never knowing serenity of repose, always panting and sweating in his struggles with opponents," while "the ordinary citizen" rests "content with his strictly limited resources" and "enjoys the serenity of a good conscience."[168] "I do not think," Augustine concluded, "anyone would be fool enough to hesitate about which he would prefer." Nor was this conclusion limited to individuals. It applied equally to "to families, to peoples, to realms."[169] Thus, Augustine asked rhetorically, "[i]s it reasonable, is it sensible, to boast of the extent and grandeur of empire, when you cannot show that men lived in happiness, as they passed their lives amid the horrors of war, amid the shedding of men's blood—whether the blood of enemies or fellow citizens—under the shadow of fear and amid the terror of ruthless ambition?"[170]

Using wealth wrongly—using it in a manner that fostered pride rather than humility—was a great sin to Augustine because it disrupted community.[171] If giving was the cement that held together Roman cities, it was for Augustine the way to obtain solidarity and cohesion in the churches. A series of sermons by Augustine recently discovered in the Erfurt cathedral library show that he preached even more extensively than previously realized on the relations between the rich and the poor. He evidently planned "entire campaigns," including "teach-ins to his own clergy" on techniques of preaching on the subject. In particular, he hoped that his clergy would become effective in shifting the giving of their congregants away from the games in the theater to Christian charity.[172] The "high-minded counterculture" of the empire had for some time criticized the games for their "sensuality, violence, and vanity," but Augustine condemned them primarily because the euergetism of the games conflicted with generosity toward the poor. More importantly, giving to the games suggested a love of the city, and that could only be "pitted against 'love of the poor.'" The object of a people's love, in true Augustinian fashion, would necessarily be a place of "social bonding." Augustine was thus led inexorably to the conclusion that the theater—the site of the games—"was a counterchurch."[173]

"Transactions with the supernatural"

Augustine considered almsgiving an obligatory practice for all Christians. He was certain that Daniel 4:27 ("Redeem your sins with alms and your injustices by compassion on the poor") should apply literally. He used this concept against the followers of Pelagius, such as the author of *De divitiis*, who argued that the rich could not be saved.[174]

The role that almsgiving played in the theologies of Ambrose and Augustine was more than a little transactional. This fact is not surprising. Pagans, Jews, and Christians in the fourth- and fifth-century empire all thought of religious giving "as a religious transaction."[175] Perhaps it was Ambrose who stated the matter most bluntly when he proclaimed that giving riches to the poor makes "God your debtor by a kind of pious loan."[176] For John Chrysostom, in Todd French's words, "the poor became the ticket to heaven."[177] The idea of placing God in one's debt fit well with the Roman Christian idea of justice, which in turn echoed the reciprocal assumptions behind Roman patronage relationships.[178] French notes that a far-from-altruistic Christian account of the "symbiotic nature of the relationship" between rich and poor had surfaced as early as the first part of the second century, in The Shepherd of Hermas, where both parties "are interested in gaining, by means of the other, those things they need."[179]

With the two options—renunciation of wealth on the one hand and an almost transactional system on the other—in place at the end of the empire's life, wealth "no longer needed to be a source of widespread, ill-defined anxiety." Brown writes: "'The wealthy' were now offered a clear-cut choice of roles. Either one remained rich and became a pillar of the church as a donor and almsgiver, or one betook oneself to a monastery."[180]

What deserves to be highlighted is the dynamic quality of the Augustinian option. In the classical world, beggars crowded around the temples to receive whatever they were given. They were not ignored, but their position as beggars reinforced their social inferiority. They were passive recipients.[181] Augustine, on the other hand, decried the tendency of the wealthy to "plunder" the possessions of others:

> For you, a man of great judgment, and of great prudence, to be sure, are daily devising methods of acquiring money, by traffic, by agriculture, by eloquence perhaps, by making yourself learned in the law, by warfare, perhaps you even add that of usury. Like a shrewd man as you are, you leave nothing untried, whereby you may pile coin on coin; and may store it up more carefully in a place of secrecy. You plunder others; you guard against the plunderer; you are afraid lest you should yourself suffer the wrong, that you yourself do; and even what you do suffer, does not correct you.[182]

French offers three possible interpretations of this passage: it may refer to practices by the rich that inevitably prevent others from gathering wealth; it may mean outright theft of the possessions of the poor; or it may be understood "as the hoarding of wealth, which distances the poor from that economic fluidity which would provide for their existence." Regardless of its meaning, "the condemnation is on the wealthy for their role in separating the poor from economic stability."[183] At the very least, Augustine considers it the gravest injustice to exclude the poor from the economy of the "whole," from the solidarity that comes through the exchange of goods.

The wealth of the church, according to Julianus Pomerius, a refugee from Africa to Gaul in the first decade of the sixth century and a loyal disciple of Augustine—"was not like any other wealth." It was "bathed in a mystical aura all its own. It was wealth piled up through innumerable transactions with the supernatural, to which all sexes and all classes had contributed. Above all, it was wealth that was collected and administered on behalf of the poor."[184]

Roman Christians knew no division between the spheres of commerce and religion. The commercial metaphors that abound in the Christian literature of the late empire were animated by a transactional understanding of the divine economy: "Sins were seen as debts. And debts could be canceled overnight by the mercy of God. Gifts to the poor could be seen as loans to God. God would repay them with unimaginable interest."[185] For Augustine, almsgiving inevitably and properly accompanied the daily prayer for forgiveness. These practices were a daily, constant kind of commerce.[186] They were part of the "economy ordained by God," in French's words; to forgive and be forgiven was part of the same theological model as give, or do not expect to receive goods.[187] Indeed, Brown shows that the word *commercium* itself did not carry for late Roman Christians the "brash and calculating overtones" with which it is associated in our world. It "evoked any form of profitable bonding. It conjured up the idea of fruitful reciprocity." The foundational act of exchange, or "commerce," was in fact the incarnation of Christ.

The economy of almsgiving was, in other words, a continual exchange and movement of riches that bound the community together as one people. Wealth, which for classical Romans was a dead letter, a static sign of the unassailable stratification of society, was brought to life in the churches as its uses drew the poor—citizen and non-citizen alike—into the Christian community.[188] When in 396, the Christian senator Pammachius gave a lavish feast on the anniversary of the death of his wife and invited and fed the poor, he did not scatter alms "to a heaving sea of faceless beggars. Rather he had brought together in miniature the twin components of a stable civic order—a rich giver was brought face-to-face with an orderly and grateful *populus*." We know of Pammachius' banquet through the writings of the Christian benefactor Paulinus. In Brown's account, Paulinus' narrative foreshadowed the circumstances of a century later, when "the poor of the church protected by the pope" came into a position analogous to that of the classical *plebs Romana*. By comparing Pammachius' banquet with the games of Rome, Paulinus had made the sixth-century arrangement thinkable.[189] And the sixth-century arrangement, in turn, foreshadowed later political theologies—most especially, as we will see, that of John Calvin.

"The salvation of the commonwealth"

The emerging link of the dynamic interchange between the rich and the poor on the one hand to social solidarity on the other supplied a perspective on poor relief that resisted demarcation between voluntary "giving" and institutionalized "justice." Augustine saw no conflict between Christian charity and the welfare of the commonwealth. He wrote to Marcellinus:

> Wherefore, let those who say that the doctrine of Christ is incompatible with the State's well-being, give us an army composed of soldiers such as the doctrine of Christ requires them to be; let them give us such subjects, such husbands and wives, such parents and children, such masters and servants, such kings, such judges — in fine, even such taxpayers and tax-gatherers, as the Christian religion has taught that men should be, and then let them dare to say that it is adverse to the State's well-being; yea, rather, let them no longer hesitate to confess that this doctrine, if it were obeyed, would be the salvation of the commonwealth.[190]

More than that, Augustine refused any distinction between an individual response and an institutional response to the needs of the poor. They necessarily operated in concert. Augustine's economy of poor relief was not only itself an institutional response to poverty, it inspired further institutional responses.[191] Three factors explain the solidification of Augustine's thinking and experiments into structures of society in the century and a half after his death. First, the dynamics of exchange that emerged in Augustine's quest of solidarity inevitably called for structure. Second, the bishops' transformation of the way in which the poor were understood put pressure on the churches to engage in social reform. Third, the church gradually and of necessity assumed many of the state's traditional acts of generosity.

"Perfection of the political economy"

The non-Christian practice of poor relief lacked a clear focus. It was driven by what Peter Brown calls a "widespread" and "general ideal of humanity," but "the actions that sprang from that ideal were scattered erratically throughout society." Almsgiving in Jewish and Christian circles, on the other hand, responded to a thought-out combination of "generosity and humanity."[192] Almsgiving enacted a vision of society.

Almsgiving was more than the practice of justice for Augustine; it was motivated by God's command to love one's neighbor. Augustine's complaint against the philosophers was not that they highlighted the role of justice in society, which was indisputable, but that they believed people could rise to justice without love for one another.[193] In an interesting paradox, Augustine's deferral to the eschaton of true and complete justice and peace enhanced rather than diminished the stress he placed on partial fulfillment of those goals in the church. The "timeless eschatological hope for the perfection of the political economy is anticipated in the here and now."[194]

"The poor of Israel"

Ambrose's reimagining of the poor people of Milan had far-reaching effects. Thinking of themselves more and more as plaintiffs than as beggars as the fifth century proceeded, the poor brought with them into the Christian churches "a sharp sense of entitlement." The way the bishops thought of them, and the way the poor began to think of themselves, placed increasing pressure on Christian communities to engage in forms of social action that would have "wider effects than mere charity to the destitute." Bishops—as Ambrose was, in the 380s, probably the first to realize—would need to assume two roles: that of almsgiver and, more dramatically, that of *auxilium civibus.* Once they took on the second role, Brown writes, "the cities would soon be theirs." [195]

That was the model that endured. It survived the end of the empire. Once the "carefully graded social statuses that protected free Romans" collapsed, the social structure that remained was "the brutal binary model in which the rich faced the poor with no intermediary classes in between." That model, however, fit exactly the Old Testament model that Ambrose and his followers had conjured up two centuries earlier. The rich could no longer be thought of as simply the wealthy; they were the powerful—the *potentes*—and what, in the final analysis, they were expected to give the poor was not money but justice.[196]

Managerial bishops

The irony for the church in the years from 350 to 550 is that it passed during that time from relative mediocrity to great affluence while the empire descended from its "age of gold" to general impoverishment.[197] With wealth came power. The church's assumption of authority was a gradual process. Even at the time of the last emperor of Rome, the 470s, it was still the state that could, should it so choose, do the greatest good for the poor. The state controlled the great warehouses. In the society at large, Christians were still thought of as almsgivers, those who could, for instance, help the poor in times of famine.[198]

Nevertheless, the transition did occur. The difference of scale between the *annona* and Christian almsgiving probably narrowed during the course of the fifth century. The church became the safety net in cities like Rome as the amount of the *annona* diminished.[199] A new alliance was emerging, this time between the Christian clergy and the newly rich families from the lower nobility. This alliance fed the power of the bishop of Rome. It gave bishops like Damasas, as early as the 370s, the authority to consolidate his own power, "to be recognized as the sole representative of the Christian churches" in the city of Rome. After divisions arising from rival fundraising campaigns, Damasas ruled that if money was going to be given to Christian causes in Rome, it would have to be given directly to him in his capacity as bishop of Rome.[200]

Damasas' move was not merely a power grab. It was in some respects a necessity under Roman law. By an edict issued in 321, Constantine had permitted bequests to the church. Such a permission, and the first Christian emperor's encouragements to Christians to give to the poor, were vague in terms of Roman law. The actual recipient was unspecified. Attempts like Augustine's to defend the growing wealth of the church by arguing that the church was not a typical owner but rather "a non-owner" presiding over "the wealth of non-persons" were awkward at best under Roman law.[201] It was not until Justinian's legal reforms that Roman law finally settled on a solution. That solution, however, had been the favored interpretation all along: the recipient had to be the bishop.[202]

Leo I, bishop of Rome from 440 until his death in 461, instituted a collection for the poor—a *collecta*—in the mid-440s. Leo's desire was for the *collecta* to express solidarity; the poor should think of their contributions as equally important as those of the wealthy. Moreover, Leo and his successors "ensured that almsgiving was sacralized and centralized." The focus was less on the destitute and more on "the cohesion of the urban community as a whole." Leo's projects, including the *collecta*, required "an unparalleled flexing of papal muscle."[203]

However, in response to the tendency of the bishops, aided by Roman law, to keep the wealth and income of the church for themselves, Pope Simplicius felt compelled to issue a ruling in 475 setting forth a fourfold division of the revenues of the church. The revenues were to be divided equally among bishop, clergy, church upkeep, and the poor.[204] Thus, the centralized and systematic redistribution of resources passed from the state to the church. By the time of Gregory I, bishop of Rome from 590 to his death in 604, the "great works" of the *annona* and the "small works" of Christian charity had merged.[205] Brown notes that this did not happen because the popes deliberately took control of the *annona* system, or what remained of it, but that the relief the popes offered happened to converge on what the people of Rome had come to expect. There was, of course, one important difference: now "the poor" and not just "the *plebs*" were considered privileged.[206]

By this time, the church was the only great landowner left in Italy. Justinian's wars of attempted reconquest, from 535 to 554, eliminated what was left of the riches of the Roman aristocracy. If individual wealth was to be had in the former lands of the empire thereafter, it would have to come through some sort of alliance with the church. It was, in fact, by "by sharing in the managerial skills" of the bishops that the large landowners of the Frankish kingdoms emerged in the seventh century as "the first truly medieval nobilities of Europe."[207]

Even taxation, at long last, fell partly under the bishops' management, though of a more local variety. In 558 or 559, Pope Pelagius I recommended that the bishop of Narni in central Italy should resign because "the gentleness which goes with such inborn simplicity as his cannot govern the patrimony of the church. He cannot stand up to the city councilors in matters of taxation."[208]

The role of providence

At the heart of the conflict between the two competing solutions to the problem of wealth among late Roman Christians—renunciation and use—lay a theological disagreement that was nothing short of an aspect of the Pelagian controversy.

Todd French provides an admirable summary of the subtle but important theological shift from Ambrose to Augustine as they grappled with the question of wealth and poverty. For Ambrose, helping the poor was a relatively straightforward transaction between the wealthy person and God; Ambrose saw the poor "as God's mediating body for salvation through physical exchange." As we have seen, Ambrose's understanding informed Augustine's treatment of the question, but Augustine also saw the poor "as God's mediating example of theological truths at work in society." Augustine, deeply concerned as always with "the question of how God's will was being worked out in the world," concluded that the poor must play a specific role in society. After all, Christians were told that the poor would always be with them. "If God wanted a person or community poor, it was certainly for a reason, and to meddle with this was tantamount to mistrusting God's will."[209] There were spiritual lessons to be learned; God could instruct the people through the interplay of wealth and poverty.

Wealth became in one sense unproblematic in the Augustinian view. Its origins were "opaque." Wealth, like everything else, resulted from "the hidden providence of God." All that mattered to the Christian was how to respond to wealth, that is, how wealth (and every other divine gift) should be used.[210]

The Pelagian author of *De divitiis* could not have disagreed more. There was no such thing as guiltless wealth for that writer. Riches, even if inherited from a remote past, could not have been acquired without at least some injustice and were, therefore, tainted in the hands of those currently holding them. God's providence played no role in the accumulation of great wealth, and God certainly did not give it to some so that they could give it back to God in some sort of salvific exchange mediated by the poor.[211]

The competing points of view persisted through the fifth and sixth centuries. John Cassian (c. 360–c. 435) refused to allow "the infection of a single coin" to adhere to a monk entering his monastery on the Iles d'Hyères in Gaul. He saw no mystery in the origins of wealth. He denounced social inequality as the result of "occupying" things that had been granted to all in common. However, renunciation "was for experts only." What mattered to Cassian "was that no trace of such inequality should linger in the sterile environment of his monastery."[212]

To Prosper of Aquitaine (390–455), this Pelagian outlook contained a paradox. If Christians believed that they had come to God of their own free will, it would be a small step for them to think, and persuade others to think, that they had brought with them "culture, class, and ascetic know-how" achieved through their own, superior free wills as well. The church might well become ruled by a small, elite class of self-righteous and self-proclaimed saints. Prosper attacked Cassian around 430, using strongly Augustinian language. Cassian, he argued, had assumed that free will was an abstract, sociologically neutral concept, whereas in reality it "could act as a shorthand for the possession of social and cultural advantages." Prosper insisted on the "utter leveling of all wills before God."[213] Cassian, to Prosper's way of thinking, had imposed complete social equality in his monastery, but at the risk of constructing a hierarchy of wills.

Leo I, of *collecta* fame, also took Augustine's side. He preached that wealth was simply "a providential fact of life . . . to be accepted on a 'No questions asked' basis."[214] Brown argues that in echoing Augustine more than Ambrose, Leo was able to subtly shift the Christian use of wealth away from a single-minded focus on the poor. He used the wealth of the church "to steady the city of Rome as a whole."[215] Thanks to Augustine's placement of the origins of wealth in the mysterious providence of God, Augustinians like Leo were relieved of the urgency of giving wealth exclusively to the poor in order to remove the taint from the riches they held. Wealth could now be distributed and redistributed with the whole of society in mind.

R. J. Hernández-Díaz demonstrates that *order* is "part of God's providential work in the world." That order, though temporary, expresses itself through hierarchy, that is, the order in which parents govern their children and nations govern their citizens. "Augustine makes the case," he writes, "that Christians are part of this hierarchical order, rendering service and paying taxes to the earthly kingdoms."[216] Augustine was not intent on eliminating social inequality in the world. That order would be leveled in the eschaton.

Augustine wrote:

> Consider the virtue of justice. The function of justice is to assign to each his due; and hence there is established in man himself a certain just order of nature, by which the soul is subordinated to God, and the body to the soul, and thus both body and soul are subordinated to God. Does not justice demonstrate, in performing this function, that she is still labouring at her task rather than resting after reaching its completion? For, we may be sure, the less the soul has God in mind in all its thinking, the less it is subordinated to God; and the more the desires of the flesh oppose the spirit, the less subordinate is the body to the soul.[217]

In the same way, the earthly city—"a household of human beings"—"limits the harmonious agreement of citizens concerning the giving and obeying of orders to the establishment of a kind of compromise between human wills about the things relevant to mortal life."[218]

The providential order that Augustine was at pains to elucidate in Book XIX of the *City of God* was no static hierarchy. Even in the in-between times, the virtue of justice labors to subordinate all things at the individual, household, and "large household" level to God in the correct order. The picture is one of household administration or management, a ceaseless activity of justice that moves all creatures and things around as order gradually emerges but never, in this age, completes its ceaseless striving.

Economic theology

Political theology, according to philosopher Giorgio Agamben, "founds the transcendence of sovereign power on the single God," while *economic theology* replaces that transcendence with "an immanent ordering" that is "domestic" rather than "political." In the distinction between the *oikia* and the *polis* in Aristotle's *Politics*, according to Agamben, economic relations consisted of "activity that is not bound to a system of rules" and thus is not "a science in the proper sense." They were, instead, decisions that responded to specific problems arising in the functioning of the *oikos*.[219] As the semantic sphere of the term *oikonomia* became defined by the "administrative paradigm," it extended analogically beyond the *oikos*.[220] It came to mean "providing for the needs of life" or "nourishing," as in Matthew 6:26 ("your heavenly Father feeds them").[221] There is, Agamben argues, no truly theological sense of the term *oikonomia*; its denotation, however, was displaced into the theological field and there acquired a new meaning,[222] that of *dispositio*, *dispensatio*, or "divine activity of administration and government."[223]

Agamben's goal in *The Kingdom and the Glory* is to uncover the theological processes by which power in the West "assumed the form of an *oikonomia*," i.e., a government of people,[224] instead of a "political" form characterized by sovereignty. The economic paradigm is currently dominant, as evident in the supremacy of "economy and government" over all other aspects of social life.[225] The consequence of the economic paradigm's triumph over the political paradigm is that Western history has turned out to be an "administrative" or "governmental" problem.[226]

Central to Agamben's account is the role that *oikonomia* played in articulating the Trinitarian problem before "an appropriate philosophical vocabulary" developed in the fourth and fifth centuries. The Trinity was first described in economic rather than "metaphysico-theological" terms.[227] In its Trinitarian function, the term *oikonomia* took on a connotation of mystery. Economy "is now the activity—as such truly mysterious—that articulates the divine being into a trinity and, at the same time, preserves and 'harmonizes' it into a unity."[228] The Fathers used the doctrine of the *oikonomia* to avoid fracturing monotheism in a way that would have reintroduced polytheism. Hippolytus carefully distinguished between *dynamis*, according to which God is one, and the divine economy, according to which God is triple. Tertullian, meanwhile, insisted "that the mere 'disposition' of the economy does not at all mean the separation of the substance."[229] Nicholas Heron encapsulates Agamben's thesis: the early Church Fathers articulated "together in a single, undivided paradigm the *deus otiosus* of Aristotle and the Epicureans with the *deus actuosus* of Plato and the Stoics" and, thus, coordinated "the unity of divine substance with the threefold procession of divine figures" in "the curious form of an *oikonomia*."[230]

The price for avoiding a caesura at the level of being, Agamben argues, was a fracture between God and God's action, "between ontology and praxis," or between God and God's "government of the world."[231] As employed by Tertullian against Praxeas' "Monarchian" objections to the doctrine of the Trinity, *oikonomia* became thoroughly "administrative-managerial or pragmatic-theoretical," with the result that the Trinity came to articulate the *praxis* rather than the being of God.[232] In more modern terms, ontology and theology correspond to the immanent Trinity and praxis and *oikonomia* correspond to the economic Trinity.[233]

Thus, the distinction between *theologia* and *oikonomia* is fundamentally that between the *being* of God and the *activity* of God.[234] Agamben, using an image that was important to both Schmitt and Peterson, summarizes the theological God, or "divine monarchy," in the phrase "Le roi règne, mais il ne gouverne pas" ("the king reigns, but he does not govern").[235]

In contrast, Agamben writes, it is because of the Christian introduction of the distinction between theology and economy that Western ethics became preoccupied with a "court of insoluble aporias" and sought to heal the suture between the two. Christian theology especially found itself in the difficult position of having to balance transcendence and immanence, to avoid the pitfalls of Gnosis and pantheism, respectively.[236] Agamben considers Augustine's reflections in *The Literal Meaning of Genesis* on the paradoxical relation between God and order the most radical articulation of the tension. There, Augustine argued that the order by which God created things cannot be a created thing itself. Measure, number, and weight, for instance, are outside of things and, thus, are in God or at least coincide with God. God, therefore, is, in God's own being, order. But in an absolute sense God *cannot* be measure, number, and weight. God "is order only in the sense of an *ordering* and *arranging*, that is, not in the sense of a substance, but in that of an activity."[237] Augustine concluded that the *dispositio* (*oikonomia*) of things is nothing other than the *dispositio* of things in God. Agamben writes, significantly:

> Immanent and transcendent order once again refer back to each other in a paradoxical coincidence, which can nevertheless be understood only as a perpetual *oikonomia*, as a continuous activity of government of the world, one that implies a fracture between being and praxis and, at the same time, tries to heal it.[238]

In Agamben's reading of Salvian, "Providence is the name of the '*oikonomia*,' insofar as the latter presents itself as the government of the world."[239] In a presentation vaguely reminiscent of the image of the Roman emperor determining, in untouchable isolation, the tax at the beginning of each year and then delegating its collection, Boethius (c. 477–524) described providence and fate as two separate powers that are hierarchically coordinated in that fate is subject to providence; "a sovereign decision determines the general principles of the organization of the cosmos, and then entrusts its administration and execution to a subordinate, yet autonomous power."[240]

Heron, following Peterson, believes that the "divine monarchy" model of political theology, developed by Philo and closely linked to Carl Schmitt, "was brought to an abrupt and definitive end" when it encountered two obstacles: the fact that the triune God had no analogue in the world, and Augustine's "eschatology of deferral."[241] Once the one true *polis* had been shifted out of this world (most decisively by Augustine), "the *saeculum* itself [had to] be conceived only in economic terms" and the public realm was transformed "into an integrally economic space, which reaches its apex with the emergence and triumph of the sphere of civil society in modernity."[242] Glory is the figure that can reconcile the political and the economic, but it must wait to do so.[243] It was, for instance, only when Augustine reached the complete inoperativity of Sabbath rest—"the full glory of the Sabbath, where nothing is in excess and nothing is lacking"—that he felt he could conclude *The City of God* (XXII, 30).[244]

What is in fact "political" may appear in the sphere of civil society to be economic. Classicist and tax scholar Maureen B. Cavanaugh has shown, for example, that Athens' progressive tax system during that city's experiment with democracy, from about 508 BC until Alexander conquered Greece in 323 BC, was not designed to redistribute wealth. Cavanaugh argues "that democratic political development in Athens corresponded with a decision to shift the burden of taxation onto the wealthy, thereby incorporating uneducated peasant-citizens into the political community as full members."[245] This move, she argues, was a strictly political one, designed not to initiate but to forestall a movement toward greater economic equality:

> With the adoption of democracy, which ensured political equality but allocated the tax burden to the wealthy, there was no need to redistribute wealth to achieve an economic equality commensurate with political equality. The inviolability of private property, attested in the Athenian constitution, was reaffirmed each year when the chief magistrate proclaimed that whatever a person possessed before the start of the year, he would possess at the end.[246]

In that proclamation, the chief magistrate would declare the unchanging and regnant quality of private property. Property would "reign" but not govern. The democratic Athenian tax system, for all of its progressivity, was not designed to "cope with problems that are each time specific"; it cannot be called "an administrative activity that is bound only to the rules of the ordered functioning of the house."[247]

The *annona* of Rome likewise had nothing to do with poor relief, as Peter Brown has shown. It rearranged nothing. It was, in fact, not an activity of any kind. It was a proclamation of social position: these are the people of Rome, the citizens, who possess the *status* of freedom from hunger. In that sense, it was political rather than economic.

Renunciation of wealth, as practiced by Jerome and Cassian, had a "political" flavor to it. One either possessed wealth or was divested of it. Poverty was absolute, in the way that Philo's monotheism was. It admitted no nuance, or, if it did, it ceased to be poverty and became wealth just as monotheism would cease to be monotheism and become polytheism. As we have seen, Christian renunciation among more Pelagian monks was at risk of partaking of the very Roman sense of natural and timeless nobility.

We have had occasion to observe the highly *political* character of taxation in the late Roman Empire. If it responded to changing circumstances, those circumstances were the state's need for revenue as decreed by the sovereign determination of the emperor. The emperor did not concern himself with the mechanics of collection, burdens on the farmers, or tortures imposed by *curiales* lest they be tortured themselves. The emperor's power contrasted sharply with the "pastoral" power, to use Michel Foucault's term, of the fourth-, fifth-, and sixth-century Christian bishops. That power was "directed to all and each"; it was wide-ranging, but it was also "specific." "The bishop," Brown writes, "was supposed to love the members of his flock. He loved each one of them equally. And he loved them all—up to the very edge of the human community."[248] Foucault, as Agamben emphasizes, recognized in "pastoral" power a governmental technique that simultaneously totalizes and individualizes government in the modern state. Pastoral power coordinates the *omnes* and the *singulatim* in the same way that Christian theology came to coordinate the "bipolar machine" of special and general providence.[249]

Not yet at the end of the Roman Empire, but eventually, taxation would become an instrument of the civil social sphere that could coordinate the "Kingdom" and the "Government," in Agamben's lexicon. It would reveal itself as a mechanism for healing the suture between the demands of the state and the needs of the people and, thus, harmonizing the political and the economic. The goal of this chapter has not been to show that the "economic" bent in Christian theology transformed the institution of taxation in fourth-, fifth-, and sixth-century Roman society. It has been to suggest that the model of the *oikonomia* influenced the way Christians in that time and place came to reimagine wealth, poverty, and the shape of society. This chapter has sought to evoke an ethos in which social and political institutions began to take on new tones and flavors. For personal understandings to evolve into systematized commitments, society's institutions often must steep in the ethos of those understandings for centuries.

Notes

1 Aurelio Bernardi, "The Economic Problems of the Roman Empire," in *The Economic Decline of Empires*, ed. Carlo M. Cipolla (London: Methuen & Co., Ltd., 1970), 54.

2 Peter Brown, *Through the Eye of a Needle: Wealth, the Fall of Rome, and the Making of Christianity in the West, 350–550 AD* (Princeton: Princeton University Press, 2012), 13; Peter Brown, *Power and Persuasion in Late Antiquity: Towards a Christian Empire* (Madison: The University of Wisconsin Press, 1992), 25–26.
3 N. J. G. Pounds, *An Economic History of Medieval Europe*, 2nd ed. (London: Longman, 1994), 34–35.
4 Pounds, *An Economic History*, 35.
5 Pounds, *An Economic History*, 35.
6 See Pounds, *An Economic History*, 24–26.
7 Charles Norris Cochrane, *Christianity and Classical Culture: A Study of Thought and Action from Augustus to Augustine* (New York: Oxford University Press, 1957), 181.
8 Cochrane, *Christianity and Classical Culture*, 175.
9 Cochrane, *Christianity and Classical Culture*, 175.
10 Cochrane, *Christianity and Classical Culture*, 175.
11 See, e.g., Pounds, *Economic History*, 3233. The empire's territorial expansion ended in AD 106 with Trajan's conquest of Dacia. Thereafter, "the windfall profits of new conquests ceased to replenish the treasury and stimulate the economy."
12 J. M. Kelly, *A Short History of Western Legal Theory* (Oxford: Clarendon Press, 1992), 91–92. Ulpian wrote, "princeps legibus solutus est" ("the emperor is not bound by statutes"). Justinian, *The Digest of Justinian*, ed. Alan Watson (Philadelphia: University of Pennsylvania Press, 1998) 1.3.31.
13 Cochrane, *Christianity and Classical Culture*, 151.
14 Brown, *Power and Persuasion*, 25–26.
15 Brown, *Through the Eye of a Needle*, 5, 24.
16 Brown, *Through the Eye of a Needle*, 24.
17 Brown, *Power and Persuasion*, 17.
18 Brown, *Through the Eye of a Needle*, 11.
19 Brown, *Through the Eye of a Needle*, 389, quoting Chris Wickham, *Framing the Early Middle Ages: Europe and the Mediterranean, 400–800* (Oxford: Oxford University Press, 2005), 711.
20 Brown, *Through the Eye of a Needle*, 389.
21 Chris Wickham, *Medieval Europe: From the Breakup of the Western Roman Empire to the Reformation* (New Haven: Yale University Press, 2016), 25.
22 Brown, *Power and Persuasion*, 134.
23 Brown, *Power and Persuasion*, 146.
24 Brown, *Through the Eye of a Needle*, 4–5, quoting P. F. Bang, "Trade and Empire: In Search of Organizing Concepts for the Roman Empire," *Past and Present* 195 (2007): 13.
25 Bernardi, "The Economic Problems of the Roman Empire," 60–61.
26 David S. Potter, *The Roman Empire at Bay, AD 180–395*, Routledge History of the Ancient World (New York: Routledge, 2004), 59–60.
27 Brown, *Through the Eye of a Needle*, 13; Brown, Power and Persuasion, 26.
28 Potter, *The Roman Empire at Bay*, 57–59.
29 Potter, *The Roman Empire at Bay*, 59; Bernardi, "The Economic Problems of the Roman Empire," *Economic Decline*, 54.
30 Carlo M. Cipolla, introduction to Cipolla, *The Economic Decline of Emperors*, 14; Bernardi, "The Economic Problems of the Roman Empire," 81.
31 Brown, *Through the Eye of a Needle*, 298.
32 Brown, *Power and Persuasion*, 26.
33 Brown, *Through the Eye of a Needle*, 393.
34 Brown, *Through the Eye of a Needle*, 187, 389–90.
35 Brown, *Through the Eye of a Needle*, 400.
36 Brown, *Through the Eye of a Needle*, 395.

37 Brown, *Through the Eye of a Needle*, 27, 400–04.
38 Brown, *Through the Eye of a Needle*, 146.
39 Brown, *Through the Eye of a Needle*, 145.
40 Brown, *Through the Eye of a Needle*, 327.
41 Brown, *Through the Eye of a Needle*, 33.
42 Brown, *Through the Eye of a Needle*, 346.
43 Brown, *Through the Eye of a Needle*, 380–81.
44 Brown, *Through the Eye of a Needle*, 381.
45 Brown, *Through the Eye of a Needle*, 382–84; Brown, *Power and Persuasion*, 147–48.
46 Brown, *Through the Eye of a Needle*, 377.
47 Brown, *Through the Eye of a Needle*, 36.
48 See, e.g., Robert M. Grant, *Augustus to Constantine: The Thrust of the Christian Movement into the Roman World* (London: Collins, 1971), 205.
49 Lactantius, *De mortibus persecutorum*, ed. and trans. J. L. Creed (Oxford: Clarendon Press, 1984) 7.5.
50 J. L. Creed, commentary on *De mortibus persecutorum*, by Lactantius (Oxford: Clarendon Press, 1984), 90n1. Creed reports that, "[a]lthough modern writers refer to [the emperor Maximian Galerius] as Galerius, Lact. always refers to him as Maximian . . . . He is Lact.'s principal villain, seen as the instigator of the persecution and also as an uneducated barbarian, an enemy both to Rome and to culture . . . ."
51 Lactantius, *De mortibus persecutorum* 7.1.
52 Lactantius, *De mortibus persecutorum* 7.8.
53 Lactantius, *De mortibus persecutorum* 7.9.
54 Lactantius, *De mortibus persecutorum* 7.10.
55 Lactantius, *De mortibus persecutorum* 7.5.
56 Lactantius, *Divine Institutes*, trans. Anthony Bowen and Peter Garnsey, Translated Texts for Historians 40 (Liverpool: Liverpool University Press, 2003) 6.18.30.
57 Lactantius, *Divine Institutes* 6.18.30. See also Bowen and Garnsey, introduction to *Divine Institutes*, by Lactantius (Liverpool: Liverpool University Press, 2003), 28–29.
58 See, e.g., Eusebius, "A Speech for the Thirtieth Anniversary of Constantine's Accession," in *From Irenaeus to Grotius: A Sourcebook in Christian Political Thought, 100-1625*, ed. Oliver O'Donovan and Joan Lockwood O'Donovan (Grand Rapids: William B. Eerdmans Publishing Co., 1999), 62:

> And in this hope our divinely favoured emperor partakes even in this present life, gifted as he is by God with native virtues and having received into his soul the outflowings of his favour. His reason he derives from the great source of all reason, he is wise, and good, and just as having fellowship with perfect wisdom, goodness and righteousness, virtuous as following the pattern of perfect virtue, valiant as partaking of heavenly strength. And truly may he deserve the imperial title who has formed his soul to royal virtues according to the standard of that celestial kingdom.

59 Lactantius, *De mortibus persecutorum* 4.
60 Lactantius, *Divine Institutes* 5.5.7.
61 Lactantius, *Divine Institutes* 6.6.19.
62 Timothy D. Barnes, *Constantine and Eusebius* (Cambridge, MA: Harvard University Press, 1981), 50.
63 Cochrane, *Christianity and Classical Culture*, 202–03.
64 Constantius exempted the clergy and their slaves from all new and special levies, permitted them to conduct business enterprises "for purposes of subsistence"

free from the *collatio lustralis*, a business tax that Constantine had imposed, and eventually exempted the clergy from the *collatio lustralis* on profits from shelters and workhouses. Cochrane, *Christianity and Classical Culture*, 256.

65 Barnes, *Constantine and Eusebius*, 258.
66 Cochrane, *Christianity and Classical Culture*, 202.
67 Cochrane, *Christianity and Classical Culture*, 203.
68 Cochrane, *Christianity and Classical Culture*, 209.
69 Cipolla, *The Economic Decline of Empires*, 56.
70 Brown, *Through the Eye of a Needle*, 433.
71 Salvian, "The Governance of God," in *The Writings of Salvian, the Presbyter*, trans. Jeremiah F. O'Sullivan (Washington: Catholic University of America, 1947) 5.4.
72 Salvian, "The Governance of God" 5.4.
73 See Jeremiah F. O'Sullivan, notes to *The Writings of Salvian, the Presbyter*, 136n14.
74 Salvian, "The Governance of God" 6.
75 Salvian, "The Governance of God" 7.
76 See O'Sullivan, notes to *The Writings of Salvian*, 136n14; Brown, *Through the Eye of a Needle*, 449.
77 O'Sullivan, notes to *The Writings of Salvian*, 142n16. Matters apparently did not improve for the poor after the final collapse of the empire in the West. Echoing Salvian, Pope Gregory wrote around the year 600 that the island of Corsica was so heavily burdened with "exactions" that the inhabitants could barely pay what was demanded of them even by selling their children. As a result, the inhabitants were fleeing "to that most cruel nation, the Lombards." What, Gregory asked rhetorically, could the inhabitants suffer from the Lombards that could be worse than—or even as bad as—having to sell their children? Gregory I, "Pope Gregory's Letter Concerning Conditions in the Islands," in *A Source Book for Medieval Economic History*, by Roy C. Cave and Herbert H. Coulson (New York: Biblo and Tannen, 1965), 357.
78 See Bernardi, "The Economic Problems of the Roman Empire," 58–59.
79 Brown, *Through the Eye of a Needle*, 447.
80 See, e.g., Augustine, Letter 153 (to Macedonius) 25, in O'Donovan and O'Donovan, 130.
81 Brown, *Through the Eye of a Needle*, 447.
82 Salvian, "The Governance of God" 4.3.30, quoted in Brown, *Through the Eye of a Needle*, 448.
83 Brown, *Through the Eye of a Needle*, 450.
84 Brown, *Through the Eye of a Needle*, 447.
85 Brown, *Through the Eye of a Needle*, 449.
86 Brown, *Through the Eye of a Needle*, 444–45.
87 Brown, *Through the Eye of a Needle*, 444–45.
88 Brown, *Through the Eye of a Needle*, 442.
89 Cochrane, *Christianity and Classical Culture*, 49.
90 See, e.g., Samuel Fleischacker, *A Short History of Distributive Justice* (Cambridge, MA: Harvard University Press, 2004), 20–22.
91 Cicero, *On Obligations*, trans. P. G. Walsh (Oxford: Oxford University Press, 2000) 2.74.
92 Cicero, *On Obligations* 2.74.
93 Cicero, *On Obligations* 2.73.
94 Cicero, *On Obligations* 2.73. This version of social-contract theory leads Charles Norris Cochrane to remark that "[i]t was indeed Cicero, rather than Locke, who first asserted that the purpose of organized society was to establish and main-

tain [the rights of property]." Cochrane, *Christianity and Classical Culture*, 45. See also Diana Wood, *Medieval Economic Thought*, Cambridge Medieval Textbooks (Cambridge: Cambridge University Press, 2002), 37 ("Cicero had seen the whole purpose and origin of cities and commonwealths as the safe-guarding of private property"). The protection of property interests dominated Cicero's political thinking to the point of excluding other governmental functions from his political philosophy. Political theorist Walter Nicgorski, while arguing that Cicero's "ultimate standard" for the political community was the common good, nevertheless acknowledges that "Cicero's fears of specific forms of government-taking of a property may have kept him from developing further a potential role of the political community in economic reform and regulation." Walter Nicgorski, *Cicero's Skepticism and His Recovery of Political Philosophy*, Recovering Political Philosophy (New York: Palgrave Macmillan, 2016), 184.

95 Cicero, *On Obligations* 2.74.

96 Cicero, *On Obligations* 2.83.

97 Henry C. Simons, *Personal Income Taxation: The Definition of Income as a Problem of Fiscal Policy* (Chicago: The University of Chicago Press, 1938), 18 ("Taxation must affect the distribution of income, whether we will it so or not").

98 Cochrane, *Christianity and Classical Culture*, 141.

99 Cochrane, *Christianity and Classical Culture*, 139.

100 Cipolla, *The Economic Decline of Empires*, 3.

101 Cipolla, *The Economic Decline of Empires*, 3.

102 Brown, *Through the Eye of a Needle*, 42–49.

103 Brown, *Through the Eye of a Needle*, 49, quoting John Bodel, "From *Columbaria* to Catacombs: Collective Burial in Pagan and Christian Rome," in *Commemorating the Dead: Texts and Artifacts in Context, Studies of Roman, Jewish, and Christian Burials*, ed. Laurie Brink and Deborah Green (Berlin: de Gruyter, 2008), 222.

104 Brown, *Through the Eye of a Needle*, 43, quoting *The Letters of St. Cyprian of Carthage*, ed. and trans. G. W. Clarke, Ancient Christian Writers 43 (New York: Newman Press, 1984) 1:165.

105 Brown, *Power and Persuasion*, 77–78.

106 Brown, *Through the Eye of a Needle*, 53.

107 Brown, *Through the Eye of a Needle*, 62.

108 Brown, *Through the Eye of a Needle*, 62.

109 Brown, *Through the Eye of a Needle*, 53.

110 Brown, *Through the Eye of a Needle*, 136–38.

111 Brown, *Through the Eye of a Needle*, 76–77.

112 Brown, *Through the Eye of a Needle*, 79.

113 Brown, *Through the Eye of a Needle*, 111.

114 Brown, *Through the Eye of a Needle*, 111.

115 Brown, *Through the Eye of a Needle*, 68.

116 Brown, *Through the Eye of a Needle*, 70.

117 Brown, *Through the Eye of a Needle*, 133.

118 Brown, *Through the Eye of a Needle*, 129–30.

119 Brown, *Through the Eye of a Needle*, 143–44.

120 Ambrose, *De officiis*, ed. and trans. Ivor J. Davidson (Oxford: Oxford University Press, 2001) 1.28.136, quoted in Brown, *Through the Eye of a Needle*, 128.

121 Brown, *Through the Eye of a Needle*, 122, 126.

122 Brown, *Through the Eye of a Needle*, 44.

123 Jennifer Hole, *Economic Ethics in Late Medieval England, 1300-1550*, Archival Insights into the Evolution of Economics, ed. Robert Leeson (Basingstoke: Palgrave Macmillan, 2016), 19.

124 Brown, *Through the Eye of a Needle*, 131. See Ambrose, *De officiis* 1.28.132.

125 Todd E. French, "Altruism or Holy Economy: Ambrose and Augustine's Care for the Poor," in *Augustine and Social Justice*, ed. Teresa Delgado, John Doody, and Kim Paffenroth (Lanham, MD: Lexington Books, 2015), 53.

126 Brown, *Through the Eye of a Needle*, 266.

127 Brown, *Through the Eye of a Needle*, 277–79.

128 Brown, *Through the Eye of a Needle*, 214–15.

129 See Brown, *Through the Eye of a Needle*, 79.

130 Jennifer A. Herdt, "Eudaimonism and Dispossession: Augustine on Almsgiving," in Delgado, Doody, and Paffenroth, 102.

131 Brown, *Through the Eye of a Needle*, 378.

132 French, "Altruism or Holy Economy," 56–57.

133 French, "Altruism or Holy Economy," 54.

134 Brown, *Through the Eye of a Needle*, 175.

135 French, "Altruism or Holy Economy," 54.

136 Brown, *Through the Eye of a Needle*, 306.

137 Brown, *Through the Eye of a Needle*, 314–16.

138 Brown, *Through the Eye of a Needle*, xx.

139 Kelly, *A Short History of Western Legal Theory* (Oxford: Clarendon Press, 1992), 107.

140 Lactantius, *Divine Institutes* 5.15.4.

141 Lactantius, *Divine Institutes* 5.5.7, 8. The turn among Christian writers toward prizing property for its *use* was apparent as early as the second century. The *First Apology* of Justin Martyr (100–165), for instance, reveals a theological shift from human participation in meeting the needs of the gods by consuming created things by fire (paganism) to human participation in God's work of meeting the needs of other humans (Christianity): "We have been taught that the only honor that is worthy of Him is not to consume by fire the things He has brought into being for our sustenance, but contribute them for ourselves and those in need." Justin Martyr, "The First Apology," in *St. Justin Martyr: The First and Second Apologies*, trans. Leslie William Barnard, Ancient Christian Writers: The Works of the Fathers in Translation, ed. Walter J. Burghardt, John J. Dillon, and Dennis D. McManus, vol. 56 (New York: Paulist Press, 1997) 13. Leslie William Barnard suggests that the contribution to those in need here is "an allusion to the Eucharistic distribution to the poor." Barnard, notes to *Justin Martyr: The First and Second Apologies*, 115n174. The emphasis on the use that Christians made of property came into sharper focus by the fourth century. Hilary of Poitiers (310–368), in his Commentary on Matthew, wrote that possessing riches was not wrongful in itself, but "the manner in which possession is used" might be wrong. Hilary of Poitiers, *Commentary on Matthew* (on Mt. 19), quoted in George O'Brien, *An Essay on Mediaeval Economic Teaching* (London: Longmans, Green, and Co., 1920), 36.

142 Ambrose, "The Story of Naboth" 36, in O'Donovan and O'Donovan, 77. See also Cochrane, *Christianity and Classical Culture*, 348 ("Thus [according to Ambrose], 'nature', as such, affords no warrant for the existence of private property, the genesis of which is attributed to the growth of social convention, while its maintenance as an institution depends on the use to which it is put").

143 Ambrose, "The Story of Naboth" 53, in O'Donovan and O'Donovan, 78.

144 Augustine, *Concerning the City of God Against the Pagans*, ed. David Knowles, trans. Henry Bettenson (Harmondsworth, UK: Penguin Books, 1972) 15.7.

145 Augustine, *City of God* 15.7. Eight centuries later, the medieval mind would still connect the right to private property to the use made of it. Even an early apologist of wealth-creation like Berthold von Regensburg (1220–1272) would find

himself unable to "recognize full and absolute right of ownership." According to Berthold, "God entrusts goods in accordance with the person of the owner and his allotted task and time on this earth. That person is the sole administrator of his wealth, and he must answer for its use." Aron Gurevich, "The Merchant," in *The Medieval World*, ed. Jacques Le Goff, trans. Lydia G. Cochrane (London: Parkgate Books, Ltd., 1990), 256.
146 Justinian, *The Digest of Justinian* 1.1.10.
147 Stephan Kuttner, "A Forgotten Definition of Justice," in *The History of Ideas and Doctrines of Canon Law in the Middle Ages* (London: Variorum Reprints, 1980), 75–76. The jurist Bulgarus (1085–1166) noted that Ulpian had narrowed the terminology from *suum* or *dignitas sua* in the non-legal texts to *ius* in the legal texts, thus making "the aim of justice identical with the aim of law." Bulgarus took the broader definition to refer to "all that is deserved (*meritum*), all that is due (*debitum*) to God, to self, and to neighbor." Kuttner, "A Forgotten Definition of Justice," 77.
148 Kuttner, "A Forgotten Definition of Justice," 81.
149 Kuttner, "A Forgotten Definition of Justice," 80.
150 Kuttner, "A Forgotten Definition of Justice," 107, referring to Lactantius, *Divine Institutes* 5.14.12.
151 Kuttner, "A Forgotten Definition of Justice," 91–92. The quotation is from Augustine's *De moribus ecclesiae et de moribus Manichaeorum* 1.15.125.
152 Thomas Aquinas, *Summa theologiae* (Latin-English Edition), trans. Fathers of the English-Dominican Province (NovAntiqua, 2013), II–II, Q. 58, Art. 1, arg. 6. The *Summa Theologiae* is cited as *ST* hereafter.
153 *ST* II–II, Q. 58, Art. 1, ad. 6.
154 Kuttner, "A Forgotten Definition," 94.
155 Kuttner, "A Forgotten Definition," 95.
156 Kuttner, "A Forgotten Definition," 107–08.
157 See Carl Joachim Friedrich, *The Philosophy of Law in Historical Perspective*, 2nd ed. (Chicago: The University of Chicago Press, 1963), 35–42.
158 Kuttner, "A Forgotten Definition," 100, 108.
159 Ambrose, "The Story of Naboth" 53.
160 Augustine, Letter 153 (to Macedonius) 23.
161 O'Brien, *Essay on Mediaeval Economic Teaching*, 83
162 Augustine, Letter 153 (to Macedonius) 26.
163 Augustine, *Homilies on the Gospel of John*, trans. John Gibb, in the Christian Classics Ethereal Library, accessed May 26, 2020, http://www.ccel.org/ccel/schaff/npnf107.iii.vii.html 6.25.
164 Brown, *Through the Eye of a Needle*, 180.
165 Brown, *Through the Eye of a Needle*, 349.
166 Herdt, "Eudaimonism and Dispossession," 101. See also Brown, *Through the Eye of a Needle*, 79.
167 Augustine, "The Way of Life of the Catholic Church," in *The Catholic and Manichaean Ways of Life*, trans. Donald A. Gallagher and Idella J. Gallagher (Washington: The Catholic University of American Press, Inc., 1966), 59, quoted in French, "Altruism or Holy Economy," 62.
168 Augustine, *City of God* 4.3.
169 Augustine, *City of God* 4.3.
170 Augustine, *City of God* 4.3. Ambrose had sounded a similar theme. The issue of whether it is good to give something to the emperor—i.e., whether it bears Caesar's or God's image—turns on whether doing so would be good for the donor (Ambrose) and good for the recipient (the emperor): "In sum, I act out of concern for the emperor's welfare; for it would neither be good for me

to hand them over, nor for him to receive them." Ambrose, "Sermon Against Auxentius" 5, in O'Donovan and O'Donovan. Ambrose emphasized enslavement to acquisitiveness in his meditation on Naboth's vineyard as well: "How far can you take this mad acquisitiveness, you rich?" Ambrose, "The Story of Naboth" 2. Ambrose's concern for the donor's welfare is consistent with his idea that the rich were simply those who fail to "use" their money and property: "You are slaves, you rich men, and what a pitiful form of slavery it is, enslaved to delusion, to grasping desire, to insatiable greed!" Ambrose, "The Story of Naboth" 52.

171 Herdt, "Eudaimonism and Dispossession," 103.
172 Brown, *Through the Eye of a Needle*, 72–73.
173 Brown, *Through the Eye of a Needle*, 73–74.
174 Brown, *Through the Eye of a Needle*, 361.
175 Brown, *Through the Eye of a Needle*, xxv.
176 Ambrose, "The Story of Naboth," 36.
177 French, "Altruism or Holy Economy," 57.
178 French, "Altruism or Holy Economy," 61. Whether Augustine's understanding of the function of almsgiving rose to quite the crass level that it did for Ambrose and Chrysostom is a matter of some debate. According to Peter Brown, "Augustine spoke of almsgiving as something as impersonal as stock-broking—as a judicious transfer of capital from this unsafe world to the next." Peter Brown, *Augustine of Hippo* (Berkeley: University of California Press, 2000), 193. Boniface Ramsey offered a similar critique of Augustine's position. Boniface Ramsey, "Almsgiving in the Latin Church: The Late Fourth and Early Fifth Centuries," *Theological Studies* 34 (1982): 252. Jennifer Herdt's more nuanced reading is that we are always, in Augustine's view, called to love God because God is good, not because God is good for us. It is only in learning to love God in this way that we become able to love others for their own sakes, and part of loving them for their own sakes "involves seeing that there are claims that others or the needs of others make on us that we are bound to recognize, or blameworthy for not responding to or recognizing." Augustine, in other words, did not view giving to the poor primarily as a benefit to the giver. Though almsgiving was enjoined on all Christians, it was *not*, for Augustine, "a way of asserting one's own control over the economy of grace." Herdt, "Eudaimonism and Dispossession," 98–106.
179 French, "Altruism or Holy Economy," 58.
180 Brown, *Through the Eye of a Needle*, 419.
181 Brown, *Through the Eye of a Needle*, 59.
182 Augustine, *Exposition of Psalm 39:7*, ed. A. Cleveland Coxe, in the Christian Classics Ethereal Library, accessed May 27, 2020, https://ccel.org/ccel/schaff/npnf108/npnf108.ii.XXXIX.html.
183 French, "Altruism or Holy Economy," 64.
184 Brown, *Through the Eye of a Needle*, 485.
185 Brown, *Through the Eye of a Needle*, 85.
186 See Brown, *Through the Eye of a Needle*, 362–63.
187 French, "Altruism or Holy Economy," 64–65.
188 See Brown, *Through the Eye of a Needle*, 234.
189 Brown, *Through the Eye of a Needle*, 233–35.
190 Augustine, Letter 138 (to Marcellinus), in New Advent, accessed May 27, 2020, https://www.newadvent.org/fathers/1102138.htm.
191 See Herdt, "Eudaimonism and Dispossession," 110.
192 Brown, *Through the Eye of a Needle*, 62.
193 Mary T. Clark, "Augustine on Justice," in Delgado, Doody, and Paffenroth, 4, 8.

194 R. J. Hernández-Díaz, "Augustine and Political Economy," in Delgado, Doody, and Paffenroth, 120.
195 Brown, *Through the Eye of a Needle*, 81.
196 Brown, *Through the Eye of a Needle*, 508–09.
197 Brown, *Through the Eye of a Needle*, 529.
198 Brown, *Through the Eye of a Needle*, 462–63.
199 Brown, *Through the Eye of a Needle*, 462–63.
200 Brown, *Through the Eye of a Needle*, 280.
201 Brown, *Through the Eye of a Needle*, 483.
202 Brown, *Through the Eye of a Needle*, 486–87.
203 Brown, *Through the Eye of a Needle*, 465–68.
204 Brown, *Through the Eye of a Needle*, 488.
205 Brown, *Through the Eye of a Needle*, 468.
206 Brown, *Through the Eye of a Needle*, 468.
207 Brown, *Through the Eye of a Needle*, 499–500, quoting Jairus Banaji, "Aristocracies, Peasantries and the Framing of the Early Middle Ages," *Journal of Agrarian Change* 9 (2009): 65–71.
208 Brown, *Through the Eye of a Needle*, 497, quoting Pelagius I, Letter 16, ed. P. M. Grassó and C. M. Batlle, *Pelagii I papae: Epistulae quae supersunt (556–61)* (Montserrat: Abbey of Montserrat, 1956), 49–50.
209 French, "Altruism or Holy Economy," 65.
210 Brown, *Through the Eye of a Needle*, 377.
211 Brown, *Through the Eye of a Needle*, 314.
212 Brown, *Through the Eye of a Needle*, 414–18.
213 Brown, *Through the Eye of a Needle*, 418–28.
214 Brown, *Through the Eye of a Needle*, 465.
215 Brown, *Through the Eye of a Needle*, 465.
216 R. J. Hernández-Díaz, "Augustine and Political Economy," 122.
217 Augustine, *City of God* 19.3.
218 Augustine, *City of God* 19.17.
219 Giorgio Agamben, *The Kingdom and the Glory: For a Theological Genealogy of Economy and Government*, trans. Lorenzo Chiesa and Matteo Mandarini (Stanford: Stanford University Press, 2011), 17–18.
220 Agamben, *The Kingdom and the Glory*, 18.
221 Agamben, *The Kingdom and the Glory*, 19.
222 Agamben, *The Kingdom and the Glory*, 21. Agamben shares Carl Schmitt's assumption that theology remains present and active in modernity, albeit in the sense that "signatures" (as opposed to concepts and signs) move between the sacred and profane fields and, in so doing, displace concepts and signs from one field to another "without redefining them semantically." Agamben, *The Kingdom and the Glory*, 4. Agamben reminds us that even Schmitt's interlocutor Erik Peterson agreed that the "ultimate formulation of a metaphysical image of the world . . . is always determined by a political decision." Agamben, *The Kingdom and the Glory*, 70. It is not necessary, according to Agamben, that we share Schmitt's (in)famous secularization thesis "to affirm that political problems become more intelligible and clear if they are related to theological paradigms." Agamben, *The Kingdom and the Glory*, 229.
223 Agamben, *The Kingdom and the Glory*, 31, 37. This displacement happened very early in the Christian tradition, according to Agamben. The "lexicon of the Pauline *ekklēsia* is 'economic,' not political," with the consequence that Christians were the first "economic" and not "political" people. In fact, Agamben insists that Paul's use of the word *oikonomia* in Ephesians could not have had a truly theological meaning—such as "plan of salvation"—and must have meant nothing more

than the activity of realizing such a plan in time and in the world. Agamben, *The Kingdom and the Glory*, 24. See also Nicholas Heron, *Liturgical Power: Between Economic and Political Theology* (New York: Fordham University Press, 2018), 25.
224 Agamben, *The Kingdom and the Glory*, xi.
225 Agamben, *The Kingdom and the Glory*, 1.
226 Agamben, *The Kingdom and the Glory*, 3.
227 Agamben, *The Kingdom and the Glory*, 36.
228 Agamben, *The Kingdom and the Glory*, 39.
229 Agamben, *The Kingdom and the Glory*, 53.
230 Heron, *Liturgical Power*, 23.
231 Agamben, *The Kingdom and the Glory*, 53.
232 Agamben, *The Kingdom and the Glory*, 40–41.
233 Agamben, *The Kingdom and the Glory*, 207.
234 Agamben, *The Kingdom and the Glory*, 5.
235 Agamben, *The Kingdom and the Glory*, 9. The image of the king who reigns but does not govern was important to both Carl Schmitt and Erik Peterson. For Peterson's development of Philo's model, see Erik Peterson, "Monotheism as a Political Problem: A Contribution to the History of Political Theology in the Roman Empire," in *Theological Tractates*, by Erik Peterson, ed. and trans. Michael J. Hollerich (Stanford: Stanford University Press, 2011), 72–77.
236 Agamben, *The Kingdom and the Glory*, 87.
237 Agamben, *The Kingdom and the Glory*, 89.
238 Agamben, *The Kingdom and the Glory*, 89. It is, in Agamben's account, this paradox that Karl Marx secularized, taking God away and putting humans in God's place. The essence of the human being becomes "nothing other than the praxis through which he incessantly produces himself." The being of the human is praxis. Agamben, *The Kingdom and the Glory*, 91.
239 Agamben, *The Kingdom and the Glory*, 111.
240 Agamben, *The Kingdom and the Glory*, 128.
241 Heron, *Liturgical Power*, 29–30.
242 Heron, *Liturgical Power*, 39.
243 Agamben, *The Kingdom and the Glory*, 230.
244 Agamben, *The Kingdom and the Glory*, 241–42.
245 Maureen B. Cavanaugh, "Democracy, Equality, and Taxes," *Alabama Law Review* 54 (2003): 443.
246 Cavanaugh, "Democracy, Equality, and Taxes," 451.
247 Agamben, *The Kingdom and the Glory*, 18.
248 Brown, *Through the Eye of a Needle*, 504.
249 Agamben, *The Kingdom and the Glory*, 110, 114.

References

Agamben, Giorgio. 2011. *The Kingdom and the Glory: For a Theological Genealogy of Economy and Government.* Translated by Lorenzo Chiesa and Matteo Mandarini. Stanford: Stanford University Press.

Ambrose. 2001. *De officiis.* Edited and translated by Ivor J. Davidson, vol. 1. Oxford: Oxford University Press.

______. 1999. "Sermon Against Auxentius." In Oliver O'Donovan and Joan Lockwood O'Donovan, *From Irenaeus to Grotius: A Sourcebook in Christian Political Thought, 100–1625*, 70–75. Grand Rapids: William B. Eerdmans.

______. 1999. "The Story of Naboth." In O'Donovan and O'Donovan, *From Irenaeus to* Grotius, 75–79.

Augustine. 1966. "The Way of Life of the Catholic Church." In *The Catholic and Manichaean Ways of Life*, translated by Donald A. Gallagher and Idella J. Gallagher, 3–64. Washington: The Catholic University of American Press, Inc..

______. 1972. *Concerning the City of God Against the Pagans*. Edited by David Knowles. Translated by Henry Bettenson. Harmondsworth, UK: Penguin Books Ltd..

______. n.d. *Exposition of Psalm 39:7*. Edited by A. Cleveland Coxe. Christian Classics Ethereal Library. Accessed May 27, 2020. https://ccel.org/ccel/schaff/npnf108/npnf108.ii.XXXIX.html.

______. n.d. *Homilies on the Gospel of John*. Translated by John Gibb. Christian Classics Ethereal Library. Accessed May 26, 2020. http://www.ccel.org/ccel/schaff/npnf107.iii.vii.html.

______. n.d. "Letter 138 (to Marcellinus)." New Advent. Accessed May 27, 2020. https://www.newadvent.org/fathers/1102138.htm.

______. 1999. "Letter 153 (To Macedonius)." In O'Donovan and O'Donovan, *From Irenaeus to Grotius*, 119–31.

Banaji, Jairus. 2009. "Aristocracies, Peasantries and the Framing of the Early Middle Ages." *Journal of Agrarian Change* 9, no. 1 (January): 59–91.

Bang P. F. 2007. "Trade and Empire: In Search of Organizing Concepts for the Roman Empire." *Past and Present* 195 (May): 3–54.

Barnes, Timothy D. 1981. *Constantine and Eusebius*. Cambridge, MA: Harvard University Press.

Bernardi, Aurelio. 1970. "The Economic Problems of the Roman Empire." In *The Economic Decline of Empires*, edited by Carlo M. Cipolla, 16–83. London: Methuen & Co., Ltd.

Bodel, John. 2008. "From *Columbaria* to Catacombs: Collective Burial in Pagan and Christian Rome." In *Commemorating the Dead: Texts and Artifacts in Context, Studies of Roman, Jewish, and Christian Burials*, edited by Laurie Brink and Deborah Green, 177–242. Berlin: de Gruyter.

Brown, Peter. 1992. *Power and Persuasion in Late Antiquity: Towards a Christian Empire*. Madison: University of Wisconsin Press.

______. 2000. *Augustine of Hippo*. Berkeley: University of California Press.

______. 2012. *Through the Eye of a Needle: Wealth, the Fall of Rome, and the Making of Christianity in the West, 350–550 AD*. Princeton: Princeton University Press.

Cavanaugh, Maureen B. 2003. "Democracy, Equality, and Taxes" *Alabama Law Review* 54: 415–81.

Cave, Roy C., and Herbert H. Coulson. 1965. *A Source Book for Medieval Economic History*. New York: Biblo and Tannen.

Cicero. 2000. *On Obligations*. Translated by P. G. Walsh. Oxford: Oxford University Press.

Cipolla, Carlo M, ed. 1970. *The Economic Decline of Empires*. London: Methuen & Co., Ltd.

Clark, Mary T. 2015 "Augustine on Justice." In *Augustine and Social Justice*, edited by Teresa Delgado, John Doody, and Kim Paffenroth, 3–10. Lanham, MD: Lexington Books.

Cochrane, Charles Norris. 1957. *Christianity and Classical Culture: A Study of Thought and Action from Augustus to Augustine*. New York: Oxford University Press.

Cyprian. 1984. *The Letters of St. Cyprian of Carthage*, edited and translated by G. W. Clarke, vol. 1. Ancient Christian Writers 43. New York: Newman Press.

Delgado, Teresa, John Doody, and Kim Paffenroth, eds. 2015. *Augustine and Social Justice.* Lanham, MD: Lexington Books.

Eusebius. 1999. "A Speech for the Thirtieth Anniversary of Constantine's Accession." In O'Donovan and O'Donovan, *From Irenaeus to* Grotius, 60–65.

Fleischacker, Samuel. 2004. *A Short History of Distributive Justice.* Cambridge, MA.: Harvard University Press.

French, Todd E. 2015 "Altruism or Holy Economy: Ambrose and Augustine's Care for the Poor." In Delgado, Doody, and Paffenroth, *Augustine and Social Justice*, 51–71.

Friedrich, Carl Joachim. 1963. *The Philosophy of Law in Historical Perspective.* 2nd ed. Chicago: The University of Chicago Press.

Grant, Robert M. 1971. *Augustus to Constantine: The Thrust of the Christian Movement into the Roman World.* London: Collins.

Gregory I. 1965. "Pope Gregory's Letter Concerning Conditions in the Islands." In Cave and Coulson, *A Source Book for Medieval Economic History*, 356–57.

Gurevich, Aron. 1980. "The Merchant." In *The Medieval World*, edited by Jacques Le Goff, and translated by Lydia G. Cochrane, 242–83. London: Parkgate Books, Ltd..

Herdt, Jennifer A. 2015 "Eudaimonism and Dispossession: Augustine on Almsgiving." In Delgado, Doody, and Paffenroth, *Augustine and Social Justice*, 97–112.

Hernández-Díaz, R. J. 2015 "Augustine and Political Economy." In Delgado, Doody, and Paffenroth, *Augustine and Social Justice*, 113–27.

Heron, Nicholas. 2018. *Liturgical Power: Between Economic and Political Theology.* New York: Fordham University Press.

Hole, Jennifer. 2016. "Economic Ethics in Late Medieval England, 1300–1550." *Archival Insights into the Evolution of Economics*, edited by Robert Leeson. Basingstoke: Palgrave Macmillan.

Justin Martyr. 1997. *St. Justin Martyr: The First and Second Apologies.* Translated by Leslie William Barnard. *Ancient Christian Writers: The Works of the Fathers in Translation*, edited by Walter J. Burghardt, John J. Dillon, and Dennis D. McManus, vol. 56. New York: Paulist Press.

Justinian. 1998. *The Digest of Justinian.* Edited by Alan Watson, vol. 1. Philadelphia: University of Pennsylvania Press.

Kelly, J. M. 1992. *A Short History of Western Legal Theory.* Oxford: Clarendon Press.

Kuttner, Stephan. 1980. "A Forgotten Definition of Justice." In *The History of Ideas and Doctrines of Canon Law in the Middle Ages*, 75–109. London: Variorum Reprints.

Lactantius. 1984. *De mortibus persecutorum.* Edited and translated by J. L. Creed. Oxford: Clarendon Press.

______. 2003. *Divine Institutes.* Translated by Anthony Bowen and Peter Garnsey. Translated Texts for Historians 40. Liverpool: Liverpool University Press.

Newhauser, Richard G. 2005. "Justice and Liberality: Opposition to Avarice in the Twelfth Century." In *Virtue and Ethics in the Twelfth Century*, edited by István P. Bejczy and Richard G. Newhauser, 295–316. Leiden: Brill.

Nicgorski, Walter. 2016. *Cicero's Skepticism and His Recovery of Political Philosophy.* Recovering Political Philosophy. New York: Palgrave Macmillan.

Nozick, Robert. 1974. *Anarchy, State, and Utopia.* Oxford: Basil Blackwell.

O'Brien, George. 1920. *An Essay on Mediaeval Economic Teaching.* London: Longmans, Green, and Co..

O'Donovan, Oliver, and Joan Lockwood O'Donovan. 1999. *From Irenaeus to Grotius: A Sourcebook in Christian Political Thought, 100–1625*. Grand Rapids: William B. Eerdmans.

Pelagius I. 1956. *Pelagii I papae: Epistulae quae supersunt* (556–61), edited by P. M. Grassó and C. M. Batlle. Montserrat: Abbey of Montserrat.

Peterson, Erik. 2011. "Monotheism as a Political Problem: A Contribution to the History of Political Theology in the Roman Empire." In *Theological Tractates*, edited by Erik Peterson, edited, and translated by Michael J. Hollerich, 68–105. Stanford: Stanford University Press.

Potter, David S. 2004. "The Roman Empire at Bay, AD 180–395." *Routledge History of the Ancient World*. New York: Routledge.

Pounds, N. J. G. 1994. *An Economic History of Medieval Europe*. 2nd ed. London: Longman.

Ramsey, Boniface. 1982. "Almsgiving in the Latin Church: The Late Fourth and Early Fifth Centuries. *Theological Studies* 34: 226–59.

Salvian. 1947. *The Writings of Salvian, the Presbyter*. Translated by Jeremiah F. O'Sullivan. Washington: Catholic University of America.

Simons, Henry C. 1938. *Personal Income Taxation: The Definition of Income as a Problem of Fiscal Policy*. Chicago: The University of Chicago Press.

Thomas Aquinas. 2013. *Summa theologiae* (Latin-English Edition). Translated by the Fathers of the English-Dominican Province. Nashville: NovAntiqua.

Wickham, Chris. 2016. *Medieval Europe: From the Breakup of the Western Roman Empire to the Reformation*. New Haven: Yale University Press.

Wood, Diana. 2002. *Medieval Economic Thought*. Cambridge: Cambridge University Press.

3 Thomas Aquinas

The interplay of natural and positive law

Introduction

Augustine's grim description of enslavement to wealth and Ambrose's concern for the effect of wealth on its possessor's soul foreshadowed the medieval consensus that being disproportionately wealthy was a sin. Isidore of Seville (560–636), following Augustine's conviction that "by wanting more than enough, the avaricious person made himself liable to lose what he already possessed," contended that almsgiving was the means of overcoming avarice.[1] Richard Newhauser writes that the idea of liberality as the antidote to greed remained popular through the seventh and eighth centuries and was presented as well in the ninth or tenth century in Adalgerus' *Admonitio ad nonsuindam reclusam*.[2] The "spiritualization of avarice and poverty" remained an important feature of medieval thought, at least until "material concerns" were "foregrounded in the High Middle Ages in the course of the development of a commercial (or profit) economy."[3] Even so, as late as the fourteenth century, Thomas Hoccleve, in *The Regiment of Princes*, decried the wearer of sumptuous clothing by a person of lower social status for being "an apparent flouter of the sumptuary law of 1363."[4] The Middle Ages came to see giving to the poor as a way to "offset the general condemnation of the attachment to wealth."[5]

The historian Jacques Le Goff considers giving to the poor the essence of the medieval "economy."[6] Following medievalist Anita Guerreau-Jalabert, Le Goff argues that "the essential act by which the use of money was justified in the Middle Ages was almsgiving." Thus, as Le Goff, Guerreau-Jalabert, and economic historian Karl Polanyi emphasize, it is impossible to speak of an independent medieval economy, since financial transactions were "imbricated into a whole dominated by religion," and it is impossible to understand the spread of money exchanges in the Middle Ages as something other than "an extension of the gift."[7]

Paradoxically, it is precisely in the interior turn—in the emphasis that Ambrose and Augustine placed on the danger that riches pose to the one who possesses them—that the seeds of a political theology were sown. The theologian Robert M. Grant argues that Christian teachings on private property were largely constructed, not on a doctrinal account of social structure, but on "response relationship," i.e., the individual's response to Jesus's sayings.[8] Grant's argument can be taken a step further: any teaching on taxation, or other appropriation of private property by the ruler, had to be built on the ruler's response to Jesus's sayings. This appears to be one of the projects in which Ambrose and Augustine were engaged. Once Ambrose claimed that he was acting "out of concern for the emperor's welfare; for it would neither be good for me to hand [churches] over, nor for him to receive them,"[9] a discussion could begin on what was appropriate for a Christian emperor to take from the people. In other words, the proper use of the institution of taxation not only affected the soul of the taxpayer; it also affected the soul of the one who had and exercised the authority to impose tax.

The idea that one could possess someone else's property by using wrongly what was putatively one's own property meant that justice, with its perennial ties to property, was a characteristic of an individual's stance toward other people. It was no longer a feature of the *polis*. Not just the wealthy, but the ruler as well, owed a debt to the poor, as illustrated by a story told by Gregory of Tours (538–594). Merovingian King Lothar, in Gregory's account, decreed that all the churches in his kingdom should pay one-third of their income to his fisc, but the bishop Injuriosus confronted him, saying "If you wish to take God's property the Lord will quickly take away your kingdom; for it is unjust that your barns should be filled through the money of the poor who ought rather to feed at your hands." The king begged for pardon and condemned what he himself had done.[10]

Tax equity could no longer be thought of in terms of a predictable income stream and overall low rates. This change is consistent with Augustine's rejection of the panoptic hubris of classical philosophy. With his *vicissitudo spatiorum temporalium* ("vicissitude of duration"), Augustine recognized that the "law" governing human thought and activity meant relinquishing "the aspiration to omniscience, recognizing that [one's] powers of apprehension are determined by the conditions of his existence as a creature in time and space."[11] Tax equity could no longer mean the aggregate tax burden on the empire considered as a collective unit (subject, of course, to the distinction between citizen and provincial). Instead, equity had come to consist of the effect that taxes had on members, and on groups of members, within society.

Necessitas and *superflua*

However, if the rich owed a debt to the poor, and the ruler was one of the "rich," then a measure was needed. Was it acceptable for an individual member of society to own any property and, if so, how much? Was it acceptable for the ruler to collect taxes and, if so, in what amount and for what purpose? What amount of the property in the ruler's possession, regardless of how it came to be there, did the ruler owe to the poor?

A balance had to be struck between the *suum cuique* of each member of society and that member's possession of things rightfully belonging to others (in the Augustinian sense). The balance that was struck turned on "necessaries"—*necessitas*—derived from Aristotle but now infused with the idea of *sufficientia* ("enough").[12] The individual's *necessitas* limited the amount of the individual's property that truly belonged to her; the rest—the *superflua*—belonged to those in need and was subject to restitution in the minds of the theologians. According to the author of the anonymous Pelagian treatise *De divitiis*, to possess *sufficientia* "was the measure of the difference between wealth and poverty." This measure had to be "calibrated and maintained with more than usual strictness" in light of the writer's "unforgiving zero-sum" conception of the distribution of wealth and poverty in society; anyone "who went beyond the measure of sufficiency could do so only by taking from the poor."[13]

A balance was also required between the *suum cuique* of the member of society and the *suum cuique* of the ruler, as well as between the ruler's *suum cuique* and the ruler's own excessive wealth. Both had to be limited. The ruler was in just possession of the necessities of the office, and could also lay just claim to the property of the subjects for the *necessitas* of the realm. The danger inherent in this formula, of course, was that *necessitas* was only a limiting factor for the subject but could easily become an enabling factor for the ruler.

Political events of the Middle Ages would reveal that the balance was often more hypothetical than real. Recounting the role of *necessitas* in legitimating medieval taxation, the cultural historian Elizabeth Brown writes:

> In view of the gap which so often exists between theory and practice, between moral standard and deed, it cannot be assumed that, interesting and persuasive as they may seem, the many statements on fiscal morality excited more than the transient interest of the rulers who heard them. In the absence of concrete evidence, it could well be imagined that they were dismissed unheeded as pious, unrealistic exhortations.[14]

Nevertheless, as Brown's account shows, the theologians persisted from the sixth through the fourteenth century to use *necessitas*, sometimes stringently, as a curb on the power to tax and, thus, to establish the grounds for tax legitimacy.[15]

On one level, the line that the theologians drew between *necessitas* and *superflua* was simply a compromise between the reality that people acquire wealth, on the one hand, and the ideals of poverty exemplified by Jesus's life on the other. The historian Jennifer Hole argues that "economic ethics" arose precisely because of this tension.[16] One of the ways of resolving the tension was for Christians to employ Aristotle's distinction between "natural" wealth-getting (acquiring those things necessary for life) and artificial wealth-getting (acquisition simply for the sake of acquisition).[17]

That Christian theologians incorporated Aristotle's distinction into their own thinking is apparent from Aquinas' reference to the distinction.[18] However, anxiety about excessive wealth did not have to wait for the High Middle Ages. Long before then, the lawyers had been concerned about superabundance. For one thing, excess wealth was associated with usury. Gratian had, with a citation to St. Jerome, introduced the concept of *superhabundantia* "to express the idea that any excess whatsoever beyond the arithmetically equal in the loan contract is to be condemned as usurious."[19]

It is reasonable to believe that the Roman and medieval economic situation played a part in giving the distinction between necessity and superabundance an important role in medieval thinking. The Roman Empire was largely agricultural. Most of the population lived at the subsistence level. After taxes and rent, the people had no reserves.[20] At the same time, however, the city of Rome had little economic activity to support it, and much of its population lived on the *annona*. Support for the city of Rome, even before the days of heavy taxation to defend the empire's crumbling borders, ensured that most of the empire remained on the edge of starvation, overtaxed and underfed.[21] The city of Rome, the government with its ever-increasing military pressures, and the overtaxed landholders all competed for the same resources. None of these three agents could hold more than the bare minimum necessary without pushing the others below the level needed for survival. Storing up goods for investment or speculation was therefore considered dishonest profit. The Capitulary of Nijmegen (806), for instance, distinguishes between keeping grain and wine to meet one's needs and storing up grain or wine until it becomes worth more. It calls the latter "greed."[22]

The situation would not change significantly until after the Middle Ages ended. The historian Giovanni Cherubini estimates that at the beginning of fourteenth-century Europe may have had as many as 73 million inhabitants, a population that would have exceeded the productive potential of its agriculture.[23] Famine was a constant threat. People continued to live close to the land; there was no margin.[24] Even in late medieval Europe nine-tenths of the population lived on what it produced by labor in the fields.[25] The peasant's concern was for self-sufficiency, i.e., to provide sufficient grain for his or her own family and for those with rights over the land and produce.[26] At the first hint of scarcity, there would be a run on food supplies, thus intensifying the scarcity and causing the poorer classes to suffer "more acutely than was necessary."[27]

Whatever the source of their concern, the theologians were deeply worried about immoderate wealth. Lactantius, for instance, denounced Diocletian's tax policies as the gratuitous accumulation of *extraordinarias*—that is, "supplementary" and "immoderate" things.[28] He saw the same dynamic at work in the individual citizen's accumulation of wealth as well. Contempt for God expressed itself in acquisitiveness, the monopolizing of "necessaries."[29]

Augustine developed the distinction between necessaries and superfluity in the context of almsgiving:

> Anoint the feet of Jesus. By living well, follow in the footsteps of the Lord. Dry them with your hair. If you have superfluity, give it to the poor and you have dried the feet of the Lord; for hair is understood to be the superfluity of the body. You have what you may do with your superfluities: they are more than you need, but they are necessary to the feet of the Lord. Perhaps on earth the Lord's feet are in need. For of whom will he speak at the end if not of his members: When you did it to one of the least of mine you did it

> to me? You bestowed your superfluities, but it was to my feet that you were gracious.[30]

Almsgiving became a focal point of the problem of superfluity. Boniface Ramsey writes: "It is often repeated that alms are due to the poor in justice, that the earth was created for all, and that the superfluity of the rich is the property of the poor."[31] In fact, almsgiving became "the point of juncture where the equality between rich and poor was re-established."[32]

Augustine, moreover, explicitly connected the problem of superfluous wealth with the principle of restitution. "The superfluity of the rich is necessary to the poor," he wrote. "If you hold onto superfluous items, then, you are keeping what belongs to someone else."[33] By advancing the *necessitas* principle, Augustine in effect argued that the economy was a zero-sum game. If one person had too little, it was because another had too much, and vice versa. The other implication of Augustine's formula—that each member of society had a quantum of *necessitas* that could be compared to another member's *necessitas*—paved the way for Aquinas later to develop a positive account of private property even as he retained the principle that superfluity belonged to the needy.

In the thirteenth century, Albertus Magnus (c. 1200–1280) wrote that the distinction between justice and charity was meaningless: "For a man to give out of his superfluities is a mere act of justice, because he is rather then steward of them for the poor than the owner."[34] Albertus Magnus was, of course, Thomas Aquinas' mentor.

Property and taxation in the *Summa*

Thomas' teachings on property rights reflect the extensive thinking of his predecessors on *superflua* and the way in which it relativizes property rights above the threshold of *necessitas*.[35] While accepting the view that property rights are conditional in the realm of *superflua*, as discussed before, Thomas defended individual rights to property. The legal historian J. M. Kelly calls Thomas' doctrine of property rights "the first elaborate justification of private property."[36] Property rights are a morally privileged baseline for Thomas in that they are "necessary to human life."[37] In Thomas' zero-sum understanding of the economy and resource allocation, however, any amounts over and above what is necessary rightfully belong, in some sense, to others. Thomas' prince, moreover, is right to "exact" from his subjects that which is due him "for the safeguarding of the common good."[38] While Thomas insisted on the importance of property rights, his is a highly nuanced account. The excavation of Thomas' philosophy of taxation in this chapter is set in the context of his balanced doctrine of property.

This chapter focuses initially on property. The implications of Thomas' ideas about property for taxation emerge later in the chapter. The account herein of Thomas' philosophy of taxation is partly constructive, as his explicit remarks about taxation are few. This chapter, therefore, follows the method represented by Jean

Porter's *Ministers of the Law*, in which the author states her intention to "offer a constructive account of legal authority as a natural relation, taking my starting points from early scholastic legal and political thought, and developing these in conversation with contemporary philosophy of law and political theology."[39]

Question 66 of Secunda Secundae of the *Summa* arises from the tension between private appropriation of exterior things and their availability for common use. Because it focuses on exterior things, Question 66 centers on theft and robbery—the sins regarding *things possessed* rather than sins against the person. Article 8 of Question 66 is particularly relevant to taxation because it considers the taking of private property by public authority.[40] The question Aquinas seeks to answer in Article 8 is whether robbery can be committed without sin, in light of the fact that robbery "implies a certain violence and coercion." The only sort of robbery that can be committed without sin turns out to be "robbery" conducted by public authority: "[I]n human society no man can exercise coercion except through public authority." Rulers, according to Thomas, are entitled to exact "that which is due to them for the safe-guarding of the common good, even if they use violence in so doing."[41]

There are limits, however. If the rulers take something "unduly," their exactions revert to the category of robbery. Thomas writes in his reply to objection 3 in Article 8: "[I]f they extort something unduly by means of violence, it is robbery even as burglary is." In other words, Aquinas carves out of private ownership a space for the public taking of property. Nevertheless, the language of private ownership remains dominant within the limited scope of Article 8.

In the broader context of Question 66 as a whole, however, the language of private ownership is balanced by the language of common property, as the possession of external things comes into tension with God's authority over things. Article 1 explains that human possession of external things is only "natural" from a certain perspective. When external things are considered in their use (*ad usum*), humans have a "natural dominion" over them, because (1) by their reason and will (2) humans are able to use them for their own profit, (3) as they were made "on account of" humankind (*quasi propter se factis*). Considered in their *nature*, however, exterior things are "not subject to the power of man, but only to the power of God Whose mere will all things obey."

Article 2 approaches the connection between humans and exterior things from a different angle: what is "relevant to man" (*competunt homini*). First, humans *can* procure and dispense external things, and the fact that humans have this power makes it lawful (*licitum est*) for them to possess things. Lawfulness proceeds, in some sense, from power. Moreover, according to Article 2, possession of things is not only lawful but also "necessary to human life" in that (1) people are more careful to procure what can be theirs than what is common to many or all, (2) order (as opposed to confusion) requires a division of labor, and (3) contentment, which ensures peace, arises from having something of one's own.

When Aquinas says in Article 2 that the human power of procurement makes possession lawful, he means "lawful" according to positive rather than natural law. Reply to objection 1 in Article 2 makes it clear that division of possessions arises from "human agreement," which is a matter of positive rather than natural law. Natural law prescribes community of goods. Natural law, however, does not preclude division of possessions. Positive law adds to natural law rather than conflicting with it. Positive law filters natural law through practical reason so that it can apply to particular circumstances.

Within Article 2, however, the matter is not that simple. Even in the use of things—in fact, especially in the use of things—a human being "ought to possess external things, not as his own, but as common, so that, to wit, he is ready to communicate them to others in their need." To import the language of Article 1, the nature of things impinges on their use. In the language of Article 2, the human power to procure and dispense is circumscribed by the common good. More generally, positive law's addition to natural law is only an addition. It does not alter the requirements of natural law in any way. Thomas is clear on this point: "But if in any point [a human law] deflects from the law of nature, it is no longer a law but a perversion of law."[42]

With respect to the ownership of property, natural law necessarily transforms the content of positive law. In terms of Article 7, "whatever certain people have in superabundance is due, by natural law, to the purpose of succoring the poor"; therefore, "each one is entrusted with the stewardship [*dispensatio*] of his own things, so that out of them he may come to the aid of those who are in need."[43]

Ownership becomes stewardship, or, more precisely, ownership of *superflua* becomes stewardship. Thomas makes this point in his discussion of liberality: "According to Ambrose . . . and Basil . . . excess of riches is granted by God to some, in order that they may obtain the merit of a good stewardship [*bonae dispensationis*]."[44] And again: "Now the use of money consists in parting with it."[45] Stewardship is an operative principle on the community's side of the equation as well. As noted above, "that which is due to" the princes is due them "for the safe-guarding of the common good."[46] The stewardship premise is implicit in the tithing context too. The pope is evidently entitled to demand tithes from anyone, even the clergy, because "natural reason dictates that he who has charge of the common estate of a multitude should be provided with all goods, so that he may be able to carry out whatever is necessary for the common welfare."[47] That tithes are "necessary for the common welfare" apparently means that they "should be employed for the assistance of the poor."[48]

A full account of the interplay of natural and positive law in Thomas' doctrine of property requires the introduction of his conceptions of justice, equality, and indebtedness as well. The next section begins by summarizing the connection in Thomas' thought between justice and right, then moves to the association of justice with a kind of equality and shows that equality is best understood in terms of indebtedness. As developed in subsequent sections, indebtedness is integral to a Thomist conception of taxation in that it supplies a moral imperative for the redistribution of resources from those in possession of them to those in need of them.

Debitum

Justice, for Thomas, is "the perpetual and constant will to render to each one his right."[49] This *suum cuique* definition, which Thomas took from Justinian's *Digest* (527),[50] points simultaneously both inward and outward. Justice is not the mere "doing of something just." It is a habit, not simply an act, and thus an inner disposition of a person. For Thomas, however, justice also focuses on external acts rather than on passions, and differs from the other moral virtues accordingly.[51] Étienne Gilson writes that, for Thomas, the moral virtues governing the passions "permit the virtuous man to keep them in a just mean in relation to himself," while the virtue of justice "seeks this just mean in the relationship between two things that are outside the virtuous man himself: his act, and the person whom his act concerns."[52] In Alasdair MacIntyre's account, Thomas' justice is the one virtue that is peculiarly concerned with relations with others.[53] Nevertheless, justice has this in common with the other moral virtues: "the just mean it seeks is the mean of reason."[54] That is what makes it a moral virtue. Although the just mean lies outside the virtuous person, in the relationship between the act and the person whom the act concerns, the relationship in question involves the virtuous person's *act* and the good of the person concerned as determined by the *reason* of the actor. In other words, the actor's own reason is a necessary component of a just act.

At least three aspects of Thomas' idea are identifiable: justice is an inner disposition that takes root as a permanent feature of the will; this inner disposition demands and finds expression in rendering to others what is due them; and what is due them is determined by a norm, i.e., a standard of "right" (*ius*). *Ius* defines the relationship of each person to other people, as in Roman law. It defines that relationship because *ius* itself "is what is rightly owed to another, either in accordance with the natural law or with positive law."[55]

The interior component of Thomas' justice means that justice produces *judgment*. Reason issues judgments about what is right for another, but only when "the origin and cause" of the decision are governed by the virtue of justice in the one pronouncing the decision.[56] That is, Aquinas does not think of justice as a static condition that inheres in things or even in acts. He thinks of it as a habit that determines rationally what is due another.

However, to speak of the judgment of judges, or the judgments of a just person, is to use language metaphorically. Strictly speaking, as Gilson points out, only a ruler issues judgments: "[T]he judgment which defines justice is the privilege of the head of the State, for it is he who establishes positive rights by promulgating laws."[57] The judgment of a judge, who applies the laws, is a judgment by extension; and the personal judgment of an individual—based on reason—is judgment by analogy.[58]

Justice, therefore, is preeminently a virtue of the ruler. Thomas says that justice "is in the sovereign as a master-virtue [*virtus architectonica*]."[59] The relationship that is informed by rights may be, and often is, one in which one person is subject to another. Thomas' prime example of this kind of "right" is the relationship between father and son. The son is "part of" the father in some way (*quodammodo est pars eius*). The English translations tend to say that the son "belongs" to the father. More literally, "the son is something of the father" (*filius est aliquid patris*).[60]

There is a relationship of "right," however, in which neither person is subject to the other. This is a relationship of "strict right," to use Gilson's term.[61] It arises when the two people are both "subjects of the ruler of the state" (*ambo sunt sub uno principe civitatis*).[62] "Right" is tied to relationship in both cases, but is more indirect in the latter, that of "civic justice."[63]

This is not to say that rights are arbitrary concessions on the part of the sovereign. The ruler's rational determination of right is guided by a principle. Thomas thought of justice as denoting "a kind of equality" (*importat enim aequalitatem quondam*).[64] The translation "equality," however, is a misleading term. The Latin original, *aequalitas*, may just as easily mean "equivalence" or "proportionality."[65]

Unlike the modern idea of equality, Thomas' *aequalitas* has content because it is connected to *debitum*, the word that is usually translated "duty." Paraphrasing Thomas, Gilson writes: "To perform an act of justice is to render someone his due in such a manner that what is rendered is equal to what is owed. Thus two notions are inseparable from that of justice, the notion of debt and the notion of equality."[66]

Debitum is inevitably translated as "duty" in English. At its root, however, *debitum* is "debt" in an accounting sense. Metaphorically, to be sure, it means "duty," but in the sense of the proportion of something in the law of nature. Even at this level it is far from a deontic "ought." The theologian Eugene Rogers writes: "We are not true to Aquinas if we allow *debitum* to float free of display and diagnosis and mean the great Kantian duty in the sky."[67]

When Thomas says that something is a *debitum*, he means that it has *aequalitas*, or equivalence, to something physical or something in nature. In this sense, we can say that *debitum* is objective. Political philosopher Martin Rhonheimer calls *debitum* something "given, based on objectively existing circumstances."[68] *Debitum* is objective because it denotes "indebtedness." My *debitum* to someone else is not what I ought to do for him or her, but something that I have that actually belongs to the other person. The philosopher Joseph Magee describes a *debitum* as something that is, paradoxically, both owned and yet lacking to the owner.[69] Thomas made this point in his discussion of restitution in the *Summa*, where he writes, "That which is not due to another is not his properly speaking."[70]

In the case of material possession, Magee argues, something can be *owed* to the one who *owns* it if it is temporarily in the possession of another: "I may own a car and have lent it to a friend. When he has finished using it, he owes me the return of the car in the condition that I lent it. While my friend is borrowing the car, I at once own it and am owed its safe return."[71] To anticipate the discussion below, the riches of the wealthy are in some sense "borrowed" from the poor, to whom they naturally belong and to whom they must be returned at the appropriate time, according to the terms of the "loan." The poor continue, in the meantime, to "own" what is "owed" them.

This equating of debt and ownership would have been, and remains, foreign to the categories of civil law. From a legal standpoint, it must remain paradoxical. Debt in this sense is primarily a moral concept. *Ius* is the pre-moral cognate of *debitum*. *Ius* in its broad, primary sense only takes on moral meaning—and, thus, the measure of obligation (*debitum*)—when law (entailing reason) applies to it. Elmer Gelinas explains the pre-moral quality of *ius*:

> The word *ius* is first used to signify the just thing itself. This is hardly justice in the sense of a moral virtue. It has to do with an appropriate commensuration or equality of *things*; for example, the property exchange value of a job is so many dollars. Interchangeability of *things* is the primary sense in which *ius* is used. Thus the terms "proper," "fitting," "appropriate," "even," or "equal" would seem to convey the amoral sense of *ius* as signifying the equality of things.[72]

Debitum arises once reason enters into the apprehension of what is fitting, i.e., when consequences are compared. This is another way of saying that the fitting action has now taken on a moral character: "Moral obligation is thereby acknowledged and the correlative moral character of the fitting (i.e., right) action, now seen as *debitum*, emerges."[73] The quality of *debitum*, therefore, makes *ius* a moral obligation and turns *aequalitas* into *iustitia*.

The following section ties the foregoing outline of the connection Thomas makes among *iustitia*, *ius*, *aequalitas*, and *debitum* to the measure of material goods, *necessitas*.

Natural law, positive law, and material necessity

To recapitulate, in Article 7 of Question 66 of the *Summa* human need (*necessitas*) prioritizes the natural law of common ownership over the positive law of appropriation. Thomas writes:

> Things which are of human right cannot derogate from natural right or Divine right. Wherefore the division and appropriation of things which are based on human law, do not preclude the fact that man's needs have to be remedied by means of these very things. Hence whatever certain people have in superabundance is due, by natural law, to the purpose of succoring the poor.

Article 7 can be read as a more practical harmonization of the two "rights" presented theoretically in Article 2. In Article 7, human need is connected to natural law, while "the division and appropriation of things" remains firmly a matter of human law. Aquinas implements the priority of need over procurement in two ways in Article 7: (1) the oft-cited *casus necessitatis extremae* exception permits a person in dire need, and for whom there is no other remedy, "to succor his own need by means of another's property, by taking it either openly or secretly"; and

(2) need dictates that superabundance (*res quas aliqui superabundantur habent*) be used to help the poor.

Two points emerge from Article 7. First, the need of people who do not have enough property triggers a demand on those who have too much.[74] Secondly, once natural law is triggered in that way, the superabundance of those who have too much becomes a *debitum*, as a matter of natural law, to those in need. These are disjunctive propositions. The obligation to share superabundance with the needy arises independently of the *casus necessitatis extremae* exception.

This superabundance principle appears in Aquinas' treatment of tithing as well. In Question 87, Article 1, of Secunda Secundae, Aquinas asks whether Christians are required to tithe. He identifies three kinds of Old Testament tithes: (1) the tithe set apart for the needs and uses of the Levites, which corresponds to provision for the clergy in the New Testament era; (2) the tithe reserved for the offering of sacrifices, which "has no place in the New Law"; and (3) the part of the tithe set apart to provide food for the stranger, the fatherless, and the widow. The third kind of tithe, far from being superseded, "is increased in the New Law." Christ commanded, according to Aquinas, that Christians "give to the poor not merely the tenth part, but all our surplus [*omnia superflua*]."[75]

The principle of giving *superflua* to the poor is not only a heightened commandment; it is also a dictate of natural law. Aquinas' ultimate answer in Article 1 is that tithing is required of Christians, partly as a "judicial precept"[76] (i.e., the *amount* of the tithe) and partly as a dictate of natural law (i.e., the *obligation* to pay tithes).

As an obligation imposed by natural law, tithing is a duty. Aquinas introduces his lengthy answer in Article 1 with a quote from Augustine: "'It is a duty to pay tithes, and whoever refuses to pay them takes what belongs to another.'" Aquinas writes later in Question 87 of the *ius* of ministers to receive tithes, and calls the duty to pay tithes *debitum*.[77] In other words, the tithe *belongs to* ministers of the New Testament.

The tithe is not alone in being due to its recipients. In his answer in Article 1, Aquinas explains that the people's obligation to provide for "those who minister the divine worship" is a dictate of natural reason just as "it is the people's duty to provide a livelihood for their rulers and soldiers and so forth."[78] The same point is made in Aquinas' commentary on Paul's Letter to the Romans, where Thomas states, in part, that "taxes are owed to rulers as a wage for their labors."[79]

In Question 66, *superflua* is *due* to the help of the poor as a matter of natural law.[80] In giving his answer in Article 7, Aquinas cites Ambrose and his words "embodied in the Decretals": "'It is the hungry man's bread that you withhold, the naked man's cloak that you store away, the money that you bury in the earth is the price of the poor man's ransom and freedom.'" In the case of extreme need, "that which [the one in need] takes for the support of his life become his own property by reason of that need."[81]

Need transforms private property into common property (*in necessitate sunt omnia communia*).[82] To put the matter in terms of the reading of Articles 1 and 2 outlined above, need neutralizes the reasons underlying the positive law of appropriation, thus allowing the natural law of common possession to operate as the principle of property. Porter writes:

> Hence, the institution of property is in tension, at least, with the ideal of equality implied by the virtue of justice. Aquinas's delineation of the limitations of property rights does not do away with this tension, but it does at least give practical force to the view that natural equality is more fundamental than the inequalities introduced by human society.[83]

Within the purview of positive law, when need is not at issue, taxation is a kind of robbery. In that context, Article 8 of Question 66 can only speak of robbery without sin as a taking of another's property with lawful or just violence and coercion. However, in cases of extreme need or when *superflua* is present, the language of *ius* and *debitum* drives the discourse. Proportion in taxation has two components: proportion to the needs of the commonweal and proportion to the individual's capacity to pay. In other words, the "burden of taxation must not be higher than necessity required" and should not lead to impoverishment but, rather, "preserve a necessary subsistence."[84]

The natural law of common goods surrounds and constrains the positive law of private ownership. Necessity allows the substrate of natural law to come to the surface and overpower positive law, as it were.[85] Thomas, as Alejandra Mancilla puts it, "shares with his contemporaries the view that the right of necessity is the revival of the original, pre-institutional right of common use of the earth's resources."[86] Necessity is the place where the line is drawn between private and common property—not just the necessity of the needy one, but also necessity as a function of what the possessor can use. That is, necessity serves as a limit to how much the possessor should have. "Ownership is limited by the necessities of human need," MacIntyre concludes with respect to Thomas' teaching.[87]

R. W. Dyson cautions that although Aquinas championed property ownership, his account of private property differs from modern doctrines in that human laws "do not confer an unlimited right of acquisition and use."[88] Dyson formulates Aquinas' distinction between ownership and use, alien to modern conceptions, in this way: "We are entitled to as much property as we need to enable us to meet our earthly needs comfortably. But what we have in excess of these needs we owe as a matter of moral duty to the poor."[89]

In summary, there is a duty, concretized in the relationship of natural and positive law, to dispose of *superflua*. To strip that concept of its deontological connotations, one individual's positive-law *superflua* is converted (or, more precisely, reverts) by operation of natural law into something that belongs to others. Giving it back to them is equality and, thus, justice.[90]

The measure of indebtedness

A pressing question remains: what is the measure of indebtedness?

The general answer, of course, is that I am indebted to others in the amount of my *superflua*—that is, in the amount by which my property exceeds what I need. This answer requires specification.

No doubt the line between *necessitas* and *superflua* must always remain elusive on the individual side of the equation, but conceptually there is a measure. The measure is self-sufficiency, as Aquinas explains in his commentary on Aristotle's *Nicomachean Ethics*.[91] Self-sufficiency, in turn, draws the line between *necessitas* and *superflua* in two ways.

First, the optimal point is reached when "a truly happy" person "is undisturbed by the things that are unnecessary even though attainable."[92] In other words, we arrive at the outer limit of *necessitas* when the acquisition of additional goods would do nothing to increase the happiness of one whose desires are "controlled by reason." Question 2, Article 1, of Prima Secundae is quite specific, enumerating the items that "serve as a remedy" for natural wants. They are "food, drink, clothing, *vehicula*, dwellings, and such like."

Secondly, there is a point at which the accumulation of property begins to undermine, rather than promote, self-sufficiency. "Superabundance," Thomas writes in his *Ethics* commentary, "makes people less self-sufficient since a man must have the help or service of many servants to guard and manage excessive possessions."[93]

Necessitas on the *community's* side has three components: "that the community be established in the unity of peace," that the community "be guided to act well," and "that, through the industry of the ruler, there be a plentiful supply of those things necessary to living well."[94] *Necessitas* and *superflua* provide the measurement of these components as well. To return to this chapter's starting point—Article 8 of Question 66—if "princes" exact property from their subjects "unjustly," they are bound to make restitution. This means that if they take something that is not "due" them (*indebite extorqueant*), they have violated justice, measured by *aequalitas*, determined by the line drawn between *necessitas* and *superflua*. Thomas' high view of individual appropriation seems to reflect his concern that the ruler could become greedy and rapacious. In a similar way, the *necessitas* of the state serves as a constraint on the limitless acquisitiveness that can beset individuals. The state and the individual do not simply keep each other honest, as we would say now. They serve as reminders to each other that the acquisition of property by either is always only instrumental; it must never become an end in itself.

To summarize the claims made here so far, *ius* ("right") implies balancing in Thomas' understanding because it demands an equivalence between what is given and what is received. *Ius*, therefore, must take into account *debitum* if it is to be an objective, moral obligation. *Debitum* in the economic sphere is measured by *necessitas*, which is worked out, in turn, by either self-sufficiency or the common good. Before turning to the implications of *balance* in Thomas' system, this chapter places the interplay of *necessitas* and *superflua* in historical context.

Between feudalism and sovereignty

The problem of private property

Awareness of the tension between the positive law of appropriation and the natural law of common ownership did not begin with Aquinas.[95] The historian Diana Wood, for instance, argues that Augustine was aware of it and concerned about it: "In the early fifth century St Augustine had recognized the problem of the conflicting laws. Rights of possession were firmly grounded on human law, whereas divine law had decreed that 'the earth and the fullness thereof' were the Lord's."[96]

The Middle Ages, according to Wood, first grappled with this lingering question of why human and divine law differed by exploiting "the flexibility of natural law" itself.[97] The twelfth-century canonist Rufinus developed "a clumsy threefold definition of natural law," in which natural law fell into three categories: *commands* ("which ordered the performance of good acts"), *prohibitions* ("which forbade the performance of bad ones"), and *demonstrations* (which provided more general advice "like 'Let all goods be held in common'" but stopped short of being obligations).[98] Custom was required for applying commands and prohibitions to specific situations. Custom could give people the liberty to say "'this is my slave, that is your field,'"[99] but custom did not thereby contradict natural law. Rather, custom was "a way of disciplining fallen humanity into following the commands and prohibitions of natural law."[100]

Thinkers who followed Rufinus quickly replaced the threefold account with a distinction between the strict letter of the natural law and its application. Alexander of Hales (d. 1254), for instance, viewed natural law as decreeing community of property in the innocent state of nature but allowing private property in the "diseased" state into which humans had fallen, in much the same way as a doctor "might think drinking wine was healthy" but "would hardly give it to a sick man."[101]

Aquinas, as we have seen, pushed the distinction further, arguing "that natural law could be changed (and Aquinas actually uses the Latin verb *mutare*, to change) in two ways, either by additions to it or subtractions from it."[102] In other words, "private possession was really for the common good."[103] In his *Commentary on the Nichomachean Ethics*, Thomas stated that "external goods that are used purposively by man have a moral character."[104]

Thomas' treatment of positive law—and, with it, his treatment of private property—is a landmark in the history of political theory, according to Walter Ullmann. Ullmann writes that Thomas was able to give us "the first exposition of the theory of the State" by integrating Aristotle's naturalism into Christian cosmology.[105] The state, for Thomas, is a natural emanation of human reason.[106] Ullmann goes so far as to say that no supernatural or divine element is necessary at all in Thomas' account, with the result that Thomas brings political science into being.[107]

In Ullmann's analysis, Aristotelian naturalism allowed Thomas to resolve the conflict between natural and positive law in a new way. Because the state is a product of nature, its laws—which are by definition positive, human laws—must also be products of nature. They are, Ullmann writes, "the channels through which the natural law finds its articulate expression."[108] Rather than placing natural law and positive law in irreconcilable conflict, Thomas holds that positive law "is an emanation of the natural law."[109]

The reemergence of taxation

Aquinas lived at a time when Europe was emerging from several centuries marked by the absence of regular taxation. Rome's crisis in the third century and then the "relative economic autarchy of the early Middle Ages and the political fragmentation following the barbarian invasions" had destroyed the sophistication of the Roman tax system as it had existed during the height of the empire.[110] The strongest and—relatively speaking—wealthiest political system in western Europe after the collapse of the Roman Empire was the Frankish kingdom, but even that was not a tax-based system.[111] The Merovingian and Gothic kings lacked any regular tax income. They had no choice but to repay "their faithful servants" by granting them benefices (land, in this context). The tendency was to add to the benefices immunity (exemption from all other jurisdiction) and commendation (the grantee's swearing of homage to the lord). In fact, the absence of regular taxation may have been one of the preconditions that allowed the elements of feudalism to fall into place.[112]

Nevertheless, the idea of the *publicum* never entirely disappeared. It was an enduring legacy of Rome, a mark of political legitimacy. "Under the empire," Chris Wickham writes, "the *publicum* was taxation, imperial property, and the bureaucracy, the collective good, just as the 'public sector' is today." Even after the wealth of the tax system disappeared, the post-Roman kings, even when weak, invoked the term "to mean rights which belonged to them."[113] Although the requirement that the lord live off the lord's own landed estates (domains) replaced the concept of regular taxation in the early Middle Ages,[114] living off the domains was only possible because the lord had a right to services, produce, and "a great number of imposts and levies."[115] These rights themselves could became property rights, as evidenced by the practices of usurping and redeeming tithes. The tithe was the most widespread form of taxation after the Carolingian rulers extended the obligation to pay it throughout western Europe in the eighth century. After the collapse of the Carolingian state, however, "the lay lords found this lucrative taxation a temptation too great to resist."[116] Even when the church managed to "redeem" its usurped tithes, the redemption typically placed the tithe in monastic hands, where it retained the character of revenue.[117] In addition, as the medieval period progressed domains at all levels of the hierarchy shrank and the lords had to concede more and more lands to the peasants; the lords found it increasingly difficult to live off their own lands.[118] Thus, the requirement that the lord live off the domains was never in reality as divorced from the practice of living off of tax revenues as it was in theory.

The reemergent institution of taxation slowly became more important as a supplement to resources from the king's own lands. This happened first in

England around 1000, with Æthelred II's Danegeld. As the eleventh century turned into the twelfth, there was a tendency for the exactions by lords from their peasants to be increasingly in money. Wickham explains that the reason for this was simple: "there was more silver around, so it was actually possible to expect that peasants might have access to it." The lords, moreover, "increasingly preferred money rent, as it was easier to use it to buy goods." Thus, when taxation returned as a regular feature of political life, it is not surprising that it too was almost always paid in money.[119] Revenue in the form of money facilitated both more bureaucracies and more wars.[120] The need for military defense, in fact, created the conditions under which *both* feudalism could develop *and* under which regular taxation could reemerge, just as the overwhelming need for military defense had contributed to the collapse of central authority and relocation of power to local landholders in the first place as the Roman Empire faded. The needs of the rulers for revenue were increasing just as their traditional sources of obtaining revenue—"the royal domain, the profits of [administering] justice, and feudal obligations"—were shrinking.[121]

The newly revived taxation "was by no means as heavy as it had been under the Roman Empire, and still was in Byzantium and the Islamic states." It was also inconsistently collected and did not become "a fundamental feature of English or French budgets" until the Hundred Years' War. Nevertheless, it helped rulers support large numbers of paid officials and increase local justice and administrative effectiveness in ways reminiscent of the Roman Empire.[122]

The principle of necessity

If a king asked for an extraordinary tax to meet an emergency or a *necessity*, any special privileges, immunities, liberties, and exemptions had to yield. They were, in fact, invalid because they amounted to nothing more than private contracts. But they were only invalid if the ruler successfully demonstrated "the existence of real necessity."[123] This early—or, rather, re-emerging—version of public law required an actual emergency or necessity to become superior to private law. In ordinary circumstances, "the king and the prerogative were subordinate to the private law of the land."[124] Necessity in this sense was, in fact, a principle of private law, but even Augustine had used the notion in his formulation of just war theory—more specifically, "the right of the kingdom to defend itself against the aggressor." According to Gaines Post, the scholastics followed and developed Augustine's thought; beginning in the twelfth century the kings of France and England appealed to necessity to justify the extraordinary taxes they demanded; and necessity became "a principle of public law in the thirteenth century."[125]

Necessity as an enabling principle, therefore, became tied to the doctrine of just war.[126] Until the thirteenth century, taxation had been a matter of private law because it was considered to be a form of appropriation and, thus, fell into the legal subject matter of property.[127] In the thirteenth century, however, taxation became a matter of public law because legitimacy of the institution came to depend on the ruler's need for funds to engage in just warfare.[128] The jurist Azo of Bologna (1190–1225), for instance, declared that just war constituted a case of necessity sufficient to permit the ruler to expropriate private property, including by the levying of taxes.[129]

The church and the theologians followed the lawyers and the politicians, at least to an extent. The Third and Fourth Lateran Councils (1179 and 1215, respectively) agreed to the rulers' use of the *necessitas* principle, but only in cases of true necessity. The 1179 Council, for instance, "decreed that bishops should not presume to burden their subjects with taxes and exactions; only in cases of great necessity, when the cause was manifest and reasonable, could modest financial aid be affectionately requested."[130] Particularly after the rediscovery of Justinian's *Digest* and of Roman law in the eleventh century and of Aristotle's political philosophy in the twelfth, the theologians began to use the concept of necessity as an enabling principle as well as a limiting principle.[131] Post argues that public law began to develop in the High Middle Ages for two reasons—because theologians began to demand that private contract "must yield to the superior rights of the public welfare,"[132] and because Roman ideas of public law re-entered the discourse right at the time in which they could be "transferred from the universal Empire to the rising feudal monarchies."[133] As Le Goff observes, there was a close connection between the reemergence of the state and the reemergence of taxation, and the impetus behind the reemergence of both was the need to fund wars.[134]

At the same time, however, the lawyers' and the theologians' commitment to *necessitas* as a limitation on the taxing power remained strong. Justinian's Code, compiled in the sixth century, forbade the imposition of new taxes without extraordinary circumstances, common utility, and the emperor's sanction. It also commanded restitution of illicit taxes and punishment of officials levying taxes beyond the limits of custom or imperial edict.[135] The *Digest* supplied a starting point for the investigations of legists and theologians into justifications of taxation when the local, irregular impositions of the early Middle Ages gave way to new revenue demands by increasingly powerful rulers in the twelfth and thirteenth centuries.[136] The theologian Peter the Chanter (d. 1197) and his Parisian colleagues, for instance, set forth "demanding criteria": money taken was robbery except in grave emergencies, and knights and other officials should be "'enjoined at confession to renounce all taxes except in cases of necessity'" or with consent.[137] The canonist Hostiensis (c. 1200–1271) demanded that taxes imposed by a ruler be necessary and just and authorized by the emperor. Even King Louis IX (1214–1270) "asserted that funds should be taken justly and used for good ends and that taxes were to be levied only in times of critical need." He insisted, in keeping with the teachings of biblical commentator and cardinal Hugues de Saint-Cher (1200–1263), "that restitution should take precedence over charitable giving, and in 1258 and 1259 he obtained papal bulls and ecclesiastical letters authorizing him to use for alms money and property which he felt bound to restore, whose owners could not be found." And the publicist Pierre Dubois (c. 1255–1321) "proclaimed it a mortal sin for the king to ask for more aid than he needed or to request support which was not absolutely essential."[138]

In summary, in the twelfth and thirteenth centuries taxation came to balance the feudal tradition, with its emphasis on property rights, against the emerging awareness of public utility.[139] Put differently, the two roles of *necessitas*—the enabling role, a function of the ruler's perspective, and the limiting role, a function of the property holder's perspective—came into a conflict that taxation was asked to mediate.

Identity of interests

These historical sketches raise the question of what tax is for. Is it primarily a means of achieving some notion of the common good, or is it the state's means of maintaining itself? In the Middle Ages, the latter purpose had not yet emerged as an independent justification for tax. Eberhard Isenmann writes: "Unlike modern taxes, which are required to meet a general financial need, medieval and early modern taxes, at least in their origins, could only be justified in terms of the general good or for more specific, and on the whole exceptional, purposes."[140] "The principal arguments justifying the levy of taxes," Isenmann concludes, "thus tended to oscillate between the necessities and claims of the prince on the one hand, and the necessities of the commonweal on the other."[141] Moreover, if the legitimate purpose of taxation was to meet "the necessities of the commonweal," what were those necessities? The idea that taxation compensated the prince for services rendered to the commonweal would serve as a bridge between the two justifications. It was a small step from the "compensation" idea to the "benefit principle" that served as the primary justification of taxation in the modern period until it ceded that role to "ability to pay."[142] Anselm of Laon (d. 1117) and, later, Henry of Ghent (d. 1293) maintained that "taxes in effect reimbursed the costs incurred by the ruler when he fought for his country and acted as judge."[143]

It would be too simplistic to conclude that medieval political leaders justified taxation as the legitimate claim of the prince while theologians justified it as payment for the necessities of the commonweal. But there appears to be a grain of truth in the suggestion that theologians hoped for greater identity between the ruler's needs and the needs of the poor than between the ruler's needs and the military defense of the realm (let alone the extravagance of the ruler's lifestyle).[144]

The ambiguity between these two necessities—needs of the poor and necessities of the prince—was explored by John of Salisbury, an adherent of Cicero's political thought,[145] and one who is numbered among the scholastic theologians concerned to employ the *necessitas* principle to limit rulers' excesses. In Book IV of his *Policraticus*, John used Deuteronomy 17:14–21 (God's warnings to the people about what would happen when they asked for a king) to argue that rulers should not multiply their "horses," i.e., should not "collect more than necessity requires," because, by doing so, the ruler would unduly burden the subjects. John described the ruler's *necessitas* as "a legitimate quantity of such things" as are "rationally demanded by necessity or utility."[146] However, John implicitly qualified his own position later, in Book VI. There he recounted a conversation he had had with his friend Pope Adrian IV (Nicholas Breakspear), the only English pope in the church's history. Adrian, according to John, asked for a candid account of the general populace's opinion of the pope. John obliged, telling him that the image of the church in Rome was suffering from a reputation for avarice and corruption. John rebuked Adrian for accepting "presents and payments" from the faithful:

> You are off the path, father, and not on the path. The city is to be maintained out of the same presents by which it was acquired. What is freely given is freely accepted. Justice is the queen of the virtues and is embarrassed to be exchanged for any amount of price. If justice is to be gracious, she is to be free of charge. She who cannot be seduced may by no means be prostituted for a price; she is entirely and forever pure. Insofar as you oppress others, you will be oppressed by even greater burdens.[147]

The pope, in John's account, laughed and responded by pointing out that the needs of the people could not be met unless the ruler, who had responsibility for meeting those needs, received the resources necessary to meet them. By way of illustration, Adrian engaged in a thought experiment in which "'all the members of the whole body conspired against the stomach, as if against that which by its voraciousness exhausted the labours of all.'"[148] After three days of withholding nourishment from the stomach to destroy it by starvation, the other members of the body found themselves faint from lack of nourishment as well. The heart spoke wisdom to them, and, in the pope's parable, they listened:

> Therefore, they all yielded to the counsel of the heart and, having deliberated thereupon, reason revealed that these evils were inflicted as a result of what had previously been denounced as a public enemy. For the tribute to it was withdrawn by them and like a public provisioner it halted nourishment to everyone. And because no one can fight without a salary, the soldiers were disabled and weakened when they did not receive a salary. But the fault cannot be traced back to the provisioner, who could hardly disburse to others what he did not receive himself. And it would be far more advisable that he should be furnished with goods for his distribution than that all the members should go hungry while getting rid of him. And so it was done; persuaded by reason, the stomach was replenished, the members were revived, and the peace of all was re-established. And so they absolved the stomach, which, although it is voracious and covetous of unsuitable things, still asks not for itself but for others which are unable to be sustained by its emptiness.[149]

The pope, we are informed, then extended his analogy to the realm of civil government, telling John that if he were to "study the matter properly," he would realize that "in the republic . . ., although the magistrates seek after a great deal, they do not accumulate it for themselves but for others."[150] John appears to have acknowledged here that the dictates of *suum cuique* justice could yield to the demands of distributive justice. The needs of the people were identified with the needs and even the wants of the ruler. Thus, the balance between the ruler's *necessitas* and the people's *necessitas* in Book IV was transformed in Book VI into a tension between the needs of the individual subject and the needs of all.

It is not known if John was satisfied with the pope's answer. What is apparent is that theologians of the Middle Ages had the luxury of raising the question of whether the ruler's interests were identical with those of the subjects. Once the state became a purely fictive person, in later centuries,[151] that question would no longer be meaningful; then the interests of the citizens would not be conceived of apart from the state that shaped and realized them.

Theologians were predisposed to remind their hearers that *necessitas* could limit as well as justify the ruler's power. They also raised the question of identity between the ruler's interests and the interests of society's needy members. The primary tax struggle, however, was between individual property interests and the needs of the ruler. In the thirteenth century, the balance between these two social goods was ripe for a comprehensive, theological articulation. As we have seen, it was Thomas who supplied that articulation.

Before exploring the ramifications of Thomas' formulation of the interplay of natural law (common property) and human law (individual property), one last piece of the historical context requires analysis: the place of Thomas' distinctive conception of property, and thus tax, in the development of ideas of political sovereignty and power.

Locating Thomas in the development of sovereignty

Arising against the feudal background, the new demands for tax revenue outstripped theoretical developments. Richard Bonney points out that the twentieth and twenty-first centuries operate with the assumption that "governments have a natural tendency to spend excessively." Bonney, with reference to Brennan and Buchanan, also observes that, "[f]or the ordinary citizen, the power to tax is the most familiar manifestation of the government's ability to coerce." Because the power to tax "does not carry with it any obligation to use the tax revenue in any particular way," the "power to 'tax' is simply the power to 'take.'" The point of fiscal rules and fiscal constitutions is "to limit and direct the coercive means of government, as embodied most conspicuously in its power to tax."[152]

In 1200, "certainly no one was yet thinking in terms of sovereignty." However, Joseph Strayer writes, "when feudal theory had been elaborated to a point where it allowed the king to regulate all justice and to tax all men, suzerainty was coming very close to sovereignty."[153] By 1300, at least in England, the king "had not only many of the attributes of sovereignty, he had, and knew that he had, sovereign power."[154] The king of England "taxed his subjects directly and repeatedly." Moreover, in a development that will play a central role in the story of the next chapter, by the early fourteenth century the English monarch "asserted his right to tax the clergy without the assent of the pope."[155]

The march toward a doctrine of political sovereignty seems to have been led in part by the special status of property rights. Even as Thomas' importation of Aristotelian naturalism strengthened the moral standing of private property, emerging theories bolstered the rulers' authority to interfere with private property. In his account of Baldus de Ubaldis' (1327–1400) treatment of the emperor's power, for instance, Joseph Canning sees a shift from Baldus' "main opinion" when the question of the emperor's right to remove or transfer his subjects' property rights arises. None of the jurists contested the fact that the emperor could remove property rights. What was in question was whether the emperor needed a *cause* to do so, lest he infringe the *ius gentium* that guaranteed those rights.[156] According to Baldus, in Canning's account, the emperor must act *with cause* in interfering with private property, but the cause can be "whatever reason motivates the emperor himself."[157] Baldus' "main opinion" consisted in a limited conception of the emperor's *potestas absoluta*. The emperor was only *legibus solutus* with respect to positive law, not natural or divine law. Canning sees this view as "distinctively medieval."[158] Baldus and other medieval thinkers did not have a modern sense of sovereignty, i.e., one in which "the sovereign's will alone expressed in a duly constitutional form makes valid law." In the medieval conception, the emperor's power had to exist "within the context of a structure of higher norms, expressed in the traditional language of *ius naturale*, *ius gentium* and *ius divinum*." These "higher norms" were rational. Reason linked the emperor, as a rational human being, along with human law to the higher norms of natural law.[159] With Baldus' assertion that the cause of the emperor's removal or transfer of his subjects' property rights could be any motivation, however, "the emperor's *potestas absoluta* has broken through the limitations of the structure of higher norms, and no longer appears as simply the restricted positive law power we have seen so far."[160]

Canning considers it "unclear" why Baldus "should adopt this view on property and leave the emperor limited in other important respects." The special treatment of property could not have been prompted by a belief that the emperor was the source of individual property rights; "the whole juristic discussion of the *princeps* and the property of his subjects arose because it became accepted that he was not the proprietor of those rights." Whatever the reason, Baldus' "treatment of private property provides a big exception to his overall view of a limited absolute power for the emperor."[161]

The thirteenth and fourteenth centuries appear to have been a time of contrary impulses with respect to private property. Baldus' bolstering of the ruler's authority to interfere with individual property occurred in the wake of Thomas' ground-clearing for a stronger justification of individual property by establishing greater continuity between natural and positive law. That Thomas himself may have unwittingly contributed to the power of rulers to "take" cannot be discounted. Walter Ullmann argues that Thomas' "naturalization" of positive law paved the way for an eventual "positivization" of natural law by Marsilius of Padua (1275/80–1342/3). Marsilius, in Ullmann's words, took "away all grounds for intervention on behalf of any ethical considerations: a law becomes a natural law through being a positive law." Positive law, moreover, is enforceable "not because it is based on natural law but because it embodies the will of the legislator."[162] Whether Ullmann is correct in saying that Marsilius "de-moralized" and "humanized" the law,[163] he argues persuasively that Marsilius' "system would not have been possible without the doctrinal preparation by Thomism."[164]

Even in Ullmann's account, however, there is a wide gulf between Thomas and Marsilius, and that gulf consists in the evacuation of theology from the discussion of politics and, thus, of law:

> We can see the advanced nature of Marsiglio's thought if for a moment we recall the Thomist view of natural law as the regulator of human positive law, and the consequential easy ingress of clerical intervention, and compare this with the Marsilian view of the will of the people as the *auctoritas humana* which is the element that confers legal, that is, enforceable character on 'natural law' and which is therefore entirely removed from the clerical sphere: no moral overtones, no appeals to the eternal truths, no reference to ethical maxims, can enter here. Here a restricted human view—there the vision of eternal life.[165]

Aquinas represents a brief and fragile stage in what Ullmann calls the "Aristotelian development." The stages are "marked by (1) hostile attitude to [Aristotle]; (2) tolerance and absorption into Christian cosmology; (3) the release of Aristotle from the Christian garb."[166] Aquinas dominated the second stage; the third stage emerged with Marsilius. If Aristotle enabled Thomas to give an unprecedentedly full and affirmative account of individual property rights, his justification for the ruler's invasion of those rights in the interest of the common good remained theological, especially in contrast to the political theories of Baldus and Marsilius.

In short, Thomas was uniquely situated to shape the dynamic between individual and common conceptions of property. In Question 66 of Secunda Secundae, Thomas writes:

> External things can be considered in two ways. First, as regards their nature, and this is not subject to the power of man, but only to the power of God Whose mere will all things obey. Secondly, as regards their use, and in this way, man has a natural dominion [*dominium*] over external things, because, by his reason and will, he is able to use them for his own profit.[167]

The human capacity to act upon external things gives humans *dominium* over those things; and this principle explains even why a piece of land should belong to one person rather than another:

> [I]f a particular piece of land be considered absolutely, it contains no reason why it should belong to one man more than to another, but if it be considered in respect of its adaptability to cultivation, and the unmolested use of the land, it has a certain commensuration to be the property of one and not of another man.[168]

For Thomas, an external thing belongs to an individual, not through sheer mastery or power, but through use guided by reason and will. Underneath the thoroughness with which he balances these two goods—individual and common property—without diminishing the importance of either, lies his unique formulation of the interplay of natural and positive law. That formulation, in turn, is made possible by Thomas' skill in balancing theology (which requires that we think of "external things" as given by God to all in common) and economic reality (which dictates that external things will contribute to the common good most effectively when invested with individual labor and rights).

From one standpoint, Thomas' reconciliation of the affirmative goods of communal and individual property is nothing other than his contribution to the articulation of the fracture "between *archē* and *dynamis* in God" in the "theological paradigm," which, by analogy, is the separation of "kingdom from government" in the "liberal political paradigm" that was to emerge.[169] Christianity, as we have seen, "split" classical ontology "into two separate realities": "theology and *oikonomia*."[170] In the theological paradigm, this aporia would be expressed in terms of immanence and transcendence. In the sphere of civil government, the gulf "lays bare the twofold structure that defines the governmental machine of the West."[171] Sovereign power becomes articulated on two levels: Kingdom and Government. In the theological realm, Kingdom and Government must be continuously separated so that the doctrine of providence can ceaselessly rejoin them.[172]

The aporia arose from Aristotle's *Metaphysics*, which, according to Agamben, bequeathed "to Western politics the paradigm of the divine regime of the world as a double system, formed, on the one hand, by a transcendent *archē*, and, on the other, by an immanent concurrence of secondary actions and causes."[173] This double system, Agamben writes, is the problem of *order*. Order (*taxis*) refers to reciprocal relation in the *Metaphysics*.[174] In the *Politics* (1298[a]), *taxis* is the reciprocal relation of the powers (*archai*). Therefore, Agamben concludes, Aristotle displaced the term "order" from its generic context to its strategic location "at the junction between ontology and politics, which makes of it a fundamental *terminus technicus* of Western politics and metaphysics."[175]

Order, in Agamben's estimation, is an ontological concept. It produces a displacement of ontology "from the category of substance to the categories of relation and praxis." Order does not presuppose being; order *is* being. The displacement of ontology from substance to praxis, Agamben argues, is "the specific legacy that medieval theology leaves to modern philosophy."[176]

This medieval move—the making of order a central ontological principle—is most pervasive in Aquinas' writings, Agamben writes. "Following an intention that deeply marked the medieval vision of the world, Thomas tried to make of order the fundamental ontological concept, which determines and conditions the very idea of being; and yet, precisely for this reason, the Aristotelian aporia reaches with him its most radical formulation."[177] After Thomas, what made human government conceptually possible was "the supposition of a *plenitudo potestatis*" that "must immediately distinguish itself from its actual exercise (its *executio*), which then constitutes the second sword."[178] The inseparability yet distinction between Thomas' natural law of common ownership and positive law of private ownership, I would suggest, maps onto the continuous fracturing and rejoining of authority and its exercise. Just as Christian theology comes close to *requiring* an aporia between the God who reigns but does not govern on the one hand and the government itself on the other, so Western politics seems to require a rupture between the ideal condition (e.g., communal property) and realistic, functioning circumstances (e.g., private property). The healing of that fracture requires a balance of the ideal condition and functional circumstances. That is, it requires civil government—and tax as a constituent part thereof.

Tax justice as equilibrium

Two types of balance have already appeared above—in connection with the equivalence that underlies *iustitia* and, thus, *aequalitas*, which depends on *debitum*, and in connection with Thomas' robust conceptions of both the natural law of common property and the positive law of individual property rights. This section links those two functions of "balance" to each other and constructively to the function of taxation.

Among the ambiguities in the medieval view of the common good is its connection to justice. Antony Black argues that for Aristotle and many of his medieval followers, to say that an action was "for the common good" was almost tantamount to saying it was just.[179] For Aquinas, however, there appears to have been a distinction. Black detects a wedge between the common good and justice in Question 96 of Prima Secundae, precisely on the issue of taxation: "'when burdens [sc., probably, taxes], even though directed at the common good, are unjustly distributed through society.'"[180] Justice (at least distributive justice) thus seems to mediate between the good of the part and the good of the whole, that is, between the individual and the community. If, as Black suggests, "burdens" are to be taken as tax burdens, then a just tax system for Thomas is one that *both* serves the collective good *and* refrains from overburdening individual property.

Black observes an ambiguity in Aquinas on the "clash" between individual and collective goods. On the one hand,

> [T]he state stands to the individual as whole to part, so that "the good of the part is referable to the good of the whole". Personal morality is interdependent with communal morality, justice itself being, on one definition, "that which directs man to the common good"—and all the virtues are related to justice.[181]

On the other hand, Black notes, Aquinas describes the collective good and the individual good as differing "not only in degree but in kind," operating according to different logics.[182] Black sees this tension within the *Summa*, the dialectic between the logic of the whole and the logic of the part as evidence that Thomas repeatedly swings between an Aristotelian "holism" and a Christian "individualism."

The synthesis, to the extent there is one, seems to be that personal and communal morality operate with different principles but that justice forms a bridge between those two sets of principles by directing individual good to the common good and ensuring that the common good honors individual good.

Justice and the common good are separate concepts in Thomas' doctrine of property because both the individual's appropriation of property and the ruler's expropriation of it can serve the common good. Something additional is required to balance these two genuine goods. The additional thing is justice. It would be an error in interpreting Aquinas to equate common ownership of property with the common good itself.[183]

In promoting individual ownership of property, Aquinas was following rather than diverging from Aristotle, who, in the name of harmony and efficiency, "had supported private property against the community of wives and property recommended by Plato in his *Republic*."[184] A distinctive feature of Aristotle's and Thomas' idea of justice, then, is the way it accommodates two positive goods. In fact, it accommodates and balances two moral goods, two *debita*. Odd Langholm writes: "As with all classical authors, the 'just' is what is 'fair': 'to give each one his due'; but with Aristotle 'fair' comes to mean 'equal', justice is an equation involving opposing 'dues.'"[185]

The full significance of *aequalitas* for Aquinas now becomes apparent. *Aequalitas* is not a formal ideal used to sanitize the compromise struck through the political process between hostile interests. Rather, it is equilibrium, the balance between two *debita* in tension. Joel Kaye, in *A History of Balance 1250–1375*, calls *aequalitas* "that aspect of justice that is quantifiable and knowable" for Aquinas.[186] In another piece, "Equalization in the Body and the Body Politic," Kaye traces the ancient analogy between the health of the body politic and the health of a human body. Kaye explains that *aequalitas* is quantifiable precisely because it is not abstract equality or an elusive numerical equivalence, but rather an equilibrium among constituent parts that are all in flux, each trying to supersede the others.[187]

Justice balances the two competing ways in which property can "belong," both ways serving the common good. Thomas' highly developed doctrine of private property as an affirmative good may have been designed to infuse the holding of individual property with moral content, working toward the goal of shoring up individual property rights against the emerging demands of increasingly powerful rulers. At the same time, he insists that the whole is greater than the part and that *necessitas* in one form or another allows the communal good both to circumscribe the individual's appropriation of goods and to limit and direct the ruler's expropriation of the individual's goods so appropriated.

Taxation itself can be a way of adjudicating between these two *debita*. *Aequalitas*, the measure of justice, in turn governed by *necessitas* on both sides of the bargain, achieves equilibrium between two real goods. This equilibrium is not a political compromise between the needs of the state and the individual freedom to generate wealth. Rather, it is justice that honors everyone's needs, and guarantees no more than that.

Although the argument has required excavation beneath the surface of Thomas' writings, I want to suggest that Thomas' highly developed equilibrium between the natural- and human-law doctrines of property imprinted a balancing function on the institution of taxation. In keeping with the assumptions of this project as a whole, Thomas' ideas about public takings in general are read as referring to taxation. That is, taxation for Thomas is a taking that is legitimated by the justice that inheres in honoring the *debita*—and, thus, the *necessitas*—of all society's members.

Justice and liberality

Why is all of this not merely an argument for generosity? Why does taxation, a kind of licit robbery by public authority, even enter Thomas' moral vision of the community of goods that circumscribes individual appropriation? Some have given liberality primacy over justice in their readings of Aquinas. Gilson writes: "No doubt those who possess these goods are free to dispose of them according to their best judgment in order to feed the hungry and clothe the naked."[188] In a similar vein, R. W. Dyson writes: "St. Thomas is content to leave the actual distribution of surplus property to the conscience of the individual proprietor. In a modern guise, however, his argument would no doubt find expression as an argument in favour of progressive or redistributive taxation."[189]

In an article titled "The Ethical Basis for Taxation in the Thought of Thomas Aquinas,"[190] Christopher Todd Meredith faults John Finnis for employing Thomas' account of *necessitas* and *superflua* in defense of redistributive taxation.[191] Meredith is surely right that no explicit grounds for the redistribution of resources through the institution of taxation can be located in Thomas' writings. Finnis would not disagree, as Meredith acknowledges. Finnis sees himself as developing principles that are implicit in Thomas' thought.[192] This project follows Finnis' "constructive" approach, and the present chapter is inspired in part by Finnis' conclusions.

In any event, use of the term "redistribution" prejudges the way tax works in relation to its baselines. While it may be impractical to do without notional baselines, the concept of redistribution implies an existing state of affairs and a different, ideal state of affairs. For Aquinas, however, there is only one state of affairs. The needy *already* own what they need and another's *superflua* is already theirs. Moreover, one should already have parted—morally, if not legally—with one's superabundance. Explicitly redistributive taxation, to the extent Thomas could have envisioned it, would have been for him nothing other than the payment of a debt.

The opposition, so natural to the modern mind, between justice and liberality would be a false one to Thomas, who wrote:

> Although liberality does not consider the legal due [*debitum legale*] that justice considers, it considers a certain moral due [*debitum quoddam morale*]. This due is based on a certain fittingness and not on an obligation [*obligatus*]: so that it answers to the idea of due in the lowest degree [*Unde minimum habet de ratione debiti*].[193]

Justice pertains by its nature to something external to the individual. The end of human existence for Thomas is a supernatural end, beatitude, an end that is "totally extrinsic to human nature."[194] Even humankind's natural end, felicity, is not generated entirely from within the individual. As the historian Anthony Parel argues, the instrumentality of things is closely linked with eschatology for Thomas. Development of an individual's natural powers (i.e., the development of virtue) is not an end in itself, but rather "culminates in man's religious development" and thus furthers the individual's "supernatural end." In the same way, the appropriation of property—far from the modern conception—is not an end in itself, but an instrument that promotes the common good, that is a constitutive element of justice, and that furthers felicity.

On the other hand, both Ullmann and Gilson argue that Thomas exploits Aristotle's grudging admission that "a good man and a good citizen are not necessarily the same thing" to elevate the status of particular justice vis-à-vis legal justice, in which the virtue of justice almost entirely consisted for Aristotle. Gilson writes:

> St. Thomas hastens to profit by this admission to make a distinction between Greek justice, which is entirely directed to the good of the city, and particular justice, enriching the soul which acquires and exercises it as one of its most precious perfections. This time it is no longer in Aristotle that St. Thomas finds the text which authorizes him to proclaim that this justice exists, it is in St. Matthew's Gospel: "Blessed are they who hunger and thirst after justice" (V, 6). Here we see how striking a metamorphosis through which Greek morality must pass in order to be able to endure in a Christian climate. Like the other virtues, justice must be interiorized if it is to become Christian.[195]

A brief summary of Thomas' conceptual framework of legal and particular, and commutative and distributive, justice can help elucidate the simultaneous internalization and externalization of justice. Justice, according to Thomas, directs people in their relations with other people. If it directs an individual in his or her relations with another individual, it is "particular justice." If it directs his or her relations to "others in general," so that it is "referable to the common good," it is "legal justice."[196] Commutative and distributive justice are the two categories of particular justice.[197] Both subcategories are "directed to the private individual, who is compared to the community as a part to the whole." Commutative justice concerns "the order of one part to another, to which corresponds the order of one private individual to another." Distributive justice describes "the order of the whole towards the parts, to which corresponds the order of that which belongs to the community in relation to each single person."[198]

Thomas' stress on particular justice requires the individual to be oriented toward another individual (in commutative justice[199]) or even for the state to be oriented toward the individual (in distributive justice[200]). True, Aquinas writes, "the good of any virtue . . . is referable to the common good," and, in that sense, justice can be called "a general virtue" and, "since it belongs to the law to direct to the common good," can be called "legal justice."[201] The force of Secunda Secundae, Question 58, Article 7, however, is that there is also another kind of justice. Article 7 is the point at which Thomas departs from Aristotle's account of justice, refers to Matthew 5:6, and concludes "so too besides legal justice there is need for particular justice to direct man in his relations to other individuals."[202] Article 7 insists that there is a kind of good that differs from the common good. Legal justice is sufficient, Thomas writes, to direct humans toward the common good, but particular justice is necessary to direct us "to the good of another individual."[203] The "common good of the realm" and "the particular good of the individual" differ, not only as "many" differs from "few," but "formally" and in their "aspect."[204]

It is possible to see the polarity of commutative and distributive justice (within particular justice) running beneath the surface of the positive-and-natural-law polarity. Thomas writes, "Distributive and commutative justice differ not only in respect of unity and multitude, but also in respect of different kinds of due [*diversam rationem debiti*]: because common property [*id quod est commune*] is due [*debetur*] to an individual in one way, and his personal property [*id quod est proprium*] in another way."[205] Thus, the entire dynamic of the two *debita*, determined for each *debitum* as the point where *necessitas* meets *superflua*, appears to be situated within particular justice. Legal justice need not enter the Thomist tax equation at all.

Thomas' bolstering of particular justice is a fundamentally theological move. In Étienne Gilson's account, Thomas both Christianized and interiorized Aristotelian justice by vivifying particular justice, with its commutative and distributive aspects, as over against legal justice.[206] From a post-Enlightenment perspective the simultaneous internalization and externalization of the virtue of justice seems incoherent. The process is intelligible, however, against the backdrop of Aristotle. In Gilson's account, it is precisely because God legislates that the law can become interior and personal:

> In [Aristotle] there is no hint of any law higher than that of the human being, we get the benefit of our address and suffer the consequences of our awkwardness; absorbed in the contemplation of his own thoughts, the First Unmoved Mover makes no attempt to legislate for man; not only is it difficult to picture him as the author of a supernatural revelation, or as the law-giver of a Decalogue, but since he is not the creator of consciences he lives his own divine life without creating any interior law to direct us or to enlighten us; our errors enslave us, and there is no Christ there to suffer on that account; the just man perseveres and the sinner repents, and there is no joy in heaven at his perseverance or welcome for his repentance; it is for man to live out his moral life and gather up the fruits; God is not interested. It seems otherwise with Plato; indeed, it is necessarily otherwise in a philosophy where the gods are the authors of nature and rule it providentially by laws. In Platonism, as in Christianity, there is a divine order which rules and defines the moral order.[207]

Aquinas follows Plato rather than Aristotle in this regard. No conflict appears between divine legislation and "interior laws." Thomas pushes the parameters of justice both inward and outward from their Aristotelian starting point.

As it is with divine government, so it is with human government. Thomas writes that "there is a certain extraneous good which awaits man after he has lived this mortal life: namely, the final blessedness to which he looks forward in the enjoyment of God after death."[208] On the plane of political theology as well, the final good also begins outside of the individual but turns out to be the individual's own good:

> If the end of man were some good existing only in himself, therefore, the final end of government would similarly be to acquire and preserve that good for the whole community. Thus if that ultimate end, whether of one man or of a community, were the life and health of the body, the physicians would have the duty of governing. And if the final end were abundant wealth, the steward would be king of the community. And if the good were that the community might achieve knowledge of the truth, the king would have the duty of a teacher. But it seems that the end for which a community is brought together is to live according to virtue; for men come together so that they may live well in a way that would not be possible for each of them living singly. For the good is life according to virtue, and so the end of human association is a virtuous life.[209]

Only in light of this extraneous interiority, or personalized externality, does it make sense to say with Thomas that "the proper effect of law is to lead its subjects to their proper virtue: and since virtue is 'that which makes its subject good,' it follows that the proper effect of law is to make those to whom it is given, good, either simply or in some particular respect."[210]

Parel writes that, for Aquinas, "the full, natural development of man can occur only through the medium of the state."[211] MacIntyre concludes that for Aquinas the optimal political regime "is that whose order best conduces to education into the virtues in the interest of the good of all."[212] More to the point of this chapter, it is "[o]nly through the mediation of the state" that "the conditional right to private property and the obligation to put privately acquired property [to] common use" can be "humanely reconciled."[213] Thomas says in section 2.4 of his *Commentary on Aristotle's Politics* that this reconciliation is the concern of the "good legislator." This statement makes practical sense. If justice is the balancing of two real goods, one arising from the individual's creative act and the other a dictate of natural law, but both promoting the common good, then an objective third party is required to effect the balance.

In the contemporary world, tax justice is achieved when the taxpayer receives something of value for the taxes paid (benefit theory) or when the burden of paying taxes is distributed fairly (sacrifice or ability theory). Tax, in either case, is a detriment to the taxpayer, something to be compensated for or minimized. In the Thomist framework, on the other hand, the equilibrium sought by the process of paying and collecting taxes benefits all parties. The injustice of holding onto *superflua* lies not only in that it is a kind of robbery; it is also the injustice of having more than one needs, of holding property that is not a ***debitum***. As the mechanism of honoring *necessitas*, taxation can train us to think of what we owe to others on the basis that it belongs to them. It can bring us to the place where justice becomes an interior, Christian virtue.

Notes

1 Richard G. Newhauser, "Justice and Liberality: Opposition to Avarice in the Twelfth Century," in *Virtue and Ethics in the Twelfth Century*, by István P. Bejczy, ed. Richard G. Newhauser (Leiden: Brill, 2005), 303.
2 Newhauser, "Justice and Liberality," 303.
3 Newhauser, "Justice and Liberality," 304.
4 Jennifer Hole, *Economic Ethics in Late Medieval England, 1300–1500*, Archival Insights into the Evolution of Economics, ed. Robert Leeson (Palgrave Macmillan, 2016), 118.
5 Hole, *Economic Ethics*, 65–66.
6 Jacques Le Goff, *Money and the Middle Ages: An Essay in Historical Anthropology*, trans. Jean Birrell (Cambridge: Polity Press, 2012), 145.
7 Le Goff, *Money and the Middle Ages*, 145.
8 Robert M. Grant, *Early Christianity and Society* (London: Collins, 1978), 98.
9 Ambrose, "Sermon against Auxentius" 5, in *From Irenaeus to Grotius: A Sourcebook in Christian Political Thought, 100–1625*, ed. Oliver O'Donovan and Joan Lockwood O'Donovan (Grand Rapids: William B. Eerdmans Publishing Co., 1999).
10 Gregory of Tours, *History of the Franks* 4.2, in *A Source Book for Medieval Economic History*, by Roy C. Cave and Herbert H. Coulson (New York: Biblo and Tannen, 1965), 353–54.
11 Charles Norris Cochrane, *Christianity and Classical Culture: A Study of Thought and Action from Augustus to Augustine* (New York: Oxford University Press, 1957), 440, referring to Augustine, *City of God* 6.5, 6.
12 Peter Brown writes that *sufficientia* was not a classical word, but one that was taken from Proverbs 30:8, "where the Hebrew *lehem huqi* referred to the daily bread allotted to each person by the hand of God." Peter Brown, *Through the Eye of a Needle: Wealth, the Fall of Rome, and the Making of Christianity in the West, 350–550 AD* (Princeton: Princeton University Press, 2012), 315.
13 Brown, *Through the Eye of a Needle*, 315.
14 Elizabeth A. R. Brown, "Taxation and Morality in the Thirteenth and Fourteenth Centuries: Conscience and Political Power and the Kings of France," *French Historical Studies* 8, no. 1 (Spring 1973): 9, accessed August 22, 2020, http://www.jstor.org/stable/285956.
15 See Brown, "Taxation and Morality," 1–6.
16 Hole, *Economic Ethics*, 22.
17 Aristotle, *Politics*, trans. Ernest Barker (Oxford: Oxford University Press, 1995) 1.3.
18 Thomas Aquinas, *Summa theologiae* (Latin-English Edition), trans. Fathers of the English-Dominican Province (NovAntiqua, 2013), I–II, Q. 2, Art. 1, resp. The *Summa Theologiae* is cited as *ST* hereafter.
19 Joel Kaye, *A History of Balance, 1250–1375: The Emergence of a New Model of Equilibrium and Its Impact on Thought* (Cambridge: Cambridge University Press, 2014), 24–25.

20 N. J. G. Pounds, *An Economic History of Medieval Europe*, 2nd ed. (London: Longman, 1994), 7.
21 Pounds, *An Economic History*, 25–26.
22 Pounds, *An Economic History*, 77.
23 Giovanni Cherubini, "The Peasant and Agriculture," in *The Medieval World*, ed. Jacques Le Goff, trans. Lydia G. Cochrane (London: Parkgate Books, Ltd., 1990), 115.
24 Pounds, *Economic History*, 134–35.
25 Cherubini, "The Peasant and Agriculture," 115.
26 Cherubini, "The Peasant and Agriculture," 118, 120.
27 Pounds, *Economic History*, 134–35.
28 Lactantius, *Divine Institutes*, trans. Anthony Bowen and Peter Garnsey, Translated Texts for Historians 40 (Liverpool: Liverpool University Press, 2003) 6.6.1.
29 Lactantius, *Divine Institutes* 6.5.1:

> To reduce the rest to servitude, they began first to withdraw the necessities of life, gathering them in and keeping them firmly locked up, so that the bounty of heaven became their bounty, not from any humanitarian impulse—they felt none—but to rake in the means of avarice and greed for themselves. In the name of justice they authorised for their own purposes laws of great unfairness and injustice, by which they could protect their greedy plunderings from mob violence.

30 Augustine, *Tractate on John* 50, 7, quoted in Boniface Ramsey, "Almsgiving in the Latin Church: The Late Fourth and Early Fifth Centuries," *Theological Studies* 43 (1982): 228, accessed August 22, 2020, http://cdn.theologicalstudies.net/43/43.2/43.2.2.pdf#:~:text=ALMSGIVING%20IN%20THE%20LATIN%20CHURCH%20231%20human%20being.,on%20the%20condition%20that%20is%20common%20to%20all.%22.
31 Ramsey, "Almsgiving in the Latin Church," 251.
32 Ramsey, "Almsgiving in the Latin Church," 256.
33 Augustine, "Exposition of Psalm 147," in *The Works of Saint Augustine: A Translation for the 21st Century* III/20, trans. Maria Boulding, ed. Boniface Ramsey (Hyde Park, NY: New City Press, 2004), 454.
34 George O'Brien, *An Essay on Mediaeval Economic Teaching* (London: Longmans, Green, and Co., 1920), 82.
35 That Thomas took a relativized, conditional view of property rights is conceded even by those who see no argument for redistributive taxation in his work. See, e.g., Christopher Todd Meredith, "The Ethical Basis for Taxation in the Thought of Thomas Aquinas," *Journal of Markets & Morality* 11, no. 1 (Spring 2008): 50.
36 J. M. Kelly, *A Short History of Western Legal Theory* (Oxford: Clarendon Press, 1992), 151.
37 *ST* II-II, Q. 66, Art. 2, resp.
38 *ST* II-II, Q. 66, Art. 8, ad. 3. Alasdair MacIntyre notes that Aquinas "inherited from the patristic tradition a view of the limitation of the right to property which would have been … vehemently rejected by some later writers, such as Hume and Blackstone. Alasdair MacIntyre, *Whose Justice? Which Rationality?* (London: Gerald Duckworth & Co. Ltd., 1988), 199.
39 Jean Porter, *Ministers of the Law: A Natural Law Theory of Legal Authority*, Emory University Studies in Law and Religion, ed. John Witte, Jr. (Grand Rapids: William B. Eerdmans Publishing Co., 2010), xv.
40 The term "property" is roughly synonymous with "exterior things" or "external things." In Roman law, particularly in Justinian's *Institutes* (533), "property"

had a broad meaning—any "thing, material or immaterial, that was owned or possessed and had some economic value." Diana Wood, *Medieval Economic Thought* (Cambridge: Cambridge University Press, 2002), 18.

41 *ST* II–II, Q. 66, Art. 8, ad. 3.
42 *ST* I–II, Q. 95, Art. 2, resp.
43 *ST* II–II, Q. 66, Art. 7, resp.
44 *ST* II–II, Q. 117, Art. 1, ad. 1.
45 *ST* II–II, Q. 177, Art. 4, resp.
46 *ST* II–II, Q. 66, Art. 8, ad. 3.
47 *ST* II–II, Q. 87, Art. 4, ad. 3.
48 *ST* II–II, Q. 87, Art. 4, ad. 4.
49 *ST* II–II, Q. 58, Art. 1.
50 Justinian, *The Digest of Justinian*, ed. Alan Watson (Philadelphia: University of Pennsylvania Press, 1998) 1.1.
51 *ST* II–II, Q. 58, Art. 10, resp. ("Therefore justice is not about the passions").
52 Étienne Gilson, *The Christian Philosophy of St. Thomas Aquinas* (London: Victor Gollancz Ltd., 1961), 309.
53 MacIntyre, *Whose Justice?*, 199.
54 Gilson, *Christian Philosophy*, 309; *ST* II–II, Q.58, Art. 10, ad. 1 ("This real mean is also the rational mean, wherefore justice satisfies the conditions of a moral virtue").
55 MacIntyre, *Whose Justice?*, 198.
56 Gilson, *Christian Philosophy*, 310.
57 Gilson, *Christian Philosophy*, 310.
58 Gilson, *Christian Philosophy*, 310; *ST* II–II, Q. 60, Art. 1.; *ST* II–II, Q. 58, Art. 6.
59 *ST* II–II, Q. 60, Art. 1, ad. 4.
60 *ST* II–II, Q. 57, Art. 4, resp.; Gilson, *Christian Philosophy*, 307. As Latin has no word or phrase for "belonging to," the genitive case in its most basic form—the possessive genitive—is typically used to express the idea of belonging. The possessive genitive easily becomes the partitive genitive: "From 'belonging to' there is an easy transition to 'part of'. Here the genitive stands to the noun defined in the relationship of the whole to its part(s)." L. R. Palmer, *The Latin Language* (London: Faber and Faber Ltd., 1954), 291. Thomas makes the connection explicitly: *[F]ilius est aliquid patris, quia quodammodo est pars eius. ST* II–II, Q. 57, Art. 4, resp.
61 Gilson, *Christian Philosophy*, 307.
62 *ST* II–II, Q. 57, Art. 4, resp.
63 *ST* II–II, Q. 57, Art. 4, resp.
64 *ST* II–II, Q. 57, Art. 1, resp.
65 Gilson, *Christian Philosophy*, 306.
66 Gilson, *Christian Philosophy*, 333.
67 Eugene F. Rogers, Jr., *Aquinas and the Supreme Court: Race, Gender, and the Failure of Natural Law in Thomas's Biblical Commentaries* (Malden, MA: Wiley-Blackwell, 2013), 89.
68 Martin Rhonheimer, "Sins Against Justice (IIa IIae, qq. 59–78)," trans. Frederick G. Lawrence, in *The Ethics of Aquinas*, ed. Stephen J. Pope (Washington: Georgetown University Press, 2002), 287 (footnotes omitted).
69 Joseph M. Magee, "Debitum and Personae: The Metaphysical Foundation of Justice," Thomistic Philosophy Page, accessed August 22, 2020, http://www.aquinasonline.com/Topics/justice.html.
70 *ST* II-II, Q. 62, Art. 1, ad. 1.
71 Magee, "Debitum and Personae."

72 Elmer T. Gelinas, "Ius and Lex in Thomas Aquinas," *American Journal of Jurisprudence* 15, no. 1 (1970): 164.
73 Gelinas, "Ius and Lex in Thomas Aquinas," 165.
74 For a contemporary reconstruction of the right of those in need to take what is needed, based on the medieval *casus necessitatis* doctrine, see Alejandra Mancilla, *The Right of Necessity: Moral Cosmopolitanism and Global Poverty* (London: Rowman & Littlefield, 2016). Mancilla calls this right of necessity "a concrete expression of the right to subsistence," "not an external but an internal limitation to any reasonable system of property rights." Mancilla, *The Right of Necessity*, 6. Mancilla argues that the right of necessity implies a concomitant duty "to rearrange global poverty arrangements in a way that does not leave millions of people in a position where they may legitimately invoke their right of necessity." Mancilla, *The Right of Necessity*, 7.
75 *ST* II–II, Q. 87, Art. 1, ad. 4.
76 "Judicial precepts" differ from "ceremonial precepts," according to Aquinas, in that it is "unlawful to observe the ceremonial precepts at the time of the New Law, whereas there is no sin in keeping the judicial precepts during the time of grace although they are not binding." In fact, however, judicial precepts may be obligatory even in the time of grace if they are commanded "by the authority of those who have power to make laws." *ST* II–II, Q. 87, Art. 1, resp.
77 *ST* II–II, Q. 87, Art. 3, resp.
78 *ST* II–II, Q. 87, Art. 1, resp.
79 Thomas Aquinas, *Commentary on Romans* 13:6, Patristic Bible Commentary, accessed September 9, 2020, https://sites.google.com/site/aquinasstudybible/home/romans/st-thomas-aquinas-on-romans/chapter-1/chapter-2/chapter-3/chapter-4/chapter-5/chapter-6/chapter-7/chapter-8/chapter-9/chapter-10/chapter-11/chapter-12/chapter-13.
80 *ST* II–II, Q. 66, Art. 7.
81 *ST* II–II, Q. 66, Art. 7, ad. 2.
82 *ST* II–II, Q. 66, Art. 7.
83 Jean Porter, "The Virtue of Justice (IIa IIae, qq. 55–122)," in *The Ethics of Aquinas*, 282.
84 Eberhard Isenmann, "Medieval and Renaissance Theories of State Finance," in *Economic Systems and State Finance*, ed. Richard Bonney (Oxford: Oxford University Press, 1995), 35.
85 See Porter, "The Virtue of Justice," 280 ("The natural law injunction that material goods should be held in common still has force, in that those who own such goods are obliged to share them with others in time of need. ... Hence, the individual's right to private property is a positive rather than a natural right, and as such it presupposes the existence of social convention.").
86 Mancilla, *The Right of Necessity*, 17.
87 MacIntyre, *Whose Justice?*, 199. See also Gilson, *Christian Philosophy*, 315.
88 R. W. Dyson, introduction to *Aquinas: Political Writings*, ed. and trans. R. W. Dyson, Cambridge Texts in the History of Political Thought (Cambridge: Cambridge University Press, 2002), xxxi.
89 Dyson, *Aquinas*, xxxi. Aquinas' account of private property owes some of its nuance to Aristotle, who wrote:

> The present system would be far preferable, if it were embellished with social customs and the enactment of proper laws. It would ... combine the merits of a system of community of property with those of the system of private property. For, although there is a sense in which property *ought* to be common, it should in general be private. When everyone has his own separate sphere of interest, there will not be the same ground for quarrels; and they will make

> more effort, because each man will feel that he is applying himself to what is his own.

Aristotle, *Politics*, trans. Ernest Barker (Oxford: Oxford University Press, 1995) 2.5.1263[a].

90 John Finnis interprets the "universal destination of goods" feature of Catholic Social Teaching (CST) in light of Thomas' *necessitas-superflua* distinction. In his critique of CST, Finnis advocates teaching "about the right to hold property ... for one's legitimate vocational purposes and responsibilities" and calls the right to hold property "a right of exclusion overridden only in circumstances of extreme necessity." But that principle, it turns out, applies only to the property holder's *necessitas*. The holder's right of exclusion should be, according to Finnis, "permanently qualified by a strict duty to distribute (via taxation and/or charitable giving) *all* one's *superflua*, all holdings beyond what one needs to discharge one's vocation." John Finnis, "A Radical Critique of Catholic Social Teaching," in *Catholic Social Teaching: A Volume of Scholarly Essays*, ed. Gerard V. Bradley and E. Christian Brugger (Cambridge: Cambridge University Press, 2019), 574. The "'universal destination' of the goods of the earth" is, Finnis later states, "essentially ... the duty to distribute one's *superflua*." Finnis, "A Radical Critique," 582n64.

Finnis' critique is designed to clarify areas in which CST has been less than clear. In Cristóbal Orrego's view as well, CST has not been entirely consistent on the question of redistribution. The tradition began, in Pope Leo XIII's *Rerum novarum* (1891), with a strong defense of "the right to private property against the overreaching of the socialist state." That position was qualified, however, in later encyclicals, which admitted "some right of the state to use legal means to redistribute riches as a requirement of the common good." Cristóbal Orrego, "The Universal Destination of the World's Resources," in *Catholic Social Teaching: A Volume of Scholarly Essays*, ed. Gerard V. Bradley and E. Christian Brugger, 272 (Cambridge: Cambridge University Press, 2019).

91 Thomas Aquinas, *Commentary on the Nicomachean Ethics*, trans. C.I. Litzinger, Library of Living Catholic Thought 1 (Chicago: Henry Regnery Co., 1964) 1.9.

92 Aquinas, *Commentary on the Nicomachean Ethics* 1.9.116.

93 Aquinas, *Commentary on the Nicomachean Ethics* 10.13.2128.

94 Thomas Aquinas and Tolomeo of Lucca, "De regimine principum" ("De regno") 1.16, in *St. Thomas Aquinas: Political Writings*, ed. and trans. R. W. Dyson, Cambridge Texts in the History of Political Thought (Cambridge, Cambridge University Press, 2002), 44. Thomas did not complete "De regimine principum" before his death; that task fell to his friend and disciple Tolomeo of Lucca. The sections of the work that are referenced here, however, are accepted as Thomas' own writings.

95 See, e.g., Augustine, *Homilies on the Gospel of John*, trans. John Gibb, in the Christian Classics Ethereal Library, accessed August 23, 2020, https://ccel.org/ccel/schaff/npnf107/npnf107.iii.vii.html:

> For by divine right, "The earth is the Lord's, and the fullness thereof." The poor and the rich God made of one clay; the same earth supports alike the poor and the rich. By human right, however, one says, This estate is mine, this house is mine, this servant is mine. By human right, therefore, is by right of the emperors. Why so? Because God has distributed to mankind these very human rights through the emperors and kings of this world.

96 Wood, *Medieval Economic Thought*, 19.

97 Wood, *Medieval Economic Thought*, 21.

98 Wood, *Medieval Economic Thought*, 21; Kelly, *Short History*, 151.
99 Wood, *Medieval Economic Thought*, 21, quoting Rufinus, *Summa decretorum*, ed. Heinrich Singer, in *Medieval Political Ideas*, ed. Ewart Lewis, vol. 1 (New York: Cooper Square, 1974), 38.
100 Wood, *Medieval Economic Thought*, 21.
101 Wood, *Medieval Economic Thought*, 22, citing Alexander of Hales, *Summa theologica* (Quaracchi: Collegium S. Bonaventurae, 1924–48) 4.2.2.3.
102 Wood, *Medieval Economic Thought*, 22, citing *ST* I–II, Q. 93, Art. 5.
103 Wood, *Medieval Economic Thought*, 23.
104 Aquinas, *Commentary on the Nicomachean Ethics* 1.3.34.
105 Walter Ullmann, *Principles of Government and Politics in the Middle Ages* (London: Methuen & Co. Ltd., 1961), 248–49.
106 *ST* I–II, Q. 71, Art. 6, ad. 4.
107 Ullmann, *Principles of Government*, 248–51.
108 Ullmann, *Principles of Government*, 249.
109 *ST* I–II, Q. 95, Art. 2.
110 Richard Bonney, introduction to *The Rise of the Fiscal State in Europe, c. 1200–1815*, ed. Richard Bonney (Oxford Scholarship Online, 2011), 9, accessed August 23, 2020, http://www.oxfordscholarship.com/view/10.1093/acprof:oso/9780198204022.001.0001/acprof-9780198204022.
111 Chris Wickham, *Medieval Europe* (New Haven: Yale University Press, 2016), 38. Taxes were still collected in Visigothic Spain in the late seventh century, but the revenue was probably small and, in any event, it would only have enriched the king since there was no standing army. Wickham, *Medieval Europe*, 40.
112 Pounds, *Economic History*, 47.
113 Wickham, *Medieval Europe*, 33.
114 John W. Baldwin, *Masters, Princes, and Merchants: The Social Views of Peter the Chanter and His Circle*, vol. 1 (Princeton: Princeton University Press, 1970), 218, 238–39.
115 Baldwin, *Masters, Princes, and Merchants*, 228.
116 Baldwin, *Masters, Princes, and Merchants*, 229.
117 Baldwin, *Masters, Princes, and Merchants*, 234.
118 Cherubini, "The Peasant and Agriculture," 125.
119 Wickham, *Medieval Europe*, 128–29.
120 Wickham, *Medieval Europe*, 140.
121 Pounds, *Economic History*, 433.
122 Wickham, *Medieval Europe*, 151–52.
123 Gaines Post, *Studies in Medieval Legal Thought* (Princeton: Princeton University Press, 1964), 18–19.
124 Post, *Studies in Medieval Legal Thought*, 20.
125 Post, *Studies in Medieval Legal Thought*, 21.
126 Post, *Studies in Medieval Legal Thought*, 21.
127 Post, *Studies in Medieval Legal Thought*, 9.
128 Post, *Studies in Medieval Legal Thought*, 21.
129 Post, *Studies in Medieval Legal Thought*, 276. See also Baldwin, *Masters, Princes, and Merchants*, 218 ("Around 1200, Roman and canon lawyers began to declare that urgent necessity of common utility justified extraordinary taxes from all subjects").
130 Brown, "Taxation and Morality," 3.
131 Kelly, *Short History*, 82.
132 Post, *Studies in Medieval Legal Thought*, 12, 18.
133 Post, *Studies in Medieval Legal Thought*, 434.
134 Le Goff, *Money and the Middle Ages*, 48–50.

135 Brown, "Taxation and Morality," 2–3.
136 Brown, "Taxation and Morality," 3.
137 Brown, "Taxation and Morality," 4.
138 Brown, "Taxation and Morality," 7.
139 See Post, *Studies in Medieval Legal Thought*, 287 (arguing that, while property rights remained tied to feudal tradition, taxation served as the paradigmatic instance of public utility; the canonists and legists "thought of 'reason of government' and 'reason of the public welfare' of the State as normal principles of the public law, but principles most obviously applicable to the necessity of extraordinary measures, such as levying taxes, in times of dire emergencies or dangers that threatened the *status regni*," their ideas thereby weakening feudal law and custom).
140 Isenmann, "Medieval and Renaissance Theories of State Finance," 32.
141 Isenmann, "Medieval and Renaissance Theories of State Finance," 30. Gaines Post, in fact, considers the medieval conception of *necessitas* to be a precursor to the later "reasons of state." Post, *Studies in Medieval Legal Thought*, 264. Although the medieval *regnum* was "achieving fictive personality," it had not yet been completely abstracted from the *status regni*. Post, *Studies in Medieval Legal Thought*, 303–4.
142 See Isenmann, "Medieval and Renaissance Theories of State Finance," 30–31.
143 Isenmann, "Medieval and Renaissance Theories of State Finance," 31.
144 See, e.g., Baldwin, *Masters, Princes, and Merchants*, 239–40 (in the opinion of the theologians, the feudal lord's necessity became more reasonable as it became more identified with the needs of the poor).
145 Cary J. Nederman and Kate Langdon Forhan, ed., *Medieval Political Theory—A Reader: The Quest for the Body Politic, 1100–1400* (London: Routledge, 1993), 27.
146 John of Salisbury, "Policraticus: Of the Frivolities of Courtiers and the Footprints of Philosophers," IV.4, in *Medieval Political Theory—A Reader: The Quest for the Body Politic, 1100–1400*, ed. Cary J. Nederman and Kate Langdon Forhan (London: Routledge, 1993), 36.
147 John of Salisbury, "Policraticus," 48.
148 John of Salisbury, "Policraticus," 48.
149 John of Salisbury, "Policraticus," 48–49. This parable has two major classical sources: Livy's *History of the Romans* and Aesop. Nederman and Forhan, introduction to "The Fable of a Man, His Belly, and His Limbs," in *Medieval Political Theory*, 24. In Livy's account, Menenius Agrippa was sent to the Plebs, who had seceded to the Sacred Mount because of those who had been enslaved for debt, to persuade them to stop their rebellion. Menenius, according to Livy, won over his audience with the parable. Livy's version emphasizes the fact that the stomach received no more than it gave back to the other members of the body. Livy, *The History of Rome*, ed. Ernest Rhys, trans. William Masfen Roberts (London: J. M. Dent & Sons, Ltd., 1905), 2.32. Aesop's version merely concludes that "the Belly in its dull quiet way was doing necessary work for the Body." Aesop, "The Belly and the Members," in *Fables*, ed. Joseph Jacobs, The Harvard Classics, ed. Charles W. Eliot (New York: P.F. Collier & Son, 1909–14) 17.1. A poetic twelfth-century version of the parable, by Marie de France, has a less happy ending:

> The belly dwindled to nothing
> And the hands and feet went too.

In Marie's poem, the moral of the story follows Livy's emphasis on social cohesion:

> No one can have honour
> Who brings shame to his lord.

Nor can his lord have it either
If he wishes to shame his people.
If either one fails the other
Evil befalls them both.

Marie de France, "The Fable of a Man, His Belly, and His Limbs," trans. Kate Forhan, in *Medieval Political Theory*, 25. By highlighting the distributive aspect of the story, John of Salisbury's telling resembles Aesop's version more than it does the other two, although Nederman and Forhan speculate that John may have heard Marie, his contemporary, tell it at the court of Henry II of England and his queen, Eleanor of Aquitaine. Nederman and Forhan, introduction to "The Fable of a Man, His Belly, and His Limbs," 24.

150 John of Salisbury, "Policratus," 49.
151 See, e.g., Quentin Skinner, *Foundations of Modern Political Thought*, vol. 2, *The Age of Reformation* (Cambridge: Cambridge University Press, 1978), 353–55.
152 Bonney, *Fiscal State*, 4–6.
153 Joseph R. Strayer, *On the Medieval Origins of the Modern State* (Princeton: Princeton University Press, 2005), 43.
154 Strayer, *Medieval Origins*, 44.
155 Strayer, *Medieval Origins*, 44, 47. 54–55.
156 Joseph Canning, *Political Thought of Baldus de Ubaldis*, Cambridge Studies in Medieval Life and Thought, Fourth Series (Cambridge: Cambridge University Press, 1987), 79.
157 Canning, *Political Thought of Baldus*, 81.
158 Canning, *Political Thought of Baldus*, 72–73.
159 Canning, *Political Thought of Baldus*, 76–77.
160 Canning, *Political Thought of Baldus*, 81.
161 Canning, *Political Thought of Baldus*, 82.
162 Ullmann, *Principles of Government*, 270.
163 Ullmann, *Principles of Government*, 276. The debate as to whether Marsilius was a full-fledged positivist is summarized in Canning, *Political Thought of Baldus*, 76.
164 Ullmann, *Principles of Government*, 268.
165 Ullmann, *Principles of Government*, 272.
166 Ullmann, *Principles of Government*, 232.
167 *ST* II–II, Q. 66, Art. 1, resp.
168 *ST* II–II, Q. 57, Art. 3, resp.
169 Giorgio Agamben, *The Kingdom and the Glory: For a Theological Genealogy of Economy and Government*, trans. Lorenzo Chiesa and Matteo Mandarini (Stanford: Stanford University Press, 2011), 73 (summarizing the "real contribution of [Erik] Peterson to political theology").
170 Agamben, *The Kingdom and the Glory*, 140.
171 Agamben, *The Kingdom and the Glory*, 99.
172 Agamben, *The Kingdom and the Glory*, 99.
173 Agamben, *The Kingdom and the Glory*, 84.
174 Agamben, *The Kingdom and the Glory*, 84.
175 Agamben, *The Kingdom and the Glory*, 82.
176 Agamben, *The Kingdom and the Glory*, 88.
177 Agamben, *The Kingdom and the Glory*, 85.
178 Agamben, *The Kingdom and the Glory*, 103.
179 Antony Black, *Political Thought in Europe 1250–1450* (Cambridge: Cambridge University Press, 1992), 25.
180 Black, *Political Thought*, 26, quoting *ST* I–II, Q. 96, Art. 4, resp. (brackets in original).

181 Black, *Political Thought*, citing *ST* I–II, Q. 92, Art. 1, ad. 1 and 3; II–II, Q. 58, Art. 5, resp.

182 Black, *Political Thought*, citing *ST* I–II, Q. 58, Art. 7, ad. 2; I–II, Q. 92, Art. 1, ad. 3.

183 Louis Hensler III argues that natural law theorists following Aquinas have overemphasized the role of the common good. They "provide a target" to identify the parts of the natural law that governments should enforce, namely, the common good. But that target, Hensler writes, "does not do much to guide or constrain the enforcement of the natural law through human law." Louis W. Hensler III, "A Modest Reading of St. Thomas Aquinas on the Connection Between Natural Law and Human Law," *Creighton Law Review* 43 (2009): 167. Citing *ST* I–II, Q. 96, Art. 2, resp. ("Wherefore human laws do not forbid all vices, from which the virtuous abstain, but only the more grievous vices, from which it is possible for the majority to abstain; and chiefly those that are to the hurt of others, without the prohibition of which human society could not be maintained ..."), Hensler argues that Thomas' own test for determining whether a part of the natural law should be enforced by the state is not whether it contributes to the common good, but whether it contributes to the maintenance of human society—a test that Hensler considers more "powerful" and "distinct" than "the prevailing and flexible 'common good' target." Hensler, "A Modest Reading," 169. Although Hensler is speaking here of prohibitions in natural and human law rather than affirmative features, such as the affirmation of property rights, his point is well taken: the idea of the common good is not sufficient on its own to guide any political theory.

184 Black, *Political Thought*, 23, citing Aristotle, *The Politics* 1.7.1255[b] and 7.3.1325[a].

185 Odd Langholm, *Price and Value in the Aristotelian Tradition: A Study in Scholastic Economic Sources* (Bergen: Universitetsforlaget, 1979), 14.

186 Kaye, *A History of Balance*, 50.

187 Joel Kaye, "Equalization in the Body and the Body Politic: From Galen to Marsilius of Padua," *Mélanges de l'École française de Rome—Moyen Âge* 125, no. 2 (2013), accessed August 24, 2020, https://journals.openedition.org/mefrm/1252. See also Rhonheimer, "Sins Against Justice," 287–88, describing Thomas' idea of injustice as an "imbalance"; citing *ST* II–II, Q. 59, Art. 1.

188 Gilson, *Christian Philosophy*, 315.

189 Dyson, introduction to *Political Writings*, xxxi–ii.

190 Meredith, "The Ethical Basis for Taxation in the Thought of Thomas Aquinas," *Journal of Markets & Morality* 11, no. 1 (Spring 2008): 41–57.

191 Meredith, "The Ethical Basis for Taxation," 43–46. In Meredith's account, relying on Thomas' commentary on Romans, Thomas thought of taxes as "salary" for the prince's "ministry."

192 Meredith, "The Ethical Basis for Taxation," 45; Finnis, *Aquinas*, 191–95.

193 *ST* II–II, Q. 117, Art. 5, ad. 1.

194 Anthony Parel, "The Thomistic Theory of Property, Regime, and the Good Life," in *Calgary Aquinas Studies*, ed. Anthony Parel (Toronto: Pontifical Institute of Medieval Studies, 1978), 85.

195 Gilson, *Christian Philosophy*, 308. See also Ullmann, *Principles of Government*, 234, 248.

196 *ST* II–II, Q. 58, Art. 5, resp.

197 *ST* II–II, Q. 61, Art. 1, resp.

198 *ST* II–II, Q. 61, Art. 1, resp.

199 See *ST* II–II, Q. 61, Art. 1, resp.

200 See *ST* II–II, Q. 61, Art. 1, resp.

201 *ST* II–II, Q. 58, Art. 5, resp.
202 *ST* II–II, Q. 58, Art. 7, resp.
203 *ST* II–II, Q. 58, Art. 7, ad. 1.
204 *ST* II–II, Q. 58, Art. 7, ad. 2.
205 *ST* II–II, Q. 61, Art. 1, ad. 5.
206 Gilson, *Christian Philosophy*, 308.
207 Étienne Gilson, *The Spirit of Mediaeval Philosophy*, trans. A.H.C. Downes (London: Sheed & Ward, 1936), 331–32.
208 Thomas Aquinas, "De regimine" 1.15.
209 Thomas Aquinas, "De regimine" 1.15.
210 *ST* I–II, Q. 92, Art. 1, resp.
211 Parel, "Thomistic Theory," 100.
212 MacIntyre, *Whose Justice?*, 201.
213 Parel, "Thomistic Theory," 101.

References

Aesop. 1909–14. "The Belly and the Members." In *Fables*, edited by Joseph Jacobs. *The Harvard Classics*, edited by Charles W. Eliot. New York: P.F. Collier & Son.

Agamben, Giorgio. 2011. *The Kingdom and the Glory: For a Theological Genealogy of Economy and Government*. Translated by Lorenzo Chiesa and Matteo Mandarini. Stanford: Stanford University Press.

Alexander of Hales. 1924–48. *Summa theologica*. Quaracchi: Collegium S. Bonaventura.

Ambrose. 1999. "Sermon Against Auxentius." In Oliver O'Donovan and Joan Lockwood O'Donovan, *From Irenaeus to Grotius: A Sourcebook in Christian Political Thought, 100–1625*, 70–75. Grand Rapids: William B. Eerdmans.

Aristotle. 1995. *Politics*. Translated by Ernest Barker. Oxford: Oxford University Press.

Augustine. 1972. *Concerning the City of God Against the Pagans*. Edited by David Knowles. Translated by Henry Bettenson. Harmondsworth, UK: Penguin Books Ltd.

———. 2004. "Exposition of Psalm 147." In *The Works of Saint Augustine: A Translation for the 21st Century III/20*, edited by Boniface Ramsey, and translated by Maria Boulding, 441–76. Hyde Park, NY: New City Press.

———. n.d. *Homilies on the Gospel of John*. Translated by John Gibb. Christian Classics Ethereal Library. Accessed August 23, 2020. https://ccel.org/ccel/schaff/npnf107/npnf107.iii.vii.html.

Baldwin, John W. 1970. *Masters, Princes, and Merchants: The Social Views of Peter the Chanter and His Circle*, vol. 1. Princeton: Princeton University Press.

Black, 1992. Antony. *Political Thought in Europe 1250–1450*. Cambridge: Cambridge University Press.

Bonney, Richard, ed. 1995. *Economic Systems and State Finance*. Cambridge Studies in the History and Theory of Politics. New York: Oxford University Press.

———, ed. 2011. *The Rise of the Fiscal State in Europe, c. 1200–1815*. Oxford Scholarship Online. Accessed August 23, 2020. http://www.oxfordscholarship.com/view/10.1093/acprof:oso/9780198204022.001.0001/acprof-9780198204022.

Bradley, Gerard V., and E. Christian Brugger, eds. 2019. *Catholic Social Teaching: A Volume of Scholarly Essays*. Cambridge: Cambridge University Press.

Brown, Elizabeth A. R. 1973. "Taxation and Morality in the Thirteenth and Fourteenth Centuries: Conscience and Political Power and the Kings of France." *French Historical Studies* 8, no. 1 (Spring): 1–28. Accessed August 22, 2020. http://www.jstor.org/stable/285956.

Brown, Peter. 2012. *Through the Eye of a Needle: Wealth, the Fall of Rome, and the Making of Christianity in the West, 350–550 AD*. Princeton: Princeton University Press.

Canning, Joseph. 1987. *The Political Though of Baldus de Ubaldis*. Cambridge Studies in Medieval Life and Thought, Fourth Series. Cambridge: Cambridge University Press.

Cave, Roy C., and Herbert H. Coulson. 1965. *A Source Book for Medieval Economic History*. New York: Biblo and Tannen.

Cherubini, Giovanni. 1997. "The Peasant and Agriculture," in *The Medieval World*, edited by Le Goff, 113–37.

Cochrane, Charles Norris. 1957. *Christianity and Classical Culture: A Study of Thought and Action from Augustus to Augustine*. New York: Oxford University Press.

Dyson, R. W., ed. and trans. 2002. *Aquinas: Political Writings*. Cambridge Texts in the History of Political Thought, edited by Raymond Guess and Quentin Skinner. Cambridge: Cambridge University Press.

Finnis, John. 1998. *Aquinas: Moral, Political, and Legal Theory*. Oxford: Oxford University Press.

———. 2019 "A Radical Critique of Catholic Social Teaching." In *Catholic Social Teaching: A Volume of Scholarly Essays*, edited by Gerard V. Bradley and E. Christian Brugger, 548–84. Cambridge: Cambridge University Press.

Gelinas, Elmer T. 1970. "Ius and Lex in Thomas Aquinas." *American Journal of Jurisprudence* 15, no. 1: 154–70.

Gilson, Étienne. 1936. *The Spirit of Mediaeval Philosophy*. Translated by A.H.C. Downes. London: Sheed & Ward.

———. 1961. *The Christian Philosophy of St. Thomas Aquinas*. London: Victor Gollancz Ltd.

Grant, Robert M. 1978. *Early Christianity and Society*. London: Collins.

Gregory of Tours. 1965. *History of the Franks 4.2*. In Cave and Coulson, *A Source Book for Medieval Economic History*, 353–54.

Hensler, Louis W., III. 2009. "A Modest Reading of St. Thomas Aquinas on the Connection Between Natural Law and Human Law." *Creighton Law Review* 43: 153–74.

Hole, Jennifer. 2016. *Economic Ethics in Late Medieval England, 1300–1550*. Archival Insights into the Evolution of Economics, edited by Robert Leeson. Basingstoke: Palgrave Macmillan.

Isenmann, Eberhard. 1995. "Medieval and Renaissance Theories of State Finance." In *Economic Systems*, edited by Bonney, 21–52.

John of Salisbury. 1993. "Policraticus: Of the Frivolities of Courtiers and the Footprints of Philosophers." In *Medieval Political Theory—A Reader: The Quest for the Body Politic, 1100–1400*, edited by Cary J. Nederman and Kate Langdon Forhan. London: Routledge.

Justinian. 1998. *The Digest of Justinian*. Edited by Alan Watson, vol. 1. Philadelphia: University of Pennsylvania Press.

Kaye, Joel. 2013. “Equalization in the Body and the Body Politic: From Galen to Marsilius of Padua.” *Mélanges de l’École française de Rome—Moyen Âge* 125, no. 2. Accessed August 24, 2020. https://journals.openedition.org/mefrm/1252.

———. 2014. *A History of Balance 1250–1375: The Emergence of a New Model of Equilibrium and Its Impact on Thought.* Cambridge: Cambridge University Press.

Kelly, J. M. 1992. *A Short History of Western Legal Theory.* Oxford: Clarendon Press.

Lactantius. 2003. *Divine Institutes.* Translated by Anthony Bowen and Peter Garnsey. Translated Texts for Historians 40. Liverpool: Liverpool University Press.

Langholm, Odd. 1979. *Price and Value in the Aristotelian Tradition: A Study in Scholastic Economic Sources.* Bergen: Universitetsforlaget.

Le Goff, Jacques, ed. 1980. *The Medieval World.* Translated by Lydia G. Cochrane. London: Parkgate Books, Ltd.

———. 2012. *Money and the Middle Ages: An Essay in Historical Anthropology.* Translated by Jean Birrell. Cambridge: Polity Press.

Livy. 1905. *The History of Rome.* Edited by Ernest Rhys. Translated by William Masfen Roberts. London: J. M. Dent & Sons, Ltd.

MacIntyre, Alasdair. 1988. *Whose Justice? Which Rationality?* London: Gerald Duckworth & Co. Ltd.

Magee, Joseph M. n.d. “Debitum and Personae: The Metaphysical Foundation of Justice.” Thomistic Philosophy Page. Accessed August 22, 2020. http://www.aquinasonline.com/Topics/justice.html.

Mancilla, Alejandra. 2016. *The Right of Necessity: Moral Cosmopolitanism and Global Poverty.* London: Rowman & Littlefield.

Meredith, Christopher Todd. 2008. “The Ethical Basis for Taxation in the Thought of Thomas Aquinas.” *Journal of Markets & Morality* 11, no. 1 (Spring): 41–57.

Newhauser, Richard G. 2005. “Justice and Liberality: Opposition to Avarice in the Twelfth Century.” In *Virtue and Ethics in the Twelfth Century*, edited by Richard G. Newhauser and István P. Bejczy, 295–316. Leiden: Brill.

O’Brien, George. 1920. *An Essay on Mediaeval Economic Teaching.* London: Longmans, Green, and Co.

O’Donovan, Oliver, and Joan Lockwood O’Donovan. 1999. *From Irenaeus to Grotius: A Sourcebook in Christian Political Thought, 100–1625.* Grand Rapids: William B. Eerdmans.

Orrego, Cristóbal. 2019. “The Universal Destination of the World’s Resources.” In Bradley and Brugger, *Catholic Social Teaching*, 267–99.

Palmer, L. R. 1954. *The Latin Language.* London: Faber and Faber Ltd.

Parel, Anthony. 1978. “The Thomistic Theory of Property, Regime, and the Good Life.” In *Calgary Aquinas Studies*, edited by Anthony Parel, 77–104. Toronto: Pontifical Institute of Medieval Studies.

Pope, Stephen J., ed. 2002. *The Ethics of Aquinas.* Washington: Georgetown University Press.

Porter, Jean. 2010. *Ministers of the Law: A Natural Law Theory of Legal Authority.* Emory University Studies in Law and Religion, edited by John Witte, Jr. Grand Rapids: William B. Eerdmans Publishing Co.

———. 2002. “The Virtue of Justice (IIa IIae, qq. 58–122).” In Pope, *The Ethics of Aquinas*, 272–86.

Post, Gaines. 1964. *Studies in Medieval Legal Thought.* Princeton: Princeton University Press.

Pounds, N. J. G. 1994. *An Economic History of Medieval Europe.* 2nd ed. London: Longman.

Ramsey, Boniface. 1982. "Almsgiving in the Latin Church: The Late Fourth and Early Fifth Centuries." *Theological Studies* 43: 226–59.Accessed August 22, 2020. http://cdn.theologicalstudies.net/43/43.2/43.2.2.pdf#:~:text=ALMSGIVING%20IN%20THE%20LATIN%20CHURCH%20231%20human%20being.,on%20the%20condition%20that%20is%20common%20to%20all.%22.

Rhonheimer, Martin. 2002. "Sins Against Justice (IIa IIae, qq. 59–78)." Translated by Frederick G. Lawrence. In Pope, *The Ethics of Aquinas,* 287–303.

Rogers, Eugene F., Jr. 2013. *Aquinas and the Supreme Court: Race, Gender, and the Failure of Natural Law in Thomas's Biblical Commentaries.* Malden, MA: Wiley-Blackwell.

Rufinus. 1974. *Summa decretorum.* Edited by Heinrich Singer, vol. 1, *Medieval Political Ideas,* edited by Ewart Lewis. New York: Cooper Square.

Skinner, Quentin. 1978. *The Foundations of Modern Political Thought, vol. 2, The Age of Reformation.* Cambridge: Cambridge University Press.

Strayer, Joseph R. 2005. *On the Medieval Origins of the Modern State.* Princeton: Princeton University Press.

Thomas Aquinas. 1964. *Commentary on the Nicomachean Ethics.* Translated by C. I. Litzinger. Library of Living Catholic Thought 1. Chicago: Henry Regnery Co.

———. 2013. *Summa Theologiae* (Latin-English Edition). Translated by the Fathers of the English-Dominican Province. Nashville: NovAntiqua.

———. 2000 *Commentary on Romans.* Patristic Bible Commentary. Accessed September 9, 2020. https://sites.google.com/site/aquinasstudybible/home/romans/st-thomas-aquinas-on-romans.

Thomas Aquinas, and Tolomeo of Lucca. 2002. "De regimine principum" ("De regno"). In *St. Thomas Aquinas: Political Writings,* edited and translated by R. W. Dyson, 5–52. Cambridge Texts in the History of Political Thought. Cambridge, Cambridge University Press.

Ullmann, Walter. 1961. *Principles of Government and Politics in the Middle Ages.* London: Methuen & Co. Ltd.

Wickham, Chris. 2016. *Medieval Europe.* New Haven: Yale University Press.

Wood, Diana. 2002. *Medieval Economic Thought.* Cambridge: Cambridge University Press.

4 William of Ockham

Repudiation of power and wealth

Introduction

The balance between appropriation and expropriation in Thomas' writings can be seen as equilibrium between two *dominia*. The term *dominium* came to mean at least two separate things in the Middle Ages: (1) ownership, or any of various property rights clustering around the idea of ownership; and (2) political power. This ambiguity is present in Aquinas' *Summa*. In Question 66 of Secunda Secundae, God has "sovereign dominion" (*principale dominium*) over all things, while humankind has dominion over things "as regards the power to make use of them" (*dominium quantum ad potestatem utendi ipsis*).[1] Human dominion over external things arises because humans are "able to use them for [their] own profit,"[2] but dominion over external things "as regards their nature" belongs to God alone.[3] Thus, in the same article, Thomas employs the term *dominium* both in the sense of "mastery," from which private ownership arises, and in the sense of "lordship." The latter meaning of *dominium* can be extended from God's dominion to a human form of lordship, something along the lines of jurisdiction. In making a distinction between *latria* (paying service to the lordship of God) and *dulia* (paying service to a human lord), Thomas nevertheless uses *dominium* for both types of lordship:

> Now servitude is due to God and man under different aspects: even as lordship [*dominium*] is competent to God and to man under different aspects. For God has absolute and paramount lordship [*plenarium et principale dominium*] over the creature wholly and singly, which is entirely subject to His power: whereas man partakes of a certain likeness to the divine lordship [*similitudinem divini dominii*], forasmuch as he exercises a particular power over some man or creature.[4]

The dual sense of the term *dominium* persisted into William of Ockham's time. In the notes on her translation of Ockham's last work, *De imperatorum et pontificum potestate*, Annabel Brett writes of the challenges posed by the word *dominium*:

> With regard to translations of specific words, I feel there are only two that the reader must be alerted to. One is *dominium*: this Latin term can cover a range of meanings from "'lordship" to "jurisdiction" to "property" to

> "mastership." Ockham, like most late-medieval writers on questions of spiritual and temporal power, occasionally exploits the ambiguity of the term . . . . In those passages where *dominium* over external goods (not persons) is clearly the issue, I have translated "ownership" or "property." In passages where the *dominium* in question is over persons, I have translated "lordship" or simply "dominion."[5]

These linguistic constraints (or opportunities) themselves suggest a linkage between the mastery that leads to property rights and the ruler's exercise of jurisdictional rights to obtain revenue. It is, perhaps, not a great step from the tension between mastery and lordship, both understood as *dominium*, to the conflict between inalienable property rights and the absolute demands of the state.

It is ironic that in the scholarly wars over the origin of the modern idea of rights (*iura*), some writers have placed Aquinas in the "objective," Aristotelian camp and Ockham in the "subjective," modern camp. Michel Villey, for instance, argued that *ius*[6] for Aristotle and Aquinas meant objective right, something observable, rather than "the rights and powers of individuals." *Ius*, in Villey's account of Aristotle's understanding, could mean either "objectively right relationship" or a "moral or legal precept," equivalent to *lex*.[7] Villey blamed the early church fathers for obscuring the first meaning of *ius*, employing the term instead to refer to divine commands. Villey maintained that this distortion continued into the medieval period, when Aquinas briefly restored "objectively right relationship" to the center of the definition of *ius*. By the fourteenth century, in Villey's account, *ius* had been bifurcated; it could mean "command" or it could mean—as in Ockham—"individual power or subjective right." The one bright spot, according to Villey, was Aquinas, who avoided both (erroneous) extremes of "subjective right" and "prescriptive law," instead restoring Aristotle's objective meaning. *Ius* was a *res*, "something existing in external nature."[8]

In Villey's view, Ockham's philosophy was "the mother of subjective right."[9] Villey's thesis in *La formation de la penseé juridique moderne* was that Ockham's nominalism and voluntarism sparked a "semantic revolution" that left "no room for any conception of objective right."[10] Tierney describes Villey's restatement of Ockham's political philosophy this way:

> At the summit is the absolute power of God. In turn God confers powers on men, primarily a power of appropriating external goods (after the Fall) and a power of instituting rulers. The ruler then has the power of legislation (*potestas condendi leges*). From human laws *dominium*, usufruct, right of use—subjective rights guaranteed by state authority. The rights are all absolute. They can be exercised or renounced at will. *And there is nothing else*. The subjective rights of individuals have filled the void left by the loss of objective natural right.[11]

In Villey's account, the subjective right that Ockham's thinking made possible is a faculty or liberty residing in the individual. Thus it is a kind of *power* rather than an objective *thing*. Villey considered this meaning of *ius* alien to Aquinas, for whom *ius* limited power.[12]

Although he insisted that Thomas thought of *ius* as an objective *res*, Villey acknowledged that *ius naturale* was also for Aquinas "a way of interpreting reality."[13] The need for an interpretive means was necessary because *ius naturale* could change as human beings change.[14] In other words, for Thomas "justice is a *problem* which always poses itself in new terms and calls for new solutions as circumstances change."[15] I take this conception of justice to be the architectonic virtue of justice that resides, as judgment, in the ruler. For purposes of the previous chapter's construction of a Thomist idea of taxation, this sort of justice adjudicates between appropriation as a creature of positive law and expropriation as a realization of the requirements of natural law. Both this appropriation and this expropriation are forms of *dominium*, or at least outgrowths of *dominium*. Thus, even in Villey's "objective" reading, Thomas sees justice as a means of restraining and balancing the excesses of power connected with private property and with political jurisdiction.

A central thesis of this chapter is that Ockham, in his understanding of taxation and his reworking of the categories and vocabulary he inherited from Aquinas and others, provided a path through the power struggle, a way to think of tax justice as something other than the equilibrium between two *dominia*.

Ockham's *An princeps* and other political writings

Ockham's political writings, including those pertaining to taxation, are ultimately a product of the dispute between his Franciscan order and the Avignon popes over property and poverty.

The controversy arose from the words of the Rule of Saint Francis:

> Let the brothers appropriate nothing to themselves, neither goods nor land nor any thing. And like pilgrims and strangers in the present world, serving God in poverty and humility, let them go trustingly forth to beg for alms, nor should they be ashamed, for the Lord for us made himself a pauper in this world.[16]

The initial question for the order itself was one of simple practicality: how could the Franciscans live if they had nothing? This practical question implied two theoretical ones: what relation did they have with the food, shelter, and clothing that they needed to survive, and, if they did not own it, who did?[17]

Donald Nielsen writes that the mendicant orders represented an interpenetration of the two poles of medieval religious life, i.e., the "religious virtuosi" and the laity.[18] The Franciscans, for instance, "allowed the principles of monastic asceticism partially to penetrate the world." They could do so only incompletely, however, and, to the extent that they did represent those principles, they "were viewed with suspicion by the Church." "If the spirit of asceticism threatened to break loose from its established bounds," Nielsen writes, "the Church did not hesitate to label it 'heresy' and act accordingly."[19]

The popes of the early thirteenth century seemed happy enough to support the Franciscan order's view of poverty; the popes favored "non-localised, mendicant clergy as an instrument against the regional hierarchies of the institutional church."[20] However, the writings of the popes led to a split within the order itself on the meaning of poverty, as well as to a quarrel with the secular clergy, who argued that the Franciscans' claims to perfection were "theologically void."[21] The Franciscans—and some Dominicans—responded. Bonaventure, for instance, wrote *Apologia pauperum*, positing different degrees of perfection. In 1279 Pope Nicholas III adopted the basics of Bonaventure's *Apologia* in his bull *Exiit qui seminat*, which contained what was intended to be the conclusive statement of Franciscan poverty: external goods could be property, possession, usufruct, or right of use, but the Franciscans had none of these rights; they had only "simple use of fact" (*simplex usus facti*), which yielded no rights at all in goods.[22] Having made his point, Nicholas forbade further discussion of the matter.[23]

Nevertheless, one particular issue refused to die. The Franciscans argued that they had renounced all rights to property, "even in things that were consumed in use."[24] In 1322, the Avignon pope John XXII, "for reasons that remain obscure," issued *Ad conditiorem*. This bull purported to be merely "interpreting" Nicholas III's decree, but in fact it directly challenged the Franciscan doctrine of apostolic poverty.[25] John argued that use could not be separated from ownership in things that were consumed in the act of using them. He also argued that "simple use of fact" was "morally impossible" because to act without right "was to act wrongly." *Ad conditiorem* was followed by three more papal bulls—*Cum inter nonnullos* in 1323, *Quia quorundam* in 1324, and *Quia vir reprobus* in 1329—all attacking the Franciscan understanding of property and ideal of poverty.[26] In *Cum inter nonnullos*, the pope "declared that henceforth it would be heretical to maintain that Jesus Christ and the apostles did not 'have' anything, individually or in common, or that they had no 'right of using' the things that they actually did have." Needless to say, the Franciscans reacted "with dismay and indignation."[27]

In the midst of this furor, William of Ockham arrived in Avignon in 1323 or 1324.[28] Ockham, who was from Surrey in England, had entered the Franciscan order around 1306 and then embarked on an academic career at Oxford. He is thought to have written his commentary on Lombard's *Sentences* between 1317 and 1319. According to the traditional account, the "Thomist-oriented" chancellor of Oxford University John Lutterrell presented 56 theses from Ockham's commentary for censure, and Ockham was summoned to Avignon to answer for them.[29] A minority view suggests that Ockham had simply relocated to Avignon as an expert lecturer.[30] In any event, as Arthur Stephen McGrade puts it, "[i]f Ockham was not a defendant when he arrived in Avignon, he became one before leaving."[31] A formal inquisition was commenced against him in 1327, but, as far as is known, no heresy was ever formally attributed to his early theological writings.[32]

Whatever the degree of philosophical controversy surrounding Ockham's first few years in Avignon, it was eclipsed by the political controversy in which he became embroiled. One of his superiors in the Franciscan order—probably the Minister General Michael of Cesena—commanded Ockham to read Pope John's pronouncements on "gospel poverty," the poverty of Christ and the apostles.[33] To the detriment of his academic career, Ockham (and, at the same time, Michael of Cesena) became convinced that the pope was teaching heresy in this matter. Ockham, Michael, and other Franciscans called for action against John in 1328.[34]

It is unclear if Ockham had been detained in Avignon for years or whether he was merely under a form of house arrest for a few days in 1328 after the dispute with John erupted in full force. It is clear, however, that Ockham and the other dissidents fled in May 1328 to the court of Ludwig of Bavaria in Pisa (later relocating to Munich). Ludwig had assumed the imperial throne after a disputed election in 1314. Pope John did not approve the election, and eventually excommunicated Ludwig, in 1324.[35] Before Ockham's arrival at his court, Ludwig had protected Marsilius of Padua and other thinkers and writers who were out of favor with the church.[36]

Ockham was excommunicated in June 1328.[37] Michael of Cesena issued a series of manifestos calling the pope a heretic; the pope responded with *Quia vir reprobus.* Ockham "entered the fray" with *Opus nonaginta dierum*, "a very detailed, word by word commentary on the pope's bull."[38]

The escape from Avignon may have ended Ockham's academic career as such, but his career as a political writer probably would never have begun without the flight to Ludwig's court.[39] Tradition has it that Ockham presented himself to Ludwig with the announcement, "Protect me with your sword, O Emperor, and I shall protect you with my pen." While these words may be apocryphal, Ockham did, in fact, devote himself to defending both the Franciscan ideal of absolute gospel poverty and Ludwig's claim to the imperial throne.[40] During the 1330s and 1340s, Ockham wrote a number of political works focused on the relation of secular government to the church. These include *Opus nonaginta dierum* (*The Work of Ninety Days*), *An princeps* ("Whether a Ruler Can Accept the Property of Churches for His Own Needs, Namely, in Case of War, Even against the Wishes of the Pope"), *Dialogus* (the *Dialogue*), *Breviloquium de principatu tyrannico* (*A Short Discourse on Tyrannical Government*), *Octo quaestiones de potestate papae* (*Eight Questions on the Power of the Pope*), and *De imperatorum et pontificum potestate* (*On the Power of Emperors and Popes*).[41]

The contours of this outpouring of political thought are already present in *An princeps*, written between late 1337 and early 1340 in response specifically to a tax dispute.[42] After some negotiation, the controversial Ludwig had entered into an alliance with King Edward III of England in 1338.[43] The alliance was prompted by hostility between the two rulers on the one hand and Philip VI of Valois on the other after Edward laid claim to the French crown in 1337.[44] Ockham's goal in writing *An princeps* was to show that Edward should be helped in his "just war" against France by subsidies from both his lay subjects and the English clergy. The latter, Ockham argued, were to pay the subsidies from their churches as well as their personal goods, even if a pope prohibited the payment. In his prologue to *An princeps*, Ockham wrote:

> I will try to illustrate, by creating a brief discussion, that our most serene and glorious ruler and lord, Lord Edward, by the grace of God King of England, legally, lawfully and indeed deservedly, must be helped, not only by laymen, but also by secular prelates, religious and other clerics within his lordship [*sui dominii*] from the property of the Church [*de bonis ecclesiae*], in his battle against enemies attacking him and usurping his rights unjustly; that if his intent is pure, no human statute, judgment or legal process, even if it should come from the pope himself, stands in his way.[45]

Disagreement over whether secular rulers could exact tribute from the clergy within their realms was nothing new. The historian John W. Baldwin describes the theological support for the two positions:

> On one hand were the examples of Christ, Who taught His disciples to render to Caesar the things which were Caesar's in specific reference to tribute money (Matt. 22:17–22) and Who paid this tribute with a coin miraculously found in the mouth of a fish in order to avoid scandal (Matt. 17:24–27). On the other hand, there had appeared by the twelfth century a canonical doctrine to the effect that since church lands were sacred to the works of charity, they were immune from taxation.[46]

Gratian, in Baldwin's account, had assembled statements concerning the obligation of ecclesiastics to contribute to war efforts. Gratian assumed that regalian lands were subject to contributions for military aid. Following his lead, both the Parisian theologians and the canonists generally held that prelates holding regalia owed military service to the king. Some of the canonists, however, "insisted on the additional condition that papal consent must be obtained." Peter the Chanter (d. 1197) "suggests that the bishop who was a count should carefully separate his regalian obligations from all other revenues which supported the works of charity and the bishop's necessary expenses." Robert of Courson (1160/70–1219), on the other hand, argued that Christ's teaching about paying tribute did not apply to ecclesiastics and, thus, that obligations of military service from regalian lands should be nullified.[47]

Cary Nederman speculates that Ockham may have been motivated to write *An Princeps* not just out of duty to his protector, Ludwig, but also out of "a special loyalty" to his native England, which, thanks to the papacy, he was never to see again.[48] The work was never finished, probably because the alliance between Edward and Ludwig broke down in 1340.[49]

Ockham and political theology

In Giorgio Agamben's account of the development of Christian political theology, what lay at the heart of the clash between Ockham and John XXII was—theologically speaking—the unique Christian problem of God's action. The classical tradition's image of the world "exploded" when it collided with the Christian conception, according to Agamben, because the latter introduced the idea that divine praxis—divine operation, creation—"does not necessarily depend on being, and nor is it founded on it, but is the result of a free and gratuitous act of the will."[50] The motif of "creation ex nihilo," Agamben continues, highlights the fact that the Christian God did not create the world out of some necessity of his nature, but because God wanted to. Agamben calls the split "between God and his government of the world" the "secret dualism that the doctrine of the *oikonomia* [in the form of the doctrine of the Trinity] has introduced into Christianity."[51] Economy, in other words, has no foundation in ontology.[52] The Patristic distinction between theology and economy—being and praxis—has proved so tenacious, according to Agamben, that it persists even now in the form of the conflict between the transcendent and immanent Trinity.[53]

Ethics, Agamben believes, occupies an "eminent place" in the Christian tradition because, "with its court of insoluble aporias," it is born of this secret dualism.[54] Agamben's placement of ethics helps explain why ethics and political theology are intertwined; they both seek the healing of the fracture between theology and economy. That fracture is an ontological *and* political crisis, introducing the problem of the legitimization of government in the West.[55] The contribution of political theology, in Agamben's estimation, is to demonstrate "the analogy between the liberal political paradigm that separates kingdom from government and the theological paradigm that distinguishes between *archē* and *dynamis* in God."[56]

These theological developments led, Agamben writes, to the canonists' elaboration of the *rex inutilis* in the twelfth and thirteenth centuries. There "the distinction between the Kingdom and the Government finds for the first time its technical formulation in the juridical field."[57] Sovereign power in "the governmental machine of the West" is articulated according to two polarities: *dignitas* and *administratio*, i.e., Kingdom and Government. The sovereign (in the realm of civil government) is *rex inutilis* or *mehaignié*. The sovereign's "dignity is measured against the possibility of its uselessness and inefficacy"; administration is "always already cut off" from the sovereign even as it "formally" continues to belong to the sovereign.[58]

Agamben narrates the most fundamental of medieval disputes—the conflict between the "two swords"—in terms of the distinction between ontology and praxis. Giles of Rome, Agamben writes, was one of the few scholastics to ask why there are two powers. After all, "[i]f the spiritual power is higher than any other and naturally extends its government to material things just as the soul governs the body, 'what need was there, then, to institute another power and another sword?'"[59] Stated differently, celestial virtue as a first cause could, according to scholastic thinking, produce its effect either with or without the aid of secondary causes, so why does it do so with the aid of secondary causes?[60] The answer that Giles proposed and that Agamben develops is that something is lacking in spiritual power, despite its perfection, "and that something is the effectiveness of the execution."[61] At the theological level, the answer to the question of whether God could have created a rational creature that could not sin is as follows: according to the divine *potentia absoluta*, God could have done so, but according to the divine *potentia ordinata*, God could not have done so because to have done so would have made providential government of the world pointless and grace useless.[62] At the level of nature, "heaven and a lion" bring about the generation of another lion; though heaven possesses the fullness of power, it cannot produce a lion without a lion.[63] At the level of civil government, "God's impotence functions to make possible a righteous government of the world."[64] Thus, in the opinion of Hostiensis and other canonists, "*de potentia ordinata*, the pontiff must abide by the law, although *de potentia absoluta* he is not bound by it."[65] It was, in any event, fitting for the papacy to delegate to the secular sword the exercise of power while retaining the fullness of power itself.[66]

Christian theology must separate divine being and divine praxis to account for praxis, even to make praxis possible. At the same time, however, there is also the need "for providential action to unceasingly rejoin them."[67] The "righteous government of the world" is part of that "providential action." It is the material execution of spiritual power. Thus, government must articulate a separation of the two kinds of power even as it seeks to reunify them. The Kingdom and the Government are distinct, but they must be connected.

Nevertheless, the manner in which the two were reconciled at the theological level and at the level of civil government developed over time, and, in Agamben's account, Ockham's dispute with John XXII represents a critical moment in that development. In the fourteenth century, the "old model of territorial sovereignty" confronted the new model of "governmental power."[68] In the territorial model, Agamben writes, sovereignty is "inseparable from its exercise"; everything happens there by necessity, nothing by contingency. In the governmental-power model, "regality is structurally divided and separate from government"; absolute power (Kingdom) always exceeds and precedes ordered power (Government).[69]

Agamben interprets the debate between the pope and Ockham against this backdrop. John, in Agamben's account, regarded God's laws as identical with God's essence and, thus, eternal and unchangeable. In other words, God cannot act in a way other than how God has acted.[70] Against the pope's position, Ockham proposed "the irreducibility of absolute power to ordered power"—not that there are two powers, but that there are "two different ways in which to say that God can or cannot do something, or two internal articulations of a single divine power in respect to the act."[71] Ockham thought it essential to preserve "the contingency of decision" against the understanding of Muslims, heretics, and "old women" that reduced acting to pure necessity.[72] In the secular realm, for John the Kingdom was fully identified with the Government, but for Ockham the two elements retain their identities "and the contingency of the acts of government corresponds to the freedom of the sovereign decision."[73]

Perhaps, then, it is not mere happenstance that so much of Ockham's later career would be devoted to justifying the institution of taxation. In the fourteenth century, as now, taxation was the clearest expression of the sovereign's power. If the doctrine of providence was needed to reconcile ontology and praxis, then it may not be too outlandish to suggest that taxation plays an analogous part in healing the aporia between the king's absolute power and the ordered power of right government. By levying taxes, as we shall see, the king in Ockham's view links his own absolute and unquestionable power to the good of his realm and his people. Taxes express both sovereignty (Kingdom) and care (Government).

Four justifications of taxation

In the course of defending Edward's right to tax the English churches, Ockham necessarily explained and justified taxation as such. *An princeps* provides four tax-related theories—an explanation of taxation as payment for services rendered, a "donation" theory of property, a doctrine of the common good, and a concept of *necessitas*—that reappear throughout the later political works, even though the latter did not arise as directly from concerns about the nature of taxation. This subsection will explore the four justifications as they emerge in *An princeps* and then evolve in some of Ockham's later writings.

Payment theory

The first six chapters of *An princeps* attack, in general terms, the "plenitude of power" (*plenitudo potestatis*) that the hierocrats attributed to the pope.[74] In the seventh chapter Ockham provided a roadmap of the direction in which he wishes to take the specific part of the argument. The eighth chapter then begins to present arguments, not just against plenitude of power in general, but specifically against the pope's alleged authority to prevent the English king from receiving subsidies from English churches.

At the most basic level, Ockham characterizes these subsidies as payments properly due for services rendered:

> It is lawful for the clergy to pay soldiers their pay for the defense of the clergy and of their property out of the goods of the Church, as can be gathered from many sacred canons. All the more, therefore, ought the clergy to give aid in defending their lord in temporal things, for the defense of the kingdom and of their own rights, as it is through him that both they and the property of the Church [*res ecclesiae*] are defended.[75]

The parallel Ockham draws is between the *stipendia* ("pay" or "tax") of the soldiers who defend person and property of the clergy and the aid that the clergy should expend (*impendere*) for their temporal lord who defends them and their property. Ockham presents the king here as a soldier on a large scale. The soldier-king protects person, property, and rights; the three are inseparable. For his work in doing so, he is entitled to pay, dues, tax.

In some respects, Ockham's parallel is reminiscent of Aquinas' analogy between tithing and paying soldiers their wages, an analogy that draws its own parallel between rulers and soldiers:

> Because natural reason dictates that the people should administer the necessaries of life to those who minister the divine worship for the welfare of the whole people [*ad salutem populi totius*] even as it is the people's duty to provide a livelihood for their rulers and soldiers and so forth [*scilicet principibus et militibus et aliis huiusmodi, stipendia victus debentur a populo*].[76]

Indeed, the force of the analogies in both passages seems to depend on the fact that *everyone* in the community is protected and so everyone must pay. Part of the reasonableness of paying the ministers of divine worship seems to lie, for Aquinas, in the fact that those ministers work "for the welfare of the whole people." Ockham, meanwhile, offers as "proof" of his payment argument the apparently unassailable fact that everyone should lend a hand in matters that affect everyone. Immediately following the "it is lawful" passage quoted above, he writes:

> Proof: because, just as "what affects everyone ought to be approved by everyone," so too what affects everyone ought to be guarded against by everyone. But an attack on the kingdom and the royal laws affects everyone in the country, clergy and laymen alike [*omnes de regno, clericos et laicos, tangit*]. Therefore everyone ought to lend a hand in defending the kingdom and the laws of the king [*ad defendendum regnum et iura regis*].[77]

The ruler, it seems, is the soldier for everyone, just as Thomas' minister of divine worship ministers for the welfare of the whole people. Thus, there is no escaping the obligation to pay for the ruler's services (or for the minister's ministrations). The clergy and their goods cannot be exempt.

If fourteenth-century taxation remained an occasional and irregular exaction for Ockham—triggered, as usual, by war—it nevertheless showed signs of becoming universal. The focus had shifted away from the feudal relationship of vassal to lord, though the king was still called "lord," to the reality of *dominium*. In *An princeps*, this lord is protector and defender of all people and all goods within his jurisdiction.

In other words, the relocation of a basis for taxation progressed in the two or three generations since Thomas wrote the *Summa*. It is no longer to be found in the judgment that strikes a balance between competing *dominia* that could be seen emerging from the ruins of feudal bonds. For Ockham, a clearer reciprocity between the protection provided by the lord of a *dominium* and the obligation to pay for that protection on the part of those within that *dominium* emerged as a basis of taxation.

Nor is that the only shift in emphasis between Question 87 in Secunda Secundae of the *Summa* and the eighth chapter of *An princeps;* the linkage between the payment of tax and the temporal goods from which it is paid has become tighter. According to Ockham, it is lawful for the clergy to pay tax to the king *de bonis ecclesiae* precisely because it is through the king that *res ecclesiae* are defended. In this part of Ockham's political writings, at least, the *necessitas* of persons is not what sets the dynamic of taxation in motion. Rather, the very property from which tax is to be paid carries within it the obligation and right of taxation. Compare, for instance, Aquinas' assertion that the *people* should provide the necessaries of life to the ministers of divine worship[78] with Ockham's insistence that the clergy should expend the goods of the church to pay the king for his defense of those very goods.

The element of *necessitas* does enter Ockham's later political theology, but as a limitation on *dominium* rather than as an authorization for the exercise of *dominium*, as it was for Aquinas. Necessity legitimizes heavy-handed behavior, even force, in the *Summa*: "It is no robbery if princes exact from their subjects that which is due to them for the safe-guarding of the common good, even if they use violence in so doing."[79] Although there is no reason to believe that Ockham would have disagreed with that statement of Aquinas', he was more likely to use the idea of *necessitas* to restrict displays of power. In *On the Power of Emperors and Popes* (written in 1347), a primary argument against the pope's alleged plenitude of power hinges on Ockham's insistence that the pope's principate is one "of service," not "of lordship":

> For that principate which ought to have an anxious care for subjects whom it cannot rightfully deprive of their possessions, rights and liberties (although it may be able to exact from them its necessary expenses, just as a mercenary and a hired man can demand their necessary expenses from those whom they serve), is recognisably instituted for the utility and advantage of its subjects rather than for the honour and advantage of the holder of the principate: and, therefore, it deserves to be called not "of lordship" but "of service."[80]

Necessity provides only a very limited sphere in which the pope can exercise lordship in the sense of exacting goods from his subjects.

This limited allowance for taking the goods of others applies, of course, only to the pope. Edward III, in *An princeps*, is hampered by no such restriction on the demands for revenue arising from his own aggression toward France. However, the difference between Ockham's treatment of the pope and his treatment of the king points precisely to the inseparability of tax revenue and the property from which tax revenue comes. The pope, unlike the king, is not in the business of defending temporal goods:

> [P]relates should strive to be loved by their subjects, in securing their utility, and not to be feared, in depriving them of their rights, liberties and possession—except to the extent that they require these possession for alleviating their own needs: so that to take their possessions in this way should be a matter of necessity, but to serve them spiritually a matter of the will.[81]

As a spiritual servant rather than a temporal lord, the pope simply has no property (or, rather, *should* have no property) to which the benefits and burdens of taxation can attach. The English churches should direct their aid of subsidy, then, to Edward, not John.

That is to say, the argument in *An princeps* is negative as well as positive. Not only does the king have a right to subsidies for his engagement with the French, but the pope has no right—beyond the limited scope of his *necessitas*—to any subsidy. This point is just the beginning of Ockham's weaving together of property and tax. His idea that the burdens and entitlements of which taxation consists somehow attach to property itself underlies all of his theories of taxation.

Donation theory

Ockham's second argument[82] is that the king's predecessors gave the church its property in the first place. Of all people, he argues in the eighth chapter of *An princeps*, the clergy should be the first to repay with gratitude the king's generosity: "They ought to help him because of the generosity of his predecessors who conferred goods on the Church. The Church ought to aid its patron when the need arises more specially than others in need."[83]

Because Edward's predecessors gave the English church its property, Ockham continues, the church holds its property according to human rather than divine law. This, indeed, is the first specific argument that Ockham made in the seventh chapter of *An princeps*: "The first of these arguments is that the prelates and clergy subject to the king of England do not possess temporal things, especially superabundant things, by divine law, but by human law emanating from the king himself."[84] Ockham returns to this theme in the ninth chapter: "For, as it was shown earlier, in Chapter 7, the clergy do not possess temporal goods, especially the surplus [*maxime superabundantes*], by divine authority [*iure divino*], but only by human authority [*solummodo iure humano*], which is the authority [*ius*] of emperor and king."[85]

The argument here is not simply that it would be ungrateful for the English church to refuse Edward his aid of subsidy since his predecessors gave the church its property. That is the mere preface to Ockham's argument that the English church has no *power* over its own temporal goods other than that which accompanied the earlier kings' grant of those goods. Ockham continues in chapter nine: "therefore the pope does not have ruling power [*regulariter . . . potestatem*] over temporal things given to the English churches, unless by the authority of the kings [*nisi iure regum*]; therefore, he has only as much as the kings have given to him, and no more."[86]

Of course, the ultimate goal of *An princeps* and much of Ockham's later political writing is to show that the pope has very little temporal power. The argument would therefore naturally run toward power. The power in question, however, is associated in some sense with property. Ruling power—presumably, in this case, the pope's power to tax or to prevent someone else (the king) from taxing—comes with temporal goods. Thus, if the pope has any ruling power with respect to the temporal goods of the English church, the kings of England had to have granted it to him. This is because they were the donors of the property: "For, as has been shown, the pope does not have any power over the temporal goods given to the English churches, unless by human authority, and as the English kings have conceded it to him."[87]

The full extent to which Ockham desacralizes the pope's temporal power (i.e., his power over temporal goods) becomes fully apparent in the *Breviloquium* (probably written in 1341 or 1342). Chapter 10 of book 1 begins:

> To know and inquire what power the pope has, not from God alone, but from men, is understood to belong chiefly by no means to theologians, but to experts in civil law and those who know what properties, possessions, jurisdictions, liberties, and rights have been granted to the Roman pontiffs by emperors, kings, princes, and anyone else: for such matters can be known, not from the sacred Scriptures, in which things of this sort are never mentioned, but from the laws of the emperors, which speak of them plentifully, and from the instruments, privileges, and charters of emperors, kings, princes, and others who have enriched the Roman Church and endowed it with liberties.[88]

Ockham does, as this quote suggests, see God as the source of some of the pope's power, but only of the pope's power that is required to fulfill his spiritual function. In chapter 7 of book 1, Ockham draws a distinction between the pope's power that comes from divine law—"the power of order, the power to teach, and the power to require temporal things for the spiritual things he sows in God's people"—and the power that the pope has "from human law and from men"—namely, "the power he claims in particular over some parts of Christendom, especially outside the bishopric of Rome."[89] It belongs to theologians to "inquire what power the pope has by divine law,"[90] but, as Ockham states in chapter 10, it belongs to "experts in civil law" to determine the power granted to the pope by humans and according to human law. Of course, the answer that the experts in civil law should give is: not much power at all.

Throughout Ockham's political works, but most explicitly in *An princeps*, the power to tax or to resist being taxed is a temporal power. Simply put, the English kings did not give the pope any such power: "[T]he English kings have not given to the highest pontiff any power, by any statute, prohibition or command, sentence or proceeding, to forbid the clergy subject to the king to give aid to him in his just war."[91]

Thus, Ockham desacralizes both property and the power to tax, and links the two to each other. As a result, property ownership is conditional, not in the same way it was for Aquinas, but because it potentially brings the burden of taxation with it wherever it goes. Cary Nederman notes that Ockham, in *An princeps*, was not simply expressing the classical Augustinian view "that all property holding is a function, not of natural or divine rights, but of human law," though he was doing that.[92] More significantly, "'An princeps' is often equated with the observation of the conditions set on the transfer of temporal goods and rights."[93] The conditions need not be restrictions; they can be privileges or powers as well. Ockham goes on to argue in the ninth chapter of *An princeps* that Edward's predecessors certainly could have attached an immunity from taxation to the property they granted the English church:

> Again, as it is clear from the preceding, anyone can impose an agreement of law with respect to one's own property as one wishes, in a donation or endowment, and consequently one can ordain how much power the one receiving, or anyone else, should have over it [*quantum recipiens vel alius in ea habere debeat potestatem*]. But the things given to the English churches were first those of the English kings, and not of the pope; hence, when the kings gave them to the English churches, they were able to ordain how they should be expended and how much power the clergy and popes should have over them [*quantum potestatem clerici et papa haberent in eis*], nor should anyone have any power over these things, except what the English kings have bestowed upon him.[94]

It is noteworthy how thoroughly relativized property becomes in Ockham's account. Not only is the king free to attach conditions and privileges to the property transferred, but the king may even designate in advance how much power the transferee will have over his or her property. This move on Ockham's part is not completely original. He depends, in making it, on "a doctrine embedded deep in the English system of government and property holding, namely, that since 'all titles were based on grants or confirmation by the King', it fell to him alone to determine the correct and incorrect uses of property and related rights."[95] Ockham's notable extension of this English doctrine in *An princeps* lies in his making it "the indispensable foundation for all power wielded in the realm—ecclesiastical as well as lay."[96]

Not surprisingly, Ockham finds no explicit grant of immunity or privilege in the English kings' donation of property to the church. That conclusion does not end the inquiry, however, because a privilege may be implicit: "[I]f the English kings gave such power to the pope through a special or even a general privilege, then either this is contained, distinctly, explicitly and specifically in some special or general privilege, which belongs to the king and not to the pope, or it is held only implicitly and in general terms."[97]

The idea that an unstated condition attached to a transfer of property to the church was well known in the Middle Ages. Nederman writes, "It had been a customary canon law precept that the goods of the churches were possessed by clerics in trust for the needy to whom they in some sense actually belonged."[98] This, indeed, was the doctrine that Edward's opponents invoked in the taxation dispute that gave rise to *An princeps*; William of Pagula, for example, argued that Edward was engaged in "extortion" of the clergy because the goods of the English churches belonged to the poor.[99]

Ockham turns the implied-condition argument on its head to respond to the position that the churches could not alienate property that they held in trust for the poor. First, he treats the implied-condition argument more as a rule of interpretation than as a precept. Ockham writes that the real implied condition was precisely this: that the grant of "contemptible privileges" (*privilegia odiosa*) should be interpreted restrictively.[100] A "contemptible privilege," it seems, is one that "diminish[es] the power and authority of others."[101] Any hypothetical temporal power granted by the English kings to the pope (e.g., a power to prevent taxation of church property), Ockham argues, would have diminished the power and authority of the clergy. The clergy "would be made subject to the pope with respect to many things, in which otherwise they would not be subject, but they would have freer administration over these things, if the kings were to concede less of such powers to the pope; for then they could do many things without the permission of the pope, even against the pope's command." Ockham concludes, therefore, that any privileges that may have been implicitly conceded to the pope "are not to be increased, but restricted."[102]

Whether or not it is a successful move, Ockham's treatment of the implied condition as a restrictive rule of construction has the effect of tightening the link between transferred property and the privileges and burdens that are transferred with it. It also has the effect of pulling temporal rights—including the right to tax and the right to resist tax—out of the sphere of metaphysical speculation into the mundane world of legal documents and rules of legal interpretation. As Nederman observes, Ockham's preoccupation with the conditions that attached to property placed the whole question in the hands of lawyers. Theological concerns, at least on the surface, has become irrelevant; "[t]he problem of clerical taxation is thus transformed by Ockham into a problem for legal judgement."[103]

That conclusion, however, may be overstated. Ockham's rule of construction opens up a troublesome question: since an implied privilege may increase some rights while diminishing others, how do we distinguish "contemptible" privileges from others? For that matter, how do we tell when a right is diminished? The English clergy, one suspects, might not have accepted Ockham's assumption that the pope's power to protect their property from Edward's war tax diminished their rights.

The common good, Ockham argues, ultimately determines which privileges are contemptible and which are not. Ockham insists that it is "not licit to impede the clergy from giving support to the king during such time of need."[104] Any such impediment would be "prejudicial to the common good of the kingdom." Therefore, his argument continues, there is no point in looking further into whether any such power was given to the pope. Because such a power would have prejudiced the common good, it *was not* granted; the English kings "did not give such power to the pope." After all, "a privilege is a private law; but a law is not a law unless it is just, a right is not a right unless it is just."[105]

Not only does an implied privilege that prejudices the common good deserve to be read restrictively—to the point of vanishing, in fact—but a privilege that promotes the common good is to be read *into* the grant of property and power.

This too is an implied condition in the sense that it must be read into the conditions attached *expressly* to grants of property. Ockham assumes, in chapter 8 of *An princeps*, that "charters" and "documents" accompanied the English kings' donation of property to the English churches. These charters and privileges would have stipulated that the churches use the property so conferred for "righteous causes."[106] The question then arises, what is a righteous cause? Ockham reads righteous causes to include defense of the realm:

> But the will and intent of the kings of England and of their subjects in conferring their temporal property on the churches was that they be used in righteous causes, especially in causes that would spill over into the common good of everyone falling under the lordship of those kings, as can be seen in the charters and privileges which the churches receive and possess concerning these matters. If these documents should only state righteous causes, for which these goods were given to the churches, in a general way, the term must be understood in a more benign and humane way . . . . But the defence of one's country and its royal laws must in no way be considered unimportant among righteous causes. Therefore charters and privileges of this sort must be interpreted in such a way that they are extended to the defence of the country and the laws of its people.[107]

Moreover, even in the absence of charters and documents accompanying the donation, an implied condition to the same effect would necessarily have attached to the donated property itself:

> Furthermore, not only the property which is handed over to secular persons, but also that which is handed to ecclesiastical persons—especially the surplus—is transferred with its condition unless the person who has the power to do so dissolves this condition. But the condition imposed on the property conferred on the churches was that it be used to aid the king in the defence of the country and the laws of the people.[108]

This line of reasoning is a response to the papalists' argument against Edward that clerical taxation would hurt the poor, and that helping the poor is the righteous cause par excellence.[109] Ockham was compelled to make defense of the realm a righteous cause. Indeed, it is a *more righteous* cause than helping the poor, because, as Aristotle said, "the common good is 'better and more divine than the individual good.'"[110] Ockham's inference from Aristotle's position is that "the good of the whole country is better and more divine than the good of the poor of that country." Indeed, "it is more pious to come to the aid of the whole country than to the aid of the poor of the country."[111]

Political theology, or at least political philosophy, continues to do some work after all. Any opinion of a civil law expert that a king had implicitly granted the pope power to resist royal taxation of the clergy would simply be overruled by the doctrine of the common good. Chapter 9 of *An princeps* concludes with these words: "But the way in which [conceded privileges] should be restricted can be made clear from what has been written before: namely, in such a way that, for the sake of the common good of the king and of those subject to the king, the pope himself should not be able to impede, by any statute, prohibition or command, procedure or sentence."[112]

Common good, including defense of the realm, rests with the king and his realm, not with the pope. What further role the common good plays in Ockham's theory of taxation is the subject of the next subsection.

Common good

In Aquinas' *Summa*, the doctrine of the common good does the work of justifying positive law by drawing it into conformity with natural law, as an addition to the latter.[113] By having human positive law contribute to the common good, Thomas tends to equalize the importance of natural and human law and, thus, significantly advance the importance of private ownership of property. This equalization on Thomas' part, however, also brings natural and human law into more explicit tension. The common good cannot effectively judge between them.[114] That role falls to justice, as we have seen.

The idea of the common good does different work in Ockham's political writings. As described above, the common good has the effect of supporting and intensifying Ockham's first two theories of taxation (1) by ensuring that all property of all people is subject to the ruler's protection and, thus, available for the ruler's needs, and (2) by bolstering the "donation theory" in adding an implied condition (defense of the realm) to any explicit conditions that may have attached. In both ways, Ockham uses the doctrine of the common good to strengthen the inherent link between property and its associated rights and liabilities of taxation.

The common good is also differently situated vis-à-vis justice in Ockham's account than it is in Aquinas'. For Aquinas, justice supplies the necessary adjudication between two "goods" of society that each support the common good. Another way of making Aquinas' point is to say that justice judges between two *dominia*. Ockham's justice, on the other hand, restricts the exercise of power—which can be thought of as the exercise of *dominium*—itself.

It does this, not by opposing two *dominia* to each other, but by inquiring into the "truth" about a ruler's jurisdiction. In book 1, chapter, 6, of the *Breviloquium*, Ockham distinguishes between the "sacrilege" of questioning the pope's jurisdiction "intending to detract from the power of the ruler" on the one hand, and disputing "about the ruler's jurisdiction intending to know the truth about it when that is not known" on the other.[115] Thus, in chapter 5 of book 1, Ockham suspects the pope of having already transgressed the bounds of justice if he is even "troubled" by his subjects' inquiry into the limits of his power over them. That is, if he intended to stay within the objective bounds of justice, he would have "rejoiced" at the inquiry.[116] Justice, in other words, is a fixed limit for Ockham, not the fluid *problem*, constantly adjusting to different circumstances, than it is for Aquinas.

The move from Aquinas to Ockham is, therefore, a move from judgment to jurisdiction, a move that occurs within the very word *iudicium* itself. McGrade believes that Ockham referenced canon and civil law sources that used the word *iudicium* in the sense of "judgment" but reinterpreted those sources to make the word mean "jurisdiction." In the first chapter of the *Breviloquium*, Ockham refers to his opponents' argument "that according to the canon and civil laws no one is permitted 'to dispute about the ruler's jurisdiction.'" The quote he includes is from Justinian's Code. McGrade says of the quote and of Ockham's use of it: "*Iudicium* can mean 'judgment' (which is probably what is meant here), or 'jurisdiction' (which is the interpretation Ockham probably has in mind)."[117] In Ockham's hands, the word slides from meaning a dynamic act of the ruler to meaning a preset boundary that applies to the ruler and that all may discern.

The effect of this move is to distinguish justice from power. Some things apply to power, others to justice (and, as is typical in the Middle Ages, equity along with it). In Ockham's arsenal of attacks on the pope's alleged plenitude of power, the attack at the beginning of book 2, chapter 6, stands out for its decisive separation of justice and power:

> For it belongs to justice [*ad iustitiam*], which the supreme pontiff should cherish above all, not to allow the workings of power, but to safeguard what is equitable . . . . The pope therefore does not have power [*potestatem*] except in things which are of equity, not power [*quae aequitatis sunt et non potestatis*]. Consequently he does not have the above-mentioned fullness of power, which relates to many things not belonging to equity [*quae ad aequitatem non pertinent*]. For if he had the above-mentioned fullness of power, he could command the rich to give up all their goods [*omnia bona*] to him, subject themselves to servile burdens, not use expensive clothes and fine food, abstain altogether from meat, and countless things of this sort which are not against divine or natural law.[118]

Ockham describes a world in which justice and power govern two distinct spheres. These spheres actually oppose each other, since the pope must safeguard "what is equitable" by not allowing "the workings of power." The pope has power only insofar as some sort of power is necessary for "things which are of equity." Operating, as he must, in the sphere of equity alone, the pope has no authority to "command the rich to give up all their goods." Taxation, it seems, belongs to the sphere of power; it is not a thing of equity.

The distinction between the two spheres is not equivalent to the division between spiritual and temporal authority. The pope lacks plenitude of power even as to spiritual matters, and "kings and secular rulers do not have such fullness of power in temporal matters." The power of both types of rulers is limited, one by the fact that the pope is "servant" rather than "lord" of the faithful, the other by the fact that the king must not make all of his subjects his slaves (i.e., must not be a "despot").[119] John Kilcullen argues, in fact, that Ockham uses the concept of plenitude of power to bring together the twin evils of heresy and tyranny, both the result of the workings of power.[120]

In Ockham's political philosophy, justice retains the connotation of *belonging-to* that it had for Aquinas. When something is someone's (expressed through use of the dative case), Ockham writes in chapter 3 of book 3 of the *Breviloquium*, it is "due" him or her "by right" (*sibi de iure debentur*).[121] However, Ockham moves beyond *debitum* to say that something belongs to someone "by right" if it is "appointed" to that person. For Aquinas, *necessitas* stood behind *debitum*, giving it its measure. For Ockham, the measure of *debitum* is what is appointed:

> Further, the Evangelist testifies that, when the tax gatherers asked John the Baptist, "Master, what will we do? He said to them: Take nothing more than is appointed [*constitutum*] to you" (Luke 3:12). Here John the Baptist did not order or advise the tax gatherers to give up their office, but to perform it justly [*iuste*], taking no more than the office requires [*requirit*] . . . . The tax gatherers rightly took the things appointed to them [*constituta erant eis*]. But they took these things in the name of unbelievers. Now they could never have taken such things rightly, especially from believers, by the authority of unbelievers, unless those unbelievers had had true authority to appoint such things. Therefore they did have true authority [*auctoritatem*] and true lordship [*dominium*] of temporal things.[122]

Ockham makes this argument in the course of showing that unbelievers can have true *dominium*, and therefore that *dominium* can come from sources other than the pope. It seems that all temporal rulers, believers and unbelievers alike, have the authority and *dominium* necessary to appoint amounts that should be paid in tax. Justice consists in the tax collector's refusal to take more than the office requires, but also in what the Roman authorities appoint. An ambiguity is obvious: does justice lie in the tax collector's taking no more than required, or in the authority of the Romans?

Setting aside that question for the moment, we can at least note that the two ideas of justice coincide in something like jurisdiction. Tribute, Ockham writes, was due Caesar by right (*Ergo tributum de iure Caesari debebatur*). Therefore, Ockham concludes, "there was true temporal jurisdiction [*vera jurisdictio temporalis*] and true lordship over temporal things [*verum dominium temporalium rerum*] among unbelievers."[123] Thus, unbelieving authorities can justly appoint an amount of tax to be paid. On the other hand, the tax collector's activities are also just if the collection does not exceed the amount so appointed. This too is a kind of jurisdiction, a power to act limited by a preset, appointed amount.

Justice and jurisdiction have almost merged, at least in the case of the tax collector. Justice and jurisdiction form an objective limit on power. As such, justice is a negative concept for Ockham. Power is the problem; it relates to many things not belonging to equity. Ockham's taxonomy of justice and power stands in stark contrast to Thomas', in which justice is the exercise of power in a sense. For Ockham, justice is knowing one's limits, not determining them.

As a negative concept, justice is unable to do the work that it did for Aquinas. For one thing, it can tell us little about tax. There is no sense in which what we know about limits on the pope's jurisdiction can help us justify Edward's exactions, let alone the amount he should demand. For that information, we need to look to the common good. The common good—or, at least, that part of it that consists in defense of the realm or aggression understood as defense of the realm—justifies the transfer of clerical and other goods to the king.

Justice and the common good have virtually switched places between Aquinas and Ockham. For Ockham, the common good is the architectonic principle, more important even than the needs of the poor. The dominance of the common good over any conception of justice surfaces in various aspects of Ockham's political philosophy. McGrade writes that Ockham "seems content" with the "standoff" at which he arrives when he tries in the *Dialogus* to determine from scripture and from the idea of justice what the right form of government might be: "It would be wrong to say that Ockham found considerations of justice (in the sense of legitimacy) irrelevant in determining what government is expedient in given circumstances. Nevertheless, the purely instrumental principle of promoting the common welfare is predominant."[124]

The predominance of the common good in Ockham's political thought arises from his "functional" view of government. McGrade summarizes this foundational aspect of Ockham's political philosophy here:

> Most basically, Ockham's natural-law orientation and his functional view of government led him to appraise existing legal institutions in terms of their benefit to society, the *congregatio fidelium* or the *communitas mortalium*. This is to say that the final test of law was not law itself or even the general idea of legally defined due process but observable usefulness to the community. Hence, although both papal and imperial power involved regular respect for the rights and liberties of others, Ockham held that such respect ought not to be absolute. For the preservation or clear benefit of the whole community the rights and liberties of individuals and subordinate officials could licitly be overriden by government. Similarly, the powers of government itself could be curtailed, transferred, or otherwise changed if the common good required it.[125]

In the final analysis, the problem with the pope's alleged plenitude of power in 1337 was that it stood in the way of the common good of Edward's realm (at least as Edward—and Ockham—understood the common good of that realm). As Nederman puts it, "The pope is to be treated no differently from any other person who claims rights within England; when the exercise of a prerogative conflicts actually or potentially with the good of the realm, or with the interests of other individuals, it is to be suppressed and erased."[126]

If we are to find an architectonic principle for a theory of taxation in Ockham, that principle will need to be the common good. A certain nuancing is in order, however.

Interplay of right and need

If justice and jurisdiction are a form of objective limit on power, how do they limit the power to appoint? In other words, what limits Caesar's power to tax? On one level, of course, the answer is the common good. A discussion of Ockham's voluntarism is beyond the scope of this book, but, at least to the extent it has been transposed to the political key, it seems to have been overemphasized. In the *Dialogus*, Ockham has the "student" quote the famous voluntarist text, "What has pleased the emperor has the force of law." The "master" replies that what the emperor wills *rationally and justly and for the common good* has the force of law. The common good, along with reason and justice, imposes limits on the exercise of will.[127]

That is not, however, a wholly satisfactory answer. For one thing, the common good itself is an open-ended variable. Nothing serves as a counterbalance to it.

Moreover, Ockham himself did not leave jurisdiction solely as an expression of the common good. When Jesus said "Give to Caesar the things which are Caesar's," Ockham writes, he meant "that some things were truly Caesar's [*vere Caesaris*]." Those things are "the things which are due him by right [*quae sibi de iure debentur*]." To be due, in Ockham's reasoning, means to be due *by right.* "Therefore tribute was due to Caesar by right [*Ergo tributum de iure Caesari debebatur*]."[128] Instead of *debitum* defining right (*ius*), *ius* now stands behind *debitum* and gives it meaning.

It is ultimately *ius* that limits power. Therefore, it is *ius* that makes justice and jurisdiction limiting concepts rather than expansive ones. Rights and power often appear in inverse proportion in Ockham's political writings. In book 1, chapter 4, of the *Breviloquium*, Ockham writes:

> Further, to neglect the rights of the community counts as a vice . . . . But what is not known is neglected. The pope's subjects must therefore know the common rights of subjects. But they cannot know this unless they know how much power the pope has, and how much he does not have, over them. They must therefore know what power the pope has over them.[129]

The implication is that once the limit of power is discerned, everything else is *ius.* Rights lie beneath the overlay of power and jurisdiction. It is probably no accident that Ockham expands the *in casu necessitatis* exception to private property—typically associated with Aquinas—in a way that reveals his constant awareness of the substrate of *ius.* Tierney writes:

> One could normally use things belonging to another only in case of extreme need. So far this was the old doctrine of the canonists; but Ockham added a refinement of his own. He argued that the underlying natural right also came into play when one used something by license of an owner. The permission of the owner did not confer any new right on the licensee; it merely removed the restrictions of human law that normally impeded the exercise of a natural right.[130]

There is a given-ness about natural rights in Ockham's political thinking. They are the starting point of political thinking and always in the background, the screen over which the workings of law, power, and jurisdiction flitter.

These rights are specifically *natural* rights. As mentioned above, no problem has attracted greater attention in the scholarship surrounding Ockham's political theology and philosophy than that of *ius*. According to Villey—and Georges de Lagarde and Michel Bastit, as well—the modern idea of subjective rights was an innovation inspired by Ockham's nominalist and voluntarist philosophy.[131] In Villey's account, Ockham's "semantic revolution" transformed the traditional idea of objective natural right into the idea of subjective natural right.[132] According to Villey, when Ulpian used the word *ius* he meant the "just share, the just due" of someone within an established structure of social relationships, varying with each person's status and role.[133] After Ockham, Villey continues, *ius* came to mean what it has meant ever since. It is "something that *subiacet*, that underlies or is inherent in a person. It is a quality of the subject, a faculty, a liberty, an ability to act. In a word, 'subjective right is a power of the individual.'"[134]

If Villey were right, then Ockham's political philosophy would be quite modern. The power of individuals would constantly seek to limit the power of the ruler, and the power of the ruler would strive to overcome the threat posed to it by individual rights. Tierney strongly resists the conclusion that Villey was right. In Tierney's view, Ockham did indeed use the term *ius* to apply to a subjective faculty in the individual but so had countless writers before him.[135] In fact, according to Tierney, understanding of the term *ius* to mean a "subjective faculty" was becoming fairly widespread by around 1300.[136] Marsilius of Padua, for instance, wrote that *ius* could mean divine or human law but, alternatively, could mean a subjective power ("any voluntary human act, power, or habit").[137] *Ius* in the subjective sense, for Marsilius, "specified an area of licit conduct allowed by law or a rightful claim to some external good."[138]

Ockham, on the other hand, does not distinguish between the objective and subjective meanings of *ius* at all, according to Tierney. What he does instead is distinguish carefully and insistently between positive rights and natural rights.[139] Ockham, in Tierney's account, argues, with his Franciscan predecessors, that the Franciscans did not have any legal right to the things they actually used.[140] To bolster this argument, he uses references to the ordinary glosses of the *Decretum* and the *Decretals* to distinguish between a positive right, the deprivation of which could lead to an action in court, and which the Franciscans claimed they had renounced, and a kind of right that was derived from nature and could never be renounced because the actual use of things was necessary to sustain life.[141] Ockham uses *ius fori* to refer to a positive right or law and *ius poli* to refer to a natural right or law, but shifts between objective and subjective senses in both categories.[142]

Tierney believes that Ockham's theory of *ius* was not derived from natural law but "from an underlying assertion of human rationality."[143] In Tierney's account, Ockham avails himself of one of Aquinas' three meanings of justice—the quality of an act that is "consonant with true reason"—to argue that an act can be just even without a positive right, so long as it conformed to right reason.[144] This is true of Ockham's refinement of the *in casu necessitatis* exception—use by license. The person who is granted the license, and thus may use another's property (without extreme necessity), exercises a right. The right exercised, however, is a natural rather than a positive right.[145] Ockham uses this argument in *Opus nonaginta dierum* to defend "simple use of fact," arguing, like Aquinas, that once private property was established by human law, "the original natural right to use any thing at all was tied, restricted, or impeded."[146] However, the moral right can be "untied" by either "situations of necessity" or "the owner's permission." Once untied, "the original moral right revives and overrides the owner's legal right to exclude use by others." The owner's permission sometimes confers a legal right, but it may confer instead a *precarium*, which is the kind of right—"simple use of fact"—that the Franciscans have. It is a "moral right to use things because the owners give them precarious permission"; precarious permission confers no enforceable legal right.[147]

Nevertheless, in the absence of necessity or permission (precarious or otherwise), "there is a moral duty to respect the legal rights of others."[148] This moral duty does not represent "the original moral right," but it does rise to the level of a kind of natural right. Thus, necessity and license (permission) are the two features of Ockham's political philosophy potentially in conflict with natural right.

Ockham's ultimate defense of clerical taxation in *An princeps* is need. Need suspends all laws, rights, and privileges:

> For if both divine and human laws stop in times of need and if need is cited as an exception to them, so much more surely should human privileges stop in times of need. Therefore, if the king now or hereafter found himself in a situation of need, the privileges of immunity conceded to the clergy by kings would cease. Now it is proven that the clergy should help the king with the property of the Church in this case. For ecclesiastics are no more exempt with respect to the property of the Church than they are with respect to their own persons.[149]

Need and the common good are clearly in close alliance. Nederman considers this an original aspect of Ockham's thinking: "This clerical obligation to provide for the king when necessary extends in a novel direction the principle that the clergy must give 'for the purpose of alleviating the needs of others.'"[150] Tierney summarizes Ockham's position this way: "Usually a person's natural and civil rights could be invoked against attempted abuses of a ruler's power; but occasionally, in cases of urgent necessity, the requirements of the common good might prevail over the rights of an individual."[151] Edward's kingdom, England itself, has become Aquinas' starving thief, violating rights—human and natural—to survive.

Are we in a position, then, to conclude that need is the counterbalance to natural rights in Ockham's understanding of taxation? In a sense, that is the right conclusion. On the one hand, a balancing of need and rights is not in view; the friction point of the two cannot tell us the amount of someone's goods that can be taxed, as the friction point between positive and natural law did in the *Summa*. On the other hand, for Ockham the authority to tax, or lack thereof, is a function of the interplay between right and need. Because the needs of the realm (i.e., the common good) exceed the natural (and positive) rights of the clergy (and even the pope), the power to tax lies with Edward. No power to resist clerical taxation remains with the pope. Taxation is an all-or-nothing proposition for Ockham. Either the pope has the right to block clerical taxation or, as in this case, he does not. Either the king has the trump card of necessity, as he does in this case, or he does not. There is no balancing or optimality here—only an absolute antithesis. Circumstances swing between rights and necessity.

Alternatively, however, circumstances may swing between rights and license. *An princeps* hints that Ockham's expanded version of the urgent-necessity exception—not merely the traditional version—applies to the situation in which the English churches find themselves. In the eighth chapter, he argues that if the kings of England in some way conceded a general immunity from taxation to the English churches, that immunity would not apply to the present situation for two reasons. First, it would be illegal and therefore void. Secondly, Ockham introduced another rule of construction:

> [J]ust as … a kinder and more reasonable interpretation must be made with respect to general donations or concessions to righteous causes, so too in the matter of the concession of immunity must a similar interpretation be made. It is reasonable and kind that the clergy help the king in his hour of need. Therefore, the general concession must be understood in this way.[152]

The boundaries of *ius* should be transgressed, not just by necessity, but by the kindness and humanity of the clergy. Just as the kindness of the property owner who grants a license lifts his or her own positive rights to release the underlying natural rights of the needy person, so the kindness of the English churches should lift their own positive rights to release the foundational natural rights of the needy realm.

In this way, necessity appears less as a moral, legal, and political principle in its own right, and more as a version of license. The one with superabundance *should* give the starving person what he needs, but, in the absence of that generosity, the starving person may become a thief. The wealth of the English churches should be offered voluntarily to Edward in his hour of need, but in the absence of that generosity he is free to exact what he needs from the churches. Thus, the true poles of Ockham's tax equation are right and kindness. Need merely determines who has right on his or her side. Kindness then renounces and removes the overlay of positive right to allow the needy one's natural right to the property in question to surface. Rather than being in conflict or even in tension, natural right and need turn out to be the same thing. Positive right may stand in tension with necessity and the common good, but natural rights underlie the latter. To understand Ockham's idea of preexisting natural rights, we turn to another prominent theme in his political writings: the law of evangelical liberty.

The law of evangelical liberty

To recapitulate, the first seven chapters of *An princeps* develop the idea that the power of the pope is limited. In the specific context of Edward III's need for subsidies, however, chapter nine introduces evangelical liberty as a kind of rule of construction.

The starting point of this argument is, as we have seen, Ockham's insistence that the pope can have no power over temporal goods other than that given to him by human authority. If the English kings gave the pope such a power, they would have had to do so either explicitly or implicitly.

No explicit royal grant, Ockham argues, can be found. Moreover, even if it could be located, it would not be valid because it would contain the "obvious vice" of effecting a transfer of "the whole treasury for the defence of the country and of the public rights from those who have enough from other sources to those who, not having other sources, are known to be wanting." This hypothetical grant, a "privilege," would have to be a private law, but no law—including a private one—is a law "unless it is just."[153]

Nor could the kings have granted the pope such a privilege implicitly and generally, because "general terms placed in a privilege of this kind should not be increased, but rather they should be restricted." Ockham considers this argument a rule of construction: "in such matters the interpretation is to be made more moderate and more generous."[154] In this case, Ockham argues, moderation and generosity require the pope to "offer the aid of subsidy to the king, when he has such need, from the goods which his predecessors liberally bestowed upon the churches, rather than that he should deny him such aid." Because moderation and generosity dictate such a result, Ockham concludes, the "general terms" of the earlier grant "are to be restricted in such a way that the power of impeding such aid may be in no way conceded to the pope."[155] Generosity as a mode of reading legal documents, therefore, has the effect of restricting the pope's power.

Ockham's move in the next paragraph is to make the rule of construction a legal principle in its own right. Apart from all questions of how to interpret prior grants of property, it simply is "not licit to impede the clergy from giving support to the king during such time of need." Therefore, "it should be presumed" that the English kings gave away "nothing vicious or dangerous or prejudicial to the common good of the kingdom." Having already elevated the "reasonableness and kindness" rule of interpretation to the status of a legal principle, Ockham now makes it a legal presumption. Consequently, he can now assert in the indicative mood and without qualification that "the English kings did not give such power to the pope in general terms."[156]

However, Ockham was not content to rest there, with an unequivocal statement that the kings did not act in a manner contrary to moderation and generosity. He proceeded in the next paragraph to supply the phrase *rationabilior et benignior* with material content. The hypothetical privileges conceded by the kings to the pope would be "contemptible" (*odiosa*) because "they diminish the rights of others" (*iura diminuunt aliena*).[157] Even the rights of the clergy would be diminished by the kings' overzealous concessions to the papacy, because then the clergy "would be made subject to the pope with respect to many things, in which otherwise they would not be subject." In fact, Ockham maintained, the prevailing, expansive understanding of the pope's power means that the clergy cannot now "do many things without the permission of the pope, even against the pope's command."[158] Ockham's point is that the clergy *should* be able to do "many things" without the permission—perhaps even against the command—of the pope.

Here the legal principle becomes fully prescriptive. If, in fact, any excessively broad privileges have been granted the pope, they should now be restricted rather than increased.[159] Ockham's final claim in chapter nine is to insist that the pope must not impede, by any means, the ability—the rights—of others to do "many things."[160]

This "negative" space, free from interference, is the law of evangelical liberty. As Ockham wrote in chapter 2, Lex enim Christiana ex institutione Christi est lex libertatis, ita quod per ordinationem Christi non est maiores nec tantae servitutis quantae fuit lex vetus.[161] It is precisely this negative space that the pope must not be permitted to invade. If the pope had such power, he could deprive his subjects of all of their things and rights.[162] Book 2, chapter 3, of the Breviloquium contains a classic statement of Ockham's use of the doctrine:

> But if the pope had by Christ's precept and ordinance such fullness of power that in temporal and spiritual matters he could by right do without exception anything not against divine or natural law, then Christ's law would involve a most horrendous servitude, incomparably greater than that of the Old Law.[163]

The doctrine of evangelical liberty is not original with Ockham, although McGrade, at least, believes that Ockham's use of the doctrine against the pope's claimed plenitude of power is original.[164] In Ockham's writings, the doctrine first appears in a position of prominence in *An princeps.* Tierney traces the development of the doctrine from the use that the English glossators made of Paul's statement in I Corinthians 10:23, "All things are licit for me." According to Tierney, the glossators and later Ockham associated this passage with the "the idea of natural right as a sphere of free choice."[165] This move, Tierney writes "broadened the apostolic teaching on Christian exemption from Jewish ceremonial precepts into a more generalized doctrine of natural liberties. It was not that Christianity first conferred rights on its followers; rather, by not imposing the restrictions of the Old Law it left them free to exercise their pre-existing natural rights."[166]

However, the law of evangelical freedom, in Ockham's account, does not take away servitude. He wrote in the *Breviloquium*:

> But the statement that the gospel law is a law of perfect freedom (from which it is clear that the pope does not have such fullness of power) can be rightly

> understood, or misunderstood. It must therefore be noted that it should not be understood to mean that the gospel law takes away all servitude and does not permit it, even to Christians . . . . The statement should rather be understood negatively—that is, that the gospel law does not impose a heavy yoke, it makes no one the slave of another, and in respect of the outward worship of God it does not impose on Christians as great a burden as weighed upon the Jews.[167]

Thus, the "gospel law" cannot free slaves; it also cannot make slaves.[168] This is why it is a negative space. It leaves rights and liberties—or the lack thereof—as it found them.

Nevertheless, the law of evangelical liberty is a *law*. It is a dictate in that it actively prohibits the pope (or anyone else) from invading the space in which one's preexisting rights and liberties prevail. Annabel Brett writes that, although the law of evangelical liberty is negative in the sense that Christians do not have to perform the tasks that the Old Testament faithful did, it nevertheless is a prescription, "a rule of life."[169] The faithful, Ockham wrote in chapter nine of *De imperatorum*, "are subject to the law of perfect liberty, viz., the evangelical law."[170] The law of evangelical liberty, precisely as a law, prohibits Christians from doing certain tasks because to do them would be to do acts of "pure externality," which are morally insignificant, unable to release a sinful human from sin. In fact, as Brett explains, such acts encourage sin by setting up "a faith in externals and a captivity of the intellect to an authority other than Christ."[171]

Brett reads Ockham's insistence on the distinction between natural and positive rights as an attempt to introduce a category beyond *ius naturale* to defend Franciscan conduct outside of cases of extreme necessity. The result, the sphere governed by license more than necessity, is a redefined *ius poli* that "is only 'metaphorically' right and just" but nonetheless natural in the sense that it is consonant with right reason.[172] Brett believes, based on her interpretation of *ius poli*, that when Ockham said it is "not right" to impose external tasks on the faithful, he not only meant that it infringes natural or civil rights. He also meant that these burdens infringe "the moral rights of individuals, that is, that sphere of external conduct which is not strictly a matter of right but of moral righteousness." This sphere of action is "evangelical liberty." It is an external sphere, but "any moral activity includes an internal dimension of which the agent must be aware for it to count as moral action at all."[173]

Ockham's use of evangelical liberty primarily targets the pope and his alleged plenitude of power. Is there an analog of evangelical liberty in the secular sphere? To some extent, yes. Ockham's argument in the *Breviloquium* that the papal office should be characterized by servanthood rather than lordship is explicitly tied to Aristotle's *Politics*:

> This argument can be confirmed and supported in many ways. For apostolic or papal rule has been set up for the common advantage of the faithful no less than tempered and just secular rule for the advantage of subjects; yet the latter has been set up for the advantage of subjects, according to the world's

> wise man in the *Politics*; papal rule was therefore not set up by Christ for the pope's own sake, but for the faithful.[174]

Brett writes that Ockham's idea of tyranny in his works before *On the Power of Emperors and Popes* suggests a parallel between the power of the pope with regard to evangelical liberty and the power of the secular ruler with regard to the liberty of natural morality.[175] McGrade also concludes that there is a parallel: "In some respects, therefore, Ockham's account of ecclesiastical government will be shown to resemble his treatment of secular government."[176]

The parallel is clearest in Ockham's clearing of a "negative space" in the secular realm just as he does vis-à-vis the power of the pope. In *Octo quaestiones*, Ockham wrote: "[Y]et [rulership] seems to be most principally instituted for this, that it may correct and punish wrongdoers."[177] McGrade takes Ockham's emphasis here on "the negative, peace-keeping function of temporal government" to be in furtherance of "his striking denial of the unitary thesis that no community is well governed unless it is subject to one supreme judge." Ockham tends to ignore—or at least demote—activities at the "ethically elevated end of politics," such as "direction of the arts" and "promotion of virtue."[178] Consequently, he "provides a buffer zone between the necessary business of temporal politics and the higher activities of Christian religious institutions."[179] McGrade writes elsewhere:

> Yet there is, I believe, something to the impression that Ockham, especially the earlier Ockham, held God's will to be a uniquely supreme, comprehensive, unrestricted moral principle, and also something to the impression that the later, political Ockham was distinctive in arguing for a secular political order operating according to a rationally ascertainable natural law but lacking any inherent religious orientation.[180]

The political and philosophical branches of Ockham's thought meet in the *ius poli*. To be morally good or bad, Ockham writes in the *Sentences*, an act must be voluntary: "Furthermore, no act is virtuous or vicious unless it is voluntary and in the power of the will."[181] That "only acts of the will are intrinsically virtuous or vicious" is, according to McGrade, "[p]erhaps the best known thesis in Ockhamist ethics."[182] To be voluntary, an act must be uncoerced. This is because intentions alone determine the moral worth of an external act. McGrade writes:

> The individual who alters his religious professions to please his superiors and not from respect for the truth would be comparable, for Ockham, to the man who goes to church *propter vanam gloriam* rather than *propter Deum*. Although his behavior might be objectively correct—the superior may be orthodox, just as going to church is a proper thing to do—the ill-intentioned act is not even morally good, let alone obligatory.[183]

McGrade concludes that this aspect of Ockham's voluntarism informs his conviction that secular government should be limited: "His limited conception of governmental functions is a natural consequence of the view that virtue and vice are centered in an inner region that the external coercion of secular power does not touch."[184]

Paradoxically, however, this is the region from which taxation arises. The tenor of *An princeps* is not that the king is within his rights to *take* anything, but rather that the pope is overriding the rights and liberties of the English people, king and clergy included. The papal impediment to clerical taxation is not only illicit; it is "impious and cruel."[185] The king's need, to be sure, guides how the people of England should direct their property. Ultimately, however, taxes will be paid to Edward because "[i]t is reasonable and kind that the clergy help the king in his hour of need."[186] Necessity, again, determines the object of kindness, the one to whom license should be granted; but it does not supply the motive of the one paying the tax. The pope himself "should offer the aid of subsidy to the king" because to do so is "more reasonable and more generous."[187]

To the modern mind, it seems perhaps contradictory for the region of rights and liberties to be the place from which generosity to the ruler and for the common good springs. This, however, is Ockham's whole point. The common good directs the focus of pope, king, clergy, and others outward. If the pope had plenitude of power, that power would be for the pope's own glory. Ockham writes in book 2, chapter 5, of the *Breviloquium*: "In setting blessed Peter over his sheep Christ therefore meant chiefly to provide, not for blessed Peter, but for the sheep."[188] Likewise, as McGrade summarizes the argument in *Octo quaestiones*, "government over the unfree is always despotic, that is, operates principally for the good of the ruler."[189]

Dominium revisited

An important caveat is in order. It would be a mistake to draw an exact parallel between the relation of the pope's power to evangelical liberty and the relation of the secular ruler's power to "the liberty of natural morality."[190] Even a non-tyrannous and non-despotic secular ruler "is inevitably an exerciser of coercive dominion equipped with wealth and physical might."[191]

The classic expression of the Franciscan idea that *dominium* (in the sense of both property and jurisdiction) is the distinguishing feature of the secular world is found in Duns Scotus' (c. 1266–1308) commentary on Distinction 15 of Book IV of the *Sentences*, which focuses on restitution and, thus, on what it means for a good to be one person's and not another's.[192] Scotus writes that community of property was at first a precept of natural law, but that God revoked the precept after the fall.[193] A "license of appropriation," according to Scotus, was granted in its place after the fall; people could take what they wanted for themselves. This resulted in an intermediate state, characterized by fear and danger, before the existence of property relations.[194] In Scotus' account, individual ownership was introduced by positive human law, established, that is, either by Adam's paternal authority or by the political authority of an elected ruler.[195] Human positive law stabilized the "distinct dominions" resulting from the intermediate appropriations, but it does not automatically justify these distinct dominions. It only does so if the law itself is just, which means that the law is authoritative and in accord with practical reason.[196]

With this legacy, Ockham began his *Opus nonaginta dierum* by distinguishing two meanings of *dominium*: a power of ruling and a power of owning.[197] Ockham's delineation of the two meanings is crucial to his development of the traditional Franciscan distinction between use and ownership. In Ockham's account, the "licit power of using" that God gave Adam and Eve was an inalienable natural right but not a right or a form of ownership. Therefore, the Franciscans could have "use of fact" without ownership.[198]

According to Ockham, there have been three epochs of human history. The first was prelapsarian, when Adam and Eve had no property but only a power of using things, i.e., "use of fact."[199] After sin but before the division of external things, Adam and Eve had a power of appropriation. Ockham introduced his idea of the *res nullius* here; humankind still did not own any property (either individually or in common) in this second epoch but had the power of appropriating things because "'what belongs to no one is conceded to the occupier.'"[200] The third epoch followed the division of things, "when individual possessions came to exist."[201]

Whether ownership was introduced by human, natural, or divine laws is a difficult issue to parse in Ockham's works. In the *Opus nonaginta* he wrote that private property was introduced "by command or permission of God."[202] He went further in the *Breviloquium*, explicitly acknowledging "a divine origin of the right to acquire property."[203] In any event, once instituted, private property became a matter of natural law. Natural law for Ockham has three meanings: (1) immutable and invariable law in conformity with right reason; (2) law that is not immutable but is observed by using natural equity without human law; and (3) conditional natural law (*ex suppositione*), derived from rational responses to contingent situations.[204] Respect for private property is a natural law of the third type, *ex suppositione*.[205]

Ockham, with his fellow Franciscans, claimed to have returned to the state of innocence, living only with "use of fact."[206] To be sure, natural law (a "dictate of reason") suggests that it is "expedient for persons to appropriate things for themselves"; but anyone, like the Franciscans, may voluntarily renounce that right.[207]

That the temporal structure of *dominium* is not morally neutral, but tainted with the sin that necessitated it in the first place, comes to the fore in *De imperatorum*, where, in chapter 7, Ockham writes:

> And so Christ said: "The kings of the Gentiles exercise lordship over them," that is, the kings of the Gentiles exercise lordship over them as slaves, not as the perfectly free. For no purely royal principate, which is in respect of free men, was ever instituted among the Gentiles, but was always mixed with despotic principate or principate of lordship; just as even the royal principate which was instituted by God had something in it of lordship.[208]

There is a fundamental asymmetry between the rule of kings and the rule of the apostles and the pope; the rights and liberties of subjects are at the mercy of secular rulers in a way that the evangelical liberty of Christians is not—or should not be—at the pope's mercy.

In the "principate of lordship," power is inversely proportionate to rights and liberties. Defining power in that sphere is a matter of limiting its "coercive ability."[209] The pope's power should not have to be addressed in terms of the "principate of lordship," in Ockham's view, but that is where Ockham found papal power in his day. He had no choice but to restrict the pope's power through appeal to the evangelical law of liberty.

A "principate of service," on the other hand, would "bolster the liberty of its subjects," rather than "diminish it." That is, if the pope's rule were one of service rather than lordship, there would be no collision between his power and the moral liberty of his subjects. "[D]efining papal power" would not have to be "a matter of pure limitation of coercive ability."[210]

The "principate of service" may be a paradoxical term, but so is the "law of evangelical liberty." In fact, the two are the "flip sides" of each other. Brett sees Ockham's political arguments, at least in *De imperatorum*, as containing two basic points: (1) "papal power must respect the evangelical liberty of its subjects"; and (2) Christ himself contrasted the relations that exist between princes and their subjects and the relations he wished to exist between the apostles.[211] In the first point, the law of evangelical liberty affirmatively limits on the pope's power. In the second, the pope himself should renounce his own power. In fact, all those who live in a "principate of service" should voluntarily relinquish their rights and liberties. McGrade notes that, "[a]s a Franciscan, Ockham believed that the highest religious ideal included renouncing all one's legal rights."[212]

Thus, in the secular sphere taxation is justified by the common good. The *ius poli* there is a place of moral liberty, where subjects—guided by the dictates of necessity—give their property to the needy. The needy may be the king. The law of evangelical liberty ensures that the pope does not override that place of moral liberty, where tax is paid for "righteous causes." The focus is outward, a giving up of property for others.

In the spiritual sphere, taxation has another justification. The "principate of service" is a place of voluntary relinquishment of all rights and, thus, all power. Rights and power thus relinquished return to where they belong, the sphere of *dominium*, a "principate of lordship." Therefore, even though renunciation of legal rights is a kind of withdrawal, it is also a "giving back" and, in that sense, even more outward in its focus.

"Giving back" is a recurring theme in Ockham's political philosophy. In both the payment theory and the donation theory of taxation, Ockham presented the payment of tax as a way of returning property or money to one who had previously given it up. For those living under the "principate of service," however, paying tax is doubly appropriate. Not only would the pope and the English churches thereby give back to the king what was originally his, but they would be placing property back in the sphere to which it belongs, that is, placing it back in the sphere of *dominium*.

Caesar's *dominium* is a real thing, according to Ockham. Ockham read Jesus's words in Matthew 22:21—"Give to Caesar what is Caesar's"—as an acknowledgment that some things are in fact Caesar's. Christ left Caesar's temporal jurisdiction undisturbed.[213]

However, there is a hint that a deeper "giving back" is at work in Ockham's treatment of the saying "Give to Caesar what is Caesar's." *Dominium*, in both senses, comes from Caesar, or from some other secular ruler, and from human law. God permits *dominium* for the common good, but that is a concession on account of sin. The things that are Caesar's are necessarily "a mesh of *dominia* . . . which [Ockham] usually refers to as *iura et libertates*, rights and liberties or immunities: these range from the property rights of subjects to the jurisdictional rights of rulers."[214] For Ockham, paying the tax or tribute is ultimately not about giving property back to its rightful owner, as it was for Aquinas, but rather about placing property back in the sphere of which it is a product.

The duty to pay tax, in Ockham's account, does not arise from how much property the payor has or whether the payor's property constitutes *superflua*. Ockham wrote: "If the son of God paid the tribute, are you so great that you do not think it is to be paid? Even he paid the tribute who possessed nothing; you who pursue worldly riches, why do you not acknowledge this worldly service?"[215] In the final analysis, the payment of tax is not about the property of the one paying at all. The payment of tax is, rather, a supererogatory act of removing oneself decisively from the principate of *dominium*.

Ockham and the tax narrative

If the phenomenon of taxation is located in a space where people are relatively free from the dynamics of *dominium*—free to act out of kindness, reasonableness, and an understanding of *necessitas* that is tied to the common good, then taxation does not belong first and foremost to the realm of power. Taxation, in Ockham's rhetoric, becomes the "right" to help the king for the common good in the kingdom's hour of need. It is easy to see how Ockham's opposition of taxation so conceived to a "plenitude of power" could help to place taxation at the service of justice while leaving the remainder of human law as the instrument of coercion.

The problem is that the *form* of Ockham's political vision has lost the theological *content* that activated it. The workings of *dominium* have seeped over into the idea of tax as a reasonable and kind "aid of subsidy." The focus has shifted from the people's (and the church's) right to "give back" for the common good, to the secular ruler's right to take for the ruler's needs (albeit needs that continue to be articulated in terms of the common good).

This is an inevitable shift once theology is withdrawn from Ockham's vision. Theology is withdrawn partly in the loss of a sense of paying tax as an act of piety, "giving back" for a righteous cause tied to the common good. At a deeper level, however, theology also disappears once the paying of tax ceases to have the spiritual significance that Ockham gives it by using it to help distinguish the principate of service from the principate of lordship. The *ius poli* is not, for us, the space where renunciation of rights takes place. Instead, it has become the focal point of a power struggle all its own. When we lose the idea of giving the world back what is the world's, Ockham's arguments become arguments for an all-powerful state and not much more.

Ockham's separation of the two principates has likely contributed to the perception that his political thinking shows modern tendencies, particularly his "respect for the normal autonomy of secular political processes."[216] McGrade argues, however, that—as unprecedented as that separation may be—it is a fundamentally theological move: "It may not occur to us to imagine that the ultimate raison d'être of politics might be (in Ockham as in Locke) to provide a framework where individuals are safe to seek God."[217]

Even more starkly with respect to Ockham's than to Thomas' political theology, the subtraction of theology reduces ideas about taxation to an inevitable conflict between absolute individual rights and liberties on the one hand and the ever-growing needs of an all-consuming state on the other.

Ockham's political philosophy of taxation formally resembles a version of the contemporary philosophy of taxation; but when placed in its proper theological context, tax has an entirely different function for Ockham. When the cluster of theological concepts centered on the law of evangelical liberty is included in Ockham's structure, that structure actually looks *less* like contemporary tax philosophy than Thomas' does. Aquinas' vision resembles contemporary optimality in that it provides a model for balancing goods through an application of justice of some sort. Ockham's vision, as we have seen, depends much less on justice. It is animated, instead, by charitable motives and, ultimately, by seeking spiritual perfection through limiting the workings of power and lordship to their own sphere, a sphere that God has conceded on account of sin. The phenomenon of taxation, for Ockham, is not so much a balance between competing social goods dictated by theology or natural law, as it is an expression of one of several legitimate theological stances toward political authority.

In Ockham's "tax theology," an echo of the radical late-Roman account of wealth returns—the account that Augustine resisted, as we saw in Chapter 2. In place of the mysterious and providential sources of wealth in the Augustinian response, Ockham provided a hint, at least, of the rejection of wealth and its taint in the Pelagian *De divitiis*. Ockham was ultimately less interested in how to reconcile theology and economy than he was to delineate the two and let the Christian choose between them.

Notes

1 Thomas Aquinas, *Summa theologiae* (Latin-English Edition), trans. Fathers of the English-Dominican Province (NovAntiqua, 2013), II–II, Q. 66, Art. 1, ad. 1. The *Summa Theologiae* is cited as *ST* hereafter.

2 *ST* II-II, Q. 66, Art. 1, resp.

3 *ST* II-II, Q. 66, Art. 1, ad. 3.
4 *ST* II-II, Q. 103, Art. 3, resp.
5 Annabel S. Brett, notes on the translation and text to *On the Power of Emperors and Popes*, by William of Ockham (Bristol: Thoemmes Press, 1998), 54. Brett's other translation issue centers on the terms *principatus* and *princeps*.
6 As merely the translation of the Greek *dikaion*.
7 Brian Tierney, *The Idea of Natural Rights*, Emory University Studies in Law and Religion, ed. John Witte, Jr., vol. 5 (Grand Rapids: William B. Eerdmans Publishing Co., 2001), 22 (summarizing Villey's work).
8 Tierney, *The Idea of Natural Rights*, 23.
9 Michel Villey, *La Formation de la Penseé Juridique Moderne* (Paris: Presses Universitaires de France, 2013), 261, 253, quoted and translated in Tierney, *Natural Rights*, 30.
10 Tierney, *Natural Rights*, 30.
11 Tierney, *Natural Rights*, 30. Tierney strongly disputes Villey's conclusions about Ockham, both because Tierney believes no semantic revolution took place and because he believes there is no conceptual connection between Ockham's philosophical work and his political writings. See Tierney, *Natural Rights*, 30–34.
12 Tierney, *Natural Rights*, 28.
13 Tierney, *Natural Rights*, 23.
14 Tierney, *Natural Rights*, 24.
15 Tierney, *Natural Rights*, 24 (emphasis in the original).
16 *Regula II (Regula bullata) Fratrum minorum*, in *Opuscula sancti patris Francisci Assisiensis. Edita cura et studio PP. collegii Saint Bonaventurae* (Quaracchi, 1904), 68. quoted in Brett, introduction to *On the Power of Emperors*, 11n14.
17 Brett, introduction to *On the Power of Emperors*, 12.
18 Donald A. Nielsen, "*The Protestant Ethic and the 'Spirit' of Capitalism* as Grand Narrative: Max Weber's Philosophy of History," in *The Protestant Ethic Turns 100: Essays on the Centenary of the Weber Thesis*, ed. William H. Swatos, Jr., and Lutz Kaelber (Boulder, CO: Paradigm Publishers, 2005), 58–59.
19 Nielsen, "The Protestant Ethic," 59.
20 Brett, introduction to *On the Power of Emperors*, 12. See the papal bulls of Gregory IX (*Quo elongati* [1230]: Franciscans used goods but had no property—individual or common—in them), Innocent IV (*Ordinem vestrum* [1245]: the Roman church had the property that the Franciscans used), Innocent IV (*Quanto studiosius* [1247]: the order enjoyed "a wide range of goods without technically having property in them").
21 Brett, introduction to *On the Power of Emperors*, 12–13.
22 Brett, introduction to *On the Power of Emperors*, 13–14.
23 Brett, introduction to *On the Power of Emperors*, 14.
24 Tierney, *Natural Rights*, 131.
25 Tierney, *Natural Rights*, 95.
26 Brett, introduction to *On the Power of Emperors*, 18.
27 Tierney, *Natural Rights*, 96.
28 Tierney, *Natural Rights*, 96; *Brett*, introduction to *On the Power of Emperors*, 8.
29 Brett, introduction to *On the Power of Emperors*, 8. See also Cary J. Nederman and Kate Langdon Forhan, introduction to "Whether a Ruler Can Accept the Property of Churches for His Own Needs, Namely, in Case of War, Even against the Wishes of the Pope," by William of Ockham, in *Medieval Political Theory—A Reader: The Quest for the Body Politic, 1100–1400*, ed. Cary J. Nederman and Kate Langdon Forhan (London and New York: Routledge, 1993), 207.
30 See Arthur Stephen McGrade, introduction to *A Short Discourse on Tyrannical Government*, by William of Ockham, ed. Arthur Stephen McGrade, trans. John

Kilcullen, *Cambridge Texts in the History of Political Thought*, ed. Raymond Geuss and Quentin Skinner (Cambridge: Cambridge University Press, 1992), xvi.

31 McGrade, introduction to *A Short Discourse*, xvi.

32 Brett, introduction to *On the Power of Emperors*, 8.

33 McGrade, introduction to *A Short Discourse*, xvii; Brett, introduction to *On the Power of Emperors*, 10

34 McGrade, introduction to *A Short Discourse*, xvii.

35 McGrade, introduction to *A Short Discourse*, xvii.

36 Nederman and Forhan, introduction to "Whether a Ruler," 207.

37 Brett, introduction to *On the Power of Emperors*, 9; McGrade, introduction to *A Short Discourse*, xvii.

38 Tierney, *Natural Rights*, 96–97.

39 McGrade, introduction to *A Short Discourse*, xvii.

40 Nederman and Forhan, introduction to "Whether a Ruler," 207–8.

41 See William of Ockham, *Opera politica*, vols. 1 and 4, ed. H. S. Offler (Manchester: Manchester University Press, 1974, 1997). See also Nederman and Forhan, introduction to "Whether a Ruler," 208; Ockham, *On the Power of Emperors*; and Ockham, *A Short Discourse*.

42 Nederman and Forhan, introduction to "Whether a Ruler," 208; Offler, introduction to *An princeps*, in *Opera politica*, 221.

43 Nederman and Forhan, introduction to "Whether a Ruler," 208.

44 Offler, introduction to *An princeps*, 221.

45 Ockham, *Whether a Ruler*, 209; Ockham, *An princeps*, 228.

46 John W. Baldwin, *Masters, Princes, and Merchants: The Social Views of Peter the Chanter and His Circle*, vol. 1 (Princeton: Princeton University Press, 1970), 216.

47 Baldwin, *Masters, Princes, and Merchants*, 216.

48 Cary J. Nederman, "Royal Taxation and the English Church: The Origins of William of Ockham's *An princeps*," 37 *Journal of Ecclesiastical History* No. 3 (1986), 388.

49 Nederman and Forhan, introduction to "Whether a Ruler," 208.

50 Giorgio Agamben, *The Kingdom and the Glory: For a Theological Genealogy of Economy and Government* (Homo Sacer *II, 2*) (Stanford, CA: Stanford University Press, 2011), 55.

51 Agamben, *The Kingdom and the Glory*, 53.

52 Agamben, *The Kingdom and the Glory*, 54.

53 Agamben, *The Kingdom and the Glory*, 62.

54 Agamben, *The Kingdom and the Glory*, 54.

55 Agamben, *The Kingdom and the Glory*, 66–67.

56 Agamben, *The Kingdom and the Glory*, 73.

57 Agamben, *The Kingdom and the Glory*, 98.

58 Agamben, *The Kingdom and the Glory*, 99.

59 Agamben, *The Kingdom and the Glory*, 99, quoting Giles of Rome, *On Ecclesiastical Power*, trans. R. W. Dyson (Woodbridge, UK: The Boydel Press, 1986), 108.

60 Agamben, *The Kingdom and the Glory*, 101–102.

61 Agamben, *The Kingdom and the Glory*, 102.

62 Agamben, *The Kingdom and the Glory*, 106.

63 Agamben, *The Kingdom and the Glory*, 102, citing Giles of Rome, *On Ecclesiastical Power*, 187–88.

64 Agamben, *The Kingdom and the Glory*, 106.

65 Agamben, *The Kingdom and the Glory*, 105.

66 Agamben, *The Kingdom and the Glory*, 103.
67 Agamben, *The Kingdom and the Glory*, 99.
68 Agamben, *The Kingdom and the Glory*, 107–108. Agamben is using Michel Foucault's terms here.
69 Agamben, *The Kingdom and the Glory*, 107–108.
70 Agamben, *The Kingdom and the Glory*, 107.
71 Agamben, *The Kingdom and the Glory*, 107.
72 Agamben, *The Kingdom and the Glory*, 108.
73 Agamben, *The Kingdom and the Glory*, 108.
74 "Plenitude of power," discussed more thoroughly below, refers to the "all-encompassing lordship over the offices and properties of the laity, which had long been a mainstay of the papacy's defence of its temporal prerogatives." Nederman and Forhan, introduction to "Whether a Ruler," 208.
75 Ockham, *An princeps*, 256 (my translation).
76 *ST* II-II, Q. 87, Art. 1, resp.
77 Ockham, "Whether a Ruler," 211; Ockham, *An princeps*, 256.
78 *ST* II-II, Q. 87, Art. 1, resp.
79 *ST* II-II, Q. 66, Art. 8, ad. 3.
80 Ockham, *On the Power of Emperors*, 87 (footnote omitted). See also Ockham, *On the Power of Emperors*, 98 ("[T]hat all those things which are possible for a mortal prince and rector, and which are necessary to procure the salvation of souls and the rule and governance of the faithful, are a matter for papal principate (in such a way, however, that the limit of moderation is in no way grossly exceeded); respecting the possession, rights and liberties of others, except that he can exact his necessary expenses from his subjects") (footnote omitted).
81 Ockham, *On the Power of Emperors*, 96.
82 The arguments are not necessarily presented here in the same order in which Ockham presents them. They are woven together in Ockham's political writings but pulled apart here for ease of analysis.
83 Ockham, "Whether a Ruler," 211.
84 Ockham, *An princeps*, 253 (my translation).
85 Ockham, "Whether a Ruler," 212; Ockham, *An princeps*, 257.
86 Ockham, "Whether a Ruler," 212; Ockham, *An princeps*, 258.
87 Ockham, "Whether a Ruler," 213.
88 Ockham, *A Short Discourse*, 15.
89 Ockham, *A Short Discourse*, 12. McGrade describes the "power of order" as "the power conferred on a priest by ordination, the sacrament of Holy Orders, e.g., the power to change bread and wine into the body and blood of Christ in the Mass." Ockham, introduction to *A Short Discourse*, n29.
90 Ockham, *A Short Discourse*, 12.
91 Ockham, "Whether a Ruler," 213.
92 Nederman, "Royal Taxation," 383.
93 Nederman, "Royal Taxation," 383.
94 Ockham, "Whether a Ruler," 212; Ockham, *An princeps*, 258.
95 Nederman, "Royal Taxation," 384, quoting Joseph R. Strayer, *On the Medieval Origins of the Modern State* (Princeton: Princeton University Press, 1970), 38.
96 Nederman, "Royal Taxation," 384.
97 Ockham, "Whether a Ruler," 213.
98 Nederman, "Royal Taxation," 381. Nederman sees this principle extending back to Augustine and Jerome. Aquinas endorsed it in his treatment of tithing. See, e.g., *ST* II–II, Q. 76, Art. 4.
99 Nederman, "Royal Taxation," 382.
100 Ockham, "Whether a Ruler," 214; Ockham, *An princeps*, 260.

101 Ockham, "Whether a Ruler," 214.
102 Ockham, "Whether a Ruler," 214.
103 Nederman, "Royal Taxation," 383.
104 Ockham, "Whether a Ruler," 214.
105 Ockham, "Whether a Ruler," 213.
106 Ockham, "Whether a Ruler," 209.
107 Ockham, "Whether a Ruler," 209–10.
108 Ockham, "Whether a Ruler," 210.
109 See Nederman, "Royal Taxation," 381–82.
110 Ockham, "Whether a Ruler," 211, citing Aristotle, *Ethics* 1.1.
111 Ockham, *Whether a Ruler*, 211.
112 Ockham, *Whether a Ruler*, 214–15.
113 See especially *ST* II–II, Q. 66, Art. 2.
114 Compare the common good argument in *ST* II–II, Q. 66, Art 2, resp. (individual ownership promotes greater care of property by all, more order in "human affairs," and a "more peaceful state") with the explicit common good language in *ST* II–II, Q. 66, Art. 8, ad. 3 (rulers may exact from their subjects, even by violence, "that which is due to them for the safe-guarding of the common good").
115 Ockham, *A Short Discourse*, 11.
116 Ockham, *A Short Discourse*, 10.
117 Ockham, introduction to *A Short Discourse*, 5n5.
118 Ockham, *A Short Discourse*, 28–29; Ockham, *Breviloquium*, 120.
119 Ockham, *A Short Discourse*, 29.
120 John Kilcullen, "The Political Writings," in *The Cambridge Companion to Ockham*, ed. Paul Vincent Spade (Cambridge: Cambridge University Press, 1999), 311.
121 Ockham, *A Short Discourse*, 77; Ockham, *Breviloquium*, 167.
122 Ockham, *A Short Discourse*, 78; Ockham, *Breviloquium*, 168.
123 Ockham, *A Short Discourse*, 77; Ockham, *Breviloquium*, 167.
124 Arthur Stephen McGrade, *The Political Thought of William of Ockham: Personal and Institutional Principles*, Cambridge Studies in Medieval Life and Thought, 3rd series, vol. 7 (Cambridge: Cambridge University Press, 1974), 126. Kilcullen goes so far as to say that the common good does the work for Ockham that general welfare does later for John Stuart Mill and his followers. Kilcullen, "Political Writings," 318–20.
125 McGrade, *Political Thought*, 215.
126 Nederman, "Royal Taxation," 385.
127 For a discussion of this passage and the tendency of historians and political theologians to attribute extreme political voluntarism to Ockham, see Tierney, *Natural Rights*, 195–203.
128 Ockham, *A Short Discourse*, 77; Ockham, *Breviloquium*, 167.
129 Ockham, *A Short Discourse*, 9.
130 Tierney, *Natural Rights*, 122.
131 Tierney, *Natural Rights*, 8, 97.
132 Tierney, *Natural Rights*, 14.
133 Tierney, *Natural Rights*, 16. Tierney describes Villey's account of the classical meaning of *ius* as fundamentally "structuralist" in its focus on patterns of relationship. Tierney, *Natural Rights*, 18.
134 Tierney, *Natural Rights*, 28, quoting Michel Villey, "La genèse du droit subjectif chez Guillaume d'Occam," in *Le droit subjectif en question*, vol. 9, *Archives de philosophie du droit* (Paris: Sirey, 1974), 100–102.

135 Even Aquinas, Tierney writes, uses the word *ius* differently in different contexts, without always specifying its meaning. Tierney notes in this connection that Thomas follows the practice of his age in occasionally using *ius* and *lex* interchangeably. Tierney, *Natural Rights*, 25. However, as Tierney acknowledges, Thomas seems deliberately to avoided using *ius* to mean "subjective right." Tierney, *Natural Rights*, 258.
136 Tierney, *Natural Rights*, 93.
137 Tierney, *Natural Rights*, 109, quoting Marsilius of Padua, *Defensor pacis*, ed. R. Scholz (Hanover: Hahn, 1933), 268.
138 Tierney, *Natural Rights*, 113. Marsilius' originality, in Tierney's opinion, lies in basing "the whole discussion on a formal distinction between *ius* as objective law and *ius* as subjective right and then [sustaining] the distinction consistently through the whole course of the ensuing argument . . . ." Tierney, *Natural Rights*, 115.
139 Tierney, *Natural Rights*, 119–20.
140 Tierney, *Natural Rights*, 121.
141 Tierney, *Natural Rights*, 121–122.
142 Tierney, *Natural Rights*, 127.
143 Tierney, *Natural Rights*, 129.
144 Tierney, *Natural Rights*, 130, quoting Ockham, *Opus nonaginta dierum*, 557.
145 Tierney, *Natural Rights*, 130–31.
146 Kilcullen, "Political Writings," 308.
147 Kilcullen, "Political Writings," 308.
148 Kilcullen, "Political Writings," 308.
149 Ockham, "Whether a Ruler," 210.
150 Nederman, "Royal Taxation," 387.
151 Tierney, *Natural Rights*, 194.
152 Ockham, "Whether a Ruler," 210.
153 Ockham, "Whether a Ruler," 213; *An princeps*, 259.
154 Ockham, "Whether a Ruler," 214; *An princeps*, 259. Ockham has already articulated this principle of interpretation in Chapter 7.
155 Ockham, "Whether a Ruler," 214; *An princeps*, 259.
156 Ockham, "Whether a Ruler," 214; *An princeps*, 260.
157 Ockham, "Whether a Ruler," 214; *An princeps*, 260.
158 Ockham, "Whether a Ruler," 214.
159 Ockham, *An princeps*, 260.
160 Ockham, "Whether a Ruler," 214–15.
161 Ockham, *An princeps*, 230.
162 Ockham, *An princeps*, 232 (*privare omnibus rebus suis et iuribus*).
163 Ockham, *A Short Discourse*, 23.
164 McGrade, *Political Thought*, 141n179.
165 Tierney, *Natural Rights*, 67.
166 Tierney, *Natural Rights*, 68.
167 Ockham, *A Short Discourse*, 24.
168 After *An princeps*, Ockham used works of supererogation as an example. These were works of Christian perfection, but the pope could not regularly command them because to do so would contravene evangelical liberty. See Tierney, *Natural Rights*, 188.
169 Brett, introduction to *On the Power of Emperors*, 38.
170 Ockham, *On the Power of Emperors*, 99.
171 Brett, introduction to *On the Power of Emperors*, 38–39.
172 Brett, introduction to *On the Power of Emperors*, 36–37.

173 Brett, introduction to *On the Power of Emperors*, 37–38.
174 Ockham, *A Short Discourse*, 26. The reference is to the following passage from *Politics* 3.6:

> The conclusion which follows is clear: those constitutions which consider the common interest are right constitutions, judged by the standard of absolute justice. Those constitutions which consider only the personal interest of the rulers are all wrong constitutions, or perversions of the right forms. Such perverted forms are despotic; whereas the city is an association of freemen.

Aristotle, *Politics*, trans. Ernest Barker, ed. R. F. Stalley (Oxford: Oxford University Press, 1995), 99.
175 Brett, introduction to *On the Power of Emperors*, 46.
176 McGrade, *Political Thought*, 148.
177 William of Ockham, *Octo quaestiones de potestatae papae*, in *Opera politica*, vol. 1, 110. The translation is taken from McGrade, *Political Thought*, 115.
178 McGrade, *Political Thought*, 115.
179 McGrade, *Political Thought*, 115–16.
180 Arthur Stephen McGrade, "Natural Law and Moral Omnipotence," in *The Cambridge Companion to Ockham*, ed. Paul Vincent Spade (Cambridge: Cambridge University Press, 1999), 273.
181 William of Ockham, *Quodlibeta* III, Q. 13, 4, in *Philosophical Writings*, by William of Ockham, ed. and trans. Philotheus Boehner (Indianapolis and Cambridge: Hackett Publishing Co., 1990), 145.
182 McGrade, *Political Thought*, 186.
183 McGrade, *Political Thought*, 187.
184 McGrade, *Political Thought*, 189.
185 Ockham, "Whether a Ruler," 214.
186 Ockham, "Whether a Ruler," 210.
187 Ockham, "Whether a Ruler," 214.
188 Ockham, *A Short Discourse*, 26.
189 McGrade, *Political Thought*, 119.
190 Brett, introduction to *On the Power of Emperors*, 46.
191 Brett, introduction to *On the Power of Emperors*, 47.
192 Brett, introduction to *On the Power of Emperors*, 14.s
193 Tierney, *Natural Rights*, 147n49, citing Duns Scotus, *Opus Oxoniense* 4.15.2, in *Joannis Duns Scoti opera omnia*, ed. L. Vivès, 26 vols. (Paris, 1891–95).
194 Brett, introduction to *On the Power of Emperors*, 14.
195 Tierney, *Natural Rights*, 147.
196 Brett, introduction to *On the Power of Emperors*, 14–15.
197 Ockham, *Opus nonaginta*, 305–308. See Tierney, *Natural Rights*, 160.
198 Ockham, *Opus nonaginta*, 492–93; Tierney, *Natural Rights*, 161.
199 Tierney, *Natural Rights*, 166; Kilcullen, "Political Writings," 306.
200 Ockham, *Opus nonaginta*, 434–35; Tierney, *Natural Rights*, 163.
201 Ockham, *Opus nonaginta*, 439; Tierney, *Natural Rights*, 166.
202 Ockham, *Opus nonaginta*, 664; Tierney, *Natural Rights*, 165.
203 Tierney, *Natural Rights*, 165.
204 See Tierney, *Natural Rights*, 177–79.
205 Tierney, *Natural Rights*, 178–79.
206 See Tierney, *Natural Rights*, 156; Kilcullen, "Political Writings," 306.
207 Tierney, *Natural Rights*, 164.
208 Ockham, *On the Power of Emperors*, 91.
209 Brett, introduction to *On the Power of Emperors*, 50.
210 Brett, introduction to *On the Power of Emperors*, 50.

211 Brett, introduction to *On the Power of Emperors*, 41.
212 McGrade, *Political Thought*, 213.
213 Ockham, *A Short Discourse*, 51–52.
214 Brett, introduction to *On the Power*, 43.
215 Ockham, *A Short Discourse*, 52.
216 McGrade, "Natural Law and Moral Omnipotence," 290.
217 McGrade, "Natural Law and Moral Omnipotence," 292.

References

Agamben, Giorgio. 2011. *The Kingdom and the Glory: For a Theological Genealogy of Economy and Government* (Homo Sacer *II, 2*). Stanford, CA: Stanford University Press.

Aristotle. 1995. *Politics*. Translated by Ernest Barker. Edited by R. F. Stalley. Oxford: Oxford University Press.

Baldwin, John W. 1970. *Masters, Princes, and Merchants: The Social Views of Peter the Chanter and His Circle*, vol. 1. Princeton: Princeton University Press.

Bonaventure. 1904. *Regula II (Regula bullata) Fratrum minorum*, in *Opuscula sancti patris Francisci Assisiensis. Edita cura et studio PP. collegii Saint Bonaventurae.* Florence: Quarracchi.

Duns Scotus. 1891–95. "Opus Oxoniense." In *Joannis Duns Scoti opera omnia*, edited by Luke Wadding, vol. 26. Paris: L. Vivès.

Giles of Rome. 1986. *On Ecclesiastical Power*. Translated by R. W. Dyson. Woodbridge, UK: The Boydel Press.

Kilcullen, John. 1999. "The Political Writings." In *The Cambridge Companion to Ockham*, edited by Paul Vincent Spade, 302–25. Cambridge: Cambridge University Press.

Marsilius of Padua. 1933. *Defensor pacis*. Edited by R. Scholz. Hanover: Hahn.

McGrade, Arthur Stephen. 1974. *The Political Thought of William of Ockham: Personal and Institutional Principles*. Cambridge Studies in Medieval Life and Thought, 3rd series, vol. 7. Cambridge: Cambridge University Press.

———. 1999. "Natural Law and Moral Omnipotence." In Spade, *The Cambridge Companion to Ockham*, 273–301.

Nederman, Cary J. 1986. "Royal Taxation and the English Church: The Origins of William of Ockham's *An princeps*." *Journal of Ecclesiastical History* 37, no. 3: 377–88.

Nielsen, Donald A. 2005. "The Protestant Ethic and the 'Spirit' of Capitalism as Grand Narrative: Max Weber's Philosophy of History." In *The Protestant Ethic Turns 100: Essays on the Centenary of the Weber* Thesis, edited by William H. Swatos, Jr., and Lutz Kaelber, 53–75. Boulder, CO: Paradigm Publishers.

Spade, Paul Vincent, ed. 1999. *The Cambridge Companion to Ockham*. Cambridge: Cambridge University Press.

Strayer, Joseph R. 1970. *On the Medieval Origins of the Modern State*. Princeton: Princeton University Press.

Thomas Aquinas. 2013. *Summa Theologiae* (Latin-English Edition). Translated by the Fathers of the English-Dominican Province. Nashville: NovAntiqua.

Tierney, Brian. 2001. *The Idea of Natural Rights*. Emory University Studies in Law and Religion, edited by John Witte, Jr., vol. 5. Grand Rapids: William B. Eerdmans Publishing Co.

Villey, Michel. 1974. "La genèse du droit subjectif chez Guillaume d'Occam." In *Le droit subjectif en question*, vol. 9, *Archives de philosophie du droit*. Paris: Sirey.

———. 2013. *La Formation de la Penseé Juridique Moderne*. Paris: Presses Universitaires de France, 2013.

William of Ockham. 1974, 1997. *Opera politica*. Edited by H. S. Offler, vols. 1 and 4. Manchester: Manchester University Press.

———. 1990. *Philosophical Writings*. Edited and translated by Philotheus Boehner. Indianapolis: Hackett Publishing Co.

———. 1992. *A Short Discourse on Tyrannical Government*. Edited by Arthur Stephen McGrade, Translated by John Kilcullen. Cambridge Texts in the History of Political Thought, edited by Raymond Geuss and Quentin Skinner. Cambridge: Cambridge University Press.

———. 1993. "Whether a Ruler Can Accept the Property of Churches for His Own Needs, Namely, in Case of War, Even against the Wishes of the Pope." In *Medieval Political Theory—A Reader: The Quest for the Body Politic, 1100–1400*, edited by Cary J. Nederman and Kate Langdon Forhan, 207–20. London: Routledge.

———. 1998. *On the Power of Emperors and Popes*. Translated by Annabel S. Brett. Bristol: Thoemmes Press.

5 Martin Luther's redistributive theology of the Lord's Supper

Introduction

It is well established that Ockham's nominalism was an influence on Martin Luther, but how much of an influence it may have been is disputed. It was probably one of many currents that shaped Luther's thinking. Heiko Oberman and Michael Laffin argue that any complete identification of Luther's thought with Ockham's nominalism must be nuanced; "Augustinianism, humanism, and even mysticism" shaped Luther's theology as well.[1]

In some ways, the two theologians' political theologies have suffered similar fates. Supposedly cut off by sociopolitical circumstances from the theology and philosophy for which Ockham and Luther are known, any political reflections that the two thinkers may have had are sometimes regarded as uninteresting at best, dangerous at worst. Most treatments of Luther, according to Laffin, neglect the connection between Luther's political views and the deeper structures of his theology, with the result that his political views are interpreted as nominalistic, individualistic, and quietistic or authoritarian.[2]

Luther's "two kingdoms" theology surfaced strongly after the Peasants' War (1524–1525) and has often been read as instituting a split in Luther's understanding of the human being. Each individual believer, according to a thoroughgoing two kingdoms theology, has an "inner" person and an "outer" person who dwell in two different kingdoms and therefore follow different principles.[3] This reading requires correction in two ways. First, as Bernd Wannenwetsch notes, readers like Weber, Troeltsch, and Marcuse mistakenly supposed that the "inner" and "outward" person in Luther's writings "represent anthropological provinces *within* 'man.'" In reality, Luther assigned these designations "to man *as a whole*, only in different perspectives, either facing God (*coram Deo*) or facing the world (*coram mundo*)."[4]

More importantly, Luther's two kingdoms theology serves as "a merely emancipative purpose," as a bulwark against conflation of secular and ecclesial authority "and illegitimate borrowings of one side from the other."[5] Although Luther used the two kingdoms in a "polemical" way to ensure that politics and the church do not absorb each other, in the case of godly rulers, at least, "the secular authority acts directly as a servant of the church," and, in all events, "one rule and reign of God . . . is being expressed."[6] Luther wrote in 1526, "Thus, in the end, all authority comes from God, whose alone it is; for he is emperor, prince, count, noble, judge, and all else, and he assigns these offices to his subjects as he wills, and takes them back again for himself."[7] Thus, in Laffin's words, the two kingdoms "refer to the one rule of God over His kingdom in a twofold manner over and against the kingdom of the devil." They are not autonomous spheres, but rather highlight an eschatological tension.[8] In Laffin's view, the only way to make sense of Luther's political theology is to uphold a distinction, without separation, between God's acts of grace in redemption and God's general providential care for creation.[9]

This chapter seeks to explore the connection between Luther's political views, specifically with respect to taxation, and the deeper structures of his theology, starting with a preface that Luther wrote to an actual piece of legislation.

"Preface to the Ordinance of a Common Chest"

Luther's concern to provide for the poor through both charity and social assistance first surfaced in his sermons on usury in 1519 and 1520.[10] He elaborated these calls for social reform in his "Open Letter to the Christian Nobility of the German Nation Concerning the Reform of the Christian Estate" (1520), in which he urged the princes and nobility to eliminate the mendicant orders in their territories to help erase begging from the land[11] and expressed hope for the liberation of Germany from the pope's "intolerable taxing and fleecing."[12]

The Wittenberg town council responded to Luther's "Open Letter" by drafting an ordinance that would "ensure the regulation of public assistance to the city's house poor and . . . make begging unnecessary." Luther's then-colleague and later-adversary Andreas Bodenstein von Karlstadt assisted in the preparation of the ordinance while Luther was detained in the Wartburg Castle after the Diet of Worms.[13] The resulting ordinance, "The Order of the City of Wittenberg," was published in 1522. It resolved to gather the property of the "cloisters" and "all the income from the churches, all of the brotherhoods, and the guilds" into a common chest, which would be used "to provide for the poor people" under the supervision of two town council delegates, two delegates from the community, and a secretary. Beggars were to be either urged to work or expelled from the city, except that those who had fallen into poverty through age, sickness, or misfortune were to be provided for from the common chest. The common chest would also make loans to "poor artisans" and was to "provide for poor orphans, the children of poor people, and maidens who shall be given an appropriate dowry for marriage." Wittenberg's common chest was also designed to provide loans to "citizens and residents" who were burdened by high interest rates, "for example, five to six percent." The chest would offer refinancing at a four-percent rate.[14]

The Wittenberg ordinance did not directly refer to the need for ongoing taxation, but it did acknowledge that the income from churches, brotherhoods, and guilds might become insufficient at some point to meet the city's goal of providing for the poor through the common chest. In that case "shall others, be they priests or citizens, according to what they have, yearly contribute a sum of money for the maintenance of the multitude of the poor."[15] This provision reflects the way in which Luther's idea of distributive and redistributive justice, discussed in more detail below, took into consideration both the abundance of those with more and the needs of those with less. The amount of the priests' and citizens' contributions would depend on "what they have," but, at the same time, "[t]he only criterion for distribution of loans or outright gifts was to be the need of the recipient."[16]

Luther's ideas about social assistance embodied in the Wittenberg ordinance were well received elsewhere. Other towns approached him hoping for his assistance in drafting legislation. One of the first was Leisnig, a town south of Wittenberg with a parish that also included eleven surrounding villages. Jurisdiction of the city had been granted to the abbot of Buch, a nearby Cistercian monastery, in 1191 and confirmed repeatedly thereafter.[17] From its earliest moments, the evangelical movement in Leisnig found itself in conflict with the monastery, as the abbot in Luther's day was hostile to the Reformation.[18] In 1522 the town appealed to Luther. In response, he spent a week in Leisnig preparing a church order that included a common chest.[19] The congregation proceeded to take over all the church properties in the parish and set up an organization to administer them for the assistance of "the poor and needy."[20] Five months later, in January 1523, the town council and the congregation sent Luther a formal letter requesting his advice on a proposed ordinance to codify these measures.[21] Luther responded with his "Preface to the Ordinance of a Common Chest" and had the ordinance printed and published with his preface.[22]

The Leisnig common chest was to have ten elected directors—two from the nobility, two from the town council, three from the citizenry, and three from the rural peasantry. The directors were to meet on a weekly basis and give triennial reports to the whole community.[23]

The Leisnig ordinance, unlike its Wittenberg precursor, explicitly provided for ongoing taxation.[24] The Leisnig tax provision stated in full:

> Wherever the rents, collections, revenues, and contributions to the resources and stores of our common chest, as itemized above, should prove insufficient for the maintenance and support of our pastoral office, office of sacristan, schools, needy poor, and the buildings owned in common, as these have been daily set forth in orderly sequence, we the nobility, council, craft supervisors, gentry, and commoners dwelling in the city and villages of our whole parish, for ourselves and our posterity, and by virtue of our fraternal agreement, have unitedly resolved and consented that every noble, townsman, and peasant living in the parish shall, according to his ability and means, remit in taxes for himself, his wife, and his children a certain sum of money to the chest each year, in order that the total amount can be arrived at and procured which the deliberations and decisions of the general parish assembly, on the basis of investigation in and experience with the annual statements, have determined to be necessary and sufficient. To this end, throughout the entire

> extent of our parish, every householder, domestic servant, journeyman of the various handicrafts, and other persons who are not home owners but who share in the enjoyment and use of our parish rights shall individually contribute annually one silver groschen; that is, three new pennies, the fourth part of the groschen, every quarter at the Ember fast. Each master or mistress shall diligently collect this money and turn it over to the ten directors at each Ember fast. The parish assembly solemnly purposes and promises that to the honor of God and the love of our fellow Christians we shall never spare ourselves this trifling annual contribution in view of the fact that hitherto, since time out of mind, both residents and nonresidents throughout our common parish have by many methods and devices been overburdened and fleeced incessantly the year round with exorbitant and intolerable impositions and assessments. By the grace of God these practices have now been restored to the true freedom of the Christian spirit. It is the duty of every Christian to see that such Christian liberty is not misused as a cover for shameful avarice.[25]

The provision contains patent ambiguities: whether the tax is an emergency measure designed to maintain chest resources at a certain level or a regular contribution from the inception of the program, whether the amount of the tax is set or means-tested, and whether the assembly has the authority to adjust the amount. Nevertheless, several themes emerge. First, as in the Wittenberg ordinance, ability and needs were both in view. The tax was to be paid (at least in the first paragraph) according to each taxpayer's "ability and means" but explicitly for the maintenance of the "needy poor" (among other purposes). Secondly, the tax provision purported to be the product of "fraternal agreement" among all affected classes of local society.[26] It was a "united" resolve, entered into with full consent. Thirdly, the levy was to be measured and consistent, not overly burdensome and arbitrary like the impositions to which the parish was accustomed.

Another feature is the implicit redistributive structure of the Leisnig ordinance's annual tax provision. The resources of the common chest were required to be maintained at a level sufficient to meet the needs of the poor, as determined by the investigation and experience of the parish assembly. Luther himself, in the preface, lauded the ordinance's elevation of need over all other worthy causes. The confiscated property of the Leisnig parish monasteries can be distributed in a number of ways, he wrote, but need-based administration of that property in the common chest is preferable to the others:

> The third way is the best, however, to devote all the remaining property to the common fund of a common chest, out of which gifts and loans could be made in Christian love to all the needy in the land, be they nobles or commoners . . .. Now there is no greater service of God than Christian love which helps and serves the needy, as Christ himself will judge and testify at the last day, Matthew 25. This is why the possessions of the church were formerly called *bona ecclesiae*, that is, common property, a common chest, as it were, for all who were needy among the Christians.[27]

If we think of taxation as implicating three interests—the needs of the state, the needs of the poor, and the interests of property owners—Luther linked the needs of the state to the needs of the poor rather than to the interests of property owners. He also subordinated the state's other revenue needs to the necessities of the poor. "If we have to spend such large sums every year on guns, roads, bridges, dams, and countless similar items to insure the temporal peace and prosperity of a city," Luther asked, "why should not much more be devoted to our poor neglected youth?"[28] Luther considered the ruler's protection a means to the state's ultimate end, which is the provision of life's basic necessities. He wrote in his explanation of the fourth petition of the Lord's Prayer in his Large Catechism:

> It would therefore be fitting if the coat of arms of every upright prince were emblazoned with a loaf of bread instead of a lion or a wreath of rue, or if a loaf of bread were stamped on coins, in order to remind both princes and subjects that it is through the princes' office that we enjoy protection and peace and that without them we could neither eat nor preserve the precious gift of bread.[29]

The contrast between Luther's insistence on an axis between the ruler and the poor, on the one hand, and the modern alliance of the state's interest in efficiency with the taxpayer's economic liberty, on the other, deserves emphasizing. Luther saw a reorientation underway in the economy of his day, away from the needs of the poor as its highest priority. He observed a new profit economy emerging in his place and time, an economy that he was sure would divorce the possession of money from its use for human needs, feed avarice, and erode the common good.[30] Abandonment of the focus on need could only mean capitulation to the idea that economic principles and laws are autonomous—a perspective that Luther considered "idolatrous."[31]

More was at stake in the redistribution of monastic property than merely a decision about what to do with surplus assets suddenly on hand; at issue was a theological reappraisal of poverty. Even in the "Ninety-five Theses," Luther was already reacting against the idea that the poor are the treasure of the church, supplying the rich with the opportunity to do good works through almsgiving.[32] Luther's forceful opposition to begging marked a shift from the late medieval efforts merely to control begging to a stance that insisted on the abolition of begging. This shift, Lindberg argues, may have been prompted by sensitivity to the "deleterious effects of widespread begging," but responded equally to an awareness of the implications of Luther's "theology of justification by grace alone, which precludes any salvific benefits to poverty and to alms."[33]

Paul Warde's detailed study of state formation in Germany in the sixteenth and seventeenth centuries, which pays particular attention to the Duchy of Württemberg in the southwestern part of the German world, demonstrates that by 1568 legislation of the Lutheran period had already established a state church, created a school system in which the use of the vernacular was becoming widespread, and "codified the tax, property, poor relief and inheritance systems."[34]

A "secularization of charity" was already underway before the 1520s, when the focus shifted suddenly in German towns that embraced the evangelical cause from alleviating poverty through voluntary giving to centrally administered welfare.[35] However, the earlier changes had resulted from a push to correct abuses in the system of almsgiving.[36] Once salvation came to be perceived as the foundation rather than the goal and achievement of life, "the energy and resources poured into acquiring other-worldly capital" could be "redirected to this-worldly activities."[37] A theology highlighting salvation as purely the gift of God had the effect of deflating the soteriological significance of both poverty and almsgiving.[38] Thus, the Lutheran towns' establishment of common chests could be considered an expression of the "brotherly love" that was the "fruit" of realizing that "all temporal and eternal blessings won by our Lord and Savior Christ out of pure grace and mercy are granted unto us by the eternal God."[39]

Anthropological studies of the type popular in the 1970s tended to assume that welfare states began to emerge in early modern Europe as collective management of the land gave way to "private-property-based agriculture" that produced "casualties" requiring "collectively sponsored welfare provision." More recent accounts, however, are "far less inclined to privilege single forms of explanation."[40] Hans-Christoph Rublack argues that new principles guiding social change and legislation in the early modern period typically began as a form of "social action" in response to "pre-theoretical" concerns of daily life but were then legitimized and converted to social policies through the use of "verbal" or "integrative" norms.[41] Codification of law in late fifteenth-century Germany, for instance, made frequent use of the norms of justice, peace, unity, and the common weal, all four "directed towards 'the praise of God.'"[42] For all that, appeals to these norms are no less genuine and the rhetoric no less sincere.[43] The impact of theological and philosophical ideas on legislation is hard to gauge. It seems plausible, however, that ideas are often criticisms of, and reactions to, social, economic, and political circumstances[44] and that these criticisms and reactions can, and sometimes do, influence actions and decisions. Although more work is called for to establish the exact path that Luther's teachings on poor relief and his endorsement of the Leisnig ordinance followed in influencing the emergence of the modern welfare state in Germany and the Nordic countries, Luther seems to have done more than articulate changing circumstances. The rhetorical power with which he insisted on justification by grace through faith infused the secularization of charity with energy in ways that the rest of this chapter will suggest.

Despite the power of Luther's rhetoric in his preface, the shift proved difficult in Leisnig. The town council was reluctant to levy taxes for poor relief[45] and claimed that it could not relinquish its right to dispose of endowments without the elector's express permission. The congregation appealed to the elector, who appointed a tax commission to hear the dispute. After several weeks of negotiation, a compromise was reached in which the parties would present their differences to the elector as they arose. Luther himself traveled to Leisnig again in August 1523, probably at the elector's request, and found that the town council was still withholding funds. Luther was unable to break the impasse. He asked the elector to enforce the Leisnig ordinance, but the elector, characteristically, hesitated.[46] In November 1524, Luther wrote to the elector's advisor Georg Spalatin that he "deeply regretted that the Leisnig attempt, the first of its kind, which should have been such an example of success, had turned out to be such a miserable example of failure." It was not until 1529 that the Saxon visitation committee, a Lutheran revival of a medieval custom, confirmed the common chest at the same time that it recognized Leisnig's independence from the abbot of Buch.[47]

The transition from individual to centralized poor relief was challenging for a number of reasons, not the least of which was that almsgiving rather than redistribution through tax-and-transfer systems had been the central instrument of poor relief in the Middle Ages. Taxation often had a different purpose, that of funding the state. As previous chapters have shown, in the feudal period kings were expected to live off their own resources, but in the thirteenth and fourteenth centuries an increase in the number of servants prompted interest in taxation. The first justification of exceptional taxes was war, particularly the crusades. By the end of the thirteenth century, however, it was typical of rulers to extend these taxes to maintain order.[48] Towns were also in a difficult situation, as they often arose outside the feudal structure. They could meet their revenue needs only by expanding their territories and levying taxes on their new citizens.[49] By the fifteenth century, "the income drawn directly from the landed estates of the prince was overtaken by taxation as the main source of finance for the activities of central governments."[50]

Thus, Luther's support for regular, general, and centralized taxation coincided with the emergence of precisely that kind of taxation as the main—perhaps only—way of funding the increasingly expensive governments of Europe. However, the tax revenue needed for poor relief was in direct competition with the tax revenue needed to sustain the administrations of territories and towns. Luther (and Calvin after him) saw this tension. Luther's chief charge against the princes and nobility in his "Admonition to Peace" (1525) was that they collected taxes "for their own profit and advantage" rather than for "the welfare of their subjects."[51] It is little wonder that even Leisnig, a town of only 1500 people,[52] took seven years to implement the terms of its own ordinance. Taxation in Luther's thinking may have been conceptually rooted in theology, but the general impulse behind collecting taxes in the 1520s was pragmatic: the needs of administration. The story of competing visions of taxation—redistributive versus administrative—had begun in earnest.

As noted, the Leisnig ordinance anticipated a deliberately redistributive role for taxation. The ordinance assumed a Christian consensus in which "the nobility, council, craft supervisors, gentry, and commoners dwelling in the city and villages of the assembly and parish of Leisnig, . . . upon the considered and mature counsel of men learned in the divine Scriptures" (i.e., Luther) agreed fraternally "that, according to human opinion, all the internal and external possessions of Christian believers are to serve and contribute to the honor of God and the love of the fellow-Christian neighbor."[53] Redistribution of resources for the benefit of the poor was a spiritually motivated act for Luther. After the initial failure of the Leisnig ordinance, Luther preached a sermon in which he offered ideas on how a city could establish a system of poor relief. He added ruefully, "But we do not have the personnel for this, therefore I do not think we can put it into effect until God makes Christians."[54]

The precise connection between the love of neighbor and relief of the poor depended, for Luther, on the logic of redistribution in his overall theology. To that connection we turn.

The redistributive logic of Luther's theology

For Luther, as for Aquinas, material goods are subject to redistribution because they are, in the final analysis, held in common. Luther's grammar of distribution and redistribution, however, began with Christ and his work, whereas Aquinas saw redistribution as a human activity undertaken in response to natural law. Aquinas wrote that "[c]ommunity of goods is ascribed to the natural law."[55] He also stated:

> Things which are of human right cannot derogate from natural right or Divine right . . . Wherefore the division and appropriation of things which are based on human law, do not preclude the fact that man's needs have to be remedied by means of these very things. Hence whatever certain people have in superabundance is due, by natural law, to the purpose of succoring the poor.[56]

Luther, on the other hand, wrote:

> In this sacrament [of the Lord's Supper], therefore, man is given through the priest a sure sign from God himself that he is thus united with Christ and his saints and has all things in common, that Christ's sufferings and life are his own, together with the lives and sufferings of all the saints. . . . But in times past this sacrament was so properly used, and the people were taught to understand this fellowship so well, that they even gathered food and material goods in the church, and there—as St. Paul writes in I Corinthians 11—distributed among those who were in need.[57]

In what Luther called the third "power of faith," the human soul is united through faith with Christ "as a bride is united with her bridegroom."[58] "[I]t follows," Luther wrote, "that everything they have they hold in common, the good as well as the evil." The poor become rich through the power of faith in a spiritual distribution from Christ to sinner: "Here this rich and divine bridegroom Christ marries this poor, wicked harlot, redeems her from all her evil, and adorns her with all his goodness."[59]

The communicatio idiomatum

This "happy exchange" (*fröhliche Wechsel*) in Luther's theology between Christ and the believer is based on the originally Christological doctrine of the *communicatio idiomatum* (communication of attributes).[60] The doctrine is not original with Luther, but he placed it in the center, not just of his Christology, but of his whole theology.[61] As a result of the *communicatio*, Luther wrote, "whatever is said about [Christ] as a human being must also be said about him as God, namely, "Christ has died," and, as Christ is God, it follows that 'God has died." Likewise, "whatever is said of God must also be attributed to the human being. Thus 'God created the world and is almighty,' and the human being Christ is God; therefore, the human being Christ created the world and is almighty."[62]

Luther's understanding of relationships among believers mirrors his Christological formulation of the *communicatio idiomatum*.[63] The exchange between bridegroom and bride (Christ and the believer) models the exchange between the two natures of Christ.[64] Thus, according to Luther, Christ distributes to Christians the "prerogatives" of "priesthood" and "kingship" that he obtained. The prerogative of kingship is a spiritual kingship that means that the believer is, in the space of faith and liberty, subject to none. Christ "obtained" this prerogative, and the believer receives it because Christ "imparts" and "shares" it through the legal consequences of the act of "marrying" the believer.[65] This sharing of all things comes about in Christ's action rather than in human action that responds to an underlying created order, as Aquinas would have it.

The grammar of redistribution applies as well to the other prerogative that Christ has won and now distributes: priesthood. However, priesthood itself implies a redistribution of what is received. By virtue of the priesthood of all believers—bestowed on Christians by Christ—Christians in turn distribute to others what they have received.[66] The grace of being a distributor is, as it were, distributed.

The believer, who is *distributee* as well as *distributor*, lives in a place of abundance, free from all the anxieties that her own distributing of good things would cause her if she were in a place of scarcity. Faith is "produced" through the preaching of "why Christ came, what he brought and bestowed, what benefit it is to us to accept him." This preaching, in turn, "is done when that Christian liberty which [Christ] bestows is rightly taught."[67]

The force of this freedom to distribute, and the starting point of the place of abundance that it implies, is thrown into relief by the material scarcity that characterized Luther's setting. The economy of rural and small-town Germany at the beginning of the early modern period was a zero-sum game, dependent on a fixed set of naturally given resources. The land was capable of supporting only so much material wealth; there came a point at which increased production could no longer support higher consumption, and the only way to support one person's higher level of consumption was to take the resources that had previously gone to someone else.[68] In Warde's words, Luther's was "a world profoundly worried about the scarcity of resources."[69]

Population grew more rapidly than food supplies in the sixteenth century, and peasants consequently could no longer rely on local regulation to survive. Their lives were increasingly absorbed into the "broader political economy of market controls" and poor relief. Warde demonstrates that, in Württemberg, ordinances addressing poverty and begging began to appear in 1531 and "from 1562 onwards dearth and its consequences became a regular concern of the central government."[70] These measures were the result of a certain "moral panic" that settled in when it became apparent that the decision-making processes of village life could not grapple successfully with new forms of the "limited good." Warde writes that "the impetus was thus created for the development of a poor-relief system to pick up this slack of poverty." Nevertheless, the responses were deeply conservative. Even though the distribution of taxable wealth did become marginally less unequal in the century following Luther's time, "at no point did this society collectively alter the balance of land use on any scale, reorganize holdings, or move systematically to shift the balance of livestock and cultivated land."[71]

The tenor of the Leisnig ordinance and Luther's preface is all the more striking against their pervasive backdrop of scarcity. Universal applicability and regular imposition of the annual tax, along with the Leisnig assembly's apparent concern to tailor the amount to the exact needs of the common chest, explicitly arose from a restoration of "the true freedom of the Christian spirit."[72] Faith is liberty because faith is the place where law is not needed.[73] Luther's believer renounces not only her legal rights but *all* rights as superfluous and unnecessary.[74] The connection between the "Christian spirit" and the scarcity or abundance of material resources is dissected in the following discussion.

Freedom, faith, and love

All the good things Christ has won he distributes to believers, who receive them by faith, and that by having this faith a believer dwells in a place of freedom from law and obligation because Christ has fulfilled the law and has distributed to the believer the benefits of that fulfillment. The faith and liberty bestowed by Christ would represent the entirety of Luther's distributive narrative if humans were nothing but spiritual beings. Because of the outer person, however, Scripture contains "commandments" as well as the "promise." The commandments are for the outer person, who is called to obey and conform to the inner person. Works are necessary for the outer person to control the body and, thus, accomplish this conforming. The "spirit of faith . . . with joyful zeal . . . attempts to put the body under control and hold it in check."[75]

From the discussion of "works in general," Luther's perspective in "The Freedom of a Christian" shifts to "the works which a Christian does for himself." The perspective then shifts a second time when Luther turns to those "things which [a Christian] does toward his neighbor."[76] Even here, Luther insisted, works arise from the place of liberty:

> Although the Christian is thus free from all works, he ought in this liberty to empty himself, take upon himself the form of a servant, be made in the likeness of men, be found in human form, and to serve, help, and in every way deal with his neighbor as he sees that God through Christ has dealt and still deals with him.[77]

In Luther's theology, all believers become like Ockham's spiritual Franciscans.

A Christian's obedience to the political authorities follows the same pattern. "Christians should be subject to the governing authorities and be ready to do every good work," Luther wrote, "not that they shall in this way be justified, . . . but that in the liberty of the Spirit they shall by so doing serve others and the authorities themselves and obey their will freely and out of love." The Matthew 17 passage on paying the Temple tax appears at this point in Luther's explanation. "This incident," he wrote, "fits our subject beautifully for Christ here calls himself and those who are his children sons of the king, who need nothing; and yet he freely submits and pays the tribute." The Christian should voluntarily be subject to the government by paying taxes (as in other ways), because in being subject the Christian is doing works that "are free and are done only to serve others."[78]

From the perspective of the subject who lives *without* faith, taxation is an obligation in the full sense of the word. It is for Luther part of the reality of temporal authority, falling in the same category as the "temporal sword," thus restraining "the un-Christian and wicked so that—no thanks to them—they are obliged to keep still and to maintain an outward peace." The sword "is not a terror to good conduct but to bad. And Peter says it is for the punishment of the wicked."[79] It is a heavy burden whose purpose is to be precisely that—a burden.[80] The burden of taxation also functions as a kind of restraint, an enforcement of moderation, working against the non-Christian's natural tendency toward luxury and excess.[81]

The believing subject, on the other hand, submits to taxation but is not burdened by it, as with all aspects of temporal authority. Luther developed the paradox of the believer's freedom most comprehensively in "The Freedom of a Christian," where he wrote:

> To make the way smoother for the unlearned—for only them do I serve—I shall set down the following two propositions concerning the freedom and bondage of the spirit: A Christian is a perfectly free lord of all, subject to none. A Christian is a perfectly dutiful servant of all, subject to all.[82]

To explain this paradox, Luther offered the "contradiction" that each human being has two "natures"—a spiritual nature and a bodily one.[83] This twofold nature explains why Scripture contains both commandments (which tell us what we ought to do) and promises (which supply the power that the commandments lack).[84] Luther goes so far as to say that "this diversity of nature" makes Scripture "assert contradictory things concerning the same man, since these two men in the same man contradict each other."[85]

Taxation is an instrument from the believing subject's perspective.[86] The Christian "uses" taxation to express and implement love for others and to act for their benefit. Both the burdens and the benefits of taxation itself are irrelevant to Christians because for them taxation is "not essential." They can and should, however, use it to benefit non-believers.[87] "[The Christian] uses the forbidden sword to serve another," Luther wrote concerning the Christian.[88]

The only-for-others quality of the outer person's actions in community both frees the Christian from worrying about benefits received in return for serving others and allows the Christian to serve the neighbor without concern for how much the neighbor deserves to be served: "For a man does not serve that he may put men under obligations. He does not distinguish between friend and enemies or anticipate their thankfulness or unthankfulness, but he most freely and most willingly spends himself and all that he has, whether he wastes all on the thankless or whether he gains a reward."[89] Luther's rejection of reciprocity in acts of neighbor-love lies at the heart of his criticism of medieval charity, which he regarded as centered on the "sin-redeeming quality" of almsgiving and the benefits that accrued to the donor instead of the needs of the recipient.[90] Medieval theology had interpreted the second table of the Decalogue in line with natural law and the golden rule, thus reading it as implying reciprocity. Luther, in contrast, offered a sharp alternative: "either self-love or love of neighbor."[91]

Luther's preface to the Leisnig ordinance refuses to distinguish between the "worthy" and "unworthy" poor.[92] The ordinance itself contains remnants of those distinctions—anticipating, for instance, disbursements from the common chest to those "who are impoverished by force of circumstances."[93] It also refers to the "needy poor,"[94] however, and in this it echoes Luther himself.

Luther made no distinction in the preface between principles that drive the spiritual realm and those that operate in the temporal sphere. In addressing the question of redistribution from the standpoint of the believing subject, he wrote that those "inmates" of the monasteries who did not wish to remain should be provided with enough funds "to make a fresh start in life," even if they brought nothing with them when they entered the monastery. As for those who did bring something with them when they entered, "it is no more than right in the sight of God that they should have it returned to them, to each his own portion, for here matters are to be determined by Christian love and not by strict human justice."[95] If a monastery founder's heirs are "impoverished and in want," it is "in harmony with Christian love that the foundation revert to them."[96] Luther anticipated the objection that acting out of Christian love in this context "'is opening the door too wide; on that basis the common chest will receive precious little, for everyone will claim the whole amount and say that his needs are so great.'" In response, he reminded his readers that he assumed he was addressing Christians and "Christians only." "We have to expect," he added, "that greed will creep in here and there. So what?"[97]

The way in which we frame the connection between faith and love in Luther's theology determines whether we will understand his political stance to be quietistic or "characterized by deep engagement in political life directed particularly at one's neighbor (i.e., at the local level)."[98] Love, Laffin argues, is properly regarded as faith's "tool" in Luther's theology. Luther puts the connection perhaps most forcefully in "The Freedom of a Christian":

> We conclude, therefore, that a Christian lives not in himself, but in Christ and in his neighbor. Otherwise he is not a Christian. He lives in Christ

> through faith, in his neighbor through love. By faith he is caught up beyond himself into God. By love he descends beneath himself into his neighbor. *Yet he always remains in God and in his love.*[99]

Faith and love are, in Laffin's words, an "organic unity."[100]

Luther's distinction, in his commentary on Galatians,[101] between "abstract" and "incarnate" faith goes some way toward clarifying the connection between faith and love in his theology. Abstract faith alone justifies; it is the faith that joins the bride and bridegroom, the means by which the believer passively receives an "alien" righteousness. Incarnate faith, on the other hand, is faith working through love.[102] This is the faith that is in complete unity with love, by which the believer "descends beneath himself into his neighbor." Luther's concept of faith, consequently, is much broader than the medieval *fides caritate formata* ("faith formed by love"), according to which love has to "perfect" "mere" faith. Luther reverses the medieval formula. For him, faith is not only an "inner" state; it is "a 'work' in its own right: an inner movement that cannot rest."[103]

Necessity

In the outward focus of the outer person, the believer is free of the burden of reciprocity and of the demands of human justice, the calculating of what is due (or not due) to the believer's neighbor. Running just beneath the surface of this theme is the theme of *need*. Now, however, the idea of necessity is not rooted in a measure of debt or of the just amount of goods a person should possess (as in Aquinas), let alone the payment rightly and cheerfully rendered to the ruler for the common good (as in Ockham), but rather consists in the neighbor's necessity that can now become the sole, consuming focus of the believer. For Luther, the goods of the church are (or should be) common property, not explicitly because of a pre-existing state of communal ownership, but because "there is no greater service of God than Christian love which helps and serves the needy." The common chest, therefore, is "for all who were needy among the Christians."[104]

Historian Renate Blickle brilliantly summarizes the role of the concept of material need—*necessitas domestica*—in late medieval and early modern Germany. "Domestic necessity," Blickle writes, was a legal norm, not just a moral and social norm (though it was that), dictating that economic resources in what was a society of scarcity should be distributed according to the principle of *need*.[105] "Need" referred to the subsistence of a household, but subsistence was not the same for every household. "Need" encompassed the ideas of "fitness" and "suitability" as well as of subsistence. It was both an expansion and a constraint, a sword against lords who lived too luxuriously to the detriment of others and a shield against poverty for peasants.[106] *Necessitas domestica* was an egalitarian principle—one to which all households of all ranks could appeal—but it was not tied, and must not be tied retroactively, to class.[107]

Necessitas or "need" (*Notdurft* in German) was, in fact, one of the two main ways of justifying claims in early modern Germany. The claim that one had a basic "right" to subsistence was encapsulated in the idea of *Notdurft*. Even the quantities of wood that households could purchase might be limited by *Notdurft*, but, again, those quantities depended on the size of a household's "economy."[108] A claim of need was rarely so crass as to omit reference to the wider good, the *gemein nutz* or "common weal." Warde notes that it was easy in this culture of reciprocal services and protection for the duke to refer to the *gemein nutz* in justifying his actions; but the poor also made use of the concept, claiming the maintenance of good order required that their needs be met for the *gemein nutz*.[109] The legitimacy of any legal procedure rested on the fact that *Notdurft* or the *gemein nutz* was being satisfied.[110] Indeed, as the emerging states came to realize, even the power of "custom" could be broken when it was shown that custom could not guarantee necessities, or when it was demonstrated that customary practices had to be changed for the benefit of the common weal.[111]

"Need," Blickle writes, gained legitimizing power through the concept of "subsistence," just as freedom would later be justified by the idea of "property." Need and property are both answers to the question "to whom do the goods of the world legitimately belong?"[112] To those who need them, or to those who possess them legally but do not need them? The question remains the same; the two answers are based on different foundational principles.

Blickle argues that the legitimizing concept of subsistence gradually gave way to the legitimizing principle of property because of the tension inherent within the early modern German concept of "divided property." The background to that tension was that a farmstead "usually belonged to two proprietors." The seignorial lord was the *dominus directus* (superior proprietor), while the peasant was the *dominus utilis* (using proprietor).[113] Direct right to the soil itself, *dominium directum*, belonged to the lord. Usufruct or the right to use (e.g., the right to farm the land in the form of a tenancy), *dominium utile*, belonged to the lord's subjects.[114]

The result was predictable: a conflict of property rights, even though the rights theoretically operated on different planes. Each party

> wanted to enjoy sole proprietorship, free from encroachments by the other . . . . Around the middle of the eighteenth century this goal was reached. At that time, . . . the property both parties were contending for . . . was parceled up and the actual parcels were portioned to the contestants. From this point on the rights of both proprietors were no longer qualitatively different; now they were identical.[115]

"Property as a private right," according to Blickle, no longer included "any kind of responsibility toward another person. It was the legitimate right of its owner regardless of the needs of others." From there, property became "a material guaranty and a manifestation" of the civil individual's freedom, with the consequence that property was finally "elevated into a sacrosanct human right."[116]

Luther lived before those developments, and his thinking bore the imprint of *necessitas domestica*. It did not do so to the exclusion of property rights, of course.

His treatment of the commandment "Thou shalt not steal" in the *Large Catechism* is expansive, comprehending "all kinds of advantage in all sorts of trade to the disadvantage of our neighbor." But the "far-reaching" impact of the commandment lies in its import, not for Christians, but mostly for "knaves and scoundrels, to whom it would be more fitting for judges, jailers, or [the executioner] to preach."[117]

With respect to Christians, Luther regarded material goods as something to be held lightly. In his treatment of the Magnificat, Luther described Mary's "low estate" as a place of material poverty that we must not spiritualize.[118] Luther wrote: "The word 'low estate' has been translated 'humility' by some, as though the Virgin Mary referred to her humility and boasted of it . . . . But that is very wide of the mark, for no one can boast of any good thing in the sight of God without sin and perdition."[119] If Luke refers to Mary as "humble," Luther continued, that is because "humility" in Scripture "is nothing else than a disregarded, despised, and lowly estate, such as that of men who are poor, sick, hungry, thirsty, in prison, suffering, and dying."[120] God, without warning, can make of Luther's believer an Ockhamite renouncer of goods.

Luther's interaction with the redistribution of property, through taxation in the case of the Leisnig ordinance, is noteworthy not simply because it centers on the idea of *necessitas* but more because of the theological content with which Luther infused that idea.

Sign and sacrament

Luther's theology of the Lord's Supper anchors the distributive logic of his overall theology by providing an extended political metaphor of redistribution, and then crossing that metaphorical barrier, connecting spiritual and material distribution through Luther's understanding of sign and sacrament.

The Lord's Supper

As early as 1519, in "The Blessed Sacrament of the Holy and True Body of Christ, and the Brotherhoods," Luther drew a parallel between communion in the sacrament of the Lord's Supper on the one hand and the common citizenship of those in political community on the other. In this extended metaphor, which he calls a "homely figure," the fellowship with Christ and the saints in the Lord's Supper "is like a city where every citizen shares with all the others the city's name, honor, freedom, trade, customs, usages, help, support, protection, and the like, while at the same time he shares all the dangers of fire and blood, enemies and death, losses, taxes, and the like."[121] More than just a "figure" of solidarity and commonality, however, the Lord's Supper is also a "sign" that the believer does, in fact, hold all things in common with Christ and the saints: "In this sacrament, therefore, man is given through the priest a sure sign from God himself that he is thus united with Christ and his saints and has all things in common, that Christ's sufferings and life are his own, together with the lives and sufferings of all the saints."[122]

"Things in common" are both spiritual and material. Distribution of material goods is a proper "use" of the Lord's Supper: "But in times past this sacrament was so properly used, and the people were taught to understand this fellowship so well, that they even gathered food and material goods in the church, and there—as St. Paul writes in I Corinthians 11—distributed among those who were in need."[123] The sacrament is of no "benefit" to those who approach it selfishly, paradoxically seeking only their own benefit from it and refusing to share in the spiritual and material burdens it imposes: "[T]hey are unwilling in their turn to belong also to this fellowship. They will not help the poor, put up with sinners, care for the sorrowing, suffer with the suffering, intercede for others, defend the truth, and at the risk of life, property, and honor seek the betterment of the church and of all Christians."[124]

The Lord's Supper is paradigmatic of the continuity between "the sacred and profane spheres." The sacrament erases that distinction, according to Martin Wendte, because it is the most salient example of the way in which "God and God's Word are always working for humankind in a materially mediated way." disclosing the "structure of God's way of acting with all creation."[125] Mary Gaebler calls this continuity "Luther's panentheistic understanding of God's presence in, with, and under the created order."[126]

A distinction is to be found in Luther's theology of the Lord's Supper—not, however, between spiritual and physical distribution, but rather between the Lord's Supper as "testament and sacrament" and "the sacrifice and good works" that may be done "in connection with it."[127] This is the distinction between *sacrament* and *sign*. The Lord's Supper, according to Luther, is both—something "external" yet containing "something spiritual."[128]

Augustine had written that a "sign is a thing which of itself makes some other thing come to mind, besides the impression that it presents to the senses,"[129] so that "one thing is seen, another is understood."[130] A sign, according to Augustine, is a sensible and intelligible reality that refers to something else beyond itself, the "signified." A sacrament was, for Augustine, a particular kind of sign—one that bore a likeness or similitude to the signified. In the case of a sign that is also a sacrament, then, "the signifier truly resembles the signified."[131] To Augustine's definition, the scholastic theologians of the twelfth and thirteenth centuries added a third component: to be a sacrament, a sign must also be *efficacious*, i.e., it must be "effective of the reality that it signifies."[132]

Luther flattened the medieval definition in that he took many things in the world, including many things that are not sacraments, to be spiritual "signs." The signs that God provides, according to Luther, are all efficacious, although sacraments are signs that are efficacious in a special way. Michael Laffin, in his discussion of Luther's three "estates" (or "institutions," sometimes "orders"), argues that the estates' "quasi-sacramental character" comes from their "connection with the Word." They are not sacraments, because they are not means of salvation, but they are "means of God's self-giving, that is, . . . means of grace."[133]

According to Luther, God gives many signs "in addition to the word . . . for the greater assurance and strengthening of our faith." Scripture, Luther writes, is full of these signs "given along with the promises"—the sign of the rainbow given to Noah, the sign of circumcision given to Abraham, the rain on Gideon's fleece, to name just three.[134] These signs, in Michael Laffin's words, intermingle "the Word with the elemental world." Luther's recognition of quasi-sacramental signs reflect his "discovery of the positive meaning of worldly reality and its spiritual importance."[135] For Luther the physical and material world mediates the Word in a sense, so that there is something accompanying the Word "to which we may cling and around which we may gather."[136]

Distributive logic undergirds Luther's theology of the Lord's Supper, understood as both sign and sacrament. Only the distribution of the spiritual benefits Christ has won is a means of salvation in the sacrament, but the distribution of material goods to the needy is also a means of grace. The formal logic is the same; what changes in the shift from sacrament to sign is the soteriological content. Thus, Luther can affirm on the one hand that distributing "alms to the poor" and "food and other necessities . . . to the needy" is "quite another thing from the testament and sacrament, which no one can offer or give either to God or to men," while bemoaning with equal force the fact that "the custom of gathering food and money at the mass has fallen into disuse" and that, in the mass, possessions are no longer "given, with thanksgiving to God and with his blessing, to the needy who ought to be receiving them."[137]

In summary, the tangible distribution of material goods to the needy not only reflects the distribution of good things won by Christ and distributed to believers with the words "This is my body, this is my blood," but also accompanies those words themselves. The recipients of Christ's body and blood further the distributive dynamic in the "overflow" to others of the "superfluity" those recipients have in "God's gifts."[138]

Transposition

Although Luther insisted that the believer's distribution of material goods flows from the distribution of goods won by Christ, he emphasizes that one is only *sign* while the other is also *sacrament.* In "A Treatise on the New Testament" (1520), he drove a wedge between *receiving* the sacrament itself and *giving* to the needy, which he nonetheless insisted should be made "in connection with" the mass.[139] Much of the treatise is devoted to banishing the language of "sacrifice" and "offering" from the sacrament:[140] "Now if you ask what is left in the mass to give it the name of a sacrifice, since so much is said in the office about the sacrifice, I answer: Nothing is left."[141]

In the *sign* that accompanies the sacrament, however, there is offering and sacrifice, even the believer's offering and sacrifice. We must not "presume to give God something in the sacrament, when it is he who in it gives us all things"; but we should bring sacrifices: "What sacrifices, then, are we to offer? Ourselves, and all that we have, with constant prayer. . . ."[142] Taken as a whole, then, the sign *and* sacrament of the Lord's Supper involve an exchange. Passive receipt is not the sum total of the believer's experience in the Lord's Supper, even if the sacrament itself asks only for passive receipt: "[I]n the mass we give nothing to Christ, but only receive from him; unless they are willing to call this a good work, that a person sits still and permits himself to be benefited, given food and drink, clothed and healed, helped and redeemed."[143]

Confusion between the sacrament and sign aspects of the Lord's Supper has led to contemporary theological debate about the exact alignment of *exchange* and *gift* in Luther's sacramental theology. In a 2001 essay, "Eucharistic Sacrifice and the Social Imagination in Early Modern Europe," William Cavanaugh argues that Luther's reaction "against what he saw as the exchangist character of late medieval piety" led him "into a dualism of exchange and gift"—a dualism that prefigures "the modern anxiety to quarantine the gift from the logic of exchange."[144] Luther's particular worry, in Cavanaugh's account, was that "[t]o imply a human return given to God in the form of sacrifice would annul the gift by proffering a human work in exchange for it."[145]

Cavanaugh rightly highlights Luther's rejection of what Carter Lindberg calls the "mendicant 'do ut des' ideology."[146] Reciprocity, the ancient idea that "[w]hen I sacrifice to the gods, I expect a return of some value," marked both the medieval symbiosis between rich and poor (at least in Luther's opinion) and the prevalence of what Luther called "usury," a term that Lindberg considers shorthand for "selling on time and credit, manipulating the market by withholding or dumping goods, developing cartels and monopolies, falsifying bankruptcies, trading in futures, and just plain misrepresenting goods."[147] This recognition is the basis for Lindberg's contention that Luther was fighting against "contractual thinking" in society on two fronts—that of the medieval symbiosis as well as that of the emerging profit economy.

However, as will be apparent from the discussion above, Luther's exclusion of mercantile logic from his eucharistic theology does not translate into a wholesale rejection of "exchangist" thinking. Luther's concept of *communicatio idiomatum* places exchange at the core of his theology, but the exchange in view is the exchange of persons rather than of goods. It is difficult to maintain Cavanaugh's thesis in light of statements from Luther like the following: "And in this way it is permissible, yes, profitable, to call the mass a sacrifice; not on its own account, but because we offer ourselves as a sacrifice along with Christ."[148] Laffin writes: "Luther is correct when he argues that some 'thing' is not exchanged in the Eucharist. Rather, there is a communication of persons (in Luther's terms a 'fortunate exchange')."[149] According to Laffin, "[w]hat is given is a return of our God-given self in Christ and a giving of ourselves to other believers, also in Christ. I do not merely offer the 'benefits' of my justification, but rather Christ whose presence is precisely the benefit of justification."[150]

In *Political Worship*, Wannenwetsch calls this exchange of persons "transposition." Transposition occurs in two ways. "This transposition process (of 'the inner man')," Wannenwetsch writes, "finds its precise correspondence in another (the transposition of the 'outward man'): the good that has been received is passed on to the Christian's neighbour." Taking transposition to be an inevitable feature of modern political philosophy, Wannenwetsch locates it in "Kant's ideal of an 'enlarged mentality,' elevated above the subjective and private sphere," in Arendt's idea of the "power of judgment," in Kohlberg's "'reversible role-making,'" and in Rawls' "'original state.'" All of these formulations fall short, because "the attempt to transpose oneself into the other almost unavoidably means transferring the other into oneself," with the result that the other's "difference" or "'strangeness'" "gets lost along the way." In contrast, Luther's theology "has a peculiar indirectness"; the believer finds herself transposed "into" her neighbor not directly but "as a Christ."[151]

Because it is mediated rather than direct, Luther's transposition is particular rather than universal. The logic of *communicatio idiomatum* implies that all that the two persons have *in particular* are exchanged. Exchange means something more here than relocating the two persons. As in the "happy exchange" between Christ and the believer, the specific attributes of one become the attributes of the other.

In an excursus on John Rawls' *Theory of Justice*, Wannenwetsch argues that Rawls had no choice but to impose the "veil of ignorance" on his fictitious "original position," "so that no one out of an assessment of his own possibilities can plant the germ of the promotion of his own advantage into the idea of justice." In other words, Rawlsian justice requires that the original position be a place of *abstraction* so that it can be purged of any tendency toward "appropriation."[152] Contrary to the abstraction of Rawlsian transposition, transposition in Luther's theology is concrete. For Luther, the one who is "as a Christ" "will neither remain for the other an ultimately untouched and detached person, nor will the one forcibly invade the other." The one who is "as a Christ" makes "the *need* of the other person his own, and not just 'the person' in a diffused sense."[153]

Luther's version of transposition fights abstraction on two fronts. It contemplates the exchange of persons rather than of things, thus resisting the tendency (so manifest in modern tax philosophies) to treat all members of society as identical economic units. At the same time, it safeguards against the danger that the distributor will define her neighbor and the neighbor's needs in terms of the distributor's own set of interests and requirements. The distributor is *as a Christ* to the neighbor; they exchange each other's attributes perfectly. The other's particular and concrete needs become one's own needs:

> See, according to this rule the good things we have from God should flow from one to the other and be common to all, so that everyone should "put on" his neighbor and so conduct himself toward him as if he himself were in the other's place. From Christ the good things have flowed and are flowing into us. He has so 'put on' us and acted for us as if he had been what we are. From us they flow on to those who have need of them so that I should lay before God my faith and my righteousness that they may cover and intercede for the sins of my neighbor which I take upon myself and so labor and serve in them *as if they were my very own.*[154]

The Lutheran systematization of taxation

It seems perhaps paradoxical that the concreteness of transposition in Luther's theology should lead him to advocate institutionalized welfare in the form of a common chest to be funded by universal and regular taxation as circumstances require. Nevertheless, Luther's abandonment of the dualistic ethic in medieval theology in favor of a universal ethic is consistent with the restoration of "the true freedom of the Christian spirit" in the Leisnig ordinance.[155] The disappearance of the special status bestowed on spiritual authority, in the face of the doctrine of the priesthood of all believers, elevates the status of temporal authority.[156] Luther wrote that the "temporal power has become a member of the body of Christendom, and is of the 'spiritual estate,' though its work is of a temporal nature."[157]

Regularization, universalization, institutionalization

Luther's elevation of temporal authority and his freeing of it from the constraints of canon law and the church opened the way for poor relief to be handed over from the whims of charity to the orderliness of government. Luther saw that charity in the sense of almsgiving is self-focused. In his "Open Letter to the Christian Nobility," Luther described the begging of the mendicant orders and others as the demand of a kind of tribute and proposed that poor relief be placed in the hands of the governing authorities. Begging is to be completely abolished, he wrote, for two reasons: begging on the part of the mendicants is a theological deformation, and begging on the part of the "really poor" is an affront to Christian civilization. Poverty should be handled by city government. Each city should support its own poor, and, if a city is too small, it should "exhort" the surrounding villages to contribute as well.[158] "No men or women beggars shall be tolerated in our parish," the Leisnig order decrees. The common chest, it was hoped, would replace the need for begging; it was designed to support "those among us who are impoverished by force of circumstances, or are unable to work because of old age or illness."[159] The common chest is where Christian "love truly express[es] itself in deeds of tender kindness."[160] For Luther, true charity *leads to* government control of redistribution rather than detracting from it, and the increasing standardization of taxation in Germany during the course of the sixteenth century suggests that his conviction may have taken root.[161]

Transposition as it functions in Luther's theology is a deeper, more thorough interaction than the fleeting transaction between the rich and the poor in almsgiving. Sean Doherty, in his remarkable treatment of Luther's economic ethics, writes:

> Thus Luther ferociously exposed the way in which the debased forms of pre-Reformation piety reinforced the conditions of the poor by treating poverty and almsgiving as meritorious. Almsgiving meant that help for the poor was immediate, but very temporary, whereas the common chest arrangement sought a structural and durable solution to the *causes* of poverty as well as alleviating particular cases of hardship.[162]

It is precisely the complex and unique circumstances of each individual person who finds herself in material need that call for a systematic and rationalized solution.

In his paradoxical synthesis of transposition and institutionalization, Luther recaptured some of Augustine's eschatological reserve concerning wealth and poverty. The reasons for wealth and poverty are more mysterious, and their ultimate resolution more hidden in the workings of divine providence, than they are in the medieval symbiosis. Luther did not demand passive resignation of either ruler or subject, but he did require theological humility in the form of trust that the optimal outcome of all social and economic policies is under God's control. With respect to taxation, the balance—the tipping point between what the government can legitimately take and what the individual may keep—should be placed in God's hands.

Warde suggests that the Lutheran Reformation, by taking the fallen state of humankind "as a given," changed the relationship between law and morality. Rejecting as too optimistic the medieval notion that laws reflecting moral certainties can be "discovered," Lutheran civil authorities grasped "the idea that the government should actively innovate and legislate to achieve a desired result."[163]

The innovation began with Luther himself. In his treatment of tithing in Deuteronomy 14:22, Luther bemoaned the burden of "taxes" (by which he meant the imposition of a fixed sum) on the German people and wished for a replacement of these "taxes" with "tithes" (taxation according to a percentage or rate):

> And would that all other inequitable taxes were removed which today devour lands and people, and that tithes were instituted instead! If one were not sufficient, three, four, or five could be added. Thus a nation could live under its lords. This would be the most honorable and just method of income, for it would depend on the sheer goodness of God. If in a given year God were to bless richly, the people would have a rich yield, and the government rich tithes. But if He did not bless very much, the government would bear the burden equally with the subjects and would receive less. Now, however, since the annual taxes are fixed and certain and the bountiful years are few, the subjects are forced to pay the full taxes even if throughout a ten-year period or longer they do not have a single bountiful year.[164]

Before standardization of German taxation began in the mid-sixteenth century, taxes were typically allotted to the communes by district authorities, and then apportioned among households by the commune. Amounts paid by inhabitants, consequently, were not consistent "from settlement to settlement."[165] The aspect that particularly bothered Luther was the lump sum. Donald Shriver and Richard Knox write:

> Germany's tax structure called for set payments of established fees akin to ancient Rome's. No matter how much income one earned in a good or bad

> economic year, one paid the same amount of tax. In bad economic times, this created a great strain on the people. Luther called for the removal of all set taxes—a more specific tax policy view than any to be found in the New Testament. Instead he suggested that the concept of the proportional tithe be adopted by the government . . . . For him this system of raising public funds had the benefit of linking directly the income of the people with the income of the government. If the people had a bad economic year, the government also would have a bad economic year, a principle that most modern tax systems assume.[166]

A more standardized approach emerged, but not until 1544–45, when the "Turk tax" was imposed on behalf of the emperor to counter the Ottoman threat on the Austrian frontier.[167] The Turk tax was a proportional ("flat") wealth tax levied at a rate of one-half of one percent on assessed wealth, but with an exemption for the very poorest members of society.[168] Proportional taxes would have represented the furthest advances of tax equity in the mid-sixteenth century.

Luther's primary concern, in fact, was that the government and the taxpayer share equally in natural abundance or lack, and his goal of restructuring taxation along the lines of the three Old Testament tithes[169] inevitably introduces the ideas of proportionality and ability-to-pay as well. Progressive taxation was not yet in view in the early sixteenth century, but for Luther taxation in the form of an annual fixed sum, imposed without regard to circumstances or means, is the quintessence of inequity: "Do you, then, call these taxes just? Would you consider these laws equitable? No wonder the people are devoured and hounded from every place! What is the kingdom of Germany today but sheer tyranny?"[170] The injustice of this "barbarity" arises from the "shameful avarice" of the rulers, who have "fleeced" the people "incessantly the year round with exorbitant and intolerable impositions and assessments," according to the Leisnig ordinance.[171]

Luther articulated the ideas of proportionality and ability-to-pay in tax policy, not in terms of greater efficiency or even fairness, but rather in terms of the theological conviction that both ruler and subject should defer to God as the final arbiter of the benefits and burdens of taxation. In Luther's framework, the need of one person, the abundance of another, the overall wealth of the community, are all set by God. Human policy is to take the form of a chastened response to those parameters set by God. As such, human laws are freed to innovate within providential confines, to build the structures needed to respond to circumstances of poverty.

Bureaucracy

At the same time, the solutions put in place are not to be regarded as foreclosing the hidden providential purposes behind wealth and poverty. Rather than collapsing into one, immediate exchange between a wealthy donor and a poor recipient—or being refined into one simply stated (if abstract) formula such as the "universal destination of goods," as Catholic Social Teaching would have it—redistributive taxation does what it can to alleviate need in the time before a final resolution appears. And in that time "intermediary office-holders" increase in number as intermediate solutions spread out to meet the various and diverse needs of the whole population. The emergence of the modern state, as Warde observes, meant the emergence as well of infrastructure—both physical and institutional. For a state to establish itself as effective, it needed to have "people on the ground who could reasonably order others to do things"; and "[t]he larger this body of people became, the more they became associated with the 'machinery' of government."[172] The consequence was a detachment of the notion of "lordship" "from simply being the top-down exercise of one's will over another" to a diffuse group of people tasked with the duty of applying laws.[173]

"The angel," Giorgio Agamben writes, "is the figure of the government of the world par excellence," as evidenced by Paul's identification of angelic names with terms describing worldly powers: *arkai*, *exousiai*, *kyriotētes*.[174] Worldly and angelic powers are indistinguishable in Paul and elsewhere in Christian thinking, Agamben maintains, because they both "stem from God" and are both "figures of the divine government of the world."[175] We could say that the objective and subjective genitive almost merge here; does the activity of these intermediaries reflect God's providential government of the world or the government that the world has put in place for itself? Agamben traces "the parallels between celestial and worldly bureaucracy" from Athenagoras to Tertullian's *Adversus Praxean* and Clement of Alexandria's *The Stromata*, and from there to the Pseudo-Dionysius and, finally, Thomas' *Summa*.[176] The two hierarchies take on each other's qualities, so that the "celestial messengers" become "organized according to offices and ministries" while "worldly functionaries . . . become capable of cleansing, enlightening, and perfecting."[177] In Agamben's account, angelology provided the model on which Western politics developed and articulated the categories of administration, hierarchy, systematization, and government itself. The celestial bureaucracy is part of the providential machine that tirelessly works to suture the wound in Christian theology between the immanent and economic trinity.

In the here and now, however, theology "never manages truly to get to the bottom of the fracture between immanent trinity and economic trinity, between *theologia* and *oikonomia*."[178] Christian theology ensured that its God took the *oikonomia* within Godself, in Agamben's account, by tying "the Trinitarian economy . . . to the action of God and his practice of providential government of the world."[179] The goal of Trinitarian theology was to heal "in a single God" the "Gnostic division" between the hidden God and the active God.[180] The ultimate telos of the law and its angelic ministers "is to be deactivated and made inoperative" in the finality of Sabbath rest, "where nothing is in excess and nothing is lacking," which Augustine chose as the final image in *The City of God*.[181]

But by taking the *oikonomia* into Godself, the Christian God made divine inoperativity an embarrassment to Christian theologians in a way that it was not to Jewish theologians and to Gnostics. The Trinitarian economy, Agamben maintains, is "a figure of action and government."[182] It cannot account for divine inoperativity, and for this reason Christian theology typically falls silent "in the face of the glorious figure of power."[183] Hence too the brittle replies of—not surprisingly, based on what we have seen—Augustine and Luther to the question, "What was God doing before God made heaven and earth?" "Getting hell ready for people who pry too deep." Augustine answered. "Sitting in the forest, cutting rods to beat those who ask impertinent questions," said Luther.[184] The great difficulty for Trinitarian theology, according to Agamben, is that it can only know God in terms of the economy or the "Government" rather than inoperativity or the "Kingdom," even though "the Government is nothing but a brief interval running between the two eternal and glorious figures of the Kingdom."[185]

"Eternal government," Agamben writes, "is the paradigm of modern politics."[186] It is that because the "modern conception of history that takes up without reservation the theological model in many of its aspects" is faced with a parallel embarrassment. On the one hand, it "abolishes the eschatology and infinitely prolongs" government; on the other hand, "it finds that the finite character of its paradigm returns ceaselessly."[187] Like that of the angelic powers, the telos of "the profane powers"—to the chagrin of the Western account of worldly government—"is to be deactivated and made inoperative."[188]

This embarrassment explains some of the puzzling quality of the welfare state, which continually seeks to redress injustice but never escapes the cycle that creates economic injustice in the first place. There is no wholesale redistribution of property in Luther's political theology, and, indeed, the "collective institutions" that developed in sixteenth-century Germany were inherently conservative in the sense that, though they had "redistributory effects," at no point did they "alter the balance of land use on any scale" or "reorganise holdings."[189] It is as if the Lutheran welfare state incorporated a kind of Augustinian eschatological reserve, anticipating in a shadowy way the Sabbath rest "where nothing is in excess and nothing is lacking"—but only anticipating it.

At the same time, the institution of redistributive taxation has a Sisyphean quality about it as it ceaselessly works to address needs. It has no end-point in Luther's version, no stage at which the right balance of equity and productivity will be reached and the task completed. Equilibrium is neither restored nor achieved in the way it seems in the exercise of judgment by Thomas' ruler or in the giving of alms by the medieval donor. Redistributive taxation represents the "eternal government" on which Agamben remarks. It also works to heal the suture between Sabbath inoperativity toward which justice moves and the endless, "in-time" reactions that characterize the mechanics of the economy. Constantly responding to need (in the Leisnig system), yet never reaching equity, Luther's embryonic welfare state bridged the gap, through the ceaseless activity of ministerial officers, between Augustine's true justice in the heavenly city and the immutable status of the poor in imperial Rome.

The material realities of existence

It may, of course, be objected that the simplicity and idealism of an early sixteenth-century common chest in a small town in Saxony has little to say to a tax system codified in 3.4 million words, interpreted in pages beyond count, and built on the foundations of three centuries of research into the science of economics. But it would be a mistake to think that the two systems lack a connection. It is not at all clear to Paul Warde, based on his exhaustive research into the early modern economy of Württemberg, that the emerging states of that time and place "saw the world much differently from the producers of village by-laws."[190] The measures taken to respond to the increasing crisis of the "limited good" were "transposed" from the village to the state, developed hand in hand at both levels, and were in the end similar at both levels.[191] Warde cautions against opposing the state and the communes.[192] The difference was primarily one of scale.[193]

Transposition from sixteenth-century "states" to twenty-first-century America is in some ways more complex, but the complexity is greater than it appears. I want to suggest that the apparent gulf between the two economic and political worlds can be reduced to one factor: our contemporary understanding and treatments of taxation are infused with abstract concepts. Even to frame the success of tax systems in terms of "efficiency" and "equity" is to abandon the material in favor of ideas. We, in our "world of abundance," view government in "immaterial" categories, such as "authority, divinity, sovereignty or community." It is difficult for us, from our vantage point, to see the application of these ideas as Luther and his contemporaries would have, i.e., in terms of "material things" like "fodder for cows, sheep and pigs; the holding of property; hail; death at the end of a wretchedly hard life." For them, the "relevance and power of the immaterial rested upon its intersection with the material realities of existence."[194] This is why, to us, sixteenth-century civil authority seems both "invasive" and "weak," interrogating "young boys about their night-time visions" and dissecting "the comments of an angel as relayed by the village do-gooders," on the one hand, but unable to articulate a theory of sovereignty, or even to see the benefit of doing so, on the other.[195]

Perhaps it is our world, not Luther's, that is fundamentally naïve. To think that we have done our duty to our neighbor by striking the optimal balance between equity and efficiency requires a remarkable degree of cognitive indirectness. Although this chapter argues that Luther contributed to the development of such a mediated form of neighbor-love, his vision for redistributive taxation operated with an end-point that was fixed and yet specific to each person, one that we lack: that of *need*.

Precisely because need was thoroughly material for Luther, it could serve as an end-point of any discussion, in much the same way that property rights often operate in U.S. policy discussions. That is to say that, in Luther's conception, "need" is a kind of foundational ethical term. It does not require a metaphysical explanation or legal defense, because none is available. Stanley Hauerwas' remarks on "perception" are helpful here. He points to Aristotle's assertion that we simply "perceive the ultimate figure in mathematics to be a triangle," and "there will be a halt."[196] In theological ethics, according to Hauerwas, a term like "murder" is similar to a figure like *triangle* in mathematics. "As a Christian," he writes, "I want to say that 'murder' or 'suicide' marks when our perception should come to a halt." "It is . . . a philosophical mistake," Hauerwas continues, "to ask what is wrong with murder. If we rightly understand the grammar of the word murder, we understand that the only issue is whether this or that killing is a case of murder." The impulse "to give a further reason why murder is wrong" is a "besetting" temptation "of modern philosophy," in Hauerwas' view, and its effect has been "to corrupt our morality through the attempt to give reasons when no reason is required and has the effect of undercutting our true judgments."[197]

Aristotle and Hauerwas are perhaps unlikely aids in the interpretation of Luther, but I submit that *need* is a foundational term and figure, like *murder* or *triangle*, in the understanding of Luther's version of redistributive taxation. It reorients the idea of social justice away from equilibrium among competing social commitments, to interpersonal duties. Tax justice need not be an arbitrary point on a spectrum between equity and efficiency.

It is, in the end, appropriate that the anticipatory (if indefinitely extended) role of redistributive taxation should be closely linked to Luther's theology of the Eucharist. The *ekklēsia*, Erik Peterson wrote, "is the assembly of the citizens of the heavenly city for the accomplishment of specific cultic acts."[198] The *ekklēsia* and the heavenly city must be distinguished, of course, but they are also connected through their worship and sacraments. The church has left the earthly Jerusalem and is now on its way to the heavenly Jerusalem. As it draws near, the church's cultic acts become a kind of participation in the activity of the angels.[199] Luther would add that the church's acts participate in the angels' ministrations to those with needs of all kinds.

Notes

1 Michael Richard Laffin, *The Promise of Martin Luther's Political Theology: Freeing Luther from the Modern Political Narrative*, T&T Enquiries in Theological Ethics, ed. Brian Brock and Susan F. Parsons (London: Bloomsbury T&T Clark, 2016), 38.
2 Laffin, *The Promise of Martin Luther's Political Theology*, 4.
3 Max Weber, for instance, described Luther's early thinking on "calling" as characterized by "an attitude closely related, in so far as the form of world activity was concerned, to the Pauline eschatological indifference." This indifference, however, gave way to a more "traditionalistic" understanding of calling as Luther "became increasingly involved in the affairs of the world." Weber regarded this shift as the product of a growing "and more intense belief in divine providence" on Luther's part—a belief "which identified absolute obedience to God's will, with absolute acceptance of things as they were." Max Weber, *The Protestant Ethic and the Spirit of Capitalism*, trans. Talcott Parsons (Mineola, NY: Dover Publications, Inc., 2003), 84–86. "Luther's harsh opposition to the peasant revolts," Donald Nielsen writes, "is rooted in this idea [of absolute acceptance], one that ultimately helped foster the authoritarian character of Lutheranism and German life that troubled Weber." Donald A. Nielsen, "The Protestant Ethic and the 'Spirit' of Capitalism as Grand Narrative: Max Weber's Philosophy of History," in *The Protestant Ethic Turns 100: Essays on the Centenary of the Weber Thesis*, ed. William H. Swatos, Jr., and Lutz Kaelber (Boulder: Paradigm Publishers, 2005), 60n22.

4 Bernd Wannenwetsch, "Luther's Moral Theology," in *The Cambridge Companion to Martin Luther*, ed. Donald K. McKim (Cambridge: Cambridge University Press, 2003), 127.
5 Wannenwetsch, "Luther's Moral Theology," 132.
6 Laffin, *The Promise of Martin Luther's Theology*, 107.
7 Martin Luther, "Whether Soldiers, Too, Can Be Saved," *LW* 46:126. Unless otherwise noted, citations from the works of Martin Luther are from *Luther's Works* (*LW*) (American Edition), ed. Jaroslav Pelikan and Helmut T. Lehmann, 55 vols. (Philadelphia: Muehlenberg Press and Fortress Press, and St. Louis: Concordia, 1955–86).
8 Laffin, *The Promise of Martin Luther's Theology*, 108–10. Wannenwetsch insists that the two kingdoms doctrine "be theologically embedded" in the framework of the three estates, "lest it be misunderstood in terms of a separation of spheres. The "Two" distinguishes the different ways in which God exercises God's rule, while the "Three" expresses "how God's rule and faith *penetrate* the elementary forms of social life alike, bringing the worldly (politics and economics) and the spiritual (religion) into line." Wannenwetsch, "Luther's Moral Theology," 132.
9 Laffin, *The Promise of Martin Luther's Theology*, 130.
10 Carter Lindberg, *Beyond Charity: Reformation Initiatives for the Poor* (Minneapolis: Fortress Press, 1993), 119.
11 Martin Luther, "An Open Letter to the Christian Nobility of the German Nation Concerning the Reform of the Christian Estate," *LW* 44:172–73. It is estimated that between 15 and 30 percent of the population of towns were "paupers and vagrants" at the time of the Reformation. Walther I. Brandt, introduction to "Ordinance of a Common Chest, Preface," *LW* 45:161.
12 Luther, "Open Letter to the Christian Nobility," *LW* 44:211.
13 Lindberg, *Beyond Charity*, 119–20. Carter Lindberg considers the resulting ordinance "the first effort to translate Luther's theological ethics into social legislation."
14 "Order of the City of Wittenberg," trans. Carter Lindberg, in *Beyond Charity*, by Carter Lindberg, 200–202.
15 "Order of the City of Wittenberg," trans. Carter Lindberg, in *Beyond Charity*, by Carter Lindberg, 201.
16 Lindberg, *Beyond Charity*, 120.
17 Lindberg, *Beyond Charity*, 123–24.
18 Brandt, introduction to "Ordinance of a Common Chest, Preface," *LW* 45:163. The struggle between parish and monastery continued, although the main point of contention was whether the abbot or congregation had the authority to name the congregation's preacher. The parish's independence from the monastery was not formally recognized by religious and temporal authorities until 1529. Brandt, introduction to "Ordinance of a Common Chest, Preface," *LW* 45:163–64.
19 Lindberg, *Beyond Charity*, 124.
20 Brandt, introduction to "Ordinance of a Common Chest, Preface," *LW* 45:165.
21 Lindberg, *Beyond Charity*, 124; Brandt, introduction to "Ordinance of a Common Chest, Preface," *LW* 45:165.
22 Brandt, introduction to "Ordinance of a Common Chest, Preface," *LW* 45:165.
23 Carter Lindberg, "Luther and the Common Chest," in *The Forgotten Luther: Reclaiming the Social-economic Dimension of the Reformation*, ed. Carter Lindberg and Paul A. Wee (Edina, MN.: Lutheran University Press, 2016), 20–21.
24 Lindberg, *Beyond Charity*, 123–25. Lindberg asserts that Luther "initiated social welfare programs that provided the seeds for the later welfare state." Carter

Lindberg, "Luther on a Market Economy," *Lutheran Quarterly* 30 (2016): 379. Social and theological historian Samuel Torvend concurs, writing that Luther "brought considerable energy to this project [of economic reform] that would be imitated throughout Germany and the Nordic countries and, in time, become what North Americans and Western Europeans know as stated-funded social assistance." Samuel Torvend, "'Greed Is an Unbelieving Scoundrel,'" in Lindberg and Wee, 38.

25 "Fraternal Agreement on the Common Chest," *LW* 45:192.

26 It was the *parish* that Luther saw as having the "right" to establish the common chest. Luther's word for "church," *Gemeinde*, illustrates the fact that the civil and church communities were coextensive in his society and in his thinking. In Wittenberg, on the other hand, the town council had formulated the ordinance. The later conflict in Leisnig over implementation of the common chest arose, as discussed below, precisely between the town council and the parish, with Luther taking the side of the parish. Lindberg, *Beyond Charity*, 119, 123.

27 Martin Luther, "Ordinance of a Common Chest, Preface," *LW* 45:172–73. Carter Lindberg highlights the fact that the "only criterion for distribution of loans or outright gifts" from the common chest "was to be the need of the recipient." Carter Lindberg, "Luther and the Common Chest," 19.

28 Martin Luther, "To the Councilmen in All Germany That They Should Establish and Maintain Christian Schools," *LW* 45:350. See Lindberg, "Luther on a Market Economy," 384.

29 Robert Kolb and Timothy J. Wengert, eds., *The Book of Concord* (Minneapolis: Fortress Press, 2000), 450. See Lindberg, "Luther and the Common Chest," 22.

30 Lindberg, "Luther on a Market Economy," 380.

31 Lindberg, "Luther on a Market Economy," 382; Lindberg, *Beyond Charity*, 113.

32 See, e.g., Martin Luther, "The Ninety-Five Theses" 59, in *Documents of the Christian Church*, ed. Henry Bettenson, 2nd ed. (London: Oxford University Press, 1963) ("Saint Lawrence said that the poor were the treasures of the Church, but in speaking thus he was using the language of his own time"). See also Lindberg, *Beyond Charity*, 99.

33 Lindberg, *Beyond Charity*, 106. Lindberg writes that "Luther's attack on begging was directed not merely to abuses but to the heart of the medieval theological and ecclesiological system. This fact did not escape the notice of the papacy; in Leo X's bull . . . " Exsurge Domine," this was one of the articles for which Luther was condemned."

34 Paul Warde, *Ecology, Economy and State Formation in Early Modern Germany*, Cambridge Studies in Population, Economy and Society in Past Time 41 (Cambridge: Cambridge University Press, 2006), 27.

35 Lindberg, *Beyond Charity*, 43–51.

36 Lindberg, *Beyond Charity*, 52.

37 Lindberg, *Beyond Charity*, 97.

38 Lindberg, *Beyond Charity*, 106.

39 "Fraternal Agreement on the Common Chest," *LW* 45:178.

40 Warde, *Ecology, Economy and State Formation*, 15–16.

41 Hans-Christoph Rublack, "Political and Social Norms in Urban Communities in the Holy Roman Empire," in *Religion, Politics and Social Protest: Three Studies on Early Modern Germany*, ed. Kaspar von Greyerz (London: George Allen & Unwin, 1984), 50–52.

42 Rublack, "Political and Social Norms," 26–28. At the heart of a codification in Nuremberg in 1478 and the 1498 Reformation of Worms, Rublack shows, was

an appeal to justice. Equally central to these and other formulations of the time were Augustine's "notion of 'pax et iustitia'" and Aquinas' phrase *Bonum et salus consociatae multitudinis est, ut eius unitas conservetur quae dicitur pax.*

43 Rublack, "Political and Social Norms," 50–52.

44 For statements of a similar methodological position, see Jennifer Hole, *Economic Ethics in Late Medieval England, 1300–1550,* Archival Insights into the Evolution of Economics, ed. Robert Leeson (Basingstoke: Palgrave Macmillan, 2016), 19.

45 Lindberg, *Beyond Charity*, 127.

46 Brandt, introduction to "Ordinance of a Common Chest, Preface," *LW* 45:166.

47 Brandt, introduction to "Ordinance of a Common Chest, Preface," *LW* 45:167. See Lindberg, *Beyond Charity*, 132–45, for a summary of later common chest statutes inspired by the Wittenberg and Leisnig orders.

48 Jacques Le Goff, *Money and the Middle Ages: An Essay in Historical Anthropology*, trans. Jean Birrell (Cambridge: Polity Press, 2012), 90–91.

49 Le Goff, *Money and the Middle Ages*, 91, 102.

50 Le Goff, *Money and the Middle Ages*, 96.

51 Martin Luther, "Admonition to Peace," *LW* 46:22–23.

52 Lindberg, *Beyond Charity*, 123.

53 "Fraternal Agreement on the Common Chest," *LW* 45:177.

54 Brandt, introduction to "Ordinance of a Common Chest, Preface," *LW* 45:167, quoting Luther, "Sermon for St. Stephen's Day, Dec. 26, 1522," *Weimarer Ausgabe* (WA) 12:693.

55 Thomas Aquinas, *Summa theologiae* (Latin-English Edition), trans. Fathers of the English-Dominican Province (NovAntiqua, 2013), II–II, Q. 66, Art. 2, ad. 1. The *Summa Theologiae* is cited as *ST* hereafter.

56 *ST* II-II, Q. 66, Art. 7, resp.

57 Martin Luther, "The Blessed Sacrament of the Holy and True Body of Christ, and the Brotherhoods," *LW* 35:52, 57.

58 Martin Luther, "The Freedom of a Christian," *LW* 31:351. Luther analyzed the three "powers of faith" in "The Freedom of a Christian." The "promises of God," he wrote, are "holy, true, righteous, free, and peaceful words." As such, they are full of "power." A soul shares "in all their power" by "cling[ing] to them with a firm faith." The first power of faith is that faith alone is sufficient for righteousness and salvation. The second power is that faith alone is true obedience, complete fulfillment of the commandments, thus rendering "the law and works" unnecessary and the believer free. Luther, "The Freedom of a Christian," *LW* 31:349–51.

59 Luther, "The Freedom of a Christian," *LW* 31:350–52.

60 See Wannenwetsch, "Luther's Moral Theology," 120; Martin Wendte, "Mystical Foundations of Politics? Luther on God's Presence and the Place of Human Beings," *Studies in Christian Ethics*, August 7, 2018, accessed June 17, 2020, journals.sagepub.com/doi/10.1177/0953946818792628.

61 Oswald Bayer, *Martin Luther's Theology: A Contemporary Interpretation*, trans. Thomas H. Trapp (Grand Rapids: William B. Eerdmans Publishing Co., 2008), 236.

62 Martin Luther, "On the Councils and the Church," in *The Christian Theology Reader*, ed. Alister E. McGrath, 2nd ed. (Malden, MA: Blackwell Publishing, 2001), 281.

63 Wannenwetsch, "Luther's Moral Theology," 134.

64 Wendte, "Mystical Foundations of Politics," 7.

65 Luther, "The Freedom of a Christian," *LW* 31:354.

66 Luther, "The Freedom of a Christian," *LW* 31:355.

67 Luther, "The Freedom of a Christian," *LW* 31:357.

68 Warde, *Ecology, Economy and State Formation*, 35.
69 Warde, *Ecology, Economy and State Formation*, 38.
70 Warde, *Ecology, Economy and State Formation*, 97.
71 Warde, *Ecology, Economy and State Formation*, 98, 120.
72 "Fraternal Agreement on the Common Chest," *LW* 45:192. As Paul Wee and Conrad Braaten note, "Luther himself viewed the means to be employed in addressing hunger and poverty to be in the area of Christian freedom." Paul A. Wee and Conrad Braaten, introduction to *The Forgotten Luther*, 11.
73 Luther, "The Freedom of a Christian," *LW* 31:349–50.
74 Luther, "The Freedom of a Christian," *LW* 31:367–68.
75 Luther, "The Freedom of a Christian," *LW* 31:358–59.
76 Luther, "The Freedom of a Christian," *LW* 31:364.
77 Luther, "The Freedom of a Christian," *LW* 31:366. See Laffin, *The Promise of Martin Luther's Political Theology*, 27 (Luther "directs us to the place of divine promise where humans are freed in faith for responsiveness to life in communion with God and neighbor").
78 Luther, "The Freedom of a Christian," *LW* 31:369.
79 Martin Luther, "Temporal Authority: To What Extent It Should Be Obeyed," *LW* 45:91.
80 Martin Luther, "The Seventh Commandment: Thou Shalt Not Steal," in *Large Catechism* (1529), in the Christian Classics Ethereal Library, accessed June 17, 2020, http://www.ccel.org/ccel/luther/largecatechism.pdf.
81 Luther, "Open Letter to the Christian Nobility," *LW* 44:112. When writing from the perspective of a subject without faith, Luther can indeed sound "Hobbesian." See J. M. Porter, "The Political Thought of Martin Luther," introduction to *Luther: Selected Political Writings*, ed. J. M. Porter (Lanham, MD: University Press of America, 1974), 1.
82 Luther, "The Freedom of a Christian," *LW* 31:344.
83 Luther, "The Freedom of a Christian," *LW* 31:344.
84 Luther, "The Freedom of a Christian," *LW* 31:348. Faith is Christian liberty because it depends on "the second part of Scripture," the "promises of God." The promises of God lead the believer to a place of freedom; "[t]hat which is impossible for you to accomplish by trying to fulfill all the works of the law—many and useless as they all are—you will accomplish quickly and easily through faith." Luther, "The Freedom of a Christian," *LW* 31:348–49.
85 Luther, "The Freedom of a Christian," *LW* 31:344.
86 J. M. Porter writes: "Analogous to the relation between the inner and outer man, faith and good works, the Christian does not require temporal authority but he willingly serves his neighbor through it." Porter, "Political Thought of Martin Luther," 1.
87 Luther, "Temporal Authority," *LW* 45:94. Here again Luther mentions the temple tax: "Thus in Matthew 17 Christ paid the half-shekel tax that he might not offend them, although he had no need to do so."
88 Luther, "Temporal Authority," *LW* 45:103.
89 Luther, "The Freedom of a Christian," *LW* 31:367. As Bernd Wannenwetsch writes concerning the believer's redistribution of Christ's bestowal, "The purpose is more than simply to pass on what has been received. Luther is saying at the same time that the giver must not himself control, measure out, or condition the giving in order to protect himself from loss of self." Bernd Wannenwetsch, *Political Worship*, trans. Margaret Kohl, Oxford Studies in Theological Ethics, ed. Oliver O'Donovan (Oxford: Oxford University Press, 2004), 332.
90 Jacob Viner, *Religious Thought and Economic Society*, ed. Jacques Melitz and Donald Winch (Durham, NC: Duke University Press, 1978), 76.

91 Wannenwetsch, "Luther's Moral Theology," 124.

92 For a discussion of this and other medieval distinctions among the poor, see Lindberg, *Beyond Charity*, 47–51.

93 "Fraternal Agreement on the Common Chest," *LW* 45:189.

94 "Fraternal Agreement on the Common Chest," *LW* 45:192.

95 Luther, "Ordinance of a Common Chest, Preface," *LW* 45:172.

96 Luther, "Ordinance of a Common Chest, Preface," *LW* 45:173.

97 Luther, "Ordinance of a Common Chest, Preface," *LW* 45:173. Ryan P. Cumming sees Luther's de-emphasis on merit as a distinctive that can serve as a counter-vision in today's economic discussions. Cumming argues that the current American conception of the economy depends in part on a system of merit, that "benefits accrue to those who most deserve them." Luther provided the resources, Cumming believes, to "question whether the economy ought to be founded on a system of merit at all." Ryan P. Cumming, "A New Vision," in Lindberg and Wee, 89–90. Carter Lindberg echoes the same hope—that Luther can redirect our thinking away from capitalism as a system of rewards and punishments—but also connects Luther's distaste for the medieval symbiosis between rich and poor to his recoil against the emerging profit economy of the sixteenth century. The same defect lay at the heart of both, as the medieval symbiosis was itself a profit economy: "He realized that an 'imitation of Christ' theology that idealized poverty as the ideal Christian state and viewed alms as the means to purchase paradise supported a profit economy that rationalized itself with charity." Lindberg, "Luther and the Common Chest," 18. See also Lindberg, "Luther on a Market Economy," 375 ("The medieval church had become quite clever in wedding the market economy to the economy of salvation and exploiting a mercantile logic for the purchase of paradise"). Merit-oriented economies, against which Luther reacted, are a perennial temptation: "[B]oth medieval theology and the rise of the profit economy were based on achievement-oriented meritocracy, the old Aristotelian drive from vice to virtue." Lindberg, "Luther on a Market Economy," 177.

98 Laffin, *The Promise of Martin Luther's Political Theology*, 46–47.

99 Luther, "The Freedom of a Christian," *LW* 31:371 (italics added).

100 Laffin, *The Promise of Martin Luther's Political Theology*, 49. Laffin's discussion interacts with Eric Voegelin's thesis in volume 4 of Voegelin's *History of Political Ideas*, that Luther had to make a place for works lest the idea of faith, which is nothing other than the certainty of salvation, become an excuse for licentiousness. The motivation for good works, according to Voegelin, had to be love, but love based on gratitude. Nevertheless, faith was primary and love its consequence. Love comes in, not with respect to our relationship with God, but in social obligations toward neighbors. Voegelin sees this logic intensified in Calvin, and then, in modern times, faith drops out of the picture, leaving love to "degenerate in practice into the aggressive, utilitarian welfare society." Laffin, *The Promise of Martin Luther's Political Theology*, 48. Hints of the coming divorce between faith and love can perhaps be seen already in the sixteenth century, as state-administered programs for poor relief responded to the "moral panic" resulting from increased consumption of limited resources. See Warde, *Ecology, Economy and State Formation*, 35. Luther, however, insisted on a redistributive logic that starts with a place of abundance. Faith is essential to that starting point, because it is only through faith that the believer can believe and trust that she is free from the threat of deprivation that might otherwise come from "loving" one's neighbor through a redistribution of scarce resources.

101 Martin Luther, "Lectures on Galatians," *LW* 26:264–65.

102 See Laffin, *The Promise of Martin Luther's Political Theology*, 54–55.

103 Wannenwetsch, "Luther's Moral Theology," 128.
104 Luther, "Ordinance of a Common Chest, Preface," *LW* 45:172–73.
105 Renate Blickle, "From Subsistence to Property: Traces of a Fundamental Change in Early Modern Bavaria," *Central European History* 25, no. 4 (1992): 381.
106 Warde accounts for the strict planning rules that applied to house decorations in early modern Germany by reference to the *necessitas* principle. "In a world where resources were perceived to be scarce," he writes, "the form or decoration of one's home or farmstead were not simply matters of taste, but 'luxury', or 'superfluity' or 'need' to be balanced against the overall needs of the community." Warde, *Ecology, Economy and State Formation*, 44.
107 Blickle, "From Subsistence to Property," 377–82.
108 Warde, *Ecology, Economy and State Formation*, 325. Similar appeals were made to *Schaden* (damage, injury, or loss) and *Nachteil* (detriment or disadvantage). A *Schaden* could be the shadow cast by a tree over one's garden and thus inhibiting the growth of grass. It could also be a tax (*Landschaden*) or simply a loss incurred when someone else's animals ate one's crop. Warde, *Ecology, Economy and State Formation*, 325.
109 Warde, *Ecology, Economy and State Formation*, 336.
110 Warde, *Ecology, Economy and State Formation*, 337.
111 Warde, *Ecology, Economy and State Formation*, 345.
112 Blickle, "From Subsistence to Property," 377.
113 Blickle, "From Subsistence to Property," 384.
114 Warde, *Ecology, Economy and State Formation*, 38–39.
115 Blickle, "From Subsistence to Property," 384.
116 Blickle, "From Subsistence to Property," 384.
117 Luther, "The Seventh Commandment: Thou Shalt Not Steal."
118 Laffin, *The Promise of Martin Luther's Political Theology*, 168–69.
119 Martin Luther, "The Magnificat," *LW* 21:312–13.
120 Luther, "The Magnificat," *LW* 21:313.
121 Luther, "The Blessed Sacrament," *LW* 35:50–52.
122 Luther, "The Blessed Sacrament," *LW* 35:52. Wannenwetsch describes the "inner logic of this citizenship" as an instance of the *communicatio idiomatum*, observing that "Luther makes clear that celebrating the Eucharist is nothing less than a political act in which the communicants actualize and suffer the citizenship that has been bestowed on them by baptism." Wannenwetsch, "Luther's Moral Theology," 134.
123 Luther, "The Blessed Sacrament," *LW* 35:57.
124 Luther, "The Blessed Sacrament," *LW* 35:57.
125 Wendte, "Mystical Foundations of Politics?," 9.
126 Mary Gaebler, "U.S. Property Law Reconsidered in Light of the Lutheran *Finitum Capax Infiniti*," in *On Secular Governance: Lutheran Perspectives on Contemporary Legal Issues*, ed. Ronald W. Duty and Marie A. Failinger (Grand Rapids: William B. Eerdmans Publishing Co., 2016), 81.
127 Martin Luther, "A Treatise on the New Testament, That Is, the Holy Mass," *LW* 35:102.
128 Luther, "A Treatise on the New Testament," *LW* 35:86.
129 Augustine, *De doctrina christiana* 2.1.1, ed. and trans. R. P. H. Green (Oxford: Clarendon Press, 1995), 56–57.
130 See Nicholas Heron, *Liturgical Power: Between Economic and Political Theology* (New York: Fordham University Press, 2018), 94.
131 Heron, *Liturgical Power*, 94–95.
132 Heron, *Liturgical Power*, 95.

133 Laffin, *Promise of Martin Luther's Political Theology*, 170. See also Wannenwetsch, "Luther's Moral Theology," 131 ("For the reformer, these stations [estates] are 'holy' in that they are instituted by God and sanctified through his work—holy though not *media salutis* or means of salvation. Rather, they are like the elements in sacramental theology: 'natural material' created by God and entrusted to humankind, always in danger of being misread.").
134 Luther, "Treatise on the New Testament," *LW* 35:86.
135 Laffin, *Promise of Martin Luther's Political Theology*, 170.
136 Luther, "Treatise on the New Testament," *LW* 35:86.
137 Luther, "Treatise on the New Testament," *LW* 35:93–96.
138 Wannenwetsch, *Political Worship*, 335.
139 See Luther, "Treatise on the New Testament," *LW* 35:94, 102.
140 Luther, "Treatise on the New Testament," *LW* 35:94.
141 Luther, "Treatise on the New Testament," *LW* 35:97.
142 Luther, "Treatise on the New Testament," *LW* 35:98.
143 Luther, "Treatise on the New Testament," *LW* 35:93.
144 William T. Cavanaugh, "Eucharistic Sacrifice and the Social Imagination in Early Modern Europe," *Journal of Medieval and Early Modern Studies* 31, no. 3 (Fall 2001): 597–98.
145 Cavanaugh, "Eucharistic Sacrifice," 597. Michael Laffin, in *The Promise of Martin Luther's Political Theology*, describes Cavanaugh's concern as a rejection of what Cavanaugh sees as Luther's "sharp contrast of gift and exchange," which contributed to the modern conception of individuals as "radically differentiated," who only enter into relations with one another on a contractual basis—"relations of exchange for mutual benefit" instead of "exchange based on mutual obligation." Laffin, *Promise of Martin Luther's Political Theology*, 80.
146 Lindberg, "Luther on a Market Economy," 376.
147 Lindberg, "Luther on a Market Economy," 381.
148 Luther, "Treatise on the New Testament," *LW* 35:99.
149 Laffin, *Promise of Martin Luther's Political Theology*, 83.
150 Laffin, *Promise of Martin Luther's Political Theology*, 81–82.
151 Wannenwetsch, *Political Worship*, 327–28.
152 Wannenwetsch, *Political Worship*, 330–31.
153 Wannenwetsch, *Political Worship*, 331 (emphasis in original).
154 Luther, "The Freedom of a Christian," *LW* 31:371 (emphasis added).
155 See Nielsen, "Max Weber's Philosophy of History," 61–62, for a discussion of Max Weber's attention to Luther's rejection of the "ethical dualism" in Roman Catholic theology and his substitution of "ethical universalism."
156 Luther, "Temporal Authority," *LW* 45:100.
157 Luther, "Open Letter to the Christian Nobility," *LW* 44:54.
158 Luther, "Open Letter to the Christian Nobility," *LW* 44:95–96.
159 "Fraternal Agreement on the Common Chest," *LW* 45:186.
160 "Fraternal Agreement on the Common Chest," *LW* 45:178. Carter Lindberg argues that German cities on the eve of the Reformation were already impressed by the idea, if not the practice, of placing public before private interests. The Reformation ideal of living for others rather than oneself, he continues, fit the social situation of the cities, and that synergy, coupled with the doctrine of the priesthood of all believers, brought about a redirection of the "many foundations and testaments of churchly organizations" through "community legislation toward charitable goals." Lindberg, *Beyond Charity*, 91, 94.
161 See Warde, *Ecology, Economy and State Formation*, 121–22, 132–33, 163–64, 172.

162 Sean Doherty, *Theology and Economic Ethics: Martin Luther and Arthur Rich in Dialogue* (Oxford: Oxford University Press, 2014), 201–202.
163 Warde, *Ecology, Economy and State Formation*, 166.
164 Martin Luther, "Lectures on Deuteronomy," *LW* 9:138–39.
165 Warde, *Ecology, Economy and State Formation*, 121.
166 Donald W. Shriver, Jr., and E. Richard Knox, "Taxation in the History of Protestant Ethics," *The Journal of Religious Ethics* 13, no. 1 (Spring 1985): 137.
167 Warde, *Ecology, Economy and State Formation*, 121.
168 Warde, *Ecology, Economy and State Formation*, 121.
169 The threefold tithe, as Luther described it, consisted of (1) a yearly donation "of all the fruits of the earth" to the Levites, (2) a setting apart every third year "of all those same fruits of the earth, to be expended as though for a common chest and public alms—for the Levites and the strangers, the orphans and the widows; for He wanted no paupers to be in the land," and (3) a tithe imposed upon the Levites themselves, "that of their tithes they would also give tithes to the priests." Luther, "Lectures on Deuteronomy," *LW* 9:138.
170 Luther, "Lectures on Deuteronomy," *LW* 9:139.
171 "Fraternal Agreement on the Common Chest," *LW* 45:192.
172 Warde, *Ecology, Economy and State Formation*, 22.
173 See Warde, *Ecology, Economy and State Formation*, 22–23.
174 Giorgio Agamben, *The Kingdom and the Glory: For a Theological Genealogy of Economy and Government (*Homo Sacer *II, 2)*, trans. Lorenzo Chiesa and Matteo Mandarini (Stanford: Stanford University Press, 2011), 165.
175 Agamben, *The Kingdom and the Glory*, 165.
176 Agamben, *The Kingdom and the Glory*, 156–57. See *ST* I, Q. 108, Art. 1.
177 Agamben, *The Kingdom and the Glory*, 157.
178 Agamben, *The Kingdom and the Glory*, 210.
179 Agamben, *The Kingdom and the Glory*, 161.
180 Agamben, *The Kingdom and the Glory*, 161.
181 Agamben, *The Kingdom and the Glory*, 241–42. See Augustine, *City of God* 22.30.
182 Agamben, *The Kingdom and the Glory*, 162–63.
183 Agamben, *The Kingdom and the Glory*, 163.
184 Agamben, *The Kingdom and the Glory*, 162.
185 Agamben, *The Kingdom and the Glory*, 162.
186 Agamben, *The Kingdom and the Glory*, 164.
187 Agamben, *The Kingdom and the Glory*, 163.
188 Agamben, *The Kingdom and the Glory*, 166.
189 Warde, *Ecology, Economy and State Formation*, 98.
190 Warde, *Ecology, Economy and State Formation*, 285.
191 Warde, *Ecology, Economy and State Formation*, 97–98.
192 Warde, *Ecology, Economy and State Formation*, 192.
193 Warde, *Ecology, Economy and State Formation*, 285.
194 Warde, *Ecology, Economy and State Formation*, 3.
195 Warde, *Ecology, Economy and State Formation*, 3.
196 Stanley Hauerwas, "Casuistry in Context: The Need for Tradition," in *The Hauerwas Reader*, ed. John Berkman and Michael Cartwright (Durham, NC: Duke University Press, 2001), 276 (quoting Aristotle, *Nicomachean Ethics* 1142a).
197 Hauerwas, "Casuistry in Context," 276–77.
198 Erik Peterson, "The Book on the Angels: Their Place and Meaning in the Liturgy," in *Theological Tractates*, by Erik Peterson, ed. and trans. Michael J. Hollerich (Stanford: Stanford University Press, 2011), 108.
199 Peterson, "The Book on the Angels," 108.

References

Agamben, Giorgio. 2011. *The Kingdom and the Glory: For a Theological Genealogy of Economy and Government* (Homo Sacer *II, 2*). Translated by Lorenzo Chiesa and Matteo Mandarini. Stanford: Stanford University Press.

Augustine. 1995. *De doctrina christiana*. Edited and translated by R. P. H. Green. Oxford: Clarendon Press.

Bayer, Oswald. 2008. *Martin Luther's Theology: A Contemporary Interpretation*. Translated by Thomas H. Trapp. Grand Rapids: William B. Eerdmans Publishing Co.

Blickle, Renate. 1992. "From Subsistence to Property: Traces of a Fundamental Change in Early Modern Bavaria." *Central European History* 25, no. 4: 377–85.

Cavanaugh, William T. 2001. "Eucharistic Sacrifice and the Social Imagination in Early Modern Europe." *Journal of Medieval and Early Modern Studies* 31, no. 3 (Fall): 585–606.

Cumming, Ryan P. 2016. "A New Vision." In *The Forgotten Luther: Reclaiming the Social-economic Dimension of the Reformation*, edited by Carter Lindberg and Paul A. Wee, 77–102. Edina, MN: Lutheran University Press.

Doherty, Sean. 2014. *Theology and Economic Ethics: Martin Luther and Arthur Rich in Dialogue*. Oxford: Oxford University Press.

Gaebler, Mary. 2016. "U.S. Property Law Reconsidered in Light of the Lutheran *Finitum Capax Infiniti*." In *On Secular Governance: Lutheran Perspectives on Contemporary Legal Issues*, edited by Ronald W. Duty and Marie A. Failinger, 79–101. Grand Rapids: Eerdmans Publishing Co..

Hauerwas, Stanley. 2001. "Casuistry in Context: The Need for Tradition" In *The Hauerwas Reader*, edited by John Berkman and Michael Cartwright. Durham, NC: Duke University Press.

Heron, Nicholas. 2018. *Liturgical Power: Between Economic and Political Theology*. New York: Fordham University Press.

Hole, Jennifer. 2016. *Economic Ethics in Late Medieval England, 1300–1550*. Archival Insights into the Evolution of Economics, edited by Robert Leeson. Basingstoke: Palgrave Macmillan.

Kolb, Robert, and Timothy J. Wengert, eds. 2000. *The Book of Concord*. Minneapolis: Fortress Press.

Laffin, Michael Richard. 2016. *The Promise of Martin Luther's Political Theology: Freeing Luther from the Modern Political Narrative*. T&T Enquiries in Theological Ethics, edited by Brian Brock and Susan F. Parsons. London: Bloomsbury T&T Clark.

Le Goff, Jacques. 2012. *Money and the Middle Ages: An Essay in Historical Anthropology*. Translated by Jean Birrell. Cambridge: Polity Press.

Lindberg, Carter. 1993. *Beyond Charity: Reformation Initiatives for the Poor*. Minneapolis: Fortress Press.

———. 2016. "Luther on a Market Economy." *Lutheran Quarterly* 30: 373–92.

———. n.d. "Luther and the Common Chest." In Lindberg and Wee, *The Forgotten Luther*, 17–29.

Lindberg, Carter, and Paul A. Wee, eds. 2016. *The Forgotten Luther: Reclaiming the Social-economic Dimension of the Reformation*. Edina, MN: Lutheran University Press.

Luther, Martin. 1955–86. *Luther's Works* (American Edition). Edited by Jaroslav Pelikan and Helmut T. Lehmann, vol. 55. Philadelphia: Muehlenberg Press and Fortress Press, and St. Louis: Concordia Publishing House.

———. 1963. "The Ninety-Five Theses." In *Documents of the Christian Church*, edited by Henry Bettenson. 2nd ed. London: Oxford University Press.

———. 2001. "On the Councils and the Church." In *The Christian Theology Reader*, edited by Alister E. McGrath. 2nd ed. Malden, MA: Blackwell Publishing.

———. 1883–2009. *D. Martin Luthers Werke: kritische Gesamtausgabe (Weimarer Ausgabe)*, vol. 136. Weimar: Hermann Böhlau.

———. n.d. *Large Catechism*. Christian Classics Ethereal Library. Accessed June 17, 2020. http://www.ccel.org/ccel/luther/largecatechism.i_1.html.

Nielsen, Donald A. 2005. "The Protestant Ethic and the 'Spirit' of Capitalism as Grand Narrative: Max Weber's Philosophy of History." In *The Protestant Ethic Turns 100: Essays on the Centenary of the Weber* Thesis, edited by William H. Swatos, Jr., and Lutz Kaelber, 53–75. Boulder: Paradigm Publishers.

Peterson, Erik. 2011. "The Book on the Angels: Their Place and Meaning in the Liturgy." In *Theological Tractates*, edited by Erik Peterson, edited and translated by Michael J. Hollerich. Stanford: Stanford University Press.

Porter, J. M., ed. 1974. *Luther: Selected Political Writings*. Lanham, MD: University Press of America.

Rublack, Hans-Christoph. 1984. "Political and Social Norms in Urban Communities in the Holy Roman Empire." In *Religion, Politics and Social Protest: Three Studies on Early Modern Germany*, edited by Kaspar von Greyerz, 24–60. London: George Allen & Unwin.

Shriver, Donald W., Jr., and E. Richard Knox. 1985. "Taxation in the History of Protestant Ethics." *The Journal of Religious Ethics* 13, no. 1 (Spring): 134–60.

Thomas Aquinas. 2013. *Summa Theologiae* (Latin-English Edition). Translated by the Fathers of the English-Dominican Province. NovAntiqua.

Torvend, Samuel. n.d. "'Greed Is an Unbelieving Scoundrel.'" In Lindberg and Wee, *The Forgotten Luther*, 30–42.

Viner, Jacob. 1978. *Religious Thought and Economic Society*. Edited by Jacques Melitz and Donald Winch. Durham, NC: Duke University Press.

Wannenwetsch, Bernd. 2003. "Luther's Moral Theology." In *The Cambridge Companion to Martin Luther*, edited by Donald K. McKim, 120–35. Cambridge: Cambridge University Press.

———. 2004. *Political Worship*. Translated by Margaret Kohl. Oxford Studies in Theological Ethics, edited by Oliver O'Donovan. Oxford: Oxford University Press.

Warde, Paul. 2006. *Ecology, Economy and State Formation in Early Modern Germany*. Cambridge Studies in Population, Economy and Society in Past Time 4. Cambridge: Cambridge University Press.

Weber, Max. 2003. *The Protestant Ethic and the Spirit of Capitalism*. Translated by Talcott Parsons. Mineola, NY: Dover Publications, Inc.

Wendte, Martin. August 7, 2018. "Mystical Foundations of Politics? Luther on God's Presence and the Place of Human Beings." *Studies in Christian Ethics*. Accessed June 17, 2020. journals.sagepub.com/doi/10.1177/0953946818792628.

6 John Calvin and the challenge of inequality

Introduction

John Calvin's explicit references to taxation are fewer than Luther's. He inherited an operational system of public finance in Geneva when he first arrived in 1536 and evidently saw little reason to adjust it. Embedding Calvin's few remarks about taxation in his overall political theology, however, can generate helpful insights into the shaping of modern assumptions about the institution of taxation. Because of Calvin's distinctive emphasis on poor relief, his political theology is instructive for redistributive taxation in particular.

This chapter first briefly describes Geneva's public finance system before and during Calvin's time there. It then addresses the distinct place of poor relief in Calvin's thinking, the place of redistribution in his overall conception of the economy, and finally Calvin's explicit teaching about taxation in the context of his overall political and economic theology.

Taxation and poor relief in Calvin's Geneva

The Reformation was officially proclaimed in Geneva, and the Duke of Savoy's troops chased away, in 1536. By then, the city's Syndics (magistrates) had been collecting the fines and penalties of the Prince-Bishop for almost ten years and had effectively completed a takeover of Geneva's public finances.[1] Once the Reformation was proclaimed, the new city-state tracked down all sources of revenue that had been available to its predecessor. In William Monter's words, "Geneva was 'secularized' with a vengeance in 1536, and one immediate result was an astronomical increase in municipal revenues."[2] The Syndics and the *Petit Conseil* were especially successful in obtaining revenue from the *gabelles* on wine and meat.[3] Nevertheless, it is estimated that at least one-fifth of Geneva's revenue during the last years of Calvin's life was used to pay interest and some principal on the city-state's foreign debt to Basel.[4]

One reason for Calvin's relative silence on the question of taxation is undoubtedly that he inherited a robust system of public finance in Geneva—one that had already been transferred from the church to the civil authorities. Other matters required more of Calvin's attention, already spread far and wide as it was. Robert

Kingdon concludes that if Calvin "did not work hard to resolve Geneva's social problems personally, it was probably because he thought they were already being handled by men of competence whom he trusted."[5]

Calvin's Geneva, in any event, became a model of the type of community that Luther sought. It was "one of the first attempts to establish a welfare state in modern Europe without the need for begging."[6] The theologian Graham Tomlin boldly asserts that Geneva is a prime, and successful, example of the Reformation cities that implemented "theologically motivated programs to eliminate destitution and poverty in favor of a much more egalitarian view of social life."[7]

At the center of sixteenth-century Geneva's social welfare efforts was the *Hôpital-Général*, a creation of the Reformation though not of Calvin.[8] This "general hospital" was much more than a "hospital" in the modern sense of the term; it provided assistance of various kinds to people in need for all sorts of reasons—to orphans and foundlings, the old and the sick, disabled people, even visitors requiring food and lodging. In the reorganization of Geneva's civic affairs accompanying the proclamation of the Reformation, the properties of five hospitals—formerly administered primarily by priests—were turned over to the new *Hôpital-Général*. The services of the five hospitals, the scene of financial and physical abuse, were consolidated in the new institution, which became considerably more efficient than the "quasireligious foundations" that it succeeded.[9] Properties confiscated from churches, convents, and confraternities added to the holdings of the new general hospital.[10] In fact, the headquarters of the new hospital were located in the former convent of Sainte-Claire, which had been closed (as a convent) under the influence of Calvin's teaching.[11]

Direction of the *Hôpital-Général* was placed entirely in the hands of laymen. Its *procureurs* were selected in the same way as most other officials of the Genevan Republic; the retiring *Petit Conseil* nominated four or five *procureurs* each year, and the slate was then presented to the *Conseil des Deux-Cents* (Geneva's largest legislative body) and the citizens for election (a mere formality). The *procureurs* became a sort of standing committee.[12] By 1550, members of the merchant families that effectively controlled the city expected, and even sought, to serve this "single institution that cared for all the city's poor."[13]

Calvin, again, had little to do with the creation and operation of the *Hôpital-Général*. Laicization and rationalization of social welfare had been underway in Geneva since the mid-fifteenth century.[14] Indeed, the inspiration for Geneva's sixteenth-century welfare program seems to have been the *Aumône-Général* of Lyon rather than the Reformation cities in Germany that had responded in the 1520s to Luther's call for welfare reform. Lyon's institution was established in the early 1530s and bore many similarities to Geneva's *Hôpital-Général*.[15]

However, the influence of the Reformation on Geneva's civic welfare reforms must not be discounted. The city's "decisive steps toward laicization and rationalization" were taken after 1536. Geneva's reforms did not differ in kind from those of contemporary cities, but they "were more thorough, more radical in their break with the past."[16] The Reformation did not create new welfare institutions so much as infuse them with new theological meaning. The emerging pattern of civic reform and the simultaneous redirection of theological commitments in Reformation cities influenced each other.[17]

Calvin's own concern for the social welfare of Geneva manifested itself in the creation of the *Bourse française* sometime between 1545 and 1550. The *Hôpital-Général* was not prepared to handle the influx of refugees—many of them French, like Calvin himself—that the Reformation triggered. The *Bourse* was a private institution, essentially a large fund collected from wealthy French refugees in Geneva and distributed to other French refugees who had trouble supporting themselves upon their arrival. In most years, Calvin was the largest individual contributor to the *Bourse*, and there is some evidence that he founded it.[18] That Geneva was a refugee center was important to Calvin, as reflected in the dedication in his commentary on the Gospel of John to the Council of Geneva. He wrote there that Geneva's role was "significant in light of Christ's statement that he regards the taking in of strangers as something done personally to him."[19]

The diaconate and the two kingdoms

So great was Calvin's concern about poverty in general, that a fourth church office, that of *deacon*, was created in Geneva for the express purpose of serving the needs of the poor. In *Calvin's Political Theology and the Public Engagement of the Church*, Matthew Tuininga helpfully traces the development of Calvin's understanding of the diaconate in the context of his emerging, and distinctive, two kingdoms theology. Martin Bucer, Tuininga writes, was the first of the Reformers to theorize about offices other than that of pastor and to distinguish among ecclesiastical offices. He did not do so as clearly as Calvin would, but he rejected the contention of Zwingli and Bullinger that the New Testament office of elder had been abolished once magistrates became Christian. Bucer believed that there should be an ecclesiastical office for the care of the poor.[20] Calvin arrived in Bucer's Strasbourg in 1538 and served as pastor of the French refugee church there until he returned to Geneva in 1541. Even during his initial stay in Geneva, Calvin's fundamental difficulty had stemmed from his desire to make the Genevan church "relatively autonomous," that is, "distinct—though not separate—from the commonwealth."[21] It seems almost certain that Bucer's early theories about ecclesiastical offices helped Calvin work out the structure of such a church. Bucer and Calvin retained a close working relationship even after Calvin left Strasbourg. Tuininga writes:

> For all of Bucer's efforts in Germany, Strasbourg, and later England, it was Calvin who would insist most sharply and systematically on the distinction between the two kingdoms and its necessary implications for the spiritual autonomy of the church. It was Calvin who would vigorously reject magisterial claims to headship and supremacy within the church, and it was Calvin who would articulate an enduring theological basis for the spiritual-ecclesiastical

> offices oriented toward discipline and care for the poor. Ultimately it was Calvin's two kingdoms theology that would emerge as the alternative to caesaropapism and the Zurich model of the *corpus Christianum.*[22]

Despite the apparent differences between teaching and discipline on the one hand and caring for the poor on the other, Calvin was adamant that care for the poor was part of the spiritual government of the church.[23] "Clearly Calvin was not satisfied to see civil government administer poor relief," Tuininga writes. Calvin "wanted it to be administered by the church as well, and he wanted it to be recognized as a spiritual work."[24] The *Ecclesiastical Ordinances* that Calvin drafted for the city of Geneva shortly after his return in 1541, and which would serve as a constitution for the Genevan church, distinguished four types of ministry within the church: pastors, elders, doctors, and deacons.[25]

"The care of the poor," according to Calvin, "was entrusted to the deacons."[26] But there must be two kinds of deacons: one set of deacons "who distribute the alms" and another set of deacons who devote "themselves to the care of the poor and sick."[27] The distinction was reflected in the affairs of Calvin's Geneva, where one division of the diaconate managed church funds and provided for the poor while the other cared for the sick in the *Hôpital-Général.*[28] And, indeed, Calvin's *Bourse française* was operated solely by deacons, largely under the oversight of Calvin and other pastors, without any involvement on the part of the civil authorities.[29] In a complete reversal of Luther's dismissal of the ancient image of the poor as the treasure of the church, Calvin wrote in the *Institutes*:

> From this we may also judge what use was made of church possessions and how they were disposed. You will frequently find both in the decrees of synods and in ancient writers that all that the church possesses, either in lands or in money, is the patrimony of the poor. And so this song is often sung there to bishops and deacons, that they should remember that they are not handling their own goods but those appointed for the need of the poor; and if in bad faith they suppress or waste them, they shall be guilty of blood. Accordingly, they are admonished to distribute these goods to whom they are owed, with the greatest awe and reverence, as if in God's presence, without partiality. Hence arise those grave protestations in Chrysostom, Ambrose, Augustine, and other bishops like them, by which they affirm their uprightness among the people.[30]

Calvin's insistence that there be deacons and that they serve the poor in these two ways was a firm response to an ongoing disagreement. Elsie Anne McKee observes that "the customary second office, the diaconate responsible for poor relief," was, along with the ministry of discipline, a function much disputed in the sixteenth century between civil and ecclesiastical authorities.[31] Calvin refused to follow the example of Zwingli and Bullinger, who had ceded the functions of poor relief and discipline to the civil government, and he thereby established a new version of Reformed political theology that emphasized the relative autonomy of the church.[32] As such, the development of Calvin's ideas about the diaconate was integral to the emergence of his distinctive two kingdoms theology.

Calvin articulated a version of Luther's two kingdoms doctrine in the 1536 edition of the *Institutes*, writing with respect to Romans 12:8[33] that "it has not come about by human perversity that the authority over all things on earth is in the hands of kings and other rulers, but by divine providence and holy ordinance," and that "God was pleased so to rule the affairs of men, inasmuch as he is present with them and also presides over the making of laws and the exercising of equity in courts of justice."[34] The 1539 edition, however, added a sentence clarifying that Paul is referring in Romans 12:8 to "a council of sober men, who were appointed in the primitive church to preside over the ordering of public discipline (which office is called in the letter to the Corinthians, 'governments')." The gift of ruling, therefore, can only be applied by analogy to "the civil power serving the same end."[35] Tuininga reads the added language as a sign that Calvin was breaking not only with Luther on the two kingdoms, but with Zwingli and Bullinger as well.[36]

Calvin continued to echo Luther on the dual stance that a believing citizen or subject must adopt toward civil authority. In his 1548 Commentary on Galatians and in his 1556 Commentary on James, he acknowledged both that the Christian is free from all orders, ranks, and governments, but also that the Christian is bound to submit to those manifestations of God's providence as a way of serving others. While liberty characterizes a person's relationship with God, that liberty need not be exercised—and often should not be exercised—in that person's relationship with other people.[37]

In the various editions of the *Institutes*, Calvin spoke of the "twofold government" under which human beings live. One government "resides in the soul or inner man and pertains to eternal life," while the other "pertains only to the establishment of civil justice and outward morality." "Christ's spiritual kingdom and the civil jurisdiction are things completely distinct," Calvin continued, and thus "it makes no difference what your condition among men may be or under what nation's laws you live, since the Kingdom of Christ does not at all consist of these things."[38] In his Commentary on the Psalms, Calvin spoke of God's "general" government, which manifests itself in civil authority, and God's "spiritual jurisdiction," which God exercises over the church.[39]

What distinguishes Calvin's two kingdoms theology most sharply from Zwingli's, Bullinger's, and, later, Hooker's (with their tendency "to identify the visible church with the political order") is Calvin's identification of the church (including its ministries of discipline and poor relief) with Christ's spiritual kingdom.[40] At the same time, "Calvin's emphasis on the visible expression of the kingdom of Christ in the outward ministry of the church" is the feature that most decisively set his two kingdoms theology apart from Luther's.[41]

We noted above that one reason for Calvin's comparative reticence to speak of taxation owes something to Reformation Geneva's preestablished system of public finance. The other reason for his relative silence would seem to be that he located the institution of taxation in the realm of civil authority, which is an expression of God's general government, while he placed social welfare among the tasks of the church, Christ's spiritual kingdom. A conceptual and practical gap appears between the redistribution of resources to those in need and the function of the tax system. Poor relief had not been separated from taxation in this way for Luther, who was thus able to connect the two and recommend that taxes be used to meet the needs of the poor. One might be tempted to conclude that Calvinism bequeathed an emphasis on voluntary charity as the primary form of poor relief to the societies that embraced a certain reading of Calvin's insistence on the church's autonomy, while social welfare in Lutheran states centered on government-administered systems of redistributive taxation.

However, the separation of functions in Calvin's theology must not be overstated. Already in the 1536 edition of the *Institutes*, Calvin insisted that the two government are "not at variance." "For spiritual government, indeed," he wrote, "is already initiating in us upon earth certain beginnings of the Heavenly Kingdom."[42] The spiritual government has begun to "break in" upon our lives on earth, although, in the 1536 edition, the appointed end of civil government remained steadfastly focused on those earthly lives: "to adjust our life to the society of men, to form our social behavior to civil righteousness, to reconcile us with one another, and to promote generally peace and tranquility."[43]

Calvin added another function of civil government in the 1559 edition of the *Institutes*: "to cherish and protect the outward worship of God, to defend sound doctrine of piety and the position of the church."[44] He added those words at the beginning of the litany of appointed ends, in the same sentence. Now, not only does the heavenly kingdom break in upon the earthly kingdom, but civil government is tasked with supporting and defending the spiritual kingdom (which is the church). This has become the civil government's primary task.[45] Tuininga considers even more telling the 1559 edition's expansion of the task of civil government to include matters associated with the first table of the law. The added language reads as follows: "If scripture did not teach that it extends to both Tables of the Law, we could learn this from secular writers: for no one has discussed the office of magistrates, the making of laws, and public welfare, without beginning at religion and divine worship."[46]

The result is an overlap of functions. Calvin also added these words in 1559: "The exhortation which we read in Ps. 82 has the same purpose: that [the kings] should 'give justice to the poor and needy, rescue the destitute and needy, and deliver the poor and needy from the hand of the oppressor."[47] Tuininga describes a certain "complementarity" between the magistrates and pastors. In the very last years of his life, Calvin wrote in his Commentary on Jeremiah that Old Testament Israel had a twofold government: the spiritual government of the "church" by the priests, and the management of civil affairs by the elders. "The two were sharply distinguished," Tuininga writes, "but they cooperated closely, as 'there were some things in which they ruled in common.'"[48]

Judging from the practice of Geneva's Consistory, provision for the poor and needy was foremost among "things in which they ruled in common." Established by the 1541 *Ecclesiastical Ordinances*, the Consistory was composed of pastors selected by the Company of Pastors and elders nominated by the *Petit Conseil* in consultation with the Company of Pastors. The Consistory's function was to oversee and impose church discipline, up to and including excommunication. Government officials were to assist the Consistory procedurally.[49] "The Consistory truly was a pastoral body," in Tuininga's words, and, in keeping with Calvin's understanding of ecclesiastical offices, among its functions were the imposition of discipline (often on merchants guilty of price gouging or impeding economic competition) and intervention on behalf of the poor.[50]

Calvin viewed the church as "between being and becoming," in Eva-Maria Faber's words.[51] The church's *being* depends on God's grace alone, but its *becoming* "depends on humankind." Faber writes: "[T]he church not only *is* the body of Christ but must also *coalesce* through the believers' interaction with each other."[52] Because this coalescing is incomplete and the church imperfect, Calvin endorsed civil government in his rebuke of the Anabaptists: "Our adversaries claim that there ought to be such great perfection in the church of God that its government should suffice for law. But they stupidly imagine such a perfection as can never be found in a community of men."[53] The purposes of civil government are "helps" to us as "we go as pilgrims upon the earth while we aspire to the true fatherland," and those who seek to take away those helps "deprive man of his very humanity."[54] Calvin insists that civil government does more than supply the conditions required for humans to "breathe, eat, drink, and [be kept] warm."[55] It "also prevents idolatry, sacrilege against God's name, blasphemies against his truth, and other public offenses against religion."[56] Although its functions are different from those of the church, the civil government's first and highest role is to support the church through those different functions. "For the care of equity and justice grows cold in the minds of many," Calvin wrote, "unless due honor has been prepared for virtue; and the lust of wicked men cannot be restrained except by severity and the infliction of penalties."[57] In short, Calvin wrote, as early as 1536, the civil government "provides that a public manifestation of religion may exist among Christians."[58]

Perhaps it was inevitable that the two kingdoms should meet above all in their officials' mutual care for the poor. At the end of his life, Calvin made very clear that the "sacrifice of material wealth to God in service to the needs of the poor" was characteristic of the life and *worship* of those who inhabit the kingdom of Christ.[59] Though "'religion is strictly spiritual,'" and salvation "'ought yet to be viewed as properly belonging to our souls,'" salvation also "'extends to our bodies.'"[60] Indeed, Calvin harmonizes the reference to the "poor in spirit" in Matthew 5:3 with the reference to the "poor" in Luke 6:20, so that Jesus's statement "includes the dimension of material poverty."[61]

Far from relegating poor relief to the realm of optional, personal choice, Calvin raised it to the level of a special task of the church and one that the civil government was obliged to support. It was a point of overlap between the two kingdoms. I want to suggest that the unique status of social welfare in Calvin's thinking stems, first of all, from the priority attached to it in scripture, but also from the place that *economic inequality* occupied in Calvin's understanding of how societies work.

Calvin's economic vision

William Stevenson writes: "Although [Sheldon] Wolin's description of the 'short step from Geneva to the English Levellers at Putney' may be exaggerated, it is true that Calvin's view of humankind had to feed the egalitarian impulse."[62] The sheer amount of space that reflections on economic and social inequality occupy in Calvin's sermons and commentaries suggests that his thought can be placed fruitfully in dialogue with contemporary discourse, for, as suggested in Chapter One, the egalitarian impulse in our own society is at odds with our Lockean conception of liberty, thus placing redistributive taxation in an awkward position.[63]

Economic inequality

Calvin was aware, not just of the human impulse toward equality, but even of the moral anxiety that inequality can engender. He was, nevertheless, determined to trace God's hand in the dilemma posed by inequality. Economic inequality was a challenge, in Calvin's view, but one that God uses.

The impulse toward equality, according to Calvin, begins with an awareness of economic inequality. In his commentary on Exodus 22:25 (with reference to Leviticus 25:35 as well), Calvin noted that God first mentioned the poverty and distress afflicting the poor before commanding Israel to relieve the needs of the poor. In this way, the minds of the people were to be predisposed to pity (*qua flectantur ad misericordiam animi*) before they received the command itself.[64] Similarly, in a sermon preached on Deuteronomy 24, Calvin asked, "Therefore, since God gave us that honor [to dispose of God's goods], is it not a villainous malice in us, and are we not more beasts than the beasts themselves, if we are not moved to pity [toward the poor]?"[65]

God's wish that the people relieve the needs of the poor then takes form as a command to redistribute resources. Compassion remains in view, however; Christ's command to give to his people as if giving to Christ himself must "wring pity from our inmost being."[66] Like tax philosophers after him, Calvin rested the case for redistribution on the case against inequality. Like theologians before him (including Aquinas and Luther), Calvin defined inequality in terms of necessity and abundance. "We relieve the necessity of our brethren," he wrote regarding 2 Corinthians 8:13, "from our abundance."[67] Echoing Luther, Calvin insisted that subsistence is never a cause for anxiety, because the "children of God" can "expect everything from his blessing."[68]

Although Calvin insisted that the wealthy must "consider that their abundance" is to be used "in relieving the necessities of the brethren," he did not prescribe absolute equality. He wrote that "there is not demanded of us an equality in which the wealthy have no right to live in greater elegance than the poor; nevertheless, equality should be observed to the point that no one is hungry and no one suppresses others by cheating them."[69] Calvin was aware that he was using the term "equality" in two different senses. He wrote, again with regard to 2 Corinthians 8:13: "*Equality* may be taken in two senses, either as meaning a mutual compensation, when like is given for like, or as meaning a proper adjustment. I understand *ἰσότητα* simply as meaning—an *equality of proportional right*, as Aristotle terms it."[70] Calvin believed that this is the kind of equality that Paul had in mind when he wrote to the Corinthians, "I do not mean that others should be eased and you burdened, but that as a matter of equality your abundance at the present time should supply their want, so that their abundance may supply your want, that there may be equality" (2 Cor. 8:13, 14).

In Calvin's view, the "true rule of equity,"[71] that God's people should redistribute their resources to relieve the needs of the poor, is not driven by a goal of strict equality. The rule of equity (*aequitatis regula*) turns out to be provision for the "present necessity."[72] In fact, Calvin prefers the phrase "suitable symmetry" to the word "equality":

> For this is the system of proportional right in the church, that while individuals share with each other according to the measure of their gifts and necessity, a suitable symmetry [*apta symmetria*] is produced from their mutual interaction. This is true even though some possess more and some possess less and gifts are distributed unequally.[73]

This idea of a "suitable symmetry" carries with it a flavor of mildness, moderation, and even cheerfulness, as Calvin himself said.[74] In his "Treatise Against the Libertines," he argued that the extreme teachings of "these madmen" concerning possession of temporal goods leads to the "diabolical delusion of wanting to heap all goods into a pile" and thereby cause a "confusion" that will not "leave any order among men."[75] Despite the polemics, Calvin actually sought to clear some middle ground in this treatise. In an attempt to strike the right balance, the "attitude our Lord wants us to have with respect to goods," Calvin encouraged anyone "who has hardly anything" to "thank God and eat his bread with contentment," and exhorted anyone who "has a great deal" to use it "moderately" and "employ the property that has been given to him in order to help and provide for his neighbors, seeing himself as God's steward who possesses the goods he has on condition that he must one day render an account."[76] In other words, all are to hold their possessions loosely, not necessarily selling everything but always remaining "poor in heart."[77] Calvin called this lightness with respect to possessions "the first law of equity"—i.e., "that no one make use of what belongs to another, but only use what he can properly call his own."[78] Regarding 1 Corinthians 7:30 ("Let those who buy be as those not buying"), Calvin commented that Paul "does not require the renunciation of property, but only that it be possessed as not being possessed."[79]

André Biéler observes that property is both "sacred" and "relative" for Calvin. It is sacred because it is "assigned by God as a trust" but relative because humans "are never the absolute owners" of it.[80] While the sacredness of private property makes theft a serious offense, the unavoidable reality of poverty softens the possessor's claim to property. "Through the poor," Biéler writes, "God speaks to warn everyone that their possessions do not by rights belong to themselves."[81] In

Biéler's account, Calvin charted a middle way between the "communism" that was resurgent in the sixteenth century and the modern, individualistic conception of absolute property rights.[82] The periodic redistribution of land contemplated in the Old Testament institutions of sabbatical year and jubilee represented for Calvin a way of maintaining "a middle condition" with respect to property, i.e., a way to honor the sacredness of private ownership while nevertheless ensuring that "a few persons" do not "draw everything to themselves and oppress the general body."[83]

By accepting proportionality as a definition of equality, thus following Aristotle and Aquinas, Calvin gave himself the freedom to work with the concept of inequality without the burden of defining "equality." This freedom, in turn, allowed him to retain but reformulate the symbiotic relationship between rich and poor that Luther had rejected.

Reformulation of the symbiotic relationship

We saw in the last chapter that the symbiotic relationship procuring salvation for the wealthy crumbled in the face of the doctrine of justification by grace. The Reformers' forceful opposition to begging marked a shift from the late medieval efforts merely to "control" begging to an insistence that begging be abolished.[84] Almost all trace of the symbiotic relationship disappeared in Luther, who resisted any hint of reciprocity in the act of relieving the needs of the poor.

All trace of salvific effect vanished in Calvin as well,[85] but Calvin retained a symbiotic relationship between the rich and the poor. His sermon on Deuteronomy 24 sets out the respective "ministries" of the rich and poor—the former to distribute what is God's and the latter to gather it in. Moses, in the biblical passage in question, says:

> "When you reap your harvest in your field, and have forgotten a sheaf in the field, you shall not go back to get it; it shall be for the sojourner, the fatherless, and the widow; that the Lord your God may bless you in all the work of your hands. When you beat your olive trees, you shall not go over the boughs again; it shall be for the sojourner, the fatherless, and the widow. When you gather the grapes of your vineyard, you shall not glean it afterward; it shall be for the sojourner, the fatherless, and the widow. You shall remember that you were a slave in the land of Egypt; therefore I command you to do this" (Deuteronomy 24:19–22).

In interpreting this instruction, Calvin argued first that wealth comes with a condition and that that condition is the "ability" (*faculté*) of the rich to relieve the needs of their neighbors. Even if it is not a question of "tax or impost" (*une taxe, ou quelque impost*), everyone should recognize that God has provided enough for those with resources to help those in need.[86]

God is the giver, in Calvin's account. We can say "with respect to man" (*selon les hommes*) that "this belongs to me"; but that claim evaporates in the light of the pity that moves us when we see the poor languishing in their need.[87] In a more ultimate sense, therefore, the condition attached to wealth is that *God* shall receive the gleanings from it, as a kind of royalty that God reserves.[88] Moreover, the poor are appointed as God's representatives (*mes procureurs*) to gather up the royalties.[89] The rich person too is God's agent (*lieutenant*). Because all things belong to God and are given with the condition attached, God gives the "office" along with wealth—the office of pitying and helping the poor.[90] The wealthy "should be ministers to the poor [*ut pauperum sint ministri*]."[91] As Biéler writes with respect to Calvin's views on wealth and poverty, "In one way or another we are all trustees for God."[92]

To put the matter bluntly, God permits or, more precisely, ordains economic inequality, as Calvin stated in a sermon harmonizing Matthew 4, Mark 1, and Luke 4:

> As Solomon says, God created the poor and the rich. He means by this that, if God wished it, each would have enough property and money and everything desirable in worldly terms, so that the distribution would be equal among all. But God knows why he has made poverty and wealth exist, and so matters will stand even till the world ends.[93]

According to Calvin, God has a purpose for inequality. Poverty is on one level the product of society's sins,[94] but that reality does not defeat the good use to which God puts economic inequality—namely, to bind humans together in their ministry to each other as God's agents (distributing God's goods) and God's representatives (gathering God's goods). "[W]e should know," Calvin wrote, "that God has intermixed the rich and the poor, so that we may have the opportunity to do good."[95] In fact, helping the poor is not only a condition attached to wealth, but is the actual *purpose* of wealth. Wealth is the means by which God has equipped the rich to help others: "For consider too the conditions on which God places benefits in the hands of the rich: so that they may have the opportunity and ability to help their poor neighbors."[96]

To summarize the paradox in Calvin's understanding of God's purposes in intermixing rich and poor, God purposes that all humans have an abundant share of the goods of creation, but God gives more of those goods to some than to others—yet in such a way that both the rich and the poor are God's ministers, blessing each other on behalf of God. Calvin attributes the human condition simultaneously to God's mysterious will and to the effects of human sin, and the economic inequality that results both from "a mysterious dispensation of providence" and from "the anarchy that intrudes into the human heart" is orchestrated to restore and promote human solidarity.[97] In other words, economic inequality is both a challenge and an opportunity. The starting point is not far from Luther's ongoing dynamic of (re)distribution from a place of abundance, but as Calvin's dynamic unfolds the stress is more on God's providential arrangement of economic conditions in a way that fosters mutual dependence between rich and poor.

Calvin's understanding of economics is permeated with the idea that God's plan for human economic activity is at present dedicated to restoring something of the economic interdependence that existed before sin.[98] While restoring primordial equality is not an instrument of salvation for anyone involved, it is an instrument of restoring unity. What becomes apparent from the way Calvin set up this dynamic, however, is that the unity emerging from progress toward equality becomes itself the goal. Although unity initially appears to be a happy byproduct of working toward equality, the tables are turned. The impulse toward equality, arising from the compassion to which we are moved by the sight of inequality, becomes the *means* and human solidarity the *end*.

Eschatology, providence, and command

The lack of a final resolution to the problems of poverty and economic inequality has two effects in Calvin's political theology: it places the instruments of social welfare, most especially the diaconate, on a permanent footing as far as the present age is concerned; and it heightens the importance of eschatology in Calvin's theology generally. This section first develops the importance of eschatology in Calvin's theology and then turns to the related questions of God's providence in the present age and God's commands. The goal of this, final, section of the chapter is to situate the function of taxation in Calvin's overall theological system in a way that contributes to the narrative of how taxation, as a facet of political theology, developed in Western politics.

Eschatology

It is worth noting that the diaconate's care for the poor was not a temporary measure designed to bring about a better set of social circumstances. Calvin desired a dedicated "permanent ecclesiastical office" for that purpose.[99] Poverty, and especially inequality, are not matters to be remedied in a final sense in the present age. They persist because God wills them to persist. Only God knows why they persist, but Calvin is sure that they will be with us until the end of the world as we know it.

Calvin's political theology is best understood in eschatological terms. More precisely, the two kingdoms are for Calvin primarily eschatological categories: the temporal and the eternal.[100] Tuininga believes—and this seems right—that the key to interpreting correctly Calvin's political theology and particularly his two kingdoms theology "is recognizing its fundamentally eschatological character, for underlying much of the terminology that allegedly betrays Neoplatonic influence is Calvin's Pauline commitment to the eschatological distinction between creation corrupted and creation restored, the present age and the age to come."[101] Thus, as Matthew Pereira writes: "Calvin believed that a just society would never be fully attained here on earth because of human corruption; nonetheless, civil institutions and agents were called upon to build a just social order, albeit in a partial and incomplete form."[102]

Despite the centrality of eschatology in Calvin's political theology, however, Calvin was reluctant to say much about the world to come. Tuininga identifies two reasons for Calvin's reticence: (1) his commitment to following scripture, which keeps the restoration of all things relatively hidden from sight; and (2) his tendency to identify the kingdom of Christ with the church.[103] Tuininga's explanation highlights a paradox in the structure of Calvin's theology, that is, that the kingdom of Christ is both hidden and immanent. It breaks into the present age but in a hidden way—through "the hidden work of the Holy Spirit."[104] Jesus described the kingdom as "inward," not because he wished to differentiate between the corporeal and noncorporeal, but to emphasize how close and yet how invisible the kingdom is.

In Giorgio Agamben's account, "the modern conception of history" finds itself "in a contradictory situation." It abolishes "eschatology" and "infinitely prolongs the history and government of the world," but then "it finds that the finite character of its paradigm returns ceaselessly."[105] After all, the "*oikonomia*, the providential government of the world, is not eternal but is completed on the Day of Judgment."[106]

The outcome of the effort of Western thought to heal the rift between the transcendent and the immanent is modern liberalism's rejection of the "divine pole" in favor of the *oikonomia*—the economy cut adrift from the "providential paradigm" that grounds it in the transcendent side "of the theological machine."[107] Even Ockham insisted on distinguishing ordered from absolute power precisely to defend the complete freedom of sovereign decision.[108] As discussed in Chapter 7 of this book, this attempt at "emancipation" is unsuccessful; but the attempt itself is important.

Like Augustine, Calvin was intent on bringing the mystery of God near—not, as Luther had done, by emphasizing the real presence of Christ's body in the material world—but by infusing the *oikonomia* itself with mystery and glory. Returning to an early expression of the tactic developed by Christian theology to avoid the charge of polytheism, Calvin wrote: "Nor am I displeased with Tertullian's definition, provided it be taken in the right sense, that there is a kind of distribution or economy in God which has no effect on the unity of essence."[109] And again, appealing to Tertullian: "God is one in unity of substance, and nonetheless the unity is disposed into a trinity by the mystery of dispensation."[110] In both instances, Calvin referred to Tertullian's *Against Praxeas*.[111] Calvin rejected the distinction between *latria* ("honor") and *dulia* ("servitude"), by means of which distinction "the papists" explain how they can give honor to the saints. Calvin wrote that "they wriggle out with the excuse that they keep unimpaired for God what is due him because they leave *latria* to him."[112] But "if we wish to have one God," Calvin insisted, "we should remember that we must not pluck away even a particle of his glory and that he must retain what is his own."[113] Superstition concedes the highest place to God but parcels out God's functions among "a throng of lesser gods" that surround God—i.e., saints—rending asunder his glory and leaving nothing but "a sterile notion of his supreme power."[114] Calvin was, paradoxically, preoccupied with much the same problem

Ockham had been: avoiding the sterility of a sovereign God who does nothing, who reigns but does not govern. Ockham's solution was to sever absolute and ordered power; Calvin's was to bring the sovereignty of God itself down into the realm of the *oikonomia*.

Calvin was concerned to safeguard *both* the unity and glory of God *and* the proximity of that mystery—close at hand in the form of the church. On the one hand, the "essence of God" must never be torn apart.[115] On the other hand, a distinction among the activities of the persons of the Trinity must not be suppressed; the "beginning of activity" is attributed to the Father, "wisdom, counsel, and the ordered disposition of all thing" to the Son, and "the power and efficacy of that activity" to the Spirit.[116] In Christ's work in the gospel accounts, Calvin asserted, we occasionally see him rendering glory to the Father, but "for the most part we see his own power shown to us."[117] Christ's work on earth, specifically "the searching and penetrating of the silent thoughts of hearts," belongs "to God alone."[118] The same is true of the Spirit, "who, everywhere diffused, sustains all things, causes them to grow, and quickens them in heaven and in earth."[119]

At the same time, any hint of subordination in the Trinity is expunged.[120] God's names (like "Creator") are applied to God's "outward activity," Calvin acknowledged, but no such name "intimates that anything new has happened to God in himself."[121] The Son not only participates with the Father in governing the world, but also carries out "other individual offices, which cannot be communicated to the creatures."[122]

Thus, Christ and his spiritual kingdom are immediately present in what we can call the *oikonomia*. Though the Old Testament saints had the same spiritual blessings that believers in the New Testament age have, they did not realize them with the same immediacy and clarity. Any attempt to "mediate" the blessings of the new covenant was, for Calvin, "an invasion of Christ's spiritual kingdom."[123]

Calvin's three related moves—rejecting any fissure between God's glory and activity, identifying Christ's activity in the spiritual kingdom as those fully and unequivocally proper to God, and denouncing any view that would mediate Christ's presence in the spiritual kingdom—generate a distinctive vision a God who is immediately present and active in the details of the here-and-now but nevertheless cloaked in glory and mystery. This is why, as Tuininga observes, Calvin effectively reversed the relationship between Christ and church that prevailed in the papacy. According to the latter, the Holy Spirit ruled the church "immediately"—without eschatological reserve—but by bestowing *dominium* on people. For Calvin, the Spirit rules the church in an incipient way but does so directly through the word.[124] The church's discipline, for example, "is the verdict of Christ, but it is not his final verdict."[125] Though not physically present, as in the Roman mass, or physically omnipresent, as Luther would have it, Christ is paradoxically even more immediately present in his glory, according to Calvin—present through word and Spirit after his bodily ascension.[126]

It is true that, for Calvin, Christ's presence through word and Spirit manifests itself through the ministry of human beings, but—as Tuininga phrases it—the church's authority is *ministerial* rather than *magisterial*, spiritual rather than political."[127] A pastor from the "lowest dregs of the people," Calvin wrote, must be heard by Christians "in the same manner as if he were descending from heaven or making known his will to us by angels."[128] Christ does govern the church through *means* (i.e., the ministry of human beings),[129] but—and this is a crucial point—Christ's ministers govern, not by virtue of their *office*, but through "the proclamation of his word," which is never separated from God.[130] The power that the church administers is spiritual and eternal; to make the church spiritual by virtue of its offices would be to repeat the errors of Rome, as well as of the "fanatics" and "libertines."[131]

Providence

It is no surprise in light of the foregoing discussion that Calvin's doctrine of providence is absolute. By ascending to the Father, Christ entered into possession of the authority given to him by the Father and thus *rules* and *governs* all things.[132] Christ reigns in three ways, in Calvin's view. Where his kingdom "has not been fully established,"[133] Christ binds with "chains of iron" and restrains his enemies from "exerting their fury beyond the limits which he shall assign."[134] But where obedience is voluntarily rendered to Christ, he reigns gloriously over the church "by the ministry of the word."[135] That is, one "government" is "universal," by which God "upholds, and maintains, and rules, all things," while another is "spiritual" and "belongs to the church," by which God draws people to Godself.[136]

Despite that distinction, however, Calvin rejected the idea of a "universal" providence that sets the affairs of the world in motion but remains untainted by direct involvement in the details. Carnal understanding, according to Calvin, takes us as far as understanding God to be initial creator and enables us to contemplate God's wisdom, power, and goodness; but only faith can show us that God is also "everlasting Governor and Preserver."[137] God must not be deprived of "control," Calvin insisted, and "control" is nothing other than the authority to rule.[138] *All* events and objects are governed by a "special" providence, and any created thing exercises its "own power" only insofar "as it is directed by God's ever-present land."[139] Thus, there is no distinction between God's stance toward natural events occurring in the ordinary course and God's stance toward special occurrences.[140]

Calvin categorically rejected the idea that God merely *permits* things and events. Carnal sense, he wrote, "can hardly comprehend how in acting through [Satan and "all the wicked"] he [God] does not contract some defilement from their transgression, and even in a common undertaking can be free of all blame, and indeed can justly condemn his ministers." Therefore, Calvin explained, "the distinction was devised between doing and permitting." But God, Calvin asserted, "openly declaring that he is the doer, repudiates this evasion," as humans "can accomplish nothing except by God's secret command." God is nothing other than "the author of that trial of which Satan and his wicked thieves were the ministers." From the abundant examples in scripture, "it is more than evident that they babble and talk absurdly who, in place of God's providence, substitute bare permission—as if God sat in a watchtower awaiting chance events, and his judgments thus depended upon human will."[141]

Oikonomia

Providence (or "government"), Giorgio Agamben argues, "is that through which theology and philosophy try to come to terms with the splitting of classical ontology into two separate realities: being and praxis, transcendent and immanent good, theology and *oikonomia.*" Providence is a "machine" whose purpose is to join back together "the two fragments in the *gubernatio dei*, the divine government of the world."[142] In Agamben's account, God's providential government of the world—which we call simply "providence"—must be unitary to reunite the transcendent and the immanent. For that very reason, however, providence "articulates itself ... into two different planes and levels." Christian theology has thus felt the overwhelming temptation to distinguish general or universal providence from special providence. Hence Thomas' extensive development of the relationship between first and second causes in his *Commentary on the Book of Causes.*[143] The first cause, according to Thomas, "aids" the second cause and, therefore, is primary. The causes are inseparable but distinct.[144]

In Calvin, however, the first cause is more immediately present with the second cause. Although Calvin upheld the validity of "intermediate causes,"[145] he insisted on God's "omnipotence," so that "no wind ever arises or increases except by God's express command"[146] and "not one drop of rain falls without God's sure command."[147] Calvin was willing to accommodate the idea of universal providence, so long as such an idea does not limit God's "especial care over each of his works."[148] It would, in short, "be senseless to interpret the words of the prophet [in Psalm 115:3—"he does whatever he wills"] after the manner of the philosophers, that God is the first agent because he is the beginning and cause of all motion." What comfort is the God of first causes to the believer suffering adversity? Calvin asked.[149]

Calvin's doctrine of providence does what Agamben thinks providence must do in Christian theology: it sutures the wound between divine being and divine praxes. But it does so in Calvin by refusing the wound in the first place. Calvin's picture of God's providential government of the world is one in which God's complete majesty is present in the smallest detail of earthly events, for God is the "keeper of the keys."[150] Calvin's answer to the "embarrassment" that Agamben thinks Christian theology faces in trying to make sense of the division between being and praxis, is *omnipotence.* Calvin, in effect, defined God's being in terms of his direct, immediate, and unassailable involvement in everything that happens and exists.

We cannot, in fact, know God apart from God's providential action, according to Calvin. "Hence we have then only the true knowledge of God," Calvin wrote, "when we not only acknowledge him to be the creator of the world, but when we also believe that the world is governed by him."[151] Calvin's picture of God is of a God *who works.* Even "when God works through an intermediary it is still

God who works."[152] Providence is active; "it is God's watchful, effective, active, ceaseless, total, detailed, personal, loving, wise, and holy governing of everything in this world and of everything that happens."[153]

God's omnipotence, in other words, means that God is "engaged in ceaseless activity." Omnipotence is not "a general principle," but a principle "directed toward individual and particular actions." God is not called omnipotent because God *can* act, but because God *does* act.[154]

Calvin's refusal to separate the majestic being of God from the ceaseless, detailed, and immanent praxis of God leads to a striking juxtaposition when viewed through the lens of Agamben's political theology. For Calvin, providence becomes the location of God's glory. "Yet his wonderful method of governing the universe," Calvin wrote, "is rightly called an abyss, because while it is hidden from us, we ought reverently to adore it."[155] The transcendent becomes immanent. God's will is, at one and the same time, near to humans, "sought not far off in the clouds or in abysses," but also "hidden," comparable "to a deep abyss."[156] God's will is both "for us the sole rule of righteousness, and the truly just cause of all things." It is not an "absolute" will, pure power separated from justice (as Ockham would have it), "but providence, that determinative principle of all things, from which flows nothing but right, although the reasons have been hidden from us."[157]

A "perpetual *oikonomia*, as a continuous activity of government of the world," continually tries to heal the fracture between being and praxis in Agamben's account.[158] Glory, according to Agamben, "is what remains after the machine of divine *oikonomia* has reached its completion and the hierarchy of angelic ministries has become completely inoperative."[159] In Calvin's view, however, glory dwells in the midst of providence or divine government of the world. We are to look "to God's secret providence with awe," Calvin wrote, because "God assumes the right (unknown to us) to rule the universe."[160] The "constant quiet and serenity" lie at the heart of "the disturbances in the world," which "deprives us of judgment."[161] "[O]ut of pure light"—that image into which divine glory resolves itself throughout Christian history—God directs "these very movements." The human act of *glorification*, "acclamation" in Agamben's account,[162] is not directed toward Sabbath inoperativity in Calvin's theology, but rather toward the abyss that lies close at hand, i.e., toward providence itself.[163]

But, again, these "hidden judgments of God" that we are to "hold in reverence,"[164] this "abyss," "hidden from us," that we nevertheless "ought reverently to adore,"[165] is not a divine government that "sits in idleness," but an "omnipotence" that is "engaged in ceaseless activity."[166] Divine activity, rather than inoperativity, is the locus of glory and the object of acclamation in Calvin's thinking. The king both reigns and governs. The king reigns *by* governing. The king reigns *in* the *oikonomia*. Bearing in mind Carl Schmitt's axiom—that theories of the state are "secularized theological concepts"—we can examine features of Calvin's understanding of civil society that parallel his transformation of the beatific vision into a political and economic picture of ceaseless activity that is an end in itself.

Circulation of goods

A striking feature of Calvin's teachings on material justice, when compared with those of Luther or Aquinas, is his concern that goods circulate. Continual circulation of the good things of creation among humans is a corollary to the theme that the process of achieving economic justice is the goal rather than the means of economic justice. Calvin's vision of the relationship between rich and poor—in which the poor gather and the rich distribute (and, where possible and when it can be done without sin, generate more wealth)—is a dynamic one, a cycle in which humans continually pass on what they receive.

Calvin's horror of hoarding by the wealthy reflects his insistence that the flow of goods not stagnate. Stagnation would result in a breakdown of human solidarity. "Communication"—sharing of goods—is God's design in this interim period. Calvin employed considerable invective against the failure to so communicate:

> He [God] could very well give each person plenty so that no-one would need help from anyone else, but he wants to test the love and fraternity we have together when we thus communicate with each other as he commands us to do: that is, that the rich should not be like wild beasts to eat and gobble up the poor and suck their blood and their substance—but should rather help them and always look on them with fairness, and not in order to say, "Oh! This is what I owe him; I gave him work and I paid him properly." But they should know they owe every help to those who are needy and in want, each indeed according to their means. For otherwise they are like murderers if they see their neighbours wasting away and yet do not open their hands to help them. In this, I tell you, they are certainly like murderers.[167]

Hiding goods away rather than placing them in the streams of commerce and redistribution reveals "such a spite" in the characters of these wealthy hoarders, according to Calvin, that he wondered if "it hurts them to share daylight or fresh air with other folk."[168]

Calvin referred to circulation in terms of both commerce and redistribution. Trading is a good practice, he wrote, for those who do engage in it are right "to exchange and barter with each other in order to keep the community together."[169] In fact, according to Calvin, the whole point of commerce is to "promote natural intercourse among men."[170] As Biéler writes, in summary of Calvin's position, "[A] dynamic imbalance exists, which generates the vital currents in social life. This makes the possessions of some circulate to others, to produce harmony and a happy balance among all."[171]

The "dynamic imbalance" that sets in motion the "vital currents" of economic and social life should, if "everyone freely agreed to [a] reciprocal imparting of the earth's wealth," achieve a kind of fluid goal. "Everyone," in Biéler's words, "would in turn be the other person's poor or rich person." Sin, however, causes the rich to "block the good things intended for their neighbours" and makes the rich "so much the more violently envious of what they do not have."[172] It is, therefore, the function of the rich and the poor to set goods in circulation again—the rich through attentiveness to the needs of the poor and the poor as the gatherers of benefits received. Justice, in Calvin's description, is not a static condition but consists in "legitimate modes of dealing."[173] Calvin's "economic theology" thus echoes Luther's version of transposition, but in more explicitly economic language.

In Calvin's thinking redistribution often sequentially follows the creation of wealth, as a periodic readjustment of the existing distribution of wealth. The force of Calvin's comments on the Jubilee principle is not only that redistribution defeats the concentration of wealth by keeping it in circulation, but also that this mechanism of reestablishing circulation when it has stalled primarily directs goods to the poor. Biéler describes Calvin's understanding this way: "The sharing of economic benefits in line with God's plan must therefore take place through a continual distribution that starts from the centres where wealth is created (the rich) and ends in locations where there is less affluence (the poor), by always tending towards a slightly nuanced equality."[174] In some respects, this dynamic resembles the modern settlement between wealth-production and redistributive justice, in which, as Linda Sugin writes,

> The political reality is that most . . . economic regulation is oriented towards maximization of wealth, rather than its distribution. The tax law comes in after productivity is maximized, and it should—to some extent at least—rearrange the results produced by markets that operate to concentrate wealth and opportunity.[175]

Calvin's political theology is marked by the conviction that inequality binds people together more effectively than equality, which would undermine mutual reliance. Government and its unifying function are characterized by inequality: "For as elements cohere only in unequal proportion, so countries are best held together according to their own particular inequality."[176] For Calvin, equality is not a measurable state of affairs. Rather, the impulse toward equality is just that: an impulse. This impulse is the starting point of the dynamic called redistribution, but a condition of equality is not the endpoint.[177]

This subsection has argued that, for Calvin, justice in society is an economic and political dynamic through commerce and redistribution. Commerce and redistribution are complementary, serving the same ends—circulation and, thus, solidarity. Redistribution may be accomplished through the distribution of tax revenue. In the contemporary understanding, particularly in the American and British settings, tax is often perceived as undermining wealth creation and, therefore, economic growth, while commerce unavoidably increases inequality. Calvin provides a theological viewpoint in which tax and commerce can both promote justice, which is the circulation of goods. Both should defeat the concentration of wealth.

The balancing role of circulation-as-justice and of tax as a subcategory thereof can also be recast as responsiveness to God's will expressed in different contexts (circumstances and command), rather than as the pragmatic outcome of a political struggle between competing ideas (efficiency and fairness). God ordains economic inequality but commands humans to alleviate it and equips them with compassion so that they desire to do so. That impulse, a kind of recoil against the inequity of great disparities in wealth, puts in motion the circulation of goods that fosters human solidarity and that is necessary to meet material needs. Calvin's dynamic has, perhaps, a Sisyphean quality; the human task, imperative though it is, inevitably meets with incomplete success when, through human sin and God's providence, inequality persists and spurs humans on to further action. Life is suspended between divinely ordained circumstances and divine command. The task is not hopeless, however, as the task itself is revealed to be a kind of social justice.

Will and command

In his commentary on 1 Corinthians 4:5 ("Therefore do not pronounce judgment before the time, before the Lord comes, who will bring to light the things now hidden in darkness and will disclose the purposes of the heart . . ."), Calvin wrote that the correct ordering of society and politics remains, for now, hidden in obscurity: "Matters are never so well regulated in this world but that many things remain in obscurity."[178] Among the things remaining in obscurity, as have seen, are God's reasons for decreeing economic inequality, especially in light of God's command to alleviate it. Humans are placed in between God's will and decree on the one hand and God's command on the other.

There is no distinction here between theology and politics or economics. Politics and economics are thoroughly theological for Calvin because human actions in the realm of civil government respond both to God's commands and to the circumstances that God providentially decrees. The ceaseless activity of God in governing finds its counterpart in the ceaseless activity of humans in correcting injustices. The former activity, providence in Agamben's account, seeks to heal the fracture between God's being and God's praxis.[179] The latter works to reconcile God's decree and God's command, responding to providential circumstances in a way that is faithful to what God has instructed God's people to do. The fracture is not between transcendence and immanence, or being and praxis, for Calvin, but between God's decree regarding things and events on the one hand and the haphazard way in which they appear to us on the other. God's will is a unity, just as Calvin denies the rupture between divine being and divine praxis. But "since the order, reason, end, and necessity of those things which happen for the most part lie hidden in God's purpose, and are not apprehended by human opinion, those things, which it is certain take place by God's will, are in a sense fortuitous."[180] Indeed, as Tuininga puts it, "God does not sanction all that takes place by his providence."[181] This is why Horton Davies writes that "Calvinism responds to the problem of evil with an eschatology rather than a theodicy."[182] God's will must not be confused with God's precept, Calvin wrote; the two are "utterly different."[183] In the end, "God requires of us only what he commands."[184] Thus, we are only apparently, not truly, caught between divine will and command, but our task remains to heal the apparent fracture between the two.

Calvin's theology refuses the separation between divine being and acting, locates both being and acting in the *oikonomia*, and draws divine providence down into the *oikonomia* as well. The price his theology pays for making these moves is a fracture (but only from the limited, human perspective) between divine will and divine precept. That fracture cannot be healed by providence in Calvin's theology, because providence lies entirely on one side of the gulf. The fracture can only be healed through the interplay between precept and will. This interplay is the domain of the Christian life, of ethics, of politics.

Because the fracture both appears *within* the *oikonomia* and is resolved there, the *oikonomia* takes on a more prominent role. In a sense, Calvin's theology fulfills Agamben's worst fear: "It is like saying that of God we can know and think only the economy, the Government, not the Kingdom or the inoperativity; and yet the Government is nothing but the brief interval running between the two eternal and glorious figures of the Kingdom."[185] It is not at all clear that the economy-Government is merely a "brief interval" for Calvin.

At the economic level—and it is more truly "economic" in the modern sense than it is for Calvin's predecessors—ceaseless activity comes to the fore. Implicitly in Luther and explicitly in Calvin, I want to suggest, there is a stress on process over end-result. The "universal destination of goods" of Catholic Social Teaching is not in view. Among the Reformers, we will always have the poor simply because God so wills it. There is again an almost Sisyphean quality to this political theology, though Calvin would never have countenanced any hint of a suggestion that either providence or precept is in any way spiteful or capricious.

It is not surprising, then, that redistributive taxation should assume a more prominent position in the Reformers' political theology—explicitly in Luther, less so in Calvin, but with "economic theology" on which to construct a theory of tax justice more fully developed in Calvin. Redistributive taxation is the sort of machine that continually adjusts to changing circumstances. It regularly and perpetually re-balances a society's resources. It does not anticipate reaching a final point at which it can become inoperative. It is not utopian, and it operates with a healthy measure of eschatological reserve. Its theological justification comes into its own with Calvin's reversal of the means and the ends of wealth and poverty and with his relocation of the interplay between them in the economy—"economy" in every sense of the word.

Calvin's explicit teaching on taxation

Civil law, for Calvin, depends on the "rule of charity." Because the temporal authorities themselves are God's agents, obedience to them is an act of honoring God. Thus, the driving force behind paying taxes (or engaging in any other form of obedience to the governing authorities or to civil law) is a kind of voluntary obedience to God. Calvin wrote in his Commentary on Romans 13:7: "This passage confirms what I said earlier, that kings and all other superiors are to be obeyed, not because we are compelled, but because it is a pleasing obedience to God, who wishes not only to be feared but also to be worshipped with voluntary respect."[186] Calvin routinely stated that charity is the regulative principle of political authority. For instance, he wrote that in Romans 13:8 ("owe nothing to anyone") Paul wished to refer this precept—i.e., of the authority of magistrates—"to the law of charity" (*ad dilectionis legem referre*).[187] According to Calvin, it is as if Paul had said "'When I require that you obey the rulers, I am not requiring anything other than what all the faithful should do from the law of charity.'"[188]

The extent to which Calvin thought of taxation as preeminently a political issue, integrated into the workings of civil government, is apparent in his commentary on the tribute-money passage in Matthew 22:

> The coin was stamped with *Cesar's likeness*; and thus the authority of the Roman government had been approved and admitted by the general practice. Hence it was evident that the Jews themselves had voluntarily come under obligation to pay tribute, for they had given up to the Romans the power of the sword; and there was not propriety in making a separate dispute about *the tribute-money*, for that question depended on the general arrangements of the government.[189]

Jesus's interlocutors, according to Calvin, had no genuine thought of resisting payment of the tribute money. Their purpose was only to ensnare Jesus with their question. In the context of Calvin's political theology, however, this commentary emphasizes the fact that the legitimacy of taxation is merely one aspect of the legitimacy of the government. "If you think it strange to pay tribute," he paraphrases Jesus as saying, "be not subjects of the Roman Empire."[190] Calvin refers the tax question back to the larger question of how civil government can accommodate various competing interests. Donald Shriver and Richard Knox write: "Calvin . . . reasoned that the justification for taxes or tributes can be deduced from an understanding of the office of the magistrate."[191]

Although redistribution of property expresses itself in different institutional structures in the church and in civil government, the line that Calvin drew was not between love and material distribution, as if the former belonged to the church and the latter to society and civil government. Rather, "true love must nevertheless be expressed through material actions" in both orders.[192] This, Calvin argued, is why the Old Testament prophets often attacked the social injustice of Israel's practices (or lack thereof) before turning their attention to the people's idolatries, ungodliness, and spiritual bankruptcy.[193] The separation between taxation and poor relief in Calvin's vision is an institutional, operational separation rather than a theological one.

God's giving more to some than to others is to be honored, even as God's command to relieve the needs of the poor through one's own abundance must be obeyed. The act of balancing God's provision and God's command is, for Calvin, the human task that finds expression partly through the institution of taxation. As a part of this task, the state has the responsibility of establishing a legal system that, on the one hand, safeguards private property from greed[194] and, on the other, guarantees to each person "the share of everyone's possessions to which they are entitled."[195] Preserving a legal system for property is only one-half of the state's responsibility; "[t]he authorities must also see to it that the products of that property are used for the benefit of the community,"[196] as illustrated by the Joseph narrative in Genesis.[197]

God's providential government extends to all rulers, whether or not they serve God, according to Calvin[198] However, "happily established" government is only possible when "religion takes first place" among its concerns; Christian rulers should be "ashamed of their negligence if they do not apply themselves to this concern."[199] Applying themselves to this concern means ruling justly, and justice means protecting right worship, defending the church and sound doctrine, and—significantly—adjusting individual life to collective life and reconciling "us with one another."[200] Justice, it seems, is tied closely to solidarity,[201] and solidarity is the adjustment of various needs within society to one another.

Thus, in a very general sense, Calvin lands in the tradition of thinkers who view taxation as an instrument of balancing social goods, as do Aquinas and our own contemporary proponents of the optimal tax model. Three social goods are in play in Calvin's conception of taxation-as-balance: personal property, the needs of the poor, and the honor of the ruler. Calvin emphasizes the third good more than Luther did, because he took the honor of the state to refer to the glory of God. Reflecting on why the "magnificence" of the ruler's "household" and the "dignity of the authority" that rulers exercise are so important to Calvin, particularly in comparison to Luther, Karl Barth suggests that "in the representative splendor of those in high and responsible places, which private citizens, the public, could not and should not hope to achieve, [Calvin] saw something divinely significant, a reflection of the majestic divine right that he did not wish to be assailed on obvious rational grounds."[202]

In the *Institutes*, Calvin began his brief treatment of taxation with the argument that taxes are legitimate because they support both the ruler's public office and the dignity of the ruler's elevated status:

> Lastly, I also wish to add this, that tributes and taxes are the lawful revenues of princes, which they may chiefly use to meet the public expenses of their office; yet they may similarly use them for the magnificence of their household, which is joined, so to speak, with the dignity of the authority they exercise.[203]

That Calvin should highlight the dignity of the authority that rulers *exercise* among the uses to which tax revenue should be put, conforms to the political theology outline above. Taxes are part of the suture of being and praxis. They link what has been torn apart: the obedience of the people and the majesty of the ruler. That majesty, like God's "providential" majesty, subsists precisely in the exercise of the rulers' authority.

But the analogy between God and ruler requires that rulers rule—reign and govern—justly, with mercy, and with the best interests of their subjects at heart. In the same passage of the *Institutes*, Calvin reminded rulers that taxes are "not so much their private chests as the treasuries of the entire people . . ., which cannot be squandered or despoiled without manifest injustice."[204] Tax revenue is "almost the very blood of the people, which it would be the harshest inhumanity not to spare."[205] "Moreover, let [the princes] consider," he continued, "that their imposts and levies, and other kinds of tributes are nothing but supports of public necessity; but that to impose them upon the common folk without cause is tyrannical extortion."[206]

Each of Calvin's perspectives qualifies the others and is "burdened" by them. The perspectives influence each other, even modifying each other in a way that seems foreign to Luther's thinking. The Christian's duty to respect magistrates, for instance, is the very thing that should give the magistrates comfort in the midst of their difficulties and diligence lest they admit injustice into their rulings.[207]

At the same time, Calvin's justice-as-balance carries with it normative force but without recourse to the practical difficulties inherent in a solution that assumes static values. In Aquinas' scheme, distributive justice requires a balancing of the dictates of natural law (communal property) and the benefits of positive law (private property). How the two goods should balance each other optimally is not altogether clear on a practical level. The optimal balance depends on one person's necessities and another's superabundance, which are difficult if not impossible to measure. Justice, therefore, must remain first and foremost the ruler's exercise of judgment for Aquinas.[208] Calvin, on the other hand, freed the process of justice from the impossible task of finding an exact balance, "no precise and vivid statement of which is given by any law."[209] The process of balancing, rather than the goal of balancing, is justice.

God, according to Calvin, sets the parameters of the conversation about redistribution of resources. It is God who ordains inequality and God who commands that it be alleviated, God who ensures that it will not be fully alleviated so that the interplay between God's ordaining and commanding may continue, God who appoints rulers and God who gives all things to everyone in common. Calvin's "tax policy" is a continuous response to the circumstances set by God and the amendments to them demanded by God.

Notes

1 William C. Innes, *Social Concern in Calvin's Geneva*, ed. Susan Cembalisty-Innes (Eugene, OR: Pickwick Publications, 1983), 180; Matthew J. Tuininga, *Calvin's Political Theology and the Public Engagement of the Church: Christ's Two Kingdoms* (Cambridge: Cambridge University Press, 2017), 62.

2 William Monter, *Calvin's Geneva* (Eugene, OR: Wipf and Stock Publishers, 1967), 156.

3 The *Petit Conseil* was Geneva's senate. In 1540, it consisted of four Syndics and twenty-one Conseillers. See William G. Naphy, *Calvin and the Consolidation of the Genevan Reformation* (Louisville: Westminster John Knox Press, 1994), 38.

4 Innes, *Social Concern in Calvin's Geneva*, 180; Monter, *Calvin's Geneva*, 157–58.
5 Robert M. Kingdon, "Social Welfare in Calvin's Geneva," *The American Historical Review* 76, no. 1 (February 1971): 64.
6 Graham Tomlin, "The Reformation and the Future of Europe," in *The Protestant Reformation of the Church and the World*, ed. John Witte Jr. and Amy Wheeler (Louisville: Westminster John Knox Press, 2018), 199.
7 Tomlin, "The Reformation and the Future of Europe," 199.
8 Kingdon, "Social Welfare in Calvin's Geneva," 52.
9 Monter, *Calvin's Geneva*, 156.
10 Kingdon, "Social Welfare in Calvin's Geneva," 55.
11 Kingdon, "Social Welfare in Calvin's Geneva," 55; Tomlin, "The Reformation and the Future of Europe," 198.
12 Kingdon, "Social Welfare in Calvin's Geneva," 55–56.
13 Kingdon, "Social Welfare in Calvin's Geneva," 57. Kingdon considers it somewhat surprising that the members of Geneva's power structure were willing to take on the duties of *procureur*, which consisted of attending a weekly meeting on Sunday mornings at 6:00 a.m., deciding on every proposal from the *hospitallier* for expenditures and every single application from poor families for a weekly ration of bread, caring for the properties now in the hands of the hospital, collecting rents associated with those properties, making cash loans of superfluous funds, approving contracts, legacies, and other legal instruments, arranging for apprenticeships and approving marriages of people in the care of the hospital, recommending staff appointments to the *Petit Conseil*, and—above all—begging "repeatedly, for supplementary grants of cash to finance adequately all the social programs sponsored by the Hospital." Kingdon, "Social Welfare in Calvin's Geneva," 58.
14 The last two of the five hospitals to be created, in 1434 and 1452, respectively, had lay rectors. A municipal foundation called the Box for All Souls in Purgatory was also created in 1452. Although it was initially designed to collect money to pay for masses for the dead, it quickly became a funding mechanism for three of the hospitals, for the placement of orphans in homes, and for arranging for the burial of the dead. It was controlled by laymen. Kingdon, "Social Welfare in Calvin's Geneva," 55.
15 Kingdon, "Social Welfare in Calvin's Geneva," 68.
16 Kingdon, "Social Welfare in Calvin's Geneva," 66.
17 Kingdon believes that there may be some truth to the argument "that when it came to deciding how the Christian community should institutionalize its obligation to help the poor, it was not Calvin who influenced Geneva, but rather Geneva that influenced Calvin." Kingdon, "Social Welfare in Calvin's Geneva," 61.
18 Kingdon, "Social Welfare in Calvin's Geneva," 64.
19 Wulfert de Greef, *The Writings of John Calvin: An Introductory Guide*, expanded ed. (Louisville: Westminster John Knox Press, 2008), 82–83, quoted in Carter Lindberg, "'There Will Be No Poor among You': The Reformation of Charity and Social Welfare," in Witte and Wheeler, 148–49.
20 Tuininga, *Calvin's Political Theology*, 58.
21 Tuininga, *Calvin's Political Theology*, 65–66.
22 Tuininga, *Calvin's Political Theology*, 60. "Caesaropapism," the political model originally expounded by Marsilius of Padua in the fourteenth century, held that the secular authorities possessed exclusive authority in temporal matters and ultimate authority in matters of church doctrine—"a model most famously embodied in Henry VIII's claim to the royal supremacy in the Church of

England." Tuininga, *Calvin's Political Theology*, 29. The Zurich model, which originated with Huldrych Zwingli and solidified by his successor Heinrich Bullinger, reflected a typically Swiss "commitment to the unity and integrity of the Christian commonwealth." The church did not submit to civil government as such. Rather, "the civil government was the authoritative body *within* the church." Tuininga, *Calvin's Political Theology*, 41–43 (italics in the original). By 1528, Lutherans were complaining that Zwingli had conflated the two kingdoms. Zwingli, in response, accused Luther of adopting the Anabaptist position and indirectly bringing about disorder in Germany by banishing the kingdom of Christ from this world. Tuininga, *Calvin's Political Theology*, 44–45. Tuininga points out the irony that, in the final analysis, the views of Luther and Zwingli were quite similar in their practical effects, both emphasizing "the importance of the inward, spiritual realm, while leaving the outward order of the church largely to the magistrates." Tuininga, *Calvin's Political Theology*, 46.

23 Tuininga, *Calvin's Political Theology*, 225.
24 Tuininga, *Calvin's Political Theology*, 227.
25 Kingdon, "Social Welfare in Calvin's Geneva," 60; Tomlin, "The Reformation and the Future of Europe," 198.
26 John Calvin, *Institutes of the Christian Religion*, trans. Ford Lewis Battles, ed. John T. McNeill (Philadelphia: The Westminster Press, 1960), 4.3.9.
27 Calvin, *Institutes* 4.3.9.
28 Tomlin, "The Reformation and the Future of Europe," 198.
29 Tuininga, *Calvin's Political Theology*, 77.
30 Calvin, *Institutes* 4.4.6.
31 Elsie Anne McKee, *Elders and the Plural Ministry: The Role of Exegetical History in Illuminating John Calvin's Theology* (Geneva: Librairie Droz, 1988), 190.
32 Tuininga, *Calvin's Political Theology*, 69.
33 Paul's list of gifts refers in verse 8 to the one who exhorts, gives, *rules*, or shows mercy (KJV).
34 Calvin, *Institutes* (1536) 4.20.4.
35 Calvin, *Institutes* (1539) 4.20.4.
36 Tuininga, *Calvin's Political Theology*, 67.
37 John Calvin, *Commentarius in epistolam ad Galatas*, vol. 50, *Ioannis Calvini opera quae supersunt omnia*, ed. Edouard Cunitz, Johann-Wilhelm Baum, and Eduard Wilhelm Eugen (Braunschweig: C.A. Schwetschke, 1882), 186–87. *Ioannis Calvini opera quae sunt supersunt omnia* is referred to hereafter as *CO*. See Tuininga, *Calvin's Political Theology*, 158–59.
38 Calvin, *Institutes* (1539) 4.20.1 (1536).
39 John Calvin, *Commentarii in librum psalmorum pars prior: Ps. I ad XC*, *CO* 31:618 (on Ps. 67:3). See Tuininga, *Calvin's Political Theology*, 276.
40 Tuininga, *Calvin's Political Theology*, 183.
41 Tuininga, *Calvin's Political Theology*, 185.
42 Calvin, *Institutes* 4.20.2 (1536).
43 Calvin, *Institutes* 4.20.2 (1536).
44 Calvin, *Institutes* 4.20.2 (1559).
45 See Tuininga, *Calvin's Political Theology*, 251.
46 Calvin, *Institutes* 4.20.9 (1559). Even in the 1536 edition of the *Institutes*, Calvin acknowledged the tension in his theology between putting religion "outside of human decision" and his committing "to civil government the duty of rightly establishing religion." He resolved the tension by highlighting the more negative role of civil government: the political authorities are tasked with defending religion once it is established, i.e., with preventing "the true religion which is contained in God's law from being openly and with pub-

lic sacrilege violated and defiled with impunity." The civil authorities are not tasked with making—and, in fact, must not make—"laws according to their own decision concerning religion and the worship of God." Calvin, *Institutes* 4.20.3.

47 Calvin, *Institutes* 4.20.9 (1559).

48 Tuininga, *Calvin's Political Theology*, 314, quoting Calvin, *Praelectionum in Ieremiam prophetam pars altera cap. VIII–XXXI, CO* 38:220 (on Jer. 19:1–3).

49 Tuininga, *Calvin's Political Theology*, 70.

50 Tuininga, *Calvin's Political Theology*, 74.

51 Eva-Maria Faber, "Mutual Connectedness as a Gift and a Task: On John Calvin's Understanding of the Church," trans. David Dichelle, in *John Calvin's Impact on Church and Society, 1509–2009*, ed. Martin Ernst Hirzel and Martin Sallman (Grand Rapids: Eerdmans Publishing Co., 2009), 128.

52 Faber, "Mutual Connectedness as a Gift and a Task," referring to John Calvin, *Commentarius in epistolam ad Corinthos, CO* 49:302.

53 Calvin, *Institutes* 4.20.2 (1536).

54 Calvin, *Institutes* 4.20.2 (1536).

55 Calvin, *Institutes* 4.20.3 (1536).

56 Calvin, *Institutes* 4.20.3 (1536).

57 Calvin, *Institutes* 4.20.9 (1536).

58 Calvin, *Institutes* 4.20.3 (1536). André Biéler summarizes the role of the civil government vis-à-vis the church in Calvin's theology bluntly: "[T]he church is not spiritual enough to dispense with the political order." André Biéler, *Calvin's Economic and Social Thought*, ed. Edward Dommen, trans. James Greig (Geneva: World Alliance of Reformed Churches, 2005), 311.

59 Tuininga, *Calvin's Political Theology*, 127.

60 Tuininga, *Calvin's Political Theology*, 127, quoting Calvin, *Commentarius in harmoniam evangelicam* (1555), *CO* 45:136 (on Mt. 4:10), and Calvin, *Praelectionum in Ieremiam prophetam pars altera cap. VIII–XXXI* (1563), *CO* 38:411 (on Jer. 23:5–6).

61 Tuininga, *Calvin's Political Theology*, 127n176, referring to Calvin, *Commentarius in harmoniam evangelicam* (1555), *CO* 45:161–62.

62 William R. Stevenson, Jr., *Sovereign Grace: The Place and Significance of Christian Freedom in John Calvin's Political Thought* (New York: Oxford University Press, 1999), 27.

63 Inequality, of course, has many dimensions. The term can refer to economic inequality (income and wealth disparity), social inequality (difference among social statuses), or political inequality (differentiated capacity among groups and individuals to participate in and benefit from decision-making processes), to name just three. International Social Science Council, Institution of Development Studies, and United Nations Educational, Scientific and Cultural Organization (UNESCO), *World Social Science Report 2016: Challenging Inequalities: Pathways to a Just World*, accessed July 6, 2020, http://unesdoc.unesco.org/images/0024/002458/245825e.pdf. This discussion focuses on economic inequality, as wealth and income disparity tends to be the dimension of inequality most often identified as a challenge or even threat to economies and businesses. However, instances of economic inequality typically implicate some or all of the other dimensions of inequality as well.

64 John Calvin, *Commentaries on the Four Last Books of Moses, Arranged in the Form of a Harmony* (Edinburgh: Calvin Translation Society, 1854), 3:127; John Calvin, *Mosis reliqui libri quatuor in formam harmoniae, digesti a Ioanne Calvino: cum eiusdem commentariis, CO* 24:680.

65 John Calvin, *Sermons sur le Deuteronomie: IV, CO* 28:205 (my translation).

66 Calvin, *Commentarius in harmoniam evangelicam*, *CO* 45:689 (on Mt. 25:40). The translation is from Biéler, *Calvin's Economic and Social Thought*, 288.
67 John Calvin, *Commentary on the Epistles of Paul the Apostle to the Corinthians*, trans. John Pringle (Edinburgh: Calvin Translation Society, 1849), 2:294.
68 John Calvin, *Praelectionum in duodecim prophetas minores*, *CO* 43:542 (on Hab. 2:6). The translation is from Biéler, *Calvin's Economic and Social Thought*, 275.
69 John Calvin, *Commentarius in epistolam posteriorem ad Corinthos*, *CO* 50:102 (on 2 Cor. 8:15) (my translation).
70 Calvin, *Commentary on Corinthians*, 2:294 (emphasis in the original).
71 Calvin, *Commentary on Corinthians*, 2:296.
72 Calvin, *Commentary on Corinthians*, 2:295–96.
73 Calvin, *Commentarius in epistolam posteriorem ad Corinthos*, *CO* 50:101 (my translation).
74 Calvin, *Commentary on Corinthians*, 2:294.
75 John Calvin, "Against the Fantastic and Furious Sect of the Libertines Who Are Called 'Spirituals,'" in *Treatises Against the Anabaptists and Against the Libertines*, ed. and trans. Benjamin Wirt Farley (Grand Rapids: Baker Academic, 1982), 282, 285, 290.
76 Calvin, "Against the Fantastic and Furious Sect," 285.
77 Calvin, "Against the Fantastic and Furious Sect," 286.
78 John Calvin, *Commentaries on the Epistles of Paul to the Philippians, Colossians, and Thessalonians*, ed. and trans. John Pringle, in the Christian Classics Ethereal Library, accessed July 6, 2020, https://www.ccel.org/ccel/calvin/calcom42.vii.v.i.html (on 2 Thes. 3:1–5). The "second law of equity" is "that no one swallow up, like some abyss, what belongs to him, but that he be beneficent to neighbors, and that he may relieve their indigence by this abundance."
   John McNeill notes the irony that "Luther and Melancthon, who were not trained in law, used the technical language and made equity a 'mitigation' of the *summum ius*, the limit of the law, while Calvin, the trained lawyer, avoided a definition of the term and gave it a sense virtually as inclusive as that of natural law itself." John T. McNeill, introduction to *Calvin on God and Political Duty*, 2nd ed. (Indianapolis: Bobbs-Merrill Educational Publishing, 1956), xvi.
79 Calvin, "Against the Fantastic and Furious Sect," 290.
80 Biéler, *Calvin's Economic and Social Thought*, 336.
81 Biéler, *Calvin's Economic and Social Thought*, 309.
82 Biéler, *Calvin's Economic and Social Thought*, 312, 344.
83 Calvin, *Mosis reliqui libri quatuor*, *CO* 24:697–98 (on Dt. 15:1). The translation is from Biéler, *Calvin's Economic and Social Thought*, 336.
84 Carter Lindberg, *Beyond Charity: Reformation Initiatives for the Poor* (Minneapolis: Fortress Press, 1993), 106. See also Jacques Le Goff, *Money and the Middle Ages: An Essay in Historical Anthropology*, trans. Jean Birrell (Cambridge: Polity Press, 2012), 20–21, 144, 145.
85 See Biéler, *Calvin's Economic and Social Thought*, 285.
86 Calvin, *Sermons sur le Deuteronomie: IV*, *CO* 28:199.
87 Calvin, *Sermons sur le Deuteronomie: IV*, *CO* 28:202.
88 Calvin, *Sermons sur le Deuteronomie: IV*, *CO* 28:199, 203–204.
89 Calvin, *Sermons sur le Deuteronomie: IV*, *CO* 28:203–204.
90 Calvin, *Sermons sur le Deuteronomie: IV*, *CO* 28:204–205.
91 John Calvin, *Commentarius in acta Apostolorum*, *CO* 48:265.
92 Biéler, *Calvin's Economic and Social Thought*, 285.
93 John Calvin, *Sermons sur l'Harmonie des Trois Evangelistes, S. Matthieu, S. Luc et S. Marc*, *CO* 46:632. The translation is from Biéler, *Calvin's Economic and

Social Thought, 288. Regarding taxation itself, Calvin was not as bothered by the steeply regressive nature of single-sum poll taxes as Luther is. Calvin even saw a redemptive message in the flat-sum offering that became the "temple 'poll tax'":

> [God] appointed the same sum for all [*Parem vero summam omnibus indixit*], that every one, of whatever rank, from the least, to the greatest, might know that they were altogether his. Nor need we wonder, that since this was a personal due, (as it was commonly phrased,) their condition was not taken into account, so that the rich should pay more than the poor, but that the same price should be paid per head.

Calvin, *Mosis reliqui libri quatuor*, *CO* 24:302. The translation is from Biéler, *Calvin's Economic and Social Thought*, 317.

94 See Biéler, *Calvin's Economic and Social Thought*, 287.
95 Calvin, *Sermons sur l'Harmonie des Trois Evangelistes*, *CO* 46:551 (on Mt. 3:9f). The translation is from Biéler, *Calvin's Economic and Social Thought*, 277.
96 Calvin, *Sermons sur le Deuteronomie: IV*, *CO* 28:199. The translation is from Biéler, *Calvin's Economic and Social Thought*, 284.
97 Biéler, *Calvin's Economic and Social Thought*, 287.
98 See Biéler, *Calvin's Economic and Social Thought*, 269.
99 Tuininga, *Calvin's Political Theology*, 68. See also Tuininga, *Calvin's Political Theology*, 226:

> Poor relief, likewise, is not simply something that Christians should do. It is a *sine qua non*, part of the fundamental order of the church itself.... Acts 6 teaches that although the preaching of the gospel is of the utmost importance, the cause of the poor is sufficiently important that it requires a perpetual office in Christ's spiritual government.

100 Tuininga, *Calvin's Political Theology*, 16, 18.
101 Tuininga, *Calvin's Political Theology*, 93–94.
102 Matthew J. Pereira, "Augustine and Social Justice in Calvin's Biblical Commentaries," in *Augustine and Social Justice*, ed. Teresa Delgado, John Doody, and Kim Paffenroth (Lanham, MD: Lexington Books, 2015), 230.
103 Tuininga, *Calvin's Political Theology*, 113.
104 Tuininga, *Calvin's Political Theology*, 120.
105 Giorgio Agamben, *The Kingdom and the Glory: For a Theological Genealogy of Economy and Government (*Homo Sacer *II, 2)*, trans. Lorenzo Chiesa and Matteo Mandarini (Stanford: Stanford University Press, 2011), 163.
106 Agamben, *The Kingdom and the Glory*, 160.
107 Agamben, *The Kingdom and the Glory*, 285.
108 Agamben, *The Kingdom and the Glory*, 107–108. See Chapter Four.
109 Calvin, *Institutes* 1.13.6 (1559).
110 Calvin, *Institutes* 1.13.28 (1559).
111 John T. McNeill, notes to *Institutes* 1.13.6, 128n23, and 1.13.28, 157n61.
112 Calvin, *Institutes* 1.12.2 (1550).
113 Calvin, *Institutes* 1.12.3 (1550).
114 Calvin, *Institutes* 1.12.1.
115 Calvin, *Institutes* 1.13.23.
116 Calvin, *Institutes* 1.13.18.
117 Calvin, *Institutes* 1.13.18.
118 Calvin, *Institutes* 1.13.12.
119 Calvin, *Institutes* 1.13.14.

120 David B. Calhoun, *Knowing God and Ourselves: Reading Calvin's* Institutes *Devotionally* (Edinburgh: The Banner of Truth Trust, 2016), 47. Calhoun writes:

> Any hint of causality or subordination latent in the Nicene terms of "begetting" (the "Lord Jesus Christ, the only-begotten Son of God, begotten of his Father before all worlds") and "proceeding" ("the Holy Spirit ... who proceeds from the Father and the Son") must be rejected—not the words themselves, but an unbiblical interpretation of these words. Calvin will not allow any sense of derived deity for the Son and the Spirit—the idea that the Father, who alone is truly and properly God, poured his own deity into the Son and the Spirit. Whatever the Father is as God, that the Son is as God, and that the Holy Spirit is as God. The deity of the Son and Spirit is not derived from the person (*hypostasis*) of the Father but from the being or essence (*ousia*) of the Godhead. The Son is not God because of the Father but the Son is the Son because of the Father.

121 Calvin, *Institutes* 1.13.8.
122 Calvin, *Institutes* 1.13.12.
123 Tuininga, *Calvin's Political Theology*, 263.
124 Tuininga, *Calvin's Political Theology*, 191. Tuininga writes: "In other words, like the ministry of the word, the power of church discipline is neither magisterial nor discretionary, but ministerial. It is bound up entirely with the word. There is no spiritual power of excommunication attached to the church itself, or to any ecclesiastical office." Tuininga, *Calvin's Political Theology*, 213.
125 Tuininga, *Calvin's Political Theology*, 215.
126 Tuininga, *Calvin's Political Theology*, 193–94.
127 Tuininga, *Calvin's Political Theology*, 199.
128 Calvin, *Commentarius in harmoniam evangelicam*, *CO* 45:314 (on Luke 10:16), quoted in Tuininga, *Calvin's Political Theology*, 198.
129 Tuininga, *Calvin's Political Theology*, 192.
130 Tuininga, *Calvin's Political Theology*, 192, 195, 198, 204. See Calvin, *Praelectionum in Ieremiam prophetam pars prior cap. I–VII*, *CO* 37:479–83 (on Jer. 1:9).
131 Tuininga, *Calvin's Political Theology*, 186, referring to Calvin, *Praelectiones in Ezechielis prophetae viginti capita priora*, *CO* 40:90–91.
132 John Calvin, *Commentarius in epistolam Pauli ad Ephesios*, *CO* 51:196–97 (on Eph. 4:10). See Tuininga, *Calvin's Political Theology*, 193.
133 Tuininga, *Calvin's Political Theology*, 193.
134 Calvin, *Commentarius in epistolam Pauli ad Ephesios*, *CO* 51:193–94 (on Eph. 4:8). See Tuininga, *Calvin's Political Theology*, 193.
135 Calvin, *Commentarius in epistolam Pauli ad Ephesios*, *CO* 51:196–97 (on Eph. 4:11).
136 Calvin, *Commentarius in epistolam Pauli ad Ephesios*, *CO* 51:192 (on Eph. 4:6). See Tuininga, *Calvin's Political Theology*, 193.
137 Calvin, *Institutes* 1.16.1.
138 Calvin, *Institutes* 1.16.4.
139 Calvin, *Institutes* 1.16.2.
140 Calvin, *Institutes* 1.16.7.
141 Calvin, *Institutes* 1.18.1.
142 Agamben, *The Kingdom and the Glory*, 140.
143 Agamben, *The Kingdom and the Glory*, 94.
144 Agamben, *The Kingdom and the Glory*, 94.
145 See Calvin, *Institutes* 1.17.9.
146 Calvin, *Institutes* 1.16.7.
147 Calvin, *Institutes* 1.16.5.

148 Calvin, *Institutes* 1.16.4.
149 Calvin, *Institutes* 1.16.3.
150 Calvin, *Institutes* 1.16.4.
151 John Calvin, *Commentariorum in quinque libros Mosis*, *CO* 23:52 (on Jer. 9:24).
152 Calhoun, *Knowing God and Ourselves*, 69.
153 Calhoun, *Knowing God and Ourselves*, 69.
154 Calvin, *Institutes* 1.16.3.
155 Calvin, *Institutes* 1.17.2.
156 Calvin, *Institutes* 1.17.2.
157 Calvin, *Institutes* 1.17.2.
158 Agamben, *The Kingdom and the Glory*, 89, 140.
159 Agamben, *The Kingdom and the Glory*, 239.
160 Calvin, *Institutes* 1.17.2.
161 Calvin, *Institutes* 1.17.1.
162 See Agamben, *The Kingdom and the Glory*, 256.
163 Calvin, *Institutes* 1.17.1.
164 Calvin, *Institutes* 1.17.1.
165 Calvin, *Institutes* 1.17.2.
166 Calvin, *Institutes* 1.16.3.
167 Calvin, *Sermons sur l'Harmonie des Trois Evangelistes*, *CO* 46:551 (on Mt. 3:9f). The translation is from Biéler, *Calvin's Economic and Social Thought*, 299.
168 John Calvin, *Commentarius in epistolam Iacobi*, *CO* 55:423 (on Jam. 5:2). The translation is from Biéler, *Calvin's Economic and Social Thought*, 299.
169 John Calvin, *Commentarius in harmoniam evangelicam*, *CO* 45:569. The translation is from Biéler, *Calvin's Economic and Social Thought*, 206. Biéler writes that, for Calvin, "[c]ommerce is a natural and social bond constitutive of society." Biéler, *Calvin's Economic and Social Thought*, 206.
170 Calvin, *Commentarius in harmoniam evangel*, *Sermons sur l'Harmonie des Trois Evangelistes*, *CO* 46:551 (on Mt. 3:9f). The translation is from Biéler, *Calvin's Economic and Social Thought*, 299.

John Calvin, *Commentarius in epistolam Iacobi*, *CO* 55:423 (on Jam. 5:2). The translation is from Biéler, *Calvin's Economic and Social Thought*, 299.

John Calvin, *Commentarius in harmoniam evangelicam*, *CO* 45:569. The translation is from Biéler, *Calvin's Economic and Social Thought*, 206.

171 Biéler, *Calvin's Economic and Social Thought*, 295.
172 Biéler, *Calvin's Economic and Social Thought*, 295 (Biéler's words).
173 Calvin, *Mosis reliqui libri quatuor*, *CO* 24:675–76 (on Lev. 19:35). The translation is from Biéler, *Calvin's Economic and Social Thought*, 339.
174 Biéler, *Calvin's Economic and Social Thought*, 295.
175 Linda Sugin, "Theories of Distributive Justice and Limitations on Taxation: What Rawls Demands from Tax Systems," *Fordham Law Review* 72, no. 5 (2004): 2013–14.
176 Calvin, *Institutes* 4.20.8.
177 In fact, Calvin was unwilling to opine on whether inequality would even be eradicated in heaven. In his Commentary on Matthew, he wrote:

> It is also worthy of our notice, that these words do not imply that there will be equality among the children of God, after they have been admitted to the heavenly glory, but rather that to each is promised the degree of honor to which he has been set apart by the eternal purpose of God.

Calvin, *Commentarius in harmoniam evangelicam*, *CO* 45:555 (on Mt. 20:23), quoted in Tuininga, *Calvin's Political Theology*, 158n71.

178 Calvin, *Commentarius in epistolam ad Corinthos*, *CO* 49:365–66, quoted in Tuininga, *Calvin's Political Theology*, 109.

179 Agamben, *The Kingdom and the Glory*, 140.
180 Calvin, *Institutes* 1.16.9.
181 Tuininga, *Calvin's Political Theology*, 169.
182 Horton Davies, *The Vigilant God: Providence in the Thought of Augustine, Aquinas, Calvin, and Barth*, 2nd ed. (New York: Peter Lang Publishing, 2018), 2.
183 Calvin, *Institutes* 1.18.4.
184 Calvin, *Institutes* 1.17.5.
185 Agamben, *The Kingdom and the Glory*, 162.
186 John Calvin, *Commentarius in epistolam Pauli ad Romanos*, *CO* 49:252 (my translation).
187 Calvin, *Commentarius in epistolam Pauli ad Romanos*, *CO* 49:252. See also Calvin's commentary on Exodus 22, where he also made the point that a "political law" could depend "on the rule of charity." Calvin, *Commentaries on the Four Last Books of Moses*, 127.
188 Calvin, *Commentarius in epistolam Pauli ad Romanos*, *CO* 49:252.
189 John Calvin, *Commentary on a Harmony of the Evangelists, Matthew, Mark, and Luke*, trans. William Pringle (Edinburgh: The Calvin Translation Society, 1846), 43–44 (on Mt. 22:19) (emphasis in original).
190 Calvin, *Commentary on a Harmony of the Evangelists*, 44 (on Mt. 22:21).
191 Donald W. Shriver and E. Richard Knox, "Taxation in the History of Protestant Ethics," *The Journal of Religious Ethics* 13, no. 1 (Spring 1985): 138.
192 Biéler, *Calvin's Economic and Social Thought*, 305.
193 See, e.g., John Calvin, *Praelectionum in duodecim prophetas minores*, *CO* 43:24 (on Amos 2:6).
194 See Calvin, *Institutes* 4.20.3 (Civil government "provides that each man may keep his property safe and sound").
195 Biéler, *Calvin's Economic and Social Thought*, 334.
196 Biéler, *Calvin's Economic and Social Thought*, 337.
197 See, e.g., Calvin, *Commentariorum in quinque libros Mosis*, *CO* 23:523 (on Gen. 41:35).
198 Tuininga, *Calvin's Political Theology*, 150–51, referring to John Calvin, *Praelectionum in Danielem prophetam*, *CO* 40:711–13 (on Dan. 5:18–20).
199 Calvin, *Institutes* 4.20.9.
200 Calvin, *Institutes* 4.20.2.
201 See Calvin, *Institutes* 4.20.15.
202 Karl Barth, *The Theology of John Calvin*, trans. Geoffrey W. Bromiley (Grand Rapids: William B. Eerdmans Publishing Co., 1995), 214.
203 Calvin, *Institutes* 4.20.13.
204 Calvin, *Institutes* 4.20.13.
205 Calvin, *Institutes* 4.20.13. See also Calvin, *Commentarius in epistolam Pauli ad Romanos*, *CO* 49:252, where Calvin wrote that it was not his place to prescribe to the rulers how much they should expend, but that it is right for him to remind them that whatever they do have from the people is common property.
206 Calvin, *Institutes* 4.20.13.
207 Calvin, *Institutes* 4.20.6. The difference in tone between Luther and Calvin seems to be the source of Karl Barth's statement that "Calvin wanted to avoid" Luther's "frenetic need to assure us that paying taxes, governing, and waging war are works of love," and that he avoided Luther's excesses by "quietly drop[ping] the word 'love'" in favor of the "more restrained term" equity. Barth, *Theology of John Calvin*, 215.
208 Thomas Aquinas, *Summa theologiae* (Latin-English Edition), trans. Fathers of the English-Dominican Province (NovAntiqua, 2013), II–II, Q. 60, Art. 1, ad. 4.

209 Biéler, *Calvin's Economic and Social Thought*, 344. Biéler argues that Calvin differed from his predecessors in his disinterest in deriving a law of property from natural law or a natural ethic that was supposed to express divine order. Positive law provides a "distant picture" of divine order, but ethical standards come only from "clear awareness of … personal responsibility towards the living God, incarnate in Jesus Christ." Biéler *Calvin's Economic and Social Thought*, 342.

References

Agamben, Giorgio. 2011. *The Kingdom and the Glory: For a Theological Genealogy of Economy and Government* (Homo Sacer *II, 2*). Translated by Lorenzo Chiesa and Matteo Mandarini. Stanford: Stanford University Press.

Barth, Karl. 1995. *The Theology of John Calvin*. Translated by Geoffrey W. Bromiley. Grand Rapids: William B. Eerdmans Publishing Co.

Biéler, André. 2005. *Calvin's Economic and Social Thought*. Edited by Edward Dommen. Translated by James Greig. Geneva: World Alliance of Reformed Churches.

Calhoun, David B. 2016. *Knowing God and Ourselves: Reading Calvin's Institutes Devotionally*. Edinburgh: The Banner of Truth Trust.

Calvin, John. 1846. *Commentary on a Harmony of the Evangelists, Matthew, Mark, and Luke*. Translated by William Pringle. Edinburgh: The Calvin Translation Society.

______. 1849. *Commentary on the Epistles of Paul the Apostle to the Corinthians*. Translated by John Pringle. Edinburgh: Calvin Translation Society.

______. 1854. *Commentaries on the Four Last Books of Moses, Arranged in the Form of a Harmony*. Edinburgh: Calvin Translation Society.

______. 1863–1900. *Ioannis Calvini opera quae supersunt omnia*. Edited by Edouard Cunitz, Johann-Wilhelm Baum, and Eduard Wilhelm Eugen, vol. 58. Braunschweig: C.A. Schwetschke. Accessed July 4, 2020. https://archive-ouverte.unige.ch/unige:650.

______. 1956. *Calvin on God and Political Duty*. Edited by John T. McNeill. 2nd ed. Indianapolis: Bobbs-Merrill Educational Publishing.

______. 1960. *Institutes of the Christian Religion*. Translated by Ford Lewis Battles. Edited by John T. McNeill, vol. 2. Philadelphia: The Westminster Press.

______. 1982. "Against the Fantastic and Furious Sect of the Libertines Who Are Called 'Spirituals.'" In *Treatises Against the Anabaptists and Against the Libertines*, edited and translated by Benjamin Wirt Farley. Grand Rapids: Baker Academic.

______. n.d.a. *Commentaries on the Epistles of Paul to the Galatians and Ephesians*. Translated by William Pringle. Grand Rapids: Christian Classics Ethereal Library. Accessed July 4, 2020. https://ccel.org/ccel/c/calvin/calcom41/cache/calcom41.pdf.

______. n.d.b. *Commentaries on the Epistles of Paul to the Philippians, Colossians, and Thessalonians*. Edited and translated by John Pringle. Christian Classics Ethereal Library. Accessed September 12, 2018. https://www.ccel.org/ccel/calvin/calcom42.titlepage.html?highlight=calvin,thessalonians#highlight.

Davies, Horton. 2018. *The Vigilant God: Providence in the Thought of Augustine, Aquinas, Calvin, and Barth*. 2nd ed. New York: Peter Lang Publishing.

Faber, Eva-Maria. 2009. "Mutual Connectedness as a Gift and a Task: On John Calvin's Understanding of the Church." In *John Calvin's Impact on Church and Society, 1509–2009*, edited by Martin Ernst Hirzel and Martin Sallman, translated by David Dichelle 122–44. Grand Rapids: Eerdmans Publishing Co.

Greef, Wulfert de. 2008. *The Writings of John Calvin: An Introductory Guide.* Expanded ed. Louisville: Westminster John Knox Press.

Innes, William C. 1983. *Social Concern in Calvin's Geneva.* Edited by Susan Cembalisty-Innes. Eugene, OR: Pickwick Publications.

International Social Science Council, Institution of Development Studies, and UNESCO (United Nations Educational, Scientific and Cultural Organization). 2016 *World Social Science Report 2016: Challenging Inequalities: Pathways to a Just World.* Accessed July 6, 2020. http://unesdoc.unesco.org/images/0024/002458/245825e.pdf.

Kingdon, Robert M. 1971. "Social Welfare in Calvin's Geneva." *The American Historical Review* 76, no. 1 (February): 50–69.

Le Goff, Jacques. 2012. *Money and the Middle Ages: An Essay in Historical Anthropology.* Translated by Jean Birrell. Cambridge: Polity Press.

Lindberg, Carter. 1993. *Beyond Charity: Reformation Initiatives for the Poor.* Minneapolis: Fortress Press.

______. 2018. "'There Will Be No Poor Among You': The Reformation of Charity and Social Welfare." In Witte and Wheeler, 139–58.

McKee, Elsie Anne. 1988. *Elders and the Plural Ministry: The Role of Exegetical History in Illuminating John Calvin's Theology.* Geneva: Librairie Droz.

Monter, William. 1967. *Calvin's Geneva.* Eugene, OR: Wipf and Stock.

Naphy, William G. 1994. *Calvin and the Consolidation of the Genevan Reformation.* Louisville: Westminster John Knox Press.

Pereira, Matthew J. 2015. "Augustine and Social Justice in Calvin's Biblical Commentaries." In *Augustine and Social Justice*, edited by Teresa Delgado, John Doody, and Kim Paffenroth, 227–49. Lanham, MD: Lexington Books.

Shriver, Donald W., Jr., and E. Richard Knox. 1985. "Taxation in the History of Protestant Ethics." *The Journal of Religious Ethics* 13, no. 1 (Spring): 134–60.

Stevenson, William R., Jr. 1999. *Sovereign Grace: The Place and Significance of Christian Freedom in John Calvin's Political Thought.* New York: Oxford University Press.

Sugin, Linda. 2004. "Theories of Distributive Justice and Limitations on Taxation: What Rawls Demands from Tax Systems." *Fordham Law Review* 72, no. 5: 1991–2014.

Thomas Aquinas. 2013. *Summa Theologiae* (Latin-English Edition). Translated by the Fathers of the English-Dominican Province. NovAntiqua.

Tomlin, Graham. 2018. "The Reformation and the Future of Europe." In *The Protestant Reformation of the Church and the World*, edited by John Witte, Jr., and Amy Wheeler, 191–207. Louisville: Westminster John Knox Press.

Tuininga, Matthew J. 2017. *Calvin's Political Theology and the Public Engagement of the Church: Christ's Two Kingdoms.* Cambridge: Cambridge University Press.

Witte, John, Jr., and Amy Wheeler, eds. 2018. *The Protestant Reformation of the Church and the World.* Louisville: Westminster John Knox Press.

Wolin, Sheldon S. 1960. *Politics and Vision: Continuity and Innovation in Western Political Thought.* Boston: Little, Brown and Co.

7 Triumph of the economy

Introduction

The story of theological reflection on taxation does not end with Calvin. John Knox "insisted that every parish" in Scotland "make available some portion of the Teinds to support the poor."[1] Almost two centuries later, "John Wesley criticized English tax policy, appealing to standards of economic efficiency and compassion for the poor."[2] However, that history is not the focus of this concluding chapter. Rather, the story here turns to the inversion of Calvin's theology of providence and its counterpart in the realm of civil government. After the sixteenth century, I argue, political philosophy and theology took as their starting point Calvin's stress on the immanence of Government *and* Kingdom (using Agamben's categories). What changed, this chapter shows, is the nature of providence. From Calvin's living and active, personal divine presence in the *oikonomia*, providence became a fixed set of laws of nature. This change can be described from one standpoint as secularization, or growing awareness of the laws of economics, but from another standpoint the change must be seen as theological or ontological. It is the latter standpoint that this chapter adopts.[3]

The Enlightenment inversion of Calvin's doctrine of providence

We have seen that John Calvin located the glory of God in providence, thus resolving the supposed fracture between divine being and praxis but at the cost of creating a tension between divine precept and the divine will. It is in the space between precept and will that society exists and works, or should do so. For Calvin, the healing of the fracture between will, which is providence, and precept, which is command, comes about in two ways. The ethical life of a Christian in society heals the fracture in a tentative way through ceaseless correction of injustices; ultimate resolution of the tension, however, must await the eschaton. That second resolution is not only hidden from view, but lacks continuity with most of what we can see in the present age. Thus, all we can know and all we can do now is work to heal the wound that divine providence has presented to us. That human work seems both ceaseless and endless; for as far as our perspective extends, it will reach no end-point of inoperativity and Sabbath rest. Calvin's placement of divine being, majesty, and glory in God's ceaseless providential action means that there is no static beatific vision toward which humans can aspire. The beatific vision, or what we can know of it here and now, is thoroughly dynamic.

Although the final, eschatological resolution of these mysteries looms large in Calvin's theology, it might seem only a small step to exclude eschatological resolution from the theological system altogether. It would be a small step but for one aspect of Calvin's theology: the full, immediate, and unmediated presence of all of God's being and activity in both the planning and carrying out of even the smallest detail of every event and object in the universe—in other words, the absolute character of divine providence in Calvin's theology, which is not attenuated in any way by second or intermediate causes.

The absoluteness and immediateness of providence were apparently easy to neglect or forget in the generations that followed Calvin's. Giorgio Agamben casts the debate between the Jansenists and the Jesuits in terms of providence and "the ways in which God intervenes in the government of the second causes."[4] In Agamben's account, settling on a theology of the divine government of the world requires striking a delicate balance between the action of governing and the free will of the individuals who are governed. The Jansenist position proved to be unacceptable to the church because it made the "activity of providence into an absolute and impenetrable government."[5] The same, of course, could be said of Calvin's doctrine of providence.

Agamben contends that behind their arguments about providence, the theologians of the seventeenth and eighteenth centuries were in fact discussing politics. The vast and hidden workings of providence paralleled "the government of the large baroque states, with their mysteries and their 'reasons.'"[6] For instance, philosopher and priest Nicolas Malebranche entered the debate in 1680 with the publication of his *Treatise on Nature and Grace*, which, in Agamben's account, absolutized divine government and radically transformed the idea of secondary causes.[7]

Malebranche began his inquiry into providence by distinguishing the general and particular divine will. God acts according to a general will by acting through the laws of nature, but according to particular will by producing an effect independently of a general law. Malebranche more or less excluded God's particular will from providence, thus reducing divine government of the world to the effect that God's general will has on "occasional" causes. Providence remains important, but "it is no longer necessary to distinguish it from nature."[8] Malebranche effectively located providence entirely in the *oikonomia*, as had Calvin and the Jansenists, but he did so in the opposite way, by allowing the laws of nature to absorb it instead of placing God's activity in intimate control of intermediate causes.

Attempting to define the best possible government, Malebranche sought in his *Treatise on Grace and Nature* to reconcile will and wisdom. In the theological sphere, this tension is the one with which Cornelius Jansen had struggled—how to reconcile God's will, which wishes that all persons will be saved, and God's wisdom, "which has order and constancy in its sights." The best government, in Agamben's words, "will therefore be that which is able to find the most economic relationship between will and wisdom." If God, who is sovereign, acted according to particular wills, God would have to intervene in so many ways and at so many times that "there would be neither government nor order but only chaos and what one might call a pandemonium of miracles." Agamben concludes that God therefore must reign but not govern, fixing the law and general wills and allowing "the contingent play of occasional causes and particular wills their most economical execution."[9] While preserving the economy as the locus of providential action, Malebranche thus reinstated the tension between divine being and praxis. It seemed untenable to him to place the full weight of divine being on the minutiae of economic life.

Agamben highlights Malebranche's influence on Rousseau, arguing that Malebranche's notion of the "general will" was transferred—perhaps not altogether consciously—through Rousseau from the field of theology to the field of politics.[10] Building on Michel Foucault's 1977–1978 lectures *Securité, territoire, population*, Agamben contends that the problem of sovereignty became more, rather than less, acute among Rousseau and his successor political philosophers. The "economy" was no longer modeled on the family but became the "art of government," that is, the delineation of "governing in the best possible way and with maximum efficacy in order to make men happy."[11]

The result, in Agamben's account, is "the economy's overwhelming domination of a popular sovereignty emptied of all meaning." That development was a result of Rousseau's attempt to minimize the problem of the origin and foundation of politics by presenting government "as the mere execution of the general will." The history of modern democracy has been nothing other than "the progressive coming to light of the substantial untruth of the primacy of legislative power and the consequent irreducibility of government to mere execution." In the final analysis, "the central mystery of politics is not sovereignty, but government; it is not God, but the angel; it is not the king, but ministry."[12] As we have seen, Calvin refused any distinction between the king and ministry, but that tension has recurred persistently in the history of Western theology in its broadest sense.

To be sure, the distinctive meaning of *oikonomia* was lost during the course of the Middle Ages and when the term "economy" came into use in the eighteenth century it "appears to spring, as it were, ex novo …, without any essential relation either to classical economics or to its theological past." However, there is no doubt in Agamben's mind that, though largely unexplored, the "subterranean connections that might link the economics of the moderns to the paradigm of the theological *oikonomia*" persist.[13] Agamben remains resolute: the dualism that the theological *oikonomia* transmitted to modern politics "reaches its apex in the paradigm of the government of the world that the great Western powers (in particular the United States) try today to put into practice on both a local and a global scale."[14] Though pushing "to an extreme" the supremacy of Government (economy), even to the point of almost eliminating the Kingdom (politics), liberalism nonetheless fails to emancipate itself from the providential paradigm.[15] Following Bousset, Agamben suggests that God's wish that humans be free is so intense that God's decree states that they are free and, therefore, the divine will is annulled in human freedom and human freedom in divine will. "At this point," Agamben writes, "theology can resolve itself into atheism, and providentialism into democracy, because God has made the world just as if it were without God and governs it as though it governs itself."[16]

Individualism and altruism

One aspect of Calvin's legacy endured. Calvin had insisted that God's "will is wrongly confused with his precept: innumerable examples clearly show how utterly different these two are." The reconciliation of will and precept remains hidden in divine providence and will be fully resolved eschatologically, but, for now, "[w]e ought, indeed, to hold fast by this: while God accomplishes through the wicked what he has decreed by his secret judgment, they are not excusable, as if they had obeyed his precept which out of their own lust they deliberately break."[17]

Even an economy emptied of divine presence contained this ambiguity. Do the laws of nature (de-theologized providence) tell us what we should do (de-theologized command)? This was one of the questions to which Hugo Grotius (1583–1645) applied himself.

Grotius

Grotius sutured the wound between the laws of nature and morality by constructing a whole natural order and a system of natural rights on an immanent principle of love. His idea was to start with the principle of self-preservation, which he linked to love, and demonstrate how that principle could generate a theory of ethical conduct.[18] In *De Indis*, published as *De iure praedae* (1604), he wrote:

> Therefore, since God fashioned creation and willed its existence, every individual part thereof has received from Him certain natural properties whereby that existence may be preserved and each part may be guided for its own good, in conformity, one might say, with the fundamental law inherent in its origin. From this fact the old poets and philosophers have rightly deduced that love, whose primary force and action are directed to self-interest, is the first principle of the whole natural order. Consequently, Horace should not be censured for saying, in imitation of the Academics, that expediency might perhaps be called the mother of justice and equity. For all things in nature, as Cicero repeatedly insists, are tenderly regardful of self, and seek their own happiness and security.[19]

"Love," in this sense, is the driving force behind self-interest. Grotius, in *De Indis*, went to great lengths to make clear that "one's own good takes precedence over the good of another person."[20] The only reason to show "altruism" was mutual benefit and reciprocity. Grotius did not define humans as *zoa politika*; anything beyond the minimal principle of self-preservation came about only because humans entered into civil society, where two further principles—each with a negative and a positive component—became necessary: (1) refrain from injuring others, even to the point of affirmatively protecting them individually and collectively; and (2) refrain from seizing others' possessions, and affirmatively contribute what is necessary to other individuals and to the whole.[21] Considerations of "general utility" could only weigh against the principle of self-preservation within civil society, and even then only in the service of self-preservation. "[T]he cargo cannot be saved," Grotius wrote in *De Indis*, "unless the ship is preserved."[22]

According to Grotius, the world in its natural state was and is "common" to all people, not in the sense that they owned or own it collectively, but in the sense that they can each use what they need from the common store. This interpretation of property in the state of nature—which Grotius made in the course of arguing that the sea could be neither owned nor controlled and was, thus, freely available to the Dutch—recalled that of the scholastic tradition.[23] Richard Tuck, however, argues that Grotius' theory was in fact original in that it supplies a "flexible account of the transition" from the state of nature to the modern condition of private property. Grotius eschewed any notion of a formal agreement. He wrote: "It is evident that the present-day concept of distinctions in ownership was the result, not of any sudden transition, but of a gradual process whose initial steps were taken under the guidance of nature herself."[24] Grotius avoided any hint of a social contract so that he could preserve the single guiding principle behind the laws of nature and ethics: self-preservation. Even the modern institution of private property rested simply "on the possibility of using the property in some way to benefit or protect oneself."[25]

Grotius' position had become more equivocal by the time he wrote *De iure belli ac pacis* (1625). He stressed in *De iure belli* that people seek a social existence with each other, not just to protect their own lives and property, "but because social life has a degree of value in itself."[26] Even so, Grotius was quick to distance his more nuanced account from a thoroughly Aristotelian one. He continued to define social life in terms of "the peaceable exercise by each member of his rights, and in particular his fundamental right of self-preservation."[27] Self-preservation remained the primary principle of the laws of nature and of morality.

Nevertheless, a rift did begin to appear as Grotius' thinking developed. In *De Indis*, he had called "the law of inoffensiveness" (i.e., the law against injuring others) simply God's command. There was no distinction in his thinking at that point between the laws of nature and morality on the one hand and divine precepts on the other. By bridging the gap between will and precept that characterized Calvin's theology, Grotius effectively identified the laws of nature with God's commands. By the time he wrote *De iure*, however, he had come to base the law of inoffensiveness on what Tuck calls "the desire for minimal sociability."[28] His thought developed logically in this direction because in *De Indis* he had not adequately explained exactly how the law of inoffensiveness arose from the principle of self-preservation.

Thus, self-preservation serves an even more central function in *De iure*. It displaces divine command as the source of morality, and it is thus not surprising that the most famous (or infamous) sentence in *De iure* hypothesizes the removal of God as a necessary feature of the entire discussion: “All we have now said would take place, though we should even grant, what without the greatest Wickedness cannot be granted, that there is no God, or that he takes no Care of human Affairs.”[29]

It remained unclear, however, how even the desire for minimal sociability could adequately account for the entire ethical structure of social life. Despite his efforts to produce a seamless web of natural laws and human morality, Grotius did not provide a fully persuasive theory of the “natural” development of the law of inoffensiveness. Following the pattern we have seen, the attempt to heal one conceptual wound in political theology produced yet another. Grotius’ solution to the fracture between will and precept engendered a fracture between individualism and altruism.

Hobbes

It was that fracture between individualism and altruism that Hobbes tried to heal with his contractarian theory. Hobbes departed from Grotius in maintaining that each person is an independent judge of the means of her own preservation. His pervasive skepticism left him with no universal principle of “love” to which he could appeal. The difficulty, of course, is that anyone may be mistaken about what is really in her self-interest. A series of subjective assessments about individual interests is likely to lead to social instability.[30] Hobbes readily recognized the likelihood of that outcome. His solution, fairly consistent throughout his career, was that there must be “an artificial agreement.”[31] Human intellect was advanced enough, in Hobbes’ estimation, to limit itself. A self-interested person would see the wisdom of renouncing her independence and thus become, in some sense, both independent and not independent at the same time. The precise mechanics of how individual judgments might be aligned developed over time; in *The Elements of Law Natural and Politic*, Hobbes “argued that the subjects had simply renounced their natural rights of resistance against the sovereign,” but in *Leviathan* the sovereign had become in some sense the subjects’ agent or representative.[32] In either case, some kind of “artificial agreement” is needed to bridge the gulf between self-interest and the ethics of social life.

The enduring attractiveness of social-contract theories seems to derive largely from their power to join *consent* and *justice*, which is merely a downstream version of their purported ability to overcome the disjunction between individualism and altruism. That resolution, in turn, is a function of these theories’ seeming capacity to link moral dictates to the laws of nature—that is, to heal the fracture that Grotius simply denied. Regarding the appeal of contractarian theories generally, Daniel Hausman and Michael McPherson write:

> Showing that a certain principle would be agreed to by people acting reasonably in the right circumstances increases its claim to guide people’s actions,

and showing that people in a state of nature would find it rational to agree to abide by certain principles supports the claim that the principles themselves are rationally defensible.[33]

In Hobbes' version of the social contract, "rationality" is connected to self-interest. In fact, according to Hausman and McPherson, seventeenth- and eighteenth-century philosophers referred to enlightened, rational self-interest as the "law of nature."[34] The social contract is a compromise that individuals recognize to be in their own best interests. Justice, in this view, is a matter of mutual advantage, and the agreement in question is the outcome of *bargaining*.

Rousseau and Kant

There is, I want to suggest, a measure of Hobbesian thinking in the assumptions underlying American political theory and, more particularly, underlying tax policy. At the same time, there is at least as much of Rousseau and Kant in these assumptions. Rousseau and Kant can be regarded as representing another strain of contractarian thinking, which "links rationality to the autonomous pursuit of ends ... and agreement to consensus, leading to a view of justice as *impartiality*." The governing principles of the social contract, in this approach, are determined by "impartial agents."[35] Rousseau, for instance, made clear in the *Social Contract* that by "autonomy" he meant not "whatever the agent prefers ... but what is truly in the agent's interests."[36] Understanding how, especially in the context of taxation, an impartial judge can determine what is in an individual's best interests and can thus somehow bestow "autonomy" on that individual necessitates a brief return to an earlier starting point in the historical narrative.

The medieval idea that the feudal lord, and then the monarch, ideally should live off that ruler's own lands proved tenacious, persisting well into the Enlightenment.[37] Even in Adam Smith's *Wealth of Nations*, taxation is portrayed as a last resort (if an inevitable one), an exception to the general rule of domains.[38] The assumption that the ruler should live off the ruler's own property had a constraining effect, even in the era of regular taxation: "Long after ordinary revenue had become inadequate to support the state, and supplemental taxes originally granted for short terms had become permanent, the distinction between ordinary and extraordinary revenue made it hard (but not impossible) for kings and their ministers to enlarge the revenue base."[39] Rulers resorted to confiscation. After the Reformation, the property of those whose beliefs differed from the ruler's was the main target, as evidenced by the confiscatory activity of Henry VIII, of Gustavus Vasa, and of the princes in the northern part of the Holy Roman Empire, as well as by the fate of Huguenot property following the Wars of Religion, the Hapsburg confiscation of Jewish properties, and confiscation of royal and ecclesiastical property in the French Revolution. Plunder from abroad temporarily helped the plight of the kings, but inflation soon evaporated the gain. Some states resorted to currency devaluation until the need for a stable currency became apparent.[40]

Political thinkers of the day were therefore faced with an urgent task: how to expand, conceptually, the authority of increasingly powerful rulers to take more of their subjects' property. The solution to this conundrum was usually war. Defense of the territory and then the realm served as the justification for taxation throughout much of the history of Christendom. In the Middle Ages, taxation re-emerged after the Merovingian period in response to military needs.[41] In the early modern period, warfare remained the justification for taxes. Underlying this justification was the goal of obtaining more power than neighboring states.[42] England's combined military and debt service never fell below 82 percent of total spending in any decade between 1700 and 1800, and average and median expenditure in England for the army, the navy, and debt service remained at 88 or 89 percent throughout the century.[43] Over time, the justification for taxation broadened, but only gradually, to include expenditures for "needs of general interest."[44]

Although Enlightenment thinkers clung to the fiction that taxation was a supplemental source of funds for the ruler—an emergency exception to the general rule that the ruler live off domains—it was becoming increasingly clear that regular taxation was going to have to be the norm. The medieval and Reformation idea had been that some theological principle transformed the property of the members of society into property of the ruler in extenuating circumstances. Now a new idea was needed—one that more immediately entitled the state to tax revenue, without a theological or philosophical principle to transform ownership of the property. Political sovereignty had become divorced from property rights.

This was a painful divorce, judging from the internal conflict that Jean Bodin (1530–1596) seems to have experienced. Bodin is typically considered "the first philosopher to make sovereignty the principle of the State,"[45] but taxation presents something of an inconsistency in his doctrine of absolute sovereignty.[46] Although he included taxation in his enumeration of the attributes of sovereignty in Book I of *Les six livres de la République*, in Book VI Bodin "preaches explicitly the need for consent to taxes, which does not tally with the theory established in book I ...."[47] This seeming inconsistency is Bodin's "sovereignty-taxes paradox."[48] Julian Franklin argues that Bodin perpetuated the medieval suspicion that taxes should not exist at all because the ruler was supposed to live of the ruler's own, and that the monarchy was doomed unless it lived within its means.[49] Taxation was, once again, a last resort.[50]

It took Bodin's successors—Gregory of Toulouse, Charles Loyseau, William Barclay, and Cardinal Le Bret—to remove the constellation of necessity, property, and consent that continued to restrict tax sovereignty. It took Hobbes to place the social contract prior to property rights, both logically and chronologically. Even then, the priority of property stubbornly persisted, and John Locke echoed Cicero in making the preservation of property the impetus behind the social contract.[51] Marc Leroy writes:

> The political conception of finance that Bodin defends is heterogeneous. It reflects the contradictions of the historical struggle between the royal power

> and feudality. It also shows the tension between a representation of taxes as an obligation towards a sovereign authority and as a legitimately authorized contribution to expenditure of general interest.[52]

The story represented by Bodin's successors, including Montesquieu, Rousseau, and Smith, proved to be the story of "the tension between sovereignty and legitimacy."[53]

Tax legitimacy, in Bodin's account, did not reduce taxes to a mere product of consent; legitimacy was also based on "relieving the poor," with specific reference to replacing *tailles* on real property with *tailles* on personal property, and of equity in distribution of the tax burden.[54] Bodin thereby retained something of the medieval and Reformation conception of tax, in which all property came from God and was to be used for God or for his people. Reinvigorating Cicero's version of the social contract, however, early modern thinkers made property rights original, the reason for the contract, the very thing that the government came into being to protect.

The difficulty was: if the government's task is to protect property rights, how can the government be sovereign? How can a sovereign's purpose consist in limiting what it itself can do? The conclusions of thinkers like Rousseau and Kant paradoxically strengthened both the individual citizen's claim to her own property and the government's claim that it could do as it pleased.

Jean-Jacques Rousseau (1712–1778) concluded that the state must both defeat property and defend it. By 1755, when Rousseau wrote his *Discourse on Political Economy*, taxation appeared either impossible or illegitimate, a choice that did not bode well for the state. Rousseau wrote: "[I]f contributions are voluntary, they produce nothing; if they are forced, they are illegitimate. It is in this cruel alternative of letting the state perish or attacking the sacred right of property, which supports the state, that the difficulty of a just and wise economy consists."[55] Property rights logically and chronologically preceded the state. Rousseau's social contract was based on property.[56] Rousseau wrote in *A Discourse on Inequality* (1754) that property is the surrogate of original freedom—all that remains of freedom after the social contract.[57]

Thus, property is sacred and must be protected, harmful though it is. Agreeing with "the wise Locke," Rousseau maintained that property is the source of all injury and therefore of justice.[58] Before justice—which is to say, before property rights—there was only pity. Compassion came before reflection. The virtues flowed from pity.[59]

Rousseau and Kant responded to the property paradox by positing that individual property rights somehow originated with the ruler. Property is an *a priori*, but a tentative one. The state takes property in its tentative form and then gives it back to the citizens in its confirmed, absolute form. As the grantor of confirmed property rights, the state is within its rights to take back any portion at any time.

Immanuel Kant (1724–1804) theorized that the "supreme commander" is entitled to tax revenue by virtue of being the supreme proprietor of land,[60] but that this supreme proprietorship "is only an idea of the civil union, designed to represent through concepts of right the need to unite the private property of all members of the people under a universal public owner."[61] Though the supreme commander possesses everything in one sense, in another sense all land belongs exclusively to the people. Without land, the people would be "devoid of all freedom."[62] This freedom, however, is an exchanged, derivative freedom rather than primal freedom. Through the original contract, all members of a people give up their "external," "wild and lawless" freedom "to receive it back at once as members of a commonwealth."[63] Following this exchange, the people "find again their entire and undiminished freedom in a state of lawful dependence (i.e., in a state of right), for this dependence is created by their own legislative will."[64]

As the one who "takes the duty of the people upon himself," the supreme commander has the right to tax the people—more precisely, their property or their commercial transactions—"for their own preservation." The government's task of preserving the people includes the funding of "the care of the poor," "foundling hospitals and church activities," and "what are otherwise known as charitable or pious institutions."[65]

Kant's prescription for taxation is redistributive in that society "must preserve those members of the society who cannot do so themselves," while, at the same time, the state is entitled to compel "prosperous citizens to provide the means of preserving those who are unable to provide themselves with even the most rudimentary necessities of nature" because the very "existence" of the prosperous "is an act of submission to the protection of the commonwealth." The purpose of taxation is not to meet "the needs of the state (for it is rich)," but to meet "the needs of the people."[66]

Freedom, property, prosperity, and even existence are received from the state, albeit after first being submitted to the state for ratification. Kant's guidelines for poor relief echo Luther's favoring of "compulsory political impositions" over voluntary contributions and his revulsion toward begging, "which has close affinities with robbery."[67] Relief of the needy must be effected "by lawful taxation."[68] Despite the weight that Kant attaches to taxation's redistributive function, his tax philosophy runs in a social-constructivist direction. The state preserves the poor to maintain its own existence and taxes the rich because they owe their own existence to the state.

The Kantian state does not respond to circumstances that it faces; it initiates those circumstances. Laying to rest any lingering questions of reciprocity, Kant asserts that the sovereign "has only rights in relation to the subject, and no … duties."[69] The general will of the people, expressed in the constitution and commonwealth, sets the parameters that drive taxation. In this conceptual response to the property paradox, the general will takes the place occupied by God's providence in Calvin's political theology. "The voice of the people is in fact the voice of God," Rousseau wrote.[70] Instead of healing the break between the laws of nature and morality through one architectonic principle (as Grotius did) or artificial agreement (as Hobbes did), Rousseau and Kant derived both secular "providence" and secular "precept" from the general will. That will is logically and (at least in a hypothetical sense) chronologically prior to true autonomy and the "givenness" of circumstances that determine what the state must and can do.

Three modern options

By the time the American Republic was founded, three options were available for resolving the fracture between individualism and altruism, which itself had evolved from the tension between providential will and moral precept as the latter tension lost its theological content. One option was something like an "invisible hand," Grotius' solution, in which a principle that was both immanent and transcendent, supplied a unified account of both self-interest and ethical social life. Another option was Hobbes', in which self-interest led to social life as the various self-interested parties bargained to reach an agreement that would ultimately continue to serve their self-interests. The third option, that was offered by Rousseau and Kant, offered a "constructed" autonomy, dependent entirely on the good graces of the general will and superior in some way to the wild and lawless freedom of human beings' natural state.

No pressing need to choose among these options presented itself. In the concluding paragraph of *Philosophy and Government*, Richard Tuck writes that "the story of the origins of modern political and moral theory" would undergo "various transformations" from the time of Hobbes through Kant and into the eighteenth century, "but in many ways the basic character of Enlightenment politics were already in place in 1651."[71] In other words, "the basic character of modern politics was in place: the criticisms of this tradition by Hume, Rousseau, Bentham and Kant were in many ways criticisms of its base, of its metaphysical preconceptions, rather than its superstructure." The "description of modern politics" associated with the "*ragion di stato* writers and in Grotius and Hobbes," Tuck continues, "with standing armies paid for out of taxation, with self-protective and potentially expansive states, and with citizens very unsure of the moral principles they should live by, looks like an accurate description of a world still recognisable to us."[72]

Max Weber noticed the tension in American culture, observing on the one hand an "initiative-taking, activity-oriented, and entrepreneurial 'world-mastery' (*weltbeherrschende*) individualism" but on the other a "*civic sphere* of ideals and values that pulled and guided individuals beyond self-interest calculations."[73] These impulses were seemingly opposite, but Weber refused to attribute them to happenstance. He saw "*both* orientations—to self and to community" as arising "out of deep American roots, particularly ones shaped by religious forces."[74] That observation encapsulates the theme of this chapter: that conflicting impulses drive the American orientation toward tax and justice—impulses that are incapable on their own of supplying a guiding principle but form a coherent narrative when traced back to the Enlightenment efforts to overcome the Christian fracture between will and precept that emerged so prominently in Calvin's thinking.

Weber, moreover, saw something of the three modern options when he surveyed the American scene that had developed from its Protestant and often

Calvinist roots. He saw, first of all, the "capitalist economic order" as "a monstrous cosmos into which the individual is born and which in practice is for him, at least as an individual, simply a given, an immutable shell, in which he is obliged to live."[75] The givenness of the monstrous cosmos into which the capitalist subject is born reflects the irresistible force of the secular providence that somehow unites individual self-interest and the good of the community. Its workings are mysterious; the only response available to human beings is to yield to its inexorable laws of nature and act accordingly. We can call this monstrous cosmos the *economy*.

At the same time, Weber saw a contractarian impulse in "the prominent *civic sphere* of ideals and values that pulled and guided individuals beyond self-interest calculations and toward the betterment of their communities."[76] Whether this impulse was fundamentally self-interested or genuinely altruistic, it had the form of a Hobbesian agreement. We can call this settlement the *bargain*.

And Weber saw in America the fabricated, domesticated apparatus of the general will that Rousseau had considered indispensable to government. Its manifestation was bureaucracy. Bureaucracy served individual autonomy by making it more stable and predictable. Philip Gorski writes regarding later refinements of Weber's thesis that, by "stimulating and legitimating" bureaucratic reforms in early modern states, "the Protestant Reformation contributed to the formation of less predatory and more predictable forms of government."[77] The technical qualifications of bureaucrats, in place of pre-Trent Catholic venality, ensured the correct balance between individual autonomy (represented in terms of property) and state control of private property. The tameness of bureaucracy was in everyone's interest, state and individual alike. We can call this option the *alliance*.

The three options persist with respect to tax policy, often coexisting without clear delineation. The *economic* option is most evident in the elevation of efficiency over all other values available to tax policymakers. The *balancing* option dominates utilitarian approaches to tax policy, including optimal theories. The *alliance* option comes to the fore in the assumption that greater productivity generates more revenue. The options coexist in a kind of perpetual cycle, the shortcomings of one answered by the strengths of the next, but the deficiencies in that solution pointing to the next option, and back to the original option as the cycle begins again.

Economy

With respect to taxation, a commitment to the supremacy of economic efficiency results in the elimination of any meaningful principle for tax policy, as Chapter One demonstrated. We saw that the prevailing assumptions among Americans and American policymakers dictate that income tax rates be kept low to foster economic productivity and thus increase revenue.[78] We saw that the 2017 Tax Act continues the trend that began in the 1980s, "treating efficiency as the prime normative goal of tax policy."[79]

That trend reflects the unwavering commitment to "scientific," value-free positivism on the part of economists. The Pareto standard is taken to represent the element of equity in the monstrous cosmos of the capitalist economy.[80] However, the result, as noted in Chapter One, is that policymakers are left with "an incoherent standard" for any tax system." A growth norm," after all, "favors repeal of every existing tax."[81]

This outcome, in which equity is domesticated and taxation rendered palatable to a market economy, is untenable. Even a stalwart advocate of the "law and economics" school of thought like Richard Posner recognizes that taxation cannot be wholly accommodated to an economic analysis of the law. Posner isolates his discussion of tax from his treatment of other areas of law. Posner acknowledges that tax policy places a "heavy emphasis ... on distributive considerations."[82] That is not a direction in which Posner has any interest in going: "Whether [the economist] can supply criteria, comparable to value or efficiency, for preferring one distribution over another is quite another question, but one that in many practical contexts does not have to be answered."[83] Redistributive taxation, along with laws against racial discrimination, invites considerations that simply do not belong in an economic analysis of the law. Posner admits this.[84]

The need to reintroduce equity into the tax equation having thus become apparent, the *bargain* option comes into view in the form of a utilitarian balance among interests. The bargain theory of social contract emerged, as we have seen, long before a utilitarian balancing-of-interests came to hold sway in tax philosophy. The story that runs from Hobbes to John Stuart Mill and his utilitarian descendants began because *sovereignty*, even when conceptualized as the general will of the people, had never become for the early modern thinkers a sufficient justification for taxation. Even in practice, absolutist France was an outlier. The reason for the intellectual reluctance to abandon legitimacy seems to have been the persistence of the Ciceronian connection between liberty and property rights. Locke's formulation is well known: a human being "hath by Nature a Power, ... to preserve his Property, that is, his Life, Liberty and Estate, against the Injuries and Attempts of other Men."[85] Smith wrote: "Every tax, however, is to the person who pays it a badge, not of slavery, but of liberty. It denotes that he is subject to government, indeed, but that, as he has some property, he cannot himself be the property of a master."[86]

Bargain and balance

Even though the government *confirmed* liberty and property, property rights acted as a bulwark against political absolutism. The sovereign could never forget that the purpose of the government was to guarantee the liberty and property of the members of the society. Balance was an essential aspect of tax systems in the eyes of many Enlightenment thinkers, as evidenced by Smith's fourth maxim[87] and Locke's insistence on consent.[88]

Services and money payments in feudalism originated in the relationship between vassal and lord but evolved into payments that the lord requested and a consultative assembly granted. The need for consent helped to give rise to Parliament in England. In France, "[a]s everywhere, war justifies taxes, but feudal assistance was asked within the framework of consultative assemblies."[89] In the modern state, legitimization of taxes "is sought after in the consent of taxpayers to the financing of needs of general interest," which have, in the meantime, expanded beyond military needs.[90]

Consent, or public opinion, "is the modern type of acclamation," according to Carl Schmitt.[91] Giorgio Agamben considers contemporary democracy to be a kind of democracy "that is entirely founded upon glory," by which he means that it is founded "on the efficacy of acclamation, multiplied and disseminated by the media beyond all imagination."[92] Consent is "social communication," and consensus rests on it.[93]

Taking Jürgen Habermas' work as his starting point, Agamben argues that the model of popular sovereignty in which members of society are physically present and participating is outdated. That kind of popular sovereignty has dissolved into "communicative procedures" that lack a "subject-people."[94]

Moving one step beyond Habermas' thesis, Agamben suggests that the "people-communication" model of popular sovereignty ultimately passes political power "into the hands of experts and the media."[95] In the final analysis, however, there is not much to distinguish the "people-nation" and "people-communication" models; they are the "two faces of the *doxa*" that "ceaselessly interweave and separate themselves" in today's democracies. In Agamben's account, the present-day development of *doxa* is nothing other than the latest stage in a genealogy of acclamation that can be traced back to Augustus' *Res gestae divi Augusti*, which, in concentrating the emperor's constitutional powers in his person, simply stated: "In my sixth and seventh consulates, after putting out the civil war, having obtained everybody's consent, I assumed all powers."[96]

The theological function of glory (*doxa*), as Agamben's entire book seeks to illustrate, is to "cover with its splendor the unaccountable figure of divine inoperativity"—the inoperativity that Agamben considers so embarrassing to Christian theology but only to *Christian* theology. Thus, at the level of civil government, the glory that is public acclamation, expressing itself in procedural consent mediated by experts and the media, is the end-point, the goal of the economy's ceaseless activity. It is our secular eschatology, the place where the optimal point is finally reached in the seemingly endless effort to balance the interests of all members of a society. Agamben suggests that the *oikonomia* ends, and true politics may finally begin, once glory captures inoperativity "in the guise of 'eternal life.'"[97] The right balance, as in the elusive of goal of utilitarian tax theories (both classical and optimal), is an example of the eternal life that America seeks.

Historically, and with particular reference to taxation, consent was formalized in benefit theory. Benefit theory retained the idea of relationship, rooted as it seems to have been in feudalism, but the relationship was one that simply existed. It was not necessarily expressed in consultation among the affected parties or in any procedural mechanism at all. Hobbes called taxes "nothing else but the Wages, due to them that hold the publique Sword, to defend private men in the exercise of severall Trades, and Callings."[98] More than a century later, Adam Smith wrote: "The expence of government to the individuals of a great nation, is like the expence of management to the joint tenants of a great estate, who are all obliged to contribute in proportion to their respective interests in the estate."[99]

As the closing phrase of Smith's sentence shows, the benefit principle not only legitimated taxation as such but also purported to provide guidance as to who should bear the burden of actual taxes. Hobbes made the same point:

> Now there is a proportionably to every man's ability, and there is a proportionably to his Benefit by Commonwealth: and this latter is it, which is according to the law of nature. For the burdens of the commonwealth being the price that we pay for benefit thereof, they ought to be measured thereby.[100]

The benefit principle represented a kind of distributive justice, suggesting that those who received the most from the state should pay the most back to the state.

Alliance

Benefit, however, had a tendency to move in the direction of the state's underwriting of property interests. Smith, for instance, considered "ground-rents" uniquely suited to heavy taxation because they "are altogether owing to the good government of the sovereign ...."[101] The taxpayer's property interests and the state's revenue needs no longer confronted each other in an agonistic relationship. Instead, the state was responsible for the taxpayer's wealth—not just responsible for some of the taxpayer's benefits in general, but responsible for the source of the tax revenue itself. The benefit principle extended beyond reciprocity toward an entitlement on the part of the state to a portion of the wealth that it had effectively created. At this point, a procedural mechanism for balancing the taxpayer's property interests against the state's revenue needs ceased to be relevant.

The procedural element disappeared from tax legitimation altogether when, as in absolutist France, sovereignty came to define the relationship between government and taxpayer. France's political mechanism, the Estates General, "fell into disuse after 1615, and its demise brought death to the principle that taxation requires the consent of the taxed." By the end of the seventeenth century, consent in its original form had vanished in Denmark, Sweden, and Prussia as well.[102]

There had been two strands of the "traditional" benefit principle.[103] The first, associated with eighteenth-century Enlightenment political theory, used the principle to justify republican and nondespotic government in contractarian terms. It had little to say about the details of tax systems. Locke,[104] Montesquieu,[105] and Kant[106] represent this strand in different ways.

A second strand of the "traditional" benefit principle emerged in the writings of John Stuart Mill, but only so that Mill could expose the principle as leading to regressive tax rates. Assuming a version of benefit in which individuals pay taxes in exchange for specific goods and services in situations where market exchanges are impractical, Mill concluded that the problem with the benefit principle was that the poor benefit more than the rich and, thus, should have to pay a higher share of the overall tax burden than the rich.[107]

Even before Mill's critique of the benefit principle, tax theorists in the English-speaking tradition had been working to define the ability-to-pay taxation as an alternative to benefit. The ability principle appeared fair to them: since each person incurs a loss when paying tax, the losses should be spread equitably, and, if they are spread according to individuals' ability to sustain them, then the spread can be considered equitable.[108]

Mill reformulated the ability principle in terms of equal sacrifice,[109] based on the premise that the utility of the last dollar of income falls as income rises and, thus, that high-income person X must pay more to incur a sacrifice equal to that of low-income person Y.[110] Mill also theorized that equal sacrifice among taxpayers would minimize total sacrifice, thus paving the way for a later shift in emphasis from "an *equitable* distribution by equal sacrifice to an *efficient* distribution by least total sacrifice."[111] Refinements were made to the equal-sacrifice principle as the nineteenth century progressed, and they resulted in the distinction among "equal absolute," "equal proportional," and "equal marginal" sacrifice concepts. F. Y. Edgeworth chose equal marginal sacrifice as the best measure of least total sacrifice. This version of the equal-sacrifice principle seeks to equate the marginal sacrifices incurred across taxpayers.[112]

The equality component of Mill's balance was subjective, dependent on how taxpayers *feel.* Mill believed that a taxpayer should "feel neither more nor less inconvenience from his share of payment than every other person experiences from his."[113] As the subsequent struggle to define "equal sacrifice" demonstrated, however, ability-to-pay was caught between the equitable concern to measure an individual's subjective sacrifice and the need for an objective standard that would make that measure administrable. Mill's conviction that "individual utility was the proper touchstone of equity" gave way to F. Y. Edgeworth's reframing of the question in terms of "the overall effects of taxation on society." Not coincidentally, Edgeworth "was the first to contend that morality alone could not decide the issue" of sacrifice.[114]

An "objective" ability principle assumes that everyone has the same utility schedule (i.e., that everyone with $X derives the same utility or welfare from unit Y, and that assumption, as tax theorists have observed, violates experience.[115] The ability principle, perhaps inevitably, bifurcated into a subjective version (seemingly unworkable because dependent on unobservable facts) and an objective version (necessitating the dubious claim that everyone has the same utility schedule).[116] "Welfare economics" argues that "interpersonal utility comparisons cannot be performed in a meaningful fashion" and, thus, removes altogether the "'scientific' foundation of the ability to pay." As a result, "the institution of progressive taxation must seek its support from philosophical judgements about 'ideal' taxation."[117]

Related to the objectivist turn in the ability-to-pay, pressure increased to translate individual viewpoints into social consensus.[118] Musgrave expresses skepticism about the glibness with which the utilitarians, particularly Bentham, assumed individual interest could be translated into collective interest.[119] Why, Musgrave asked, should individual X, with superior endowment, agree to a policy that requires her to pay higher taxes in order to transfer wealth to less-favored individual Y?[120]

The leap from self-interest to collective interest requires a hypothetical view from behind the veil of ignorance, a fictional construct. Treating these two perspectives as commensurable, existing along the same metric, does violence to both and to the resulting balance. They can be compared and given relative weights, but they cannot be reduced to the same unit of measurement.

Legal philosopher Cass Sunstein has explored the problem of "incommensurability." Sunstein argues that one of the roles of civil law is "reflecting and communicating particular ways of valuing human goods."[121] The law, in Sunstein's opinion, often yields to the temptation of "monistic theories of value," which leads to "superconcepts" (e.g., "happiness, utility, or pleasure").[122] Sunstein attaches this "unitary" thinking about values to thinkers as diverse as Plato, Bentham, and Posner.[123] Unitary thinking in the law, according to Sunstein, is reductionist and "jarring" in light of human experience, as in the case of money damages for torts.[124]

This artificial quality of unitary thinking results from its comparing of incommensurable goods. Goods are diverse, Sunstein writes, and they can be incommensurable,[125] by which he means that some of them "cannot be aligned along a single metric without doing violence to our considered judgments about how these goods are best characterized."[126] Unitary thinking affects law with particular frequency, because different goods can be measured by money and, thus, appear commensurable. Money itself is not fungible, however. It is dedicated to different purposes, reflecting "qualitative differences among human goods." Money in one "compartment" (i.e., dedicated for one intended use) is not equivalent to money in another compartment.[127] The error of law and economics, in Sunstein's opinion, is that it makes the mistake of assuming that the market values all goods in the same way.[128]

Sunstein does not deny that incommensurable goods can be compared or traded off against each other.[129] Incommensurability does not preclude the existence of some second-order goal, such as human flourishing, that operates at a sufficiently high level of abstraction to generate criteria that can "help in the assessment of diverse and plural goods."[130] What it does preclude is a "single metric" along which two goods that humans value differently can be measured against each other.[131] Such a metric misdescribes experience and can yield bad recommendations for ethics and politics.[132]

Utility, according to Sunstein, is such a metric.[133] A utilitarian approach to law might, for example, seek to treat economic growth and the reduction of race discrimination as commensurable goods. These goods certainly may be traded off against each other, with the result, perhaps, that a society chooses "to outlaw race discrimination even if that step involves some loss in social wealth." That decision, however, properly responds to a second-order good rather than to a concept of utility that assigns an economic value to race relations.[134]

Balancing incommensurable goods along a single metric does more than misdescribe experience. It transforms experience.[135] "Redescriptions"—like "investing" in one's children, improving "human capital," and entering the "marriage market"—"are important both because they describe in inadequate ways and because ... they have an important constitutive dimension—that is, they may help transform how ... we value or experience various events and relationships."[136] We create and alter norms by the way we describe, not least through civil law, different kinds of valuation.[137]

Equity and efficiency are valued in different ways and, thus, are incommensurable. They are valued in different ways because any concept of equity extrinsic to the positive science of public finance is impossible to measure using market assumptions. "[E]conomic analysis of nonmarket relations," Sunstein writes, "often runs into difficulty ...."[138] Equity is forced to become something different than it originally was. It becomes a version of the other aspiration, a form of efficiency in disguise, and thus commensurable with—and indistinct from—efficiency. Assuming that the positive science of taxation permits consideration of equity at all, rather than relegating it to the spending side of public finance, such a version of equity necessarily serves efficiency. It ceases to be equity for the sake of equity as a separate concept and manifests itself as a means to preserving political and economic stability and, thus, the conditions for making money. Establishing the conditions of wealth-maximization can itself be considered a form of equitable policymaking, but only if it is assumed that the opportunity to prosper financially is a definition of equity.[139]

In short, an "alliance" results from the sheer impossibility of balancing equity and efficiency. What ultimately undermined bargain, compromise, and balance in tax policy was not the theory that the state confirms freedom and property rights; it was the practical, economic alliance between state and taxpayer. Webber and Wildavsky write:

> Despotism shaded back to collectivism and accommodated growing elements of economic individualism. A working alliance between principles of hierarchy in the state and competition in the economy was in the making; we call such a combination 'the establishment.'[140]

This "alliance" would be "ultimately labeled capitalism."[141] The British thinkers had already responded to the property paradox by increasingly insisting that the government could obtain more revenue from its citizens if those citizens had more money and property and, therefore, that raising taxes was a self-defeating proposition. David Hume (1711–1776) remarked that "a prince will soon find, that an encrease of the impost is no encrease of his revenue,"[142] and Smith agreed, maintaining that "[h]igh taxes ... frequently afford a smaller revenue to government than what might be drawn from more moderate taxes."[143]

The risk of this alliance—in which the government has an interest in levying only modest taxes so as not to undermine the incentive and means of production, and the taxpayer has an interest in paying at least some taxes so that the government can provide the infrastructure that facilitates the taxpayer's creation of wealth—is that the delicate balance between taxing too much and taxing too little will unravel and one side of the equation will absorb the other, i.e., the fragile construct of efficiency will resolve into libertarianism or statism. The state's ability to take the property of its citizens is either rendered impotent or goes unchecked.

Jürgen Habermas writes that in a market-dominated system the state bears costs of goods and services that cannot be priced through the economy. These are, among others, the costs of unproductive commodities, structural costs related to production, and the costs of social welfare. These costs have to be financed through taxes, according to Habermas. The state apparatus has no choice but to skim off profits and income in such a way as to avoid disturbances in growth, while it raises taxes selectively, prioritizes their use, and performs its administrative functions in such a way "that the need for legitimation can be satisfied as it arises."[144] In other words, legitimacy and efficiency are in tension. The state is caught between expectations—that of "expected intervention" and "forced renunciation of intervention."[145] If the state responds to the fact "that economic resources are not sufficient to sustain fully capitalist victims of capitalist growth," it runs the risk of "crippling the process of growth."[146]

Thus, the capitalist state, most particularly in its taxing authority, is faced with a trade-off between the "private goals of profit maximization" and what Habermas calls "generalizable interests of the population."[147] More precisely, the state is faced with negotiating among three goals: private interests (e.g., profit-maximization), "generalizable interests" (e.g., social welfare and personal welfare), and "collective-capitalist interests" (e.g., an educational system that raises productivity).[148]

The state, according to Habermas, negotiates among its private, generalizable, and collective-capitalist goals in a number of ways, but most importantly, for purposes of this project, through compromises. A compromise is a "normed adjustment between particular interests" that "takes place under conditions of a balance of power between the parties involved."[149] Compromise requires (1) a balance of power between the parties and (2) negotiation concerning non-generalizable interests.[150] As the "nature-like development of economic processes" relocates itself inside the political system, society's collective-capitalist interests and private interests merge. Generalizable interests disappear altogether, because they were never party to the balance of power in the first place. To maintain the semblance of legitimacy, the state holds up tax policy as a balance or at least a compromise among society's aspirations; but this balance is illusory. The state's legitimacy becomes formal and largely designed to obscure conflict and contradiction in order to avoid crises.[151] Compromise is present in name only, as goals inconsistent with economic growth are excluded from view. They must be excluded because they cannot be measured in terms of growth. Their categories are observed, but the categories are empty. Only the project of turning all considerations into conditions of economic growth remains.

At this point, the third option—*alliance*—merges back into the first—*economy*—and the cycle begins again. The institution of taxation is justified to the extent that it honors the nature-like laws of the "monstrous cosmos" until it becomes apparent to everyone that efficiency can no longer sustain tax policy. At that point, a balancing of interests reemerges, until one interest absorbs the other, and then the cycle returns to its starting point. It must be emphasized that this cycle is more hypothetical than real. The three options often justify and structure the institution of taxation simultaneously. I use the concept of a cycle to illustrate how the three options blend into each other and how each one calls forth the others to rescue it before it collapses and makes a mockery of the tax system.

The cycle

Nevertheless, there is at least the hint of a real sequence in American tax policy. Glimpses of that cycle can be seen in Chapter One, as well as in this chapter. The "monstrous cosmos" dominated Americans' assumptions when the progressive income tax first came into vogue in the early part of the twentieth century. By settling on equal marginal sacrifice, Edgeworth and A. C. Pigou (1877–1959) had effectively joined the quest for tax fairness to the utilitarian goal of maximizing aggregate welfare.[152] Once the ability-to-pay became the guiding principle in tax policy, "tax fairness norms deal with a different problem than that of the legitimacy of taxes and of government in general."[153] E. R. A. Seligman, who more than anyone else persuaded Americans to adopt the ability-to-pay principle and progressive income taxation, viewed the ability principle as "a Hegelian idea working its way out in history." [154]

By the 1920s, however, the prescient economist Henry Simons (1899–1946) saw the absurdity of basing a tax system on the natural laws of the monstrous cosmos. Simons agreed with other theorists that an income tax system with a progressive rate structure represented taxation at its most just, but he denounced the prevailing explanation as to why such a system was just. Simons conceded that minimum-sacrifice doctrine, Edgeworth's formulation of utility, implied that taxes should be progressive.[155] Simons found this argument for progressivity, however, "not very illuminating" because the concept of sacrifice was lacking in content: "One derives practical implications from the criterion of equality, or proportionality, of sacrifice precisely in proportion to one's knowledge of something which no one has ever known, or ever will know, anything about."[156]

In Simons' account, the problem with sacrifice doctrines, even of the sophisticated variety advanced by Edgeworth, was both psychological and "theological." In addition to the difficulty (or, rather, impossibility) of measuring how much any given taxpayer suffers in parting with one dollar, the assumption underlying progressive tax rate policies was not based on the actual suffering of any living individual taxpayer at all. Marginal-utility principles represent a triumph of abstraction over particularity.

Furthermore, Simons asked, why should utility theory be based on suffering anyway? The theory regards a tax that impinges the least on enjoyment as a good tax. In other words, utility theory assumed "that all individuals are, or must be treated as, equally efficient as pleasure machines."[157] Hedonism, not the theory's "pseudo-scientific statement of the case against inequality," was the driving force behind utility theory.[158] Protestations of value-neutrality notwithstanding, Simons considered this hedonism a theological commitment. In supporting a connection between what is good and a quantum of pleasure, "one finds an appropriate theology not only convenient but utterly indispensable."[159]

Indeed, Simons' primary complaint against American tax theory in general was directed toward its dishonesty about ethical commitments. The "specialist in government finance" mentioned above would be better off introducing "at the outset a confession of faith or recital of preconceptions" rather than maintaining the illusion that tax theory is free of concerns about justice and equity.[160]

Simons' own "confession of faith" consisted in his avowed commitment to view tax systems as instruments for reducing economic inequality. Whether a tax system or policy is designed to foster equality is not the point, according to Simons. Taxation inevitably affects the material wealth of taxpayers, so policymakers have no choice but to base their tax policies—at least in part—on notions of distributive and redistributive justice. "Taxation," Simons wrote, "must affect the distribution of income, whether we will it so or not; and it is only sensible to face the question as to what kinds of effects are desirable."[161] Simons was convinced that any attempt to argue for progression on utilitarian, liberal economic grounds can *only* be subterfuge that disguises a person's, a political party's, or a nation's hedonistic impulses and yet suppresses a visceral but unconfessed discomfort with inequality.[162]

But by the 1950s, the Kalven-Blum position had come to dominate: taxes are "a necessary evil falling upon a distribution of money" and thus "the problem is not to use the tax system to adjust existing inequalities in that distribution but simply to leave all taxpayers equally 'worse off' after taxes."[163] It was not until the reception of Rawls' *A Theory of Justice* in the 1970s that equity again became a major concern of tax policy. As we have seen, that concern was short-lived. Various versions of a synthesis between the *alliance* and *economy* options have dominated American and British tax policy since 1980, with a brief resurgence of concern about inequality following the 2008 financial crisis and the emergence of a balancing approach to taxation in the guise of a wealth tax in the early part of the 2020 presidential campaign in the United States.

The bargaining, balancing, or compromising approaches each seem to need to come to the fore from time to time to reinvigorate the institution of taxation by making it appear more legitimate. It is worth reiterating that the bargaining option carries within it the quality of consent and consensus. It must resurface periodically to legitimate, not just the state's tax systems, but the state itself. It promises an end to the guesswork of economic planning. It assures us that an end-point can be reached, somewhere on the Laffer Curve, where economic productivity and fairness will be in perfect equilibrium. It is the hope that lies beyond the economy, the hope of an end-time, of eternal life.

Conclusion

The "realized eschatology" of contemporary American and British tax policy illustrates the political-theological shift that occurred after Calvin. The state ceased to be adjunct to the Christian project of healing the fracture between divine will and divine precept. It became instead the glorious instantiation of the resolution of that and all other theological fractures. That is, it became the locus of the Sabbath inoperativity where all strivings will cease and optimal conditions will prevail. Taxation, too, points to that place of inoperativity, provided we find just the right formula.

The ways in which taxation points to that end, however, are illusory. We have seen that a laissez-faire conception of equity and efficiency leaves us with, at best, a version of "thin equity," in which the tax burden is allocated more or less fairly and the rest will take care of itself. There is no place in that view for equity in its "thick" sense, i.e., in a redistributive sense.[164] Efficiency subsumes equity.

We have seen as well that equity and efficiency cannot, in the final analysis, be balanced against each other. They can be traded off in a way, but not measured against each other. The result is that tax policy must simply choose between them, in much the same way any other area of law must. In his 1976 Harvard Law Review article "Form and Substance in Private Law Adjudication"[165] (purportedly the tenth most oft-cited law review article in legal literature today), Duncan Kennedy claims that law in modern liberal democracies has coalesced around two rigid poles: (i) the aims of individualism and (ii) the rules of altruism. The result, according to this foundational article for critical legal studies, is an intractable conflict between individualism and altruism that is fatal to the coherence of liberalism and that creates wide-open judicial discretion and indeterminacy. Either pole has normative force but the two poles can generate divergent results. As a result, judges are free to decide any case—not according to precedent, as is supposed—but in a wide and conflicting variety of apparently legitimate ways. To state the result differently, judges are free to choose from a broad and seemingly random array of narratives. The same can be said for tax policymakers; they are free to choose from a random array of narratives. In American tax policy, at least, the choices lean heavily toward efficiency narratives. There is little in the way of compromise or balance.

The tendency to lean heavily on efficiency narratives results in the "alliance" between revenue-providers and revenue-takers. International political economist Susan Strange has commented on these alliances, which she sees arising even in the "tacit" agreements between kings and princes in medieval Europe, among the participants in the medieval trade fairs, and in local town markets.[166] Although those early forms of alliance contained a bargaining element, the full betrayal of bargain is on display in the contemporary alliance. Although the power to tax, according to Strange, has been one of the basic rights attributed to statehood, large corporations—following "the American lead"—"are such important cogs in the production structure, few politicians in any industrialized country have questioned the exceptional, preferential tax treatment given to them."[167]

In fact, Strange argues, this alliance is so strong that governments like the U.S. federal government have simply conceded the right to tax to such corporations, which have their own ways of raising revenue (e.g., passing on to consumers the costs of industrial espionage, security, advertising, market share, research, and patronage).[168]

In summary, the three options discussed in this chapter do not encompass plural values or commitments at all. Each option concedes to one and only value or commitment. The promise of compromise, bargain, or equilibrium among competing interests is illusory. The trilateral bargain among government, industry, and workers that Strange calls "neo-corporatism" has proved elusive for large democracies, and especially for the United States.[169] The theological history of taxation provides an antidote to the telescoping of ethical commitments in several ways. First, as we saw in the case of Thomas Aquinas, it nuances property rights by subjecting them to the higher demands of *necessitas* in natural law itself, thus ensuring that the needs of the poor are included in any bargain. Secondly, as in the recessive voice represented by Ockham, theology has the capacity to show that taxation can resolve the conflict between wealth and poverty; taxation can be the means of purifying oneself of the taint of the wealth that originates with Caesar. Thirdly, taxation can form part of the dynamic overflow of good things that characterizes Luther's theology of the Lord's Supper. Fourthly, Calvin—taking his cue from Augustine—teaches us that the end-point of all human striving lies with God in the age to come; all we can do in the present age is respond tentatively and temporarily to injustices and inequalities as they present themselves. One political-theological theme runs through all of these lessons to be learned: at the level of civil government, taxation is a paradigmatic instance of the suture that heals fundamental fractures—i.e., between equality and inequality, between rich and poor, between spiritual and physical needs, between abundance and scarcity, between will and precept, and between individualism and altruism. But that healing is only provisional. The hubris of regarding it as final is the source of artificiality of contemporary American tax policies, in which fractures are not, in fact, healed but the language of bargain and compromise persists, vainly promising optimal results and the best of all possible worlds.

The key question for a political theology of redistributive taxation, then, is whether such a form of taxation is a semi-permanent institution, with no foreseeable end-point in the present age, or a means to an end to be achieved in a society that will then embody an ideal of justice and equality going forward. At its core, this is the same question about wealth and poverty to which Augustine and Pelagius gave different answers. We have seen that most, but not all, of the Christian tradition has sided with Augustine. The contemporary American tax discussion has foreclosed the "eternal government" of redistributive taxation by establishing (or purporting to establish) a final *status*, as in the Laffer curve. This is the way it tries to heal the aporia between Government and Kingdom. But this solution is nothing other than an artificially accelerated eschatology. As Calvin taught, in perhaps the most thoroughgoing expression of Augustine's answer to the question of wealth and poverty, God's commands and our native impulses drive us to resist injustice and inequality, but the resulting task of resistance has no end in the present age. It is in some sense Sisyphean. The providential function of that task is not a utopian or ideal or even optimal solution to the problems of poverty, inequality, and injustice; its function is to bring about human solidarity.

Instead of balancing an abstract notion of equality against a negative concept of non-interference, tax policy would be well advised to see itself as a vehicle for accommodating the needs that all of society's members have to a subsistence minimum, the need of society's members to retain enough of their material resources to work productively, and the needs of the government to create and maintain the conditions necessary for both of the other sets of needs.

In the end, at least four perspectives on taxation and theology are available: (1) the view that taxation balances the dictates of natural and positive law, exemplified by Thomas Aquinas; (2) the view that paying tax expresses a repudiation of the world's dominion, set out most clearly by William of Ockham; (3) an approach that sees taxation as a sword against the unrighteous but a means of grace to the believer, as Luther proposed; and (4) a place for taxation, alongside other institutions, in the ongoing work of bringing closer together what God wills and what God commands, most starkly embodied in Calvin's political theology. It is for the reader to decide which of these views, or which combination of them, to adopt. And the perspective chosen determines the audience to which this book, in the end, turns out to be addressed. The Thomist view is appropriate to policymakers wondering how to relate law to morality; Ockham's vision is suitable for many Christians who see no choice but to separate themselves to the extent possible from the political and economic orders in which they find themselves; Luther's view, not surprisingly, offers a two-kingdoms perspective to believers; and Calvin's political theology approaches taxation in a way suitable to a Christian or Christian-ish commonwealth.

Notes

1 Donald W. Shriver, Jr., and E. Richard Knox, "Taxation in the History of Protestant Ethics," *The Journal of Religious Ethics* 13, no. 1 (Spring 1985): 141. The term "Teind" is roughly equivalent to "tithe." Knox used the "Pauline intra-church collection" practice as his precedent for this position, although "now in a very different social context of a parish system that defined all residents as subject to Christian standards." Knox distinguished between the poor who lacked all income and those with "meager earnings" (whom he called "poor labourers"). Knox argued that even though the poor laborers did not pay taxes directly, they were burdened by high taxes that wealthy landowners passed along "in the form of higher rents and fees." Donald Shriver and Richard Knox write: "Knox called for some form of relief for this sector of the Queen's subjects, and his activity in this sphere is a good illustration of the propensity of Calvinism for expansive concern about the details of political justice." Shriver and Knox, "Taxation in the History of Protestant Ethics," 141.

2 Shriver and Knox, "Taxation in the History of Protestant Ethics," 134. Shriver and Knox state that Wesley's interventions were made "with little reference overtly to theology."

3 See Donald A. Nielsen, "*The Protestant Ethic and the 'Spirit' of Capitalism* as Grand Narrative: Max Weber's Philosophy of History," in *The Protestant Ethic Turns 100: Essays on the Centenary of the Weber Thesis*, ed. William H. Swatos, Jr., and Lutz Kaelber (Boulder, CO: Paradigm Publishers, 2005), 74, writing about Max Weber's work:

> Weber takes us across a long historical journey in which changing human experiences are expressed in new religious, moral, and other forms. Indeed, our only access to this shifting inner experience is through those religious ideas. When the inner meaning of economic activity no longer exists, the spirit has finally fled.

4 Giorgio Agamben, *The Kingdom and the Glory: For a Theological Genealogy of Economy and Government (*Homo Sacer *II, 2)*, trans. Lorenzo Chiesa and Matteo Mandarini (Stanford: Stanford University Press, 2011), 261–62.
5 Agamben, The Kingdom and the Glory, 262.
6 Agamben, The Kingdom and the Glory, 262.
7 Agamben, The Kingdom and the Glory, 262–63.
8 Agamben, The Kingdom and the Glory, 263–65.
9 Agamben, The Kingdom and the Glory, 268–69.
10 Agamben, The Kingdom and the Glory, 272–73.
11 Agamben, The Kingdom and the Glory, 273.
12 Agamben, The Kingdom and the Glory, 276.
13 Agamben, The Kingdom and the Glory, 278.
14 Agamben, The Kingdom and the Glory, 140.
15 Agamben, The Kingdom and the Glory, 285.
16 Agamben, *The Kingdom and the Glory*, 286 (italics in original).
17 John Calvin, *Institutes of the Christian Religion*, trans. Ford Lewis Battles, ed. John T. McNeill (Philadelphia: The Westminster Press, 1960) 1.18.4. See Matthew J. Tuininga, *Calvin's Political Theology and the Public Engagement of the Church: Christ's Two Kingdoms* (Cambridge: Cambridge University Press, 2017), 169 (in Calvin's theology, "God does not sanction all that takes place by his providence").
18 Richard Tuck, *Philosophy and Government 1572–1651*, Ideas in Context, ed. Quentin Skinner, Lorraine Dstyon, Wolf Lepenies, Richard Rorty, and J. B. Schneewind (Cambridge: Cambridge University Press, 1993), 173.
19 Hugo Grotius, *De iure praedae commentarius* 1, trans. G. L. Williams (Oxford: Clarendon Press, 1950), 9, quoted in Tuck, *Philosophy and Government*, 172–73.
20 Grotius, *De iure praedae*, 21, quoted in Tuck, *Philosophy and Government*, 174.
21 Grotius, *De iure praedae*, 21, quoted in Tuck, *Philosophy and Government*, 174.
22 Grotius, *De iure praedae*, 21, quoted in Tuck, *Philosophy and Government*, 175.
23 Tuck, *Philosophy and Government*, 178.
24 Grotius, *De iure praedae*, 228, quoted in Tuck, *Philosophy and Government*, 178.
25 Tuck, *Philosophy and Government*, 179.
26 Tuck, *Philosophy and Government*, 196.
27 Tuck, *Philosophy and Government*, 197.
28 Tuck, *Philosophy and Government*, 197.
29 Grotius, *De iure praedae*, *prolegomena*, 11, quoted in Tuck, *Philosophy and Government*, 197–98. By 1622, when Grotius' poem *De veritate religionis Christianae* was first published, Grotius defended Christianity against Judaism, Islam, and paganism primarily on the basis of its utility. The usefulness of Christianity, interestingly, had the "positive advantage" of persuading people to hold their own property lightly so that they could relieve the poverty of others.

See Tuck, *Philosophy and Government*, 195. The Latin version of the poem was not published until 1640.

30 Tuck, *Philosophy and Government*, 306.

31 Tuck, *Philosophy and Government*, 307.

32 Tuck, *Philosophy and Government*, 308.

33 Daniel M. Hausman and Michael S. McPherson, *Economic Analysis, Moral Philosophy, and Public Policy*, 2nd ed. (Cambridge: Cambridge University Press, 2006), 200.

34 Hausman and McPherson, *Economic Analysis*, 200.

35 Hausman and McPherson, *Economic Analysis*, 200.

36 Hausman and McPherson, *Economic Analysis*, 162.

37 See Carolyn Webber and Aaron Wildavsky, *A History of Taxation and Expenditure in the Western World* (New York: Simon and Schuster, 1986), 262.

38 Adam Smith, *An Inquiry into the Nature and Causes of the Wealth of Nations*, ed. R. H. Campbell, A. S. Skinner, and W. B. Todd, vol. 2 (Oxford: Clarendon Press, 1979) 5.2.

39 Webber and Wildavsky, *History of Taxation*, 262.

40 Webber and Wildavsky, *History of Taxation*, 264–66.

41 Sociologist Marc Leroy writes that "licit war" became a function of the emerging state, "whose financing by taxes marks a change of logic compared to seigneurial taxes" and, following Schumpeter, that "[w]ar is used as an argument to make the traditional system of feudal assistance evolve into the establishment of taxation." Marc Leroy, *Taxation, the State and Society: The Fiscal Sociology of Interventionist Democracy*, Action Publique/Public Action 7 (Brussels: Peter Lang, 2011), 113.

42 Webber and Wildavsky, *History of Taxation and Expenditure*, 238–39.

43 Webber and Wildavsky, *History of Taxation and Expenditure*, 288.

44 Leroy, *Taxation, the State and Society*, 118–19.

45 Leroy, *Taxation, the State and Society*, 123.

46 Julian H. Franklin, *Jean Bodin and the Rise of Absolutist Theory* (Cambridge: Cambridge University Press, 1973), 86–87.

47 Leroy, *Taxation, the State and Society*, 124.

48 See Richard Bonney, "Early Modern Theories of State Finance," in *Economic Systems and State Finance*, ed. Richard Bonney, Cambridge Studies in the History and Theory of Politics (New York: Oxford University Press, 1995), 169, citing Martin Wolfe, "Jean Bodin on Taxes: The Sovereignty-Taxes Paradox," *Political Science Quarterly* 83, no. 2 (June 1968): 268–84.

49 Franklin, *Jean Bodin*, 87–89.

50 Bonney, "Early Modern Theories, 167–68.

51 Bonney, "Early Modern Theories," 169; Franklin, *Jean Bodin*, 91–92.

52 Leroy, *Taxation, the State and Society*, 125.

53 Leroy, *Taxation, the State and Society*, 123.

54 Leroy, *Taxation, the State and Society*, 123.

55 Jean-Jacques Rousseau, "Discours sur L'Oeconomie Politique," in *Oeuvres Philosophiques et Politiques: des Premiers Écrits au Contrat Social, 1735-1762*, vol. 2, *Oeuvres Complètes*, ed. Michel Launay (Paris: Éditions du Seuil, 1971), 287 (my translation).

56 Rousseau, "Discours sur L'Oeconomie Politique," 289 (my translation).

57 Jean-Jacques Rousseau, *A Discourse on Inequality*, trans. Maurice Cranston (Harmondsworth, UK: Penguin Books Ltd., 1984), 122.

58 Rousseau, *A Discourse on Inequality*, 115, 117.

59 Rousseau, *A Discourse on Inequality*, 99–100.

60 The "supreme commander," or "supreme ruler" or "ruler," is the organ of the "sovereign." Immanuel Kant, "The Metaphysics of Morals," in *Kant: Political*

Writings, ed. Hans Reiss, trans. H. B. Nisbet, Cambridge Texts in the History of Philosophy, ed. Raymond Guess, Quentin Skinner, and Richard Tuck (Cambridge: Cambridge University Press, 1991), 143. The sovereign, in turn, is the people in the person of the legislator. Kant, "The Metaphysics of Morals," 138.

61 Kant, "The Metaphysics of Morals," 147. The "civil union" is an arrangement in which people are related to one another through a constitution (i.e., a unifying will) that provides a system of laws (i.e., a system of public right). Kant, "The Metaphysics of Morals," 136. Kant used the term "right" here to refer to "the sum total of those conditions within which the will of one person can be reconciled with the will of another in accordance with a universal law of freedom." Kant, "The Metaphysics of Morals," 133.

62 Kant, "The Metaphysics of Morals," 147–48.

63 Kant, "The Metaphysics of Morals," 136–37. By "commonwealth," Kant meant "the people regarded as a state." Kant, "The Metaphysics of Morals," 140.

64 Kant, "The Metaphysics of Morals," 140.

65 Kant, "The Metaphysics of Morals," 149.

66 Kant, "The Metaphysics of Morals," 149–50.

67 Kant, "The Metaphysics of Morals," 150.

68 Kant, "The Metaphysics of Morals," 150.

69 Kant, "The Metaphysics of Morals," 143.

70 Rousseau, "L'Oeconomie Politique," 279.

71 Tuck, *Philosophy and Government*, 348.

72 Tuck, *Philosophy and Government*, 348.

73 Stephen Kalberg, "Utilizing Max Weber's 'Iron Cage' to Define the Past, Present, and Future of the American Political Culture," in *The Protestant Ethic Turns 100: Essays on the Centenary of the Weber Thesis*, ed. William H. Swatos, Jr., and Lutz Kaelber (Boulder, CO: Paradigm Publishers, 2005), 193–94.

74 Kalberg, "Utilizing Max Weber's 'Iron Cage," 194.

75 Martin Riesebrodt, "Dimensions of the *Protestant Ethic*, in Swatos and Kaelber, 31–32.

76 Kalberg, "Utilizing Max Weber's 'Iron Cage," 193–94.

77 Philip S. Gorski, "The Little Divergence: The Protestant Reformation and Economic Hegemony in Early Modern Europe," in Swatos and Kaelber, 168.

78 See Hausman and McPherson, *Economic Analysis*, 310; James R. Repetti, "The Appropriate Roles for Equity and Efficiency in a Progressive Income Tax," 24 *Florida Tax Review* (forthcoming 2020): 3.

79 Linda Sugin, "Tax Expenditures, Reform, and Distributive Justice," *Columbia Journal of Tax Law* 3 (2011): 35.

80 Hausman and McPherson, *Economic Analysis*, 159–60.

81 Sugin, "Tax Expenditures," 36.

82 Richard A. Posner, *Economic Analysis of Law* (Boston: Little, Brown and Co., 1973), 223.

83 Posner, *Economic Analysis of Law*, 212.

84 See, e.g., Richard A. Posner, *The Economics of Justice*, (Cambridge, MA: Harvard University Press, 1983), 351–63.

85 John Locke, *Two Treatises of Government*, ed. Peter Laslett, Cambridge Texts in the History of Political Thought (Cambridge: Cambridge University Press, 1988) 2.7.87.

86 Smith, *Wealth of Nations* 5.2.g.

87 The fourth maxim begins, "Every tax ought to be so contrived as both to take out and to keep out of the pockets of the people as little as possible, over and above what it brings into the publick treasury of the state." Smith, *Wealth of Nations* 5.2.b.

88 Locke, *Two Treatises* 2.11.138–40.
89 Leroy, *Taxation, the State and Society*, 117–18.
90 Leroy, *Taxation, the State and Society*, 118.
91 Carl Schmitt, *Constitutional Theory*, trans. and ed., J. Seitzer (Durham, NC: Duke University Press, 2008), 275, quoted in Agamben, *The Kingdom and the Glory*, 255.
92 Agamben, *The Kingdom and the Glory*, 256.
93 Agamben, *The Kingdom and the Glory*, 258.
94 Agamben, *The Kingdom and the Glory*, 257.
95 Agamben, *The Kingdom and the Glory*, 257.
96 Augustus, *Res gestae divi Augusti* §34, quoted in Agamben, *The Kingdom and the Glory*, 258.
97 Agamben, *The Kingdom and the Glory*, 259.
98 Thomas Hobbes, *Leviathan*, ed. C. B. Macpherson, The Penguin English Library (Harmondsworth, UK: Penguin Books Ltd., 1968) 2.30.
99 Smith, *Wealth of Nations* 5.2.b.
100 Thomas Hobbes, *The Elements of Law, Natural and Politic*, ed. Ferdinand Tönnies (London: Routledge, 1969) 2.9.5.
101 Smith, *Wealth of Nations* 5.2.e.
102 J. P. Somerville, "Absolutism and Royalism," in *The Cambridge History of Political Thought, 1450-1700*, ed. J. H. Burns (Cambridge: Cambridge University Press, 1991), 347.
103 Joseph M. Dodge, "Theories of Tax Justice: Ruminations on the Benefit, Partnership, and Ability-to-Pay Principles," *Tax Law Review* 58 (Summer 2005): 402.
104 For Locke's contractarian statement of the benefit principle, see John Locke, *Two Treatises of Government* 2.11.140 ("'Tis true, Governments cannot be supported without great Charge, and 'tis fit every one who enjoys his share of the Protection, should pay out of his Estate his proportion for the maintenance of it").
105 "The revenues of the state are a portion each citizen gives of his goods in order to have the security or the comfortable enjoyment of the rest." Montesquieu, *The Spirit of the Laws* 13.1, ed. and trans. Anne M. Cohler, Basia C. Miller, and Harold S. Stone, Cambridge Texts in the History of Political Thought (Cambridge: Cambridge University Press, 1989), 213.
106 "[I]n so far as he takes the duty of the people upon himself, the supreme commander has the right to impose taxes upon the people for their own preservation ...." Kant, *The Metaphysics of Morals*, 149.
107 John Stuart Mill, *Principles of Political Economy, with Some of Their Applications to Social Philosophy* (London: Longman, Green, Longman, Roberts, and Green, 1865) 5.2.2. See also Dodge, "Theories of Tax Justice," 404-405; Richard A. Musgrave, *The Theory of Public Finance: A Study in Public Economy* (New York: McGraw-Hill Book Co., Inc., 1959), 92.
108 Richard A. Musgrave, "Fairness in Taxation," in *The Encyclopedia of Taxation & Tax Policy*, 2nd ed., ed. Joseph J. Cordes, Robert D. Ebel, and Jane G. Gravelle (Washington: The Urban Institute Press, 2005), 136.
109 Mill, *Principles of Political Economy* 5.2.3. See Musgrave and Peacock, introduction to *Classics in the Theory of Public Finance*, ed. Richard A. Musgrave and Alan T. Peacock (London: Macmillan, 1958), x.
110 Musgrave, "Fairness in Taxation," 136.
111 Musgrave and Peacock, introduction to *Classics in the Theory*, x.
112 See Musgrave, "Fairness in Taxation," 136.
113 Mill, *Principles of Political Economy* 5.2.2. See Musgrave and Peacock, introduction to *Classics in the Theory of Public Finance*, ix–xii (describing Mill's version of equal sacrifice as a brief "subjective" interlude in the history of the ability-to-pay principle).

114 Stephen Utz, "Ability to Pay," *Whittier Law Review* 23 (2002): 896.
115 Utz, "Ability to Pay," 872.
116 See Dodge, "Theories of Tax Justice," 449; Daniel N. Shaviro, "Inequality, Wealth, and Endowment," *Tax Law Review* 53 (2000): 401; Utz, "Ability to Pay," 870.
117 Musgrave and Peacock, introduction to *Classics in the Theory of Public Finance*, xi.
118 Musgrave, "Fairness in Taxation," 136–37.
119 Bentham considered collective welfare simply to be the aggregate of individual welfare. His central proposition was that individuals will seek to pursue their own happiness, and that the interest of the community will be the sum of its members' interests. Musgrave, "Fairness in Taxation," 136–37.
120 Musgrave, "Fairness in Taxation," 137.
121 Cass R. Sunstein, "Incommensurability and Valuation in Law," in *Free Markets and Social Justice* (New York: Oxford University Press, 1999), 70.
122 Sunstein, "Incommensurability," 71, 73.
123 Sunstein, "Incommensurability," 71, 100.
124 Sunstein, "Incommensurability," 73, 79
125 Sunstein, "Incommensurability," 71.
126 Sunstein, "Incommensurability," 80.
127 Sunstein, "Incommensurability," 77.
128 Sunstein, "Incommensurability," 76.
129 Sunstein, "Incommensurability," 81.
130 Sunstein, "Incommensurability," 86.
131 Sunstein, "Incommensurability," 80, 82.
132 Sunstein, "Incommensurability," 82.
133 Sunstein, "Incommensurability," 80.
134 Sunstein, "Incommensurability," 86. For an economic analysis of race discrimination in U.S. Supreme Court decisions, see Richard A. Posner, "The Law and Economics of Discrimination," in *The Economics of Justice* (Cambridge, MA: Harvard University Press, 1983), 351–407.
135 Sunstein, "Incommensurability," 88.
136 Sunstein, "Incommensurability," 87–88.
137 Sunstein, "Incommensurability," 89.
138 Sunstein, "Incommensurability," 87.
139 See, e.g., Posner, *The Economics of Justice*, 6 ("efficiency as I define the term is an adequate concept of justice").
140 Webber and Wildavsky, History of Taxation and Expenditure, 241.
141 Webber and Wildavsky, History of Taxation and Expenditure, 241.
142 David Hume, "Essay VIII: Of Taxes," in *Essays, Moral, Political, and Literary*, ed. Eugene F. Miller (Indianapolis: Liberty Fund, Inc., 2010) 2:346, accessed June 26, 2018, http://oll.libertyfund.org/titles/hume-essays-moral-political-literary-lf-ed.
143 Smith, *Wealth of Nations* 5.2.k.
144 Jürgen Habermas, *Legitimation Crisis*, trans. Thomas McCarthy (Boston: Beacon Press, 1975), 61–62.
145 Habermas, *Legitimation Crisis*, 62–63.
146 Habermas, *Legitimation Crisis*, 65.
147 Habermas, *Legitimation Crisis*, 73.
148 Habermas, *Legitimation Crisis*, 63.
149 Habermas, *Legitimation Crisis*, 111.
150 Habermas, *Legitimation Crisis*, 112.
151 Habermas, *Legitimation Crisis*, 61.
152 Musgrave, "Fairness in Taxation," 136. To circumvent the resulting positivism, advocates of the "new benefit principle" argue that a taxpayer's total welfare correlates generally with the amount of government benefits received even though

only a portion of the taxpayer's well-being is actually attributable to government benefits. Repetti, "Democracy and Opportunity," 1136. Joseph Dodge points out that the new benefit principle is not necessarily incompatible with welfare activities on the part of the government but contends this is not where the new principle focuses its theoretical energy. Instead, efficiency—in the sense of "producing the maximum aggregate social wealth"—is the new benefit principle's core value. Dodge, "Theories of Tax Justice," 429–30. However, as Dodge argues, "[t]he idea that the government might be entitled to more taxes by doing (spending) less demonstrates the essential poverty of the benefit concept ...." Dodge, "Theories of Tax Justice," 446.

153 Dodge, "Theories of Tax Justice," 401.
154 Utz, "Ability to Pay," 912.
155 Henry C. Simons, *Personal Income Taxation: The Definition of Income as a Problem of Fiscal Policy* (Chicago: The University of Chicago Press, 1938), 8. See Chapter One, above, for a discussion of Edgeworth and minimum-sacrifice doctrine.
156 Simons, *Personal Income Taxation*, 7.
157 Simons, *Personal Income Taxation*, 11.
158 Simons, *Personal Income Taxation*, 10.
159 Simons, *Personal Income Taxation*, 13.
160 Simons, *Personal Income Taxation*, 2.
161 Simons, *Personal Income Taxation*, 18.
162 As Simons himself puts it, "Such curious methods of defending progression are commonplace. The practice typically is that of admitting progression through the back door, under the cloak of Adam Smith's first maxim [i.e., that taxes should be proportional to how much the taxpayer benefits from the state]." Simons, *Personal Income Taxation*, 17.
163 Walter J. Blum and Harry Kalven, Jr., "The Uneasy Case for Progressive Taxation," *University of Chicago Law Review* 19, no. 3 (Spring 1952): 460.
164 See Chapter One.
165 Duncan Kennedy, "Form and Substance in Private Law Adjudication," *Harvard Law Review* 89, no. 8 (June 1976): 1685–1778.
166 Susan Strange, *States and Markets*, 2nd ed. (London: Continuum, 1994), 39.
167 Strange, *States and Markets*, 86–87.
168 Strange, *States and Markets*, 87.
169 Strange, *States and Markets*, 40–41.

References

Agamben, Giorgio. 2011. *The Kingdom and the Glory: For a Theological Genealogy of Economy and Government* (Homo Sacer *II, 2*). Translated by Lorenzo Chiesa and Matteo Mandarini. Stanford: Stanford University Press.

Bentham, Jeremy. 1973. "Leading Principles of a Constitutional Code, for any State." In *Bentham's Political Thought*, edited by Bhikhu Parekh, 195–205. London: Croom Helm.

Blum, Walter J., and Harry Kalven, Jr. 1952. "The Uneasy Case for Progressive Taxation." *University of Chicago Law Review* 19, no. 3 (Spring): 417–520.

Bonney, Richard. 1995. "Early Modern Theories of State Finance." In *Economic Systems*, edited by Bonney, 163–229.

Calvin, John. 1960. *Institutes of the Christian Religion*. Edited by John T. McNeill. Translated by Ford Lewis Battles, vol. 2. Philadelphia: The Westminster Press.

Dodge, Joseph M. 2005. "Theories of Tax Justice: Ruminations on the Benefit, Partnership, and Ability-to-Pay Principles." *Tax Law Review* 58 (Summer): 399–461.

Franklin, Julian H. 1973. *Jean Bodin and the Rise of Absolutist Theory*. Cambridge: Cambridge University Press.

Gorski, Philip S. 2005. "The Little Divergence: The Protestant Reformation and Economic Hegemony in Early Modern Europe." In *The Protestant Ethic Turns 100: Essays on the Centenary of the Weber Thesis*, edited by William H. Swatos, Jr., and Lutz Kaelber, 165–90. Boulder, CO: Paradigm Publishers.

Grotius, Hugo. 1950. *De iure praedae commentarius* 1. Translated by G. L. Williams. Oxford: Clarendon Press.

Habermas, Jürgen. 1975. *Legitimation Crisis*. Translated by Thomas McCarthy. Boston: Beacon Press.

Hausman, Daniel M., and Michael S. McPherson. 2006. *Economic Analysis, Moral Philosophy, and Public Policy*. 2nd ed. Cambridge: Cambridge University Press.

Hobbes, Thomas. 1969. *The Elements of Law, Natural and Politic*. Edited by Ferdinand Tönnies. London: Routledge.

______. 1968. *Leviathan*. Edited by C. B. Macpherson. The Penguin English Library. Harmondsworth, UK: Penguin Books Ltd..

Hume, David. 2010. "Essay VIII: Of Taxes." In *Essays, Moral, Political, and Literary*, edited by Eugene F. Miller, part 2, 342–48. Indianapolis: Liberty Fund, Inc. Accessed June 26, 2018. http://oll.libertyfund.org/titles/hume-essays-moral-political-literary-lf-ed.

Kalberg, Stephen. 2005. "Utilizing Max Weber's 'Iron Cage' to Define the Past, Present, and Future of the American Political Culture," in Swatos and Kaelber, *The Protestant Ethic Turns 100*. 191–208.

Kant, Immanuel. 1996. "The Metaphysics of Morals." In *Kant: Political Writings*, edited by Hans Reiss, translated by H. B. Nisbet, 131–75. *Cambridge Texts in the History of Philosophy*, edited by Raymond Guess, Quentin Skinner, and Richard Tuck. Cambridge: Cambridge University Press.

Kennedy, Duncan. 1976. "Form and Substance in Private Law Adjudication." *Harvard Law Review* 89, no. 8 (June): 1685–1778.

Leroy, Marc. 2011. *Taxation, the State and Society: The Fiscal Sociology of Interventionist Democracy*. Action Publique/Public Action 7. Brussels: Peter Lang.

Locke, John. 1988. *Two Treatises of Government*. Edited by Peter Laslett. Cambridge Texts in the History of Political Thought. Cambridge: Cambridge University Press.

Mill, John Stuart. 1865. *Principles of Political Economy, with Some of Their Applications to Social Philosophy*. London: Longman, Green, Longman, Roberts, and Green.

Montesquieu. 1989. *The Spirit of the Laws*. Edited and translated by Anne M. Cohler, Basia C. Miller, and Harold S. Stone. Cambridge Texts in the History of Political Thought. Cambridge: Cambridge University Press.

Musgrave, Richard A. 2005. "Fairness in Taxation." In *The Encyclopedia of Taxation & Tax Policy*, edited by Joseph J. Cordes, Robert D. Ebel, and Jane G. Gravelle, 135–37. 2nd ed. Washington: The Urban Institute Press.

Musgrave, Richard A. 1959. *The Theory of Public Finance: A Study in Public Economy*. New York: McGraw-Hill Book Co., Inc.

______. 2005. "Fairness in Taxation." In *The Encyclopedia of Taxation & Tax Policy*, edited by Joseph J. Cordes, Robert D. Ebel, and Jane G. Gravelle, 135–37. 2nd ed. Washington: The Urban Institute Press.

Musgrave, Richard A., and Alan T. Peacock, eds. 1962. *Classics in the Theory of Public Finance.* London: Macmillan & Co. Ltd.

Nielsen, Donald A. 2005. "*The Protestant Ethic and the 'Spirit' of Capitalism* as Grand Narrative: Max Weber's Philosophy of History." In *The Protestant Ethic Turns 100: Essays on the Centenary of the Weber Thesis*, edited by William H. Swatos, Jr., and Lutz Kaelber, 53–75. Boulder, CO: Paradigm Publishers, 2005.

Posner, Richard A. 1973. *Economic Analysis of Law.* Boston: Little, Brown and Co.

______. 1983. *The Economics of Justice.* Cambridge, MA: Harvard University Press.

Repetti, James R. forthcoming 2020. "The Appropriate Roles for Equity and Efficiency in a Progressive Income Tax." *Florida Tax Review* 23.

Riesebrodt, Martin. 2005 "Dimensions of the Protestant Ethic." In Swatos and Kaelber, *The Protestant Ethic Turns 100.* 23–51.

Rousseau, Jean-Jacques. 1971. "Discours sur L'Oeconomie Politique." In *Oeuvres Complètes*, edited by Michel Launay, vol. 2, *Oeuvres Philosophiques et Politiques: des Premiers Écrits au Contrat Social, 1735–1762*, 276–93. Paris: Éditions du Seuil.

______. 1984. *A Discourse on Inequality.* Translated by Maurice Cranston. Harmondsworth, UK: Penguin Books Ltd.

Schmitt, Carl. 2008. *Constitutional Theory.* Translated and edited by J. Seitzer. Durham, NC: Duke University Press.

Shaviro, Daniel N. 2000. "Inequality, Wealth, and Endowment." *Tax Law Review* 53: 397–421.

Shriver, Donald W., Jr., and E. Richard Knox. 1985. "Taxation in the History of Protestant Ethics." *The Journal of Religious Ethics* 13, no. 1 (Spring): 134–60.

Simons, Henry C. 1938. *Personal Income Taxation: The Definition of Income as a Problem of Fiscal Policy.* Chicago: The University of Chicago Press.

Smith, Adam. 1979. *An Inquiry into the Nature and Causes of the Wealth of Nations*, edited by R. H. Campbell, A. S. Skinner, and W. B. Todd, vol. 2. Oxford: Clarendon Press.

Somerville, J. P. 1991. "Absolutism and Royalism." In *The Cambridge History of Political Thought, 1450-1700*, edited by J. H. Burns, 347–73. Cambridge: Cambridge University Press.

Strange, Susan. 1994. *States and Markets.* 2nd ed. London: Continuum.

Sugin, Linda. 2011. "Tax Expenditures, Reform, and Distributive Justice." *Columbia Journal of Tax Law* 3: 1–42.

Sunstein, Cass R. 1999. "Incommensurability and Valuation in Law." In *Free Markets and Social Justice*, 70–107. New York: Oxford University Press.

Swatos, William H., Jr., and Lutz Kaelber, eds. 2005. *The Protestant Ethic Turns 100: Essays on the Centenary of the Weber Thesis.* Boulder, CO: Paradigm Publishers.

Tuck, Richard. 1993. *Philosophy and Government 1572–1651.* Ideas in Context, edited by Quentin Skinner, Lorraine Dstyon, Wolf Lepenies, Richard Rorty, and J. B. Schneewind. Cambridge: Cambridge University Press.

Tuininga, Matthew J. 2017. *Calvin's Political Theology and the Public Engagement of the Church: Christ's Two Kingdoms.* Cambridge: Cambridge University Press.

Utz, Stephen. 2002. "Ability to Pay." *Whittier Law Review* 23: 867–950.

Webber, Carolyn, and Aaron Wildavsky. 1986. *A History of Taxation and Expenditure in the Western World.* New York: Simon and Schuster.

Wolfe, Martin. 1968. "Jean Bodin on Taxes: The Sovereignty-Taxes Paradox." *Political Science Quarterly* 83, no. 2 (June): 268–84.

Index

Made in the USA
Monee, IL
13 September 2026

62978987R10162